PR
8801
.F55
1976
Cop. 1

Flanagan, Thomas
J. B. 1923-

The Irish
novelists, 1800-
1850

$27.50

R0064249129

The Irish Novelists: 1800-1850

The Irish Novelists

1800-1850

By THOMAS FLANAGAN

GREENWOOD PRESS, PUBLISHERS
WESTPORT, CONNECTICUT

Library of Congress Cataloging in Publication Data

Flanagan, Thomas J   B   1923-
   The Irish novelists, 1800-1850.

    Originally presented as the author's thesis, Columbia.
    Reprint of the 1959 ed. published by Columbia Univer-
sity Press, New York.
    Bibliography: p.
    Includes index.
    1. English fiction--Irish authors--History and
criticism. 2. English fiction--19th century--History
and criticism. I. Title.
[PR8801.F55 1976]   823'.7'09   76-21874
ISBN 0-8371-9004-5

PR
8801
.F55

Copyright © 1958 Columbia University Press, New York

1976
cop. 1

Originally published in 1959 by Columbia University Press, New York

Reprinted with the permission of Columbia University Press

Reprinted in 1976 by Greenwood Press, a division of Congressional
Information Service, 88 Post Road West, Westport, Connecticut 06881

Library of Congress catalog card number 76-21874

ISBN 0-8371-9004-5

Printed in the United States of America

10 9 8 7 6 5 4 3 2

For Jean

This study, prepared under the
Graduate Faculties of Columbia
University, was selected by a
committee of those Faculties
to receive one of the Clarke F.
Ansley awards given annually
by Columbia University Press.

Preface

We and our bitterness have left no traces
On Munster grass and Connemara skies.[1]

THE CLOSING LINES of the poem which young William Butler Yeats wrote in dedication of his book of stories from the Irish novelists suggest the distance which separated these writers from his own generation. In 1889 he was much concerned to discover whatever was usable in the literary past of Ireland, and the commission from an American publisher gave him an opportunity to read the novels of a tradition which had flourished and declined during the first half of the century. "It has all quite gone now—our little tide," he wrote to Father Matthew Russell, who had helped him in his search for books which once were well known. Then, seeking to define the impression which his reading had made upon him, he wrote: "The old men tried to make one see life plainly but all written down in a kind of fiery shorthand that it might never be forgotten."[2]

Since the appearance of Maria Edgeworth's *Castle Rackrent* in 1800, Irish writers had addressed themselves to the native scene—Lady Morgan, John Banim, Gerald Griffin, William Carleton, and a small army of less conspicuous figures. In Ireland their books had been greeted with that mixture of lavish praise and hoarse indignation with which all public events, great or small, were celebrated. And abroad they had been accepted, each in turn and despite all contradictions, as the delineators of "the real Ireland." But the development of the Irish novel had been cut short by the despair and silence which

[1] William Butler Yeats, *Collected Poems*, p. 52.
[2] *The Letters of W. B. Yeats*, p. 143.

fell upon Ireland in the wake of the Famine. The decades which followed, years which are among the dreariest in Irish history, afforded barren soil for any kind of intellectual or political life.

"Banim and Griffin are gone," William Carleton wrote to a friend in 1863, "and I will soon follow them—*ultimus Romanorum,* and after that will come a lull, an obscurity of perhaps half a century. . . ." But the spell which had seized the country would be broken, he predicted, and other writers would come forward, "for in this manner the cycles of literature and taste appear, hold their day, displace each other, and make room for others." [3]

But he probably did not anticipate the extent to which this new generation would not only replace but reject his own. The wrong people, so it seemed to the stern young men of the Irish revival, admired the early Irish novelists and for the wrong reasons. Their books had been bred of a bastard art, neither Irish nor English, and presented a view of Irish life which was false alike in moral and in political terms.

Yeats, with his strong sense of the need for connections with the past and his relative freedom from doctrinaire political assumptions, could read the "fiery shorthand" of the old novelists. "There is a great want for a just verdict on these men and their use for Ireland," he wrote to Katherine Tynan in 1889.[4] But few shared his enthusiasm, and none attempted the task. The neglect persisted. Despite the attention which Irish literature has received, no scholar or critic has concerned himself with the general subject of the novelists who interpreted the life of Ireland during the years of its emergence into the modern world.[5]

The intention of this study, therefore, is to examine the works and careers of the principal Irish novelists of the early nineteenth century:

[3] *The Life of William Carleton.*
[4] Yeats, *Letters,* p. 133.
[5] There is, however, a useful bibliographical study: Stephen Brown, S. J. *Ireland in Fiction: A Guide to Irish Novels, Tales, Romances, and Folk-Lore* (Dublin, 1916). Brown brought to his work a long and affectionate familiarity with Irish letters, but his entries should be checked against a more recent and more professional bibliography: L. Leclaire, *A General Analytical Bibliography of the Regional Novelists of the British Isles, 1800–1950* (London, 1954).

Maria Edgeworth, Lady Morgan, John Banim, Gerald Griffin, and William Carleton. I have not forgotten that other writers were at work during these years, and I have drawn upon them to illuminate particular subjects, but the study is given its form by a close and detailed discussion of these five.

The Ireland of the nineteenth century was a fragmented culture, a dismaying and complicated tangle of classes, creeds, loyalties, and aspirations. In the first two of the three introductory chapters, I have set forth the historical background and have tried to recreate the social, political, and religious atmosphere. In its characteristic form the Irish novel is an attempt to define the nature of Irish society and to relate its present graces and disorders to the island's tragic past. The myths, justifications, and visions which such novels embody are attempts to reconcile in symbolic terms the conflicting elements of a culture at war with itself. It is necessary, therefore, to have some understanding not only of the immediate social and political issues, but of their historical roots.

The insistence that a group of writers constitutes a "school" or a "tradition" is often made at the expense of their individuality. The bond which joins these writers is that all of them were Irishmen, trying to come to terms with the experience of life on their maddening island. And so, having set up the necessary guideposts in the introductory chapters, I have relied upon each writer to chart for the reader his particular stretch of the country. When these charts are all before us, we may be able to define the "tradition" of the Irish novel.

Contents

Preface   vii

INTRODUCTION

1.   The Weight of the Past   3
2.   The Political and Social Scene   17
3.   The Nature of the Irish Novel   35

MARIA EDGEWORTH

4.   The Crisis of the "Protestant Nation"   53
5.   *Castle Rackrent*   69
6.   The Landlord as the Hero: *Ennui* and *The Absentee* 80
7.   In Search of a Hero: *Ormond*   92

LADY MORGAN

8.   Sentimental Patriotism: *The Wild Irish Girl*   109
9.   The Politics of an Irish Novel   125
10. The Houses of the West: *The O'Briens and the O'Flahertys* 147

JOHN BANIM

11. Irish Peasants and English Readers   167
12. The Historical Novel   188

GERALD GRIFFIN

13.   *Tales of the Munster Festivals*   205
14.   *The Collegians*   219
15.   The Dark Land: *The Rivals* and *Tracy's Ambition* 232

WILLIAM CARLETON

16.   A Pilgrim to Lough Derg and Dublin   255
17.   *Traits and Stories of the Irish Peasantry*   280
18.   The Dublin Years   300

CONCLUSION

19.   "Fiery Shorthand"   333

       Bibliography   343
       Acknowledgments   353
       Index   355

FLUELLEN: . . . I think, look you, under your correction, there is not many of your nation—

MACMORRIS: Of my nation? What ish my nation? Ish a villain, and a bastard, and a knave, and a rascal. What ish my nation? Who talks of my nation?   *Henry V,* Act III, Scene 2

—What is your nation, if I may ask, says the citizen.

—Ireland, says Bloom. I was born here. Ireland.   JAMES JOYCE, *Ulysses*

Introduction

1. The Weight of the Past

SHAKESPEARE BRINGS only one Irishman onto his stage. A Captain Macmorris makes a sudden appearance at the siege of Harfleur, behaves deplorably, and leaves in anger. He has been directing the mining operation and is much annoyed when retreat is sounded: " 'Tis shame for us all. So God sa' me, 'tis shame to stand still, it is shame, by my hand! and there is throats to be cut, and works to be done, and there ish nothing done. . . ."

Fluellen, the pedant of war, is convinced that he has no knowledge of "the true disciplines of the wars, look you." Macmorris listens with scant courtesy to a pompous but well-intentioned reproof, until he hears, "I think, look you, under your correction, there is not many of your nation—" And at this he explodes:

Of my nation? What ish my nation? Ish a villain, and a bastard, and a knave, and a rascal. What ish my nation? Who talks of my nation?

Fluellen, taken aback by this, makes a fresh try, though his own Welsh spirit prompts him to remark that he is "as good a man as yourself." This provokes another show of temper: "I do not know you so good a man as myself. So Chrish save me, I will cut off your head!" At this point a trumpet summons them back to the war against the French, thus leaving unanswered for the centuries Macmorris's truculent but plaintive cry, "What ish my nation?"

The scene compresses within a few lines the Elizabethan understanding of the Irish—touchy, moody, brave, undisciplined, and happily, casually murderous. Shakespeare's audience could remember Shane O'Neill the Proud, brave and treacherous, stalking through the London streets to make false submission to the Queen, protected by his shaggy, barbarous gallowglasses. A few, perhaps, had heard of how Garret Mor had justified to King Henry his burning of the cathedral of Cashel on the ground of his mistaken belief that the archbishop was inside. But everyone in that audience knew the stories brought back by soldiers from the Irish wars—chilling accounts of a land of quicksand bogs and vicious night raids, a land fitly symbolized by the wolves which prowled its shabby streets.

Ireland was no farther away than a short voyage over a rough sea, and yet it was in most ways as dreadful and as exotic as High Tartary. In theory it was a possession of the English Crown, but in practice it was a chaos of conflicting jurisdictions, for the English had never until the reign of Elizabeth determined upon a total conquest, and were incapable of maintaining permanent hold upon the Pale. The one certain principle upon which English rule was based was that English and Irish cultures were entirely different, that the latter was barbarous and degrading, and that because of its amazing absorptive powers it was a constant threat.

Since Norman times England had been despatching adventurers, soldiers, and officials to Ireland, only to discover that they had become, within one or two generations, *hibernis ipsis hiberniores,* more Irish than the Irish themselves. Such had been the fate of the great families of Fitzgerald and de Courcey and de Burgh. In polite parlance they were the "old English," but because they spoke Gaelic, lived by the Brehon code, and had no more use for English law than the most remote Maguire, they were called, more often, "degenerate English."

A number of attempts were made, in turn desultory, sullen, and ferocious, to halt these transformations, and always with the intention of keeping the cultures separate. Odd legalisms proliferated—Irish enemies, Irish rebels, English rebels. In the reign of Edward III, statutes were set which forbade intermarriage, the use of Gaelic, and even the entertaining by English hosts of native Irish. All proved useless; within a decade the most severe statute had become a mockery. London was forever receiving word that some de Burgh in Galway had flung off his English clothes, donned saffron kilts, and was now calling himself MacWilliam Oughter, or some other agglutination of rough syllables.

Elizabeth had inherited the full debt of the earlier centuries, together with a problem peculiar to her own generation. For a variety of reasons the Reformation had not taken root in Ireland, which remained faithful to the old religion. A resourceful and wary native ruler, Hugh O'Neill, had perceived the implications of this. He had thrown off his title as Earl of Tyrone and with it his allegiance, and now called himself The O'Neill. With a speed which suggests that the hour had been awaiting the man, he formed a coalition of Gaelic and Norman-Irish lords which defeated successive efforts to smash it. He had also, and more fatefully, sought aid from the Pope and from Catholic Spain against Elizabeth. The effect was to commit the cause of Celtic Ireland to that of the Counter-Reformation. Henceforth England was to be flanked, not by an ally, but by a seditious colony.

This was very much in the mind of Shakespeare's audience as it watched the first performance of *Henry V*. The reason is given to us in the prologue to Act V:

> Were now the general of our gracious Empress
> (As in good time he may) from Ireland coming,
> Bringing rebellion broached on his sword,
> How many would the peaceful city quit
> To welcome him!

At that moment Essex was preparing to cross the Irish Sea, though scarcely under the conditions anticipated by the Chorus. Far from skewering rebellion, he had been infected by it, and the guileful O'Neill was more secure than ever. During the few years which were left to O'Neill to reign at Dungannon, surrounded by his bards and harpers and tanists, his priests and papal legates and emissaries from Spain, the character of Celtic Ireland was being hammered and hardened. From then until the mid-eighteenth century she would be an enemy whom England, even if it would, dared not spare. "The priests are on the ocean green," as the poem has it, "They march along the deep."

O'Neill's hour struck in 1601. On the beach at Kinsale Gaelic Ireland suffered so utter a defeat that it seemed incapable of surviving.

It was in such circumstances, G. M. Trevelyan was to write, that "the Irish tribes finally became welded into the submerged Irish nation. . . . The abolition of the native upper class to make room for English landlords, begun under the Tudors and completed by Cromwell, left this peasant nation with no leaders but the priests and no sympathizers but the enemies of England." [1]

The literature of Ireland, for all its diversity, is given unity by the theme which returns, obsessively, to haunt every Irish writer. The question first posed by Macmorris phrases the theme as well as may be done: "What ish my nation?" But it involves those larger issues of culture and identity of which nationality, in the political sense, is but a shadow. For it may sometimes be the case that a man cannot really know what his culture is like, or even who he himself is, until he has answered Macmorris's question.

In 1908 Thomas Kettle wrote a short but brilliant introduction to the English translation of L. Paul-Dubois' *Contemporary Ireland*. It contains this passage:

A civilisation shaken by Norse invasion before it had quite recovered; a people plunged in an unimaginable chaos of races, religions, ideas, appetites, and provincialisms; brayed in the mortar without emerging as a consolidated whole; tenacious of the national idea, but unable to bring it to triumph; riven and pillaged by invasion without being conquered—how could such a people find leisure to grow up, or such a civilisation realise its full potentialities of development and discipline? [2]

Or where, we might add, could a writer look for a tradition; what assumptions could he take to be common to his society; how, indeed, could he be sure that Ireland boasted a society in the ordinary senses of the term? For Ireland was either not a nation at all, or it was many nations, having little in common and holding but slight discourse with each other. The first Irish novel came to be written because a young woman living on a large estate in County Longford found herself with time to spare. Her father had gone down to the

[1] *History of England*, p. 362.
[2] L. Paul-Dubois, *Contemporary Ireland*, p. vii.

Parliament in Dublin, where the "Protestant Nation," as it came to be called, was in session to decide whether or not it would continue to exist. Maria Edgeworth's class was more or less identical with the Protestant Nation, and this dramatic political crisis struck her with personal force. Her reflections found expression in one of the most profound of all Irish novels, *Castle Rackrent*.

There was thus, from the first, a deep involvement of the Irish novel with issues of nationality and of cultural identity. It often took subtle and unexpected forms, but it is the common subject of the important Irish novelists—Maria Edgeworth herself, Lady Morgan, John Banim, Gerald Griffin, and William Carleton. This book, therefore, may properly be called a study of five Irelands, for each writer had his own intense understanding of the country which he had taken as his subject.

The intention of this chapter and the one which follows it is to trace the sources and the consequences of that "unimaginable chaos of races, religions, ideas, appetites, and provincialisms" with which the Irish novelist of the early nineteenth century was confronted. We will be concerned, in the second of these chapters, with the prologue to our story, the rise and fall of the Protestant Nation; with the re-emergence of Celtic Ireland; with the vivid and bewildering transformation of Irish life during the first half of the nineteenth century. These are the issues and events which engaged the imagination of the Irish writer; in these he found his immediate subjects.

But these local issues, though sufficiently urgent, did not kindle his imagination and prompt his passions in and of themselves. He was haunted by history, and his thoughts returned, again and again, to the living bones of the past. Upon these, to an extraordinary degree, he fed his hatred and his love. We must know something, therefore, of his most constant concerns: the way in which Ireland's variety of races and religions came to exist and the reasons why Ireland's culture seemed fated to remain embittered and fragmented.

We may begin by citing a famous and terrible passage from Spenser's *View of the Present State of Ireland:*

Out of every corner of the woodes and glennes they came crepinge forth
upon theire handes, for theire legges could not beare them; they looked like
Anotomies of death, they spake like ghostes crying out of theire graves;
they did eat of the dead Carrions, happy were they could find them yea,
and one another soon after in so much as the very Carcases they spared not
to scrape out of theire graves. And yf they founde a plot of watercresses or
shamrocks, there they flocked as a feast for the tyme yet not long able to
continue therewithall that in short space there were none almost left, and
a most populous and plentiful country suddenly left voyde of man or beaste.[3]

It was hoped with some confidence by Elizabeth's Irish adminis-
trators that this program of extermination would accomplish what
earlier methods had failed to achieve, that it would settle "the Irish
question." Their plan, as Goldwin Smith has remarked, was to diffuse
English civilization "much as an American settler would diffuse it
among Red Indians, by improving them, so far as they could, from
the face of the earth."[4] The trouble with the plan, moral considerations aside, was that it did not work. Gaelic Ireland, by its perverse
and heedless refusal to perish, perpetuated the tragic conflict.

Seán O'Faoláin, in the opening chapters of his biography of Hugh
O'Neill, has shown us the problem as it appeared to the English cap-
tains. The Binghams, Broughs, and Essexes "could not so much as
conceive that behind the outer ring of port-towns, behind those wild
Irish woods, and those dark Irish bogs with their gleaming pools of
water, there was another mode of life as valid, as honourable, as cul-
tured, as complex as their own. They saw nothing there but 'savages,'
'wild hares,' 'beasts,' 'vermin,' 'churles,' 'rascals,' 'felons,' 'slaves,' either
to be 'rooted out' and 'civilized' or 'exterminated.'"[5]

Each of these methods was to be tried, but neither was pushed to
completion. Half of Gaelic Ireland was destroyed, but the other half
persisted, while its distinctive way of life was corrupted and brutalized.
Its nobility held tenaciously to stretches of boggy country in bad times,
surged forward in good. Their ancient prerogatives were the constant

---

[3] Edmund Spenser, *A View of the Present State of Ireland*, p. 135.
[4] Quoted by Paul-Dubois, p. 21.
[5] *The Great O'Neill: A Biography of Hugh O'Neill, Earl of Tyrone, 1550–1616*,
p. 10.

theme of the bardic order, which became the special object of English retaliation. "These bards," Spenser says coldly, "celebrate that which is most dangerous and desperate in all parts of disobedience and rebellious disposition . . . (to) . . . the hurt of the English and the maintenance of their own lewde libertie."

The issues of race, religion, and politics became hopelessly entangled. The policy of the government was to garrison the island on a scale not previously imagined. Elizabeth made extensive settlements in Munster. James cleared Ulster and resettled it with Scottish farmers. In most places the population of these plantations held themselves fiercely aloof from the natives. They had been warned, once by means of a ghastly massacre, that they were held by the "aboriginal inhabitants" to be heretic expropriators, and they had every reason, therefore, to commit themselves to the English interest. In the first years of the nineteenth century young William Carleton stood with his father on a rocky hill in Ulster, staring down with hatred at the prosperous farms of the Presbyterian settlers; for these two, the events of the seventeenth century were as real as yesterday.

In other sections, however, the Elizabethan families reverted to Catholicism, thus making one with the native population on religious grounds, while remaining sharply antagonistic in matters of politics and culture. This situation led directly to the confusion of the Parliamentary Wars, when five distinct armies were in the field, fighting each other in a bewildering sequence of alliances. All five were put to rout by Cromwell, with his customary thoroughness. The Catholic Celts were driven from two of the provinces which remained to them and sent beyond the Shannon to the inhospitable bogs of Connaught. Within a single generation, however, William of Orange faced the eternal problem again, for the great bulk of the Anglo-Irish swordsmen had rallied to the support of James II, and were prepared, with the help of his French allies, to win back his throne on Irish soil.

The full meaning to Irish culture of William's victory at the Boyne, on July 1, 1690, will be discussed later, for it is the theme of John Banim's most famous novel. Here it should suffice to say that the Williamite victory gave Irish life the form which it was to hold until the beginning of the nineteenth century. When Patrick Sarsfield, the Jacobite commander, sailed from Limerick, he took with him, in accordance with the treaty, the Irish army. Never again would Celtic Ireland mount a regular army in the field. But so long as the Stuarts had a cause, it was the plain intention of the Irish Brigades in the service of France to return some day at the point of an invasion. Throughout the dark century which followed, the Gaelic bards, now sunk to the wretched status of hedge poets, awaited "the crack of the sleet on the Jacobite fleet, and the lift of their sails in the morning." Yet in 1715, when the Old Pretender invaded Scotland, not an Irish sword stirred. "His cause," Swift noted in the "Seventh Drapier Letter," "is both desperate and obsolete. . . . Even the papists in general, of any substance or estate, and their priests, almost universally are what we call Whigs." [6]

After the centuries of plantation, massacre, assimilation, and reprisal, a stable and permanent community of "the English in Ireland" had at last been formed. It was composed of Cromwellian settlers— landlords great and small, who were scattered over the four provinces; Williamite grantees, to whom were assigned the estates, including those of "old English" Catholics, confiscated after the Boyne; and, finally, those Elizabethan families who had remained Protestant. To this two smaller but significant groups must be added. A number of important Gaelic families, like the O'Briens of Inchiquin and one branch of the Sligo O'Haras, had embraced Protestantism; henceforth they were to be reckoned as Anglo-Irish, their names being mere oddities. Secondly, the Scots-Irish Presbyterians of Ulster formed a distinct and self-conscious community. Taken in the aggregate, these groups constituted the "middle nation" of the Anglo-Irish.

After the Williamite Settlement far less than one twentieth of the land of Ireland was owned by Catholics, and yet these constituted the overwhelming bulk of the population. This simple but portentous fact accounts for the brutal penal legislation which was the dominant feature of eighteenth-century Ireland. In the measured words of Prendergast, the historian of the process of confiscation, "The object of the

[6] *The Drapier's Letters*, p. 161.

penal laws of the eighteenth century was to secure that the area still owned by Catholics should never be increased, and should be as far as possible diminished. These laws succeeded but too well in their object." [7] The laws were designed to keep servile a hostile population and to extirpate a detested creed.

The campaign was not one of extermination, but of systematic attrition. The public celebration of the Mass was prohibited, and bishops and members of religious orders were driven out upon pain of death. Secular priests, in scheduled numbers, were allowed to remain, provided they took an oath of abjuration. But since further ordinations were forbidden, it was assumed that their rank would vanish within a generation. Bounties were placed on the heads of clergy who refused to register, and "priest-hunting" with wolf-dogs supplanted for a time the other blood sports in which the gentry excelled.

The laws passed against the millions of laymen were equally barbarous. Some lands, even after the Act of Settlement, remained in Catholic hands. At the death of a Catholic landowner, however, his property was broken up and distributed equally among his children. To this there was one exception. Any son, if he conformed to the Church of Ireland, was permitted to dispossess his father and come into full possession. Catholics were forbidden to educate their own children, or to send them abroad. They could not carry arms nor vote nor sit on grand juries nor meet in assembly. They could practice neither law nor medicine. Intermarriage of Catholics and Protestants was strictly prohibited, which tended, as Burke wrote, "to finish the scheme for making the people not only two distinct parties forever, but keeping them as two distinct species on the same land." [8]

The apostolic purpose of the laws failed to carry. Once it had become clear that the conversion of the Irish, like that of the Jews, would take place only amidst the tumult of Judgment Day, the Garrison relaxed certain of its laws, less from tolerance than from an infuriated recognition of their ineffectiveness. Priests and bishops returned and maintained themselves, despite humiliating harassments. Masses were

[7] Quoted by William F. T. Butler in *Confiscation in Irish History*.
[8] Edmund Burke, "A Letter to a Peer of Ireland," *Works*, IV, 236.

celebrated, not, it is true, in chapels, but more publicly still, under open skies. Education was carried on behind a hundred hedges. Candidates for the priesthood and recruits for the Brigades were smuggled regularly from the Kerry coast.

Moreover, while religious hatreds did not slacken, the two peoples living cheek by jowl beside remote bays and bogs found, in time, a *modus vivendi*. The Catholic gentry of the Cork and Kerry coasts took to smuggling, and their Protestant neighbors were their best customers. They also acquired property and passed it on intact by means of friendly Protestant "fronts." Yet here, as elsewhere, the true effects of the Penal Laws were subtly corrosive. Honor itself seemed to demand connivance against the laws of the land.

But pure religious fanaticism, as Lecky has written, echoing Burke and Grattan, "does not appear ever to have played a dominant part in this legislation. The object of the Penal Laws, even in their worst period, was much less to produce a change of religion than to secure property and power by reducing to complete impotence those who had formerly possessed them." [9] In this it was a devastating success. Those with the longest heads, the Blakes and Lallys and Dillons and O'Donnells, took service abroad, where their names glittered on the army lists of six nations. Others were forced down inexorably into the ranks of the peasantry, like that unfortunate Lord Fermoy who was discovered as a stable boy on the lands which his father had ruled. A sizable remnant remained, battered survivors of a dozen traditions. Some, like The O'Conor Don and The O'Donoghue, were lineal descendants of the old kingly families. Some, like the Redmonds and the Graces, were the heirs of Strongbow's Norman aristocracy. A few, like those Brownes who were earls of Kenmare, were of Elizabethan stock. All were involved in a common ruin.

For half a century they nursed a Jacobitism which became increasingly sentimental. After 1750 even this vanished, though it burned strongly among the hedge poets and the peasantry. Charles Edward Stuart was wasting out his days in Rome, abandoned by Louis. And France, while it provided a most hospitable place to live, had no in-

[9] W. E. H. Lecky, *Leaders of Public Opinion in Ireland*, I, 20.

tention of righting Irish grievances. Their apparent hopelessness and the conspiratorial life they had to lead bred in them a timorousness which was to become notorious. "If you mention me or mine," old Maurice O'Connell cautioned Smith, the Kerry historian, "these seaside solitudes will no longer yield us an asylum. The Sassanagh will scale the mountains of Darrynane and we too shall be driven out upon the world without a home." [10] Not until the generation which produced Maurice's grandson would Irish Catholicism bring leaders forward.

Yet the full, staggering weight of the Penal Laws was social and moral, rather than political. The actual tillers of the soil were made into tenants-at-will of landlords who often were absentee. The land was let out to middle men, agents, and subagents. Since the system of primogeniture had broken down, peasants divided and subdivided their minute holdings. Taxes were heaped upon them, the most opprobrious being the tithes which they paid to an alien and enemy church. To improve their farms meant either eviction or an increase in rent, which put a positive premium upon slovenliness. By a system which amounted to slavery they were obliged to work untold "duty days" for the entire benefit of the landlords. When pasturage offered prospects of quicker profits, they were turned out to starve in their thousands on the roadside.

Thus, in the instance of peasant as of gentleman, the law existed only as an oppressor. The gentry at least understood the nature and function of law, but the peasants had been hurled straight from the clan system into a nightmare, sustained only by a religion which was itself an outlaw, and their cherished memories of a culture which others held in the highest contempt. The consequence was inevitable: having been robbed of law, they turned to violence; having been brutalized, they delivered it savagely.

Most Irishmen have a weakness for glamorous myths, and the Anglo-Irish were no exceptions. It beguiled their imaginations and provoked their fears to imagine that they were in constant danger

[10] Charles Smith, *Antient and Modern State of the County of Kerry* (Dublin, 1753), p. 120.

from an insidious Catholic Jacobite conspiracy. In this they persisted, even when the only Stuart claimant was the placid and Anglophile Cardinal York. Were not the Catholic landowners in league with those formidable swordsmen, the officers of the Irish brigades? For what other purpose did the devious Jesuits and Dominicans depart and return? How else were the terrorist societies of the peasant helots to be explained?

Since the seventeen sixties there had been agrarian disturbances which would become so intense as to dominate the Irish problem. In Munster, always the most turbulent province, bands of *bougheleen bawins,* or White Boys, leveled enclosures, burned the houses, and houghed the cattle of the landlords and of peasants who had taken land "over the head" of neighbors. They elected leaders with such fanciful names as "Captain Starlight" and "Captain Rock," drew up regulations, held trials, and passed sentences.[11]

These conspiracies, needless to say, were not organized in the interests of the house of Stuart or at the behest of Kathleen ni Houlihan. The plain fact was that the starving and rackrented poor, having been denied justice, had taken recourse to its only alternative. By the beginning of the nineteenth century, however, these local societies, cut off from one another by mountain and bog, had fallen together in a very loose and very tenuous confederacy. Themselves acting out of grievance and instinct, and possessing no set ambitions, they yet fed into the popular movements—the United Irish rebellion, O'Connell's agitations, Michael Davitt's Land War, and at last Sinn Fein.

The idea of the "Irish Nation" was born in the Ascendancy, and came to flower as the Protestant Nation. It could hardly have been otherwise, for the concept of nationality depends upon conditions which did not obtain for Irish Catholics in the eighteenth century. Barred from public life, they existed without any stake in their own land. Their gentry, who might well have congratulated themselves on being alive at all, carefully preserved their Spanish and French

11 George Cornewall Lewis, *On Local Disturbances in Ireland* (London, 1836), Chapter 1.

blades, their manuscript copies of the old annals, and the genealogies which traced back their ancestry to Noah or the Lost Tribes. They had the warrants of office of grandfathers and great-grandfathers who had served under James II. They sighed, in the long Connaught nights, that the king had not come into his own again. The old, blind harpers and bards, visiting their houses, sang their antique glory. And, on rare occasions, they would pluck up sufficient courage to submit to Dublin a humble petition of rights.[12]

The memories of the old Gaelic order had sifted down, like fine dust, into the peasant imagination. The cabins retained the stories of Ossian and the Fenians and Cuchulain, of Dark Rosaleen. Their poets sang of the Young Pretender, as later they would sing of Bonaparte and O'Connell, not as a living man, but as though in him had been made incarnate some lost, glittering ideal. But all this was locked in the helot's uncouth songs. Antiquaries like Smith and Vallencey and Ledwich would listen to them idly, now and then, just as they would pace back and forth, ruminatively, studying the Celtic crosses and the round towers.

Of the condition to which, by the middle of the eighteenth century, four fifths of the population had been brought, we have spoken. To the condition of the remaining fifth—the Anglo-Irish of the "middle nation"—we must shortly turn. We would seem to have traveled a long way from Macmorris's question, and yet we have not. Each generation posed it afresh. And to the nineteenth century, with its interest in process and historical continuity, the very fact that the question had been asked so many times was revealing.

Many of the Irish novels are loud with the clash of old battles— De Burghs against O'Conors, Kildares fighting Butlers for the mastery of Norman Ireland, McCarthy Mor raising up Munster against Elizabeth, O'Donnell's plots against Clifford, William at the Boyne, and Sarsfield at Limerick. But few of these novels are "historical" in the technical sense, and they are the less interesting ones. History operates upon and through a culture in ways too subtle and too profound to

[12] The life of the old gentry is vividly evoked in Daniel Corkery's *The Hidden Ireland: Gaelic Munster in the Eighteenth Century.*

be accommodated to military tableaux. The Irish novel, nonetheless, is saturated with history. The writer may be Lady Morgan, celebrating the traditional life of the old Catholic gentry, yet pulled in another direction by her Ascendancy loyalties. Or it may be Gerald Griffin, for whom the stones of Limerick were heavy with memory, meaning, and tragedy. However tedious this preoccupation with history became to others, however much it limited his own work, the Irish writer was yoked to it forever. His search for identity drove him relentlessly into the past.

The greatest of all Irish novels contains the cry: "History is a nightmare from which I am trying to awake." [13] It is also the novel with the most powerful and pervasive commitment to history as a determinant of character. The cry comes to the mind of Stephen Dedalus as he is talking to Deasy, a stuffy ideologue. Deasy assumes that Stephen, because of his race and creed, is a "Fenian," and gives him a little lecture on the days when Orangemen had been the only opponents of the Union with England. But it is not the lecture which prompts Stephen to protest. He is caught in the net himself. He remembers that when he went to work for Deasy there had stood on the sideboard a "tray of Stuart coins, base treasure of the bog." And snug in their "spooncase of purple plush, faded, the twelve apostles having preached to all the gentiles: world without end." As much as any nationalist or any Gaelic Leaguer, Stephen is conscious of where matters stand, historically, between his people and Deasy's. "For Ulster will fight and Ulster will be right," Deasy says, jingling out Randolph Churchill's slogan. But Stephen has remembered another Orange cry, "Croppies lie down," and the slashed bodies of Armagh peasants, and Sir John Blackwood in his shiny top boots riding down to Dublin.

[13] James Joyce, *Ulysses*, p. 35.

2. The Political and Social Scene

IN LADY MORGAN'S *Florence Macarthy* there occurs a scene which might have been taken from any of twenty novels of the period. A young Irishman, returning to his stricken country some time after 1810, rides to the graceful Georgian building which once housed the Irish Parliament. Gazing on it, he remembers the bright, heroic days of the Volunteers, the oratory of Grattan, and the patriotism of Bushe. "The descendant of some Irish exile," he thinks, "may voluntarily seek the bright green shores of his fathers, and in this mouldering structure, behold the monument of their former degradation."[1]

The language could only be that of a Morgan hero, but the sentiment was deep and widespread. No political idea had greater strength in nineteenth-century Ireland than the legend of the Protestant Nation, which rose to its swift grandeur in the seventeen seventies and perished ignominiously in 1800 when the Parliament, animated by lavish bribes, voted its own extinction. This idea was, in its fullness, a complex and self-contradictory one. It is of interest to us here because it was the embodiment of the aspirations of Ireland's "middle nation."

The battle of the Boyne had been won by a garrison of English settlers, Protestant in creed, and loyal to the principles of the Whig Revolution. As a garrison, it settled down to the enjoyment of the fruits of victory. Before many years had passed, however, it found itself asking Macmorris's fatal question: What is my nation? In 1698 William Molyneux, a friend of Locke, wrote a defense of Ireland's

[1] Lady Morgan, *Florence Macarthy: An Irish Tale*, I, 50.

claim to independence, only to have it burned by the public execu-
tioner.[2] But other writers took up the claim, and it was eventually
stated, with imperishable brilliance, by Swift.[3]

The question was one of practical and immediate moment. In
theory the island was governed by the King, Lords, and Commons
of Ireland, but the theory had become as badly compromised as the
practice was ignored. Since the days of Henry VII, no law of the
Irish Parliament could be ratified without English approval, and this
provision was now being used by England to cripple or prevent such
competition as she might be offered by her dependent. In this fashion
Irish manufactures, trade, and shipping were subjected to stiff and
often prohibitive duties.

England may have judged that since the Garrison was doing a
bully's work, it was entitled to no more than a bully's wages. In any
event she farmed out the government of Ireland to middle men, in
exactly the fashion that absentees farmed out land. Parliament was
controlled by the Primate, and by certain magnates and commoners
who were called "undertakers," a word in every way fitting, since
in exchange for Crown favors they had undertaken to keep the country quiet. It was against these men, and their principals in London,
that Swift launched his philippics. He wrote in the name of "the
Irish people" and "the Irish nation."

This "nation," which had found so noble a voice, is one of the
curiosities of political speculation. In *The Drapier's Letters,* Swift ex-
cludes from it, presumably in perpetuity, not only the Catholics, whom
he despised, but the Dissenters, whom he loathed. This left members
of the Church of Ireland, the bulk of whose clergy and members of
parliament he regarded as little better than suborned traitors. Perhaps
he chose his pseudonym wisely: only a Dublin draper could be sure
of meeting all his qualifications. Yet Swift's Irish papers are lifted
far above the absurdity of his central position by his patriotism, and by
the rage against man's inhumanity which led him to champion the
homeless poor who lined the roads.

[2] *The Case of Ireland's Being Bound by Act of Parliament in England. . . .*
[3] For Swift's position in this matter, see his *Drapier's Letters,* but also the less
celebrated papers collected in *Irish Tracts: 1728–1733.*

The situation of the Anglo-Irish contained ambiguities which became, in time, intolerable. They were not Irish, if by that term was meant the natives of the island. Indeed, from "the mere Irish" they held themselves arrogantly aloof. They had thought themselves English, but what meaning had that term if the sister island chose not to honor it? They lived, to use De Quincey's term, "amidst turbulent scenes,"[4] which demanded vigor and intrepidity of them, and they came to think themselves a special breed, entitled on their proved merits to self-government. And those men of the Ascendancy *were* a special breed—witty, gallant, coarse, brave, and profligate. Because the anarchy of Irish life was universal, affecting conqueror and conquered alike, the Anglo-Irish gentleman was as lawless as any Connemara peasant. Sir Walter Scott, who had long admired him from afar, was somewhat unnerved when he encountered him in 1825, stalking the land like a conquistador.[5] He was an inveterate duelist, and in this light-hearted fashion he proposed to win the independence of the "Irish Nation" from the British Empire.

The moment arrived in the seventeen seventies. Britain's conflicts with France and the colonies had spread her military establishment perilously thin, and forced her to leave Ireland unprotected against invasion. Into this breach stepped the nobility and gentry of Ireland, who formed yeomanry corps of infantry and cavalry, which coalesced into an army known as the Volunteers. Events did not permit them to take the field, although they were splendidly accoutred. But it occurred to them that they were in an excellent position to argue their cause against England. Sir Laurence Parsons, viewing events retrospectively, put matters in the nervous, declamatory rhetoric to which they were uniformly addicted:

The whole nation in a few years was thus arrayed. That is, every Protestant capable of bearing arms. . . . But their spirit rose with their armament and discipline. And, beginning only to assure themselves, and proceeding to protect the country against France, they concluded by vindicating their constitution and liberty against the aspiration of England.[6]

[4] Thomas De Quincey, *Autobiography from 1785 to 1803*, p. 226.

[5] John Gibson Lockhart, *Life of Sir Walter Scott*, VIII, 20.

[6] Quoted by Stephen Gwynn from an unpublished diary, in *Henry Grattan and His Times*, p. 59.

That is to say, they refused to disband. They were thus an unexpected weapon in the hands of patriots like Grattan, who had for
years been fighting a lonely and hopeless battle in Parliament. But
Grattan realized from the first that they were a dangerous weapon,
for while their zeal and high spirits were welcome innovations, their
aspirations were as shimmering and changeable as the epaulets with
which they had bedecked themselves.

A convention of the Volunteers at Dungannon in February of 1782
asserted in the firmest tones that they intended to secure their rights.
With so belligerent a force at his back, Grattan proceeded to a vigorous attack, and succeeded in wresting from London what amounted
to a concession of Ireland's right to self-government. Grattan announced the victory in language which long was remembered:

I found Ireland on her knees, I watched over her with a paternal solicitude;
I have traced her progress from injuries to arms, and from arms to liberty.
Spirit of Swift, Spirit of Molyneux, your genius has prevailed, Ireland is
now a nation; in that new character I hail her, and bowing in her august
presence, I say, *Esto perpetua.*[7]

Parliament tendered its thanks to Grattan in a graceful ceremony.
This was watched, with concern mixed with cool amusement, by a
landlord long resident in England, Richard Lovell Edgeworth, who
had just returned home with his daughter Maria. Edgeworth had
the quick-cutting, unsentimental mind of a philosophic radical, and
he saw at once the dangers which attended the rejoicing. Ireland's
"independence" meant nothing if it was not accompanied by a thor-
ough reform of Parliament, an adjustment of the land problem, and
a recognition of the rights of Catholics.

With the abruptness proper to a rational man when confronted by
exuberant heroics, he left Dublin and traveled north to his estates.
But Maria stored up the scene, as she would many others, in her sensitive and perceptive imagination.

Grattan was caught upon a dilemma. He was intent not merely on
reform but on the preservation of the constitution and the forms of
ordered government, yet the only hope for reform lay with the more

[7] *Ibid.*, p. 125.

swashbuckling elements in the Volunteers. These gentlemen, in confirmation of his apprehensions, descended upon Dublin in armed bodies. Nominally they were under the command of the wan and romantic Lord Charlemont. Their most congenial spirit, however, was the Bishop of Derry, a buoyant and unbalanced personality who had traveled to town ostentatiously protected by the cavalry troop of his nephew George Fitzgerald, later to be hanged after a long and alarming career as a ruffian.[8]

Grattan temporized for a time between Parliament and the rival body which had installed itself in the Rotunda, but he finally refused to accept the methods of the Volunteers for the accomplishment of his aims. As a result of this split he lost his backing, Parliament remained unreformed, and the management of Irish affairs returned, after a brief period, to the old, venal understrappers. The years that remained to the Protestant Nation have been much celebrated, but in fact they allowed Grattan little more than opportunity to polish his much-admired eloquence. With the minority of patriotic Whigs, he fought a dark and thankless battle.

Grattan's temperate and essentially conservative mind envisaged a nation which, while maintaining Protestant Ascendancy, would gradually admit Catholics of substance to the franchise. The Catholic lords, an exotic group of which the heads were Kenmare, Fingall, and Gormanston, had formed a committee to lobby for their rights. But since they considered mere assemblage an act sufficiently daring, they limited themselves to obsequious petitions. The rising class of Catholic tradesmen, however, decided upon a more manly course. Almost their first step was a momentous one, for in 1790 they hired as legal secretary a struggling barrister named Theobald Wolfe Tone.

His name tells us that the curtain had rung up on the last act. Tone is in many ways the most remarkable figure in modern Irish history.[9] An ambitious, dissatisfied, and intelligent young man, he embraced wholeheartedly the ideas which had blown across the sea from revolu-

[8] See Mary Macarthy, *Fighting Fitzgerald and Other Papers*, pp. 81–181.

[9] The most controversial, at any rate. But of the many who have appraised his character, he remains his own most candid critic: *The Life of Wolfe Tone; Written by Himself and Continued by His Son.*

tionary France. In association with a number of kindred spirits he
formed the society, subsequently famous, of United Irishmen. Their
reasoning was persuasive and their plan was daring.

The vicissitudes of the Protestant Nation had demonstrated with
something like the clarity of mathematics that the Irish Parliament
was incapable of winning for Ireland an independence which was
more than nominal. The majority of its members were place men
who voted on hire. Its patriotic minority were fettered by conservative
instincts. But to speak of the "Nation" was to use the language of
farce, since the great mass of the population was legally excluded from
its privileges. These were the Scots-Irish of Ulster, a tough-minded
and fractious people, and the Catholics of the South, whose peasantry
was a byword for rebellious violence. The plan of the United Irishmen was to bring these two groups into the field with the assistance
of a French invasion, overthrow the government, and establish a republic. Quite apart from the complacent ease with which they permitted government infiltrators to learn their secrets, they made two
fatal mistakes: they assumed that Ireland's religious hatreds were dead
and that peasants would fight in the name of an abstraction called
the Republic of Ireland.

The peasants did in fact join the United Irishmen, though not at
first, and not for the reasons which Tone supposed. News of the Rising quickly leaked out, and threw the landlords, always apprehensive
of rebellion, into hysterical panic. From every bogside they heard, or
imagined they heard, whispers of treason, and they struck first and
viciously. Bands of yeomanry rode over the countryside, burning,
whipping, torturing, and gibbeting, until the frenzied peasants knew
that there was no point in not rebelling. But the worst of the yeomanry
corps were composed of the Ulster Presbyterians upon whom Tone
had counted so heavily. And the Celtic counties of the West, which
had not been put to the rack, remained disappointingly apathetic.

The Rising, when it came, was immeasurably tragic. Brave, bewildered peasants marched out from Bargy and Forth and Shelmalier.
They fought well and hard, but not for Tone's Rights of Man. Their
actions were marred by ugly sectarianism; even their fine stand on

Vinegar Hill was attended by the systematic slaughter of unarmed Protestants. Yet it is hard to see what other ideals could have animated these poor wretches, steeped in their own history, and cut off from that of Europe. The Connaught peasants who told Humbert that they were fighting for Robespierre and the Blessed Virgin offer in those pathetic words a kind of justification.

The only apparent consequence of the Rebellion was the Act of Union, which Fitzgibbon and Castlereagh forced through a liberally bribed Parliament in 1800. Amidst the sordid but exciting scenes which attended the tallying of votes, the Protestant Nation perished as fact. But it had begun its long and equally dramatic career as a memory and an ideal.

One unambiguous "No!" to the motion in support of Union was spoken in the harsh, commanding tones of Richard Lovell Edgeworth. At that moment his daughter Maria was sitting at the long table in the crowded Edgeworthstown drawing room, scribbling furiously at the first Irish novel. *Castle Rackrent* was to be the brilliant requiem of the Protestant Nation, for Maria Edgeworth had seen its history as the life of a family which rose from obscurity, fought bravely, lost meanly, and at last perished in squalor and pride.

No one felt more keenly this national shame and loss than did a young farmer named Patrick Griffin, who had recently moved into the town of Limerick. Although a Catholic, he had been a militiaman in one of the companies of Volunteers, and had imbibed their heady patriotism. To his son Gerald, who was born in 1803, he told and retold the stories of those brave days. When he was writing his best novel, *The Collegians,* Gerald Griffin would remember his father's lofty, foolish sentiments with affection and anger. He had witnessed the drama and fire of O'Connell's victory in Clare, and the Volunteers seemed by contrast country squires playing with dress swords.

Indeed, of all the writers with whom this study deals, there is only one for whom the legend of Grattan's "Nation" did not hold meaning. In 1800 William Carleton was a barefoot, Gaelic-speaking urchin, following his father about from one hardscrabble Ulster farm to the next. For the Carletons the politics of 1800 had but one meaning: in that year a band of drunken Orange yeomen broke into their cabin and abused Carleton's sister. The Gaelic-speaking community, which in 1800 covered great stretches of the island, was locked in another time, almost another land. Carleton alone would give it voice before it perished in the Famine.

To understand the significance of Grattan's Nation, one might well pause upon this fact of language. The brief passages quoted above from Parsons and from Grattan himself suggest that the Patriot Party was intensely conscious of language, which it invested with much passion and moral feeling. Oratory of that sort was a prized accomplishment in eighteenth-century Ireland, the glittering, posed language of public men who had modeled themselves upon the heroes in Plutarch. Set against the stench and misery of Irish life, it marks the measure of their political failure.

But the speeches of Grattan celebrated—in a sense, they created— the idea of Irish nationality. And they did so in English. Ireland's claims to sovereignty had been many, various, and inchoate. With the Volunteers they assumed for the first time the shape and direction of modern European politics. By the same token these claims had, in the past, been advanced in a tongue quite unknown to the peoples of Europe, and regarded in England as the gabble of savages. Themselves a minority, and meanly jealous of their prerogatives, the Volunteers presented their countrymen with the only available image of the nation-state.

For this reason the Catholics of Ireland were divided and confused in their attitude toward the Protestant Nation. When the Volunteers were forming in 1779, Richard O'Connell of the Irish Brigade in France wrote to a friend, "Would to God, my dear Maurice, that we were at this moment 200,000 strong in Ireland, and that I had the command of our single company at Oak Park! I would kick the Members and their Volunteers and their Unions and their Societies to the Devil! I would make the rascally spawn of Damned Cromwell curse the hour of his Birth!" [10] But to Daniel O'Connell, Richard's distant

10 Mrs. Morgan John O'Connell, *The Last Colonel of the Irish Brigade*, I, 223.

kinsman, the Volunteers were a splendid and admirable example. Most of the Catholic gentry stood coolly apart both from the fury of the fire-eating Richard and from the admiration of his hardheaded cousin. "The Nation of Ireland" was the contrivance of their Protestant enemies; their participation in it had not been solicited, and they were indifferent to its death, as they had been to its life.

What the Nation meant to the Protestants of Ireland we will be able to trace in some detail when we turn to the novels and the career of Lady Morgan. The Nation's great monument is Lecky's many-volumed history, that stirring celebration of an independent Ireland written by the loyalist professor of history at Trinity College.[11] Perhaps that fact and its implications are all we need bear in mind for the moment. It was the tragedy of the nineteenth-century Ascendancy, which none felt more keenly than did Lecky himself, that the national cause had passed out of their hands, and into those of men who gave it a new shape, and new passions. The press of events would force upon the descendants of the Volunteers a position which was staunchly Unionist. Yet over the fireplace of many a great house would hang, in honor, the sword of a grandfather who had served in the Volunteers, and his uniform would be carefully preserved. The sword and the uniform may serve to remind us how rich in paradox was the culture of nineteenth-century Ireland, and how embittered.

"The majority of the Irish," Professor Constantia Maxwell has written, "inspired by their national tradition and stimulated by O'Connell, were henceforth determined to shape their own destiny. With the growth of the Gaelic spirit the old Ascendancy came to be regarded with disgust, and the Anglo-Irish were described as a caste who had done little but exploit their own interests. It is vain, perhaps, to solicit the attention of those who have been offended, but others will observe that . . . most of the institutions that flourish at present in Dublin date back to the Georgian period. The Irish capital as far as brick and stone are concerned is essentially a city of the past—an eloquent reminder of an old aristocratic society that, with all its faults, not only

[11] W. E. H. Lecky, *History of Ireland in the Eighteenth Century*.

achieved distinction at home, but upheld the standards of that age and even added to its culture." [12]

The chief legacy of the Protestant Nation was the city of Dublin itself. It appears in nearly all of the novels which we shall be discussing, and with a multiplicity of meanings. To some writers it was the portentous embodiment of England in Ireland; to others, the sad effigy of all that had made Ireland great. Yet few denied its loveliness, as haunting in its own way as the plains of Mayo. The Parliament House, the Four Courts, the Royal Exchange, the Custom House, the public buildings along the Liffey, the imposing vista of Sackville Street, attained in time the melancholy power of a Piranesi.[13] Here were buildings which seized the imagination of the writer, just as the shattered towers of the Desmonds did, and the Spanish houses of Galway. Here, more truly than in the Palladian mansions of the remote provinces, lived the spirit of the Ascendancy. But in Ireland the stones and bricks remain; the spirit is wasted and broken and swept into the past. In the period with which we will be dealing, the power of the eighteenth-century Ascendancy seemed as great as ever, but the nerve of its life had been cut.

The troubled, haunting past which has been sketched was the Irish writer's legacy, as it was that of all of his countrymen. But he was living also in his own time, and the first half of the nineteenth century witnessed swift and confusing political and social changes.

These changes may be summarized, somewhat paradoxically, either as the emergence of modern Ireland or as the reemergence of Celtic Ireland. For the transforming event of these decades was the appearance on the political scene of the Catholic peasantry, mobilized by O'Connell in the interest of Emancipation. It was his boast that he found a nation of slaves and made men of them, and he was nearly right. Sweeping aside the cautious, Whiggish nobility of the old Catholic Committees, he inspired and disciplined hundreds of thou-

---

[12] *Dublin Under the Georges, 1714–1830,* pp. 44–45.

[13] See, for example, the plates in James Malton's *Picturesque and Descriptive View of the City of Dublin,* 1799.

sands of peasants, many of whom knew no English, many of whom had never been beyond their own villages. When Insurrection Acts were passed to prevent his assemblies, he drove through them, to use his own phrase, with "a coach-and-six." And in 1829 he wrung Emancipation from Peel and Wellington by offering, or seeming to offer, civil war as the alternative.[14]

Years later, after having held his Agitations in abeyance, he tried to force the repeal of the Act of Union by the same tactics, and failed utterly. Facing his two old antagonists again, he summoned his army in even larger numbers, but this time his bluff was called. Now the choice between peace and war was his to make, and he retreated. A few years later, while his country lay prostrate with famine and plague, he died in Rome, a broken man, with his fame in shreds. His legacy was divided, in equal proportions, between the young Gracchi of *The Nation* and the gang of timeservers whom he had gathered about him.

In 1828 an election was held in Clare which was itself a kind of civil war, for O'Connell, a Catholic, was standing for Parliament. Clare was one of the "troubled" counties, and thirty thousand peasants were waiting for him in camps pitched in the meadows outside Ennis. He entered the town with an escort of three thousand horsemen along a road lighted with bonfires. The government, naturally apprehensive, had sent in strong cavalry detachments, but the Irish were under the rigid discipline of their priests, who acted as O'Connell's lieutenants, and no violence attended his overwhelming victory. All factions seem to agree that the absence of drunkenness was the oddest phenomenon, it having been believed that some natural law doomed the Irish to this condition whenever they met in assemblies larger than two. Peel, despairing of his own powers of evocation, wrote to Sir Walter Scott, "no pen but yours could have done justice to that fearful exhibition of sobered and desperate enthusiasm." [15]

[14] For a contemporary account of the events leading to Emancipation, see Thomas Wyse, *Historical Sketch of the Late Catholic Association of Ireland.* Two modern studies are excellent: Denis Gwynn, *The Struggle for Catholic Emancipation, 1750–1829,* and James A. Reynolds, *The Catholic Emancipation Crisis in Ireland, 1823–1829.*

[15] *Sir Robert Peel from His Private Papers,* ed. by Charles S. Parker, II, 99.

Gerald Griffin, the novelist, was present at the Clare election, and exchanged letters on the subject with a fellow writer, John Banim. Both men were young, liberal in their politics, and Catholic. But a generation separates them in feeling. Banim had all the cautious reservations of those Catholic landed gentlemen who followed O'Connell with such marked reluctance; Griffin was buoyant, confident, and prepared to put matters to the test. The Ennis victory supplied just the ending he needed for *The Collegians,* on which he was then at work.

But for two others of our novelists the changes wrought in Irish life by O'Connell's triumphs bore a different meaning entirely. Lady Morgan was a prominent member of the group of liberal Protestants who gave O'Connell support. She lived to hate him as the man who had given Ireland over to the mob, the priest, and the terrorist. And Maria Edgeworth, a much finer and more honorable member of the Anglo-Irish than Lady Morgan, found herself one day surrounded by the tumult and animal force of one of his "monster" demonstrations; she was fortified in her decision never to write again of Irish life. Once she had understood her country, but now it confused and terrified her.

To understand the period it is necessary to understand the impact of O'Connell, since for twenty years, from 1825 to 1845, he *was* Ireland.[16] In Balzac's phrase, which may sound hyperbolic, but was the common judgment of Europe, he was the incarnation of his people. But to see him clearly, and through the eyes of his Irish contemporaries, is no easy task. The English view of him may quickly be stated, for it found expression in a famous bit of doggerel printed in *The Times:*

> Scum condensed of Irish bog!
> Ruffian, liar, demagogue!
> Boundless liar, base detractor,
> Nurse of murders, treason's factor!
> Of Pope and priest the crouching slave,
> While thy lips of freedom rave.

[16] The most useful of the many biographies of O'Connell are those by Michael MacDonagh and Denis Gwynn. Seán O'Faoláin's *King of the Beggars* is a remarkable study of his personality and his career.

> Of England's fame the viprous hater,
> Yet wanting courage for a traitor. . . .[17]

But from the time of his first failures, and with a savagery which the years increased, he was attacked by nationalists at home, and their views have generally prevailed. "After his death," Professor Michael Tierney has remarked, "he was represented to his own people as a giant indeed, but one whose faults were more gigantic than his virtues, and as largely responsible by his preaching of a cowardly doctrine for the catastrophe of the Famine and even for the fiasco of 1848. This condemnation, passed and ratified by men who never had a tithe of the power over their own generation that O'Connell possessed over his, has remained in force down to this day." [18]

The terms of condemnation were compressed by John Mitchel into a few lines of vivid invective:

Poor old Dan! Wonderful, jovial, mighty, and mean old man, with silver tongue and smile of witchery and heart of melting ruth—lying tongue, smile of treachery, heart of unfathomable fraud. What a royal yet vulgar soul, with the keen eye and potent sweep of a generous eagle of Cairn Tual —with the base servility of a hound and the cold cruelty of a spider.[19]

But Mitchel understood O'Connell's Ireland as little as did Thomas Davis or the other members of Young Ireland who revolted against his control of the national party. There stand as a stain upon O'Connell's memory the words with which the old man turned loose his pack on Davis: "There is no such party as that styled 'Young Ireland.' There may be a few individuals who take that denomination on themselves. I am for Old Ireland. 'Tis time that this delusion should be put an end to. Young Ireland may play what pranks it pleases. I do not envy them the name they rejoice in, I shall stand by Old Ireland. And I have some slight idea that Old Ireland will stand by me." [20]

It was O'Connell at his most brutal, for he knew where he was cutting, and to what instincts he was making appeal. The incident oc-

[17] Quoted from Gwynn, *O'Connell*, p. 8.
[18] Preface to *Daniel O'Connell: Centenary Essays.*
[19] John Mitchel, *Jail Journal: or, Five Years in British Prisons,* p. 157.
[20] Sir Charles Gavan Duffy, *Young Ireland: A Fragment of Irish History,* p. 705.

curred during the "Godless colleges" controversy, and O'Connell was rousing up the Catholics who formed his great majority against the Protestant, Davis, who was quite blameless of sectarian animus. For this reason his appeal has been much reprehended, and rightly. Yet O'Connell himself was no bigot, though he has been so represented. The fact is, rather, that O'Connell *did* represent the "old Ireland," by which, of course, he meant the Catholic and Gaelic population of the island. And it had become clear, much to his own dismay, that their interests were substantially different from those of the Protestant Ascendancy. O'Connell had brought "old Ireland" into the light of modern history, from the darkness of feudal days and the eighteenth-century nightmare.

In 1825 and again in 1843, when O'Connell put the ingenious machinery of his "Agitation" into full operation, he summoned to life the slumbering passions of the "hidden," Gaelic Ireland. Uncanny rumors swept the peasantry. Peddlers carried from village to village garbled copies of the supposed prophecies of Pastorini and Columkill, the burden of which was that some ill-defined but pleasurable event had been destined for the year '25—it might be Emancipation or the end of heresy (and heretics with it) or the return of the Stuarts. Diarmuid O'Mahony, a hedge poet, wrote in Gaelic: "My thoughts were all of the troubles of the Gaels, harassed by taxes, rents, and wrongs, through the crooked laws of the tribes of treachery, since the true king, James, abandoned us. Poets of Munster, hear me: the army is coming over the water; Repeal will be won in the year that ends in five; Daniel O'Connell is our defender." [21]

O'Connell would have viewed such a poem with jovial skepticism, for he was notoriously of two minds as to the worth of the traditional Gaelic culture. Yet there can be no doubt that the great source of his power was the instinctive skill with which he evoked such passions. He spoke unerringly to an Ireland of which Wolfe Tone knew nothing and would have cared less, and which Thomas Davis saw through the romantic haze of conventional nationalism. To the "poets of

[21] From a translation by Gerald Murphy in his essay on "O'Connell's Gaelic Background" in Dr. Tierney's book of centenary essays.

Munster" his voice came like the distant thunder of their own past.

"The Catholic people of Ireland are a nation," he once said, thus bringing us full circle. Grattan's problem had been that of maintaining a Protestant Nation to which Catholics would gradually be admitted. The problem which faced Irish culture in the nineteenth century was the reverse of this, since O'Connell had made possible for Catholics a sense of nationality which they tended naturally to identify with their creed. The course of Irish history had made this almost inevitable. It followed that the question of the Protestant interest would be as insurmountable as the Catholic issue had been for Grattan.

For the seven years of the Tithe War (1830–1837), which is described so graphically in the novels of Griffin and Carleton, O'Connell was forced to leave the movement for Repeal in abeyance, partly because the Church, on whose organization he relied, was indifferent to Repeal, and partly because many Protestants who had been favorable to it hesitated to commit themselves to his leadership. When he finally did secure Church support for Repeal, in the eighteen forties, he found himself dependent for secular assistance upon the Young Ireland movement. A majority of its members were Protestant, and were very properly concerned that they should not become mere camp followers of a priest-dominated Catholic movement. Their sensitivity to affront, at times justified, created a fatal breach.

O'Connell himself, with his liberal views on cultural issues, was dedicated to the idea of a united nation, but he was overgenerous in his estimation of both creeds. Despite his genuine piety he was no clericalist but, wiser in this than his critics, he knew that no Irish popular movement could hope for success without Church support. The dreadful attritions of Penal Days had deprived Irish Catholicism of a class of educated, independent Catholic laymen, while the peasants were devoted, to the far side of idolatry, to the shepherds who had stood by them during the blackest of persecutions. Emancipation permitted the Church to show its less heroic side, and many Protestant liberals were shocked by its harshness and its intolerance. For the most part, of course, the Garrison was not liberal at all; its traditions of mastery and condescension would have been shocked by any popular movement. Caught between these conflicting and irreconcilable interests, O'Connell naturally chose in accordance with his oldest and deepest loyalties.

In his dark, final years he would spend more and more time, to the neglect of national affairs, at his Derrynane home, which his forefathers had built on a narrow Kerry peninsula thrust into the wild Atlantic. If Georgian Dublin fixes for us the image of Ascendancy Ireland, then Derrynane must stand for another strand in the cultural fabric. Lady Morgan's preposterous "Prince of Innismore," living in a crumbling fortress with his chaplains and retainers, pales in interest beside the accounts which have been preserved of the O'Connells of Derrynane. O'Connell had spent his youth in this house with his uncle Maurice, the shrewd old smuggler who had made his peace with the new order, though when he wanted something done he still sent out to his peasants the crooked knife which was his badge of authority.

There lived also at Darrynane Mhair ni Dhuv, O'Connell's grandmother, the dark woman from the O'Donohues. And for a time his uncle, Count Daniel, the last colonel of the Irish Brigade. Many memories lived there. Of Art O'Leary, the hot-blooded young soldier who was murdered during Penal Days, and over whose body his wife Ellen, an O'Connell, spoke the lament which was carried by poets over the length of Ireland: "Wretched Morris, sorrow on you! You killed my darling; and is there no man in Ireland to riddle you with bullets?" [22] And the memory of another O'Connell, driven to the West by Cromwell, and dying on the road.

Young Daniel O'Connell had gone from this house to the law courts of Dublin, and to the country assizes where only his bluster and guile stood between bewildered peasants and an infamous law. He had gone, at last, to the great open-air meetings where his voice rolled like honeyed thunder across the plains. And he had taken with him the entire submerged nation of Celtic Ireland. "It was one of my mother's humourous sayings," Justin McCarthy wrote, "that her

[22] The Gaelic text and a literal translation appear in the appendix to Mrs. M. J. O'Connell's book. The lines quoted here are as translated by Mr. Murphy in the essay cited above.

daughter—her name was Ely—was born a slave, while I, Justin, was born a free man, because Ely was born before the passing of the Catholic Emancipation Act, while I was born in the year after it had become law." [23] Because of this O'Connell was known, during his lifetime, as "the big beggar man" or as "the liberator"—depending on where you stood.

The Great Famine falls like a dark curtain across the age. It was preceded by the collapse of O'Connell's campaign of agitation and followed by the defeat of the Young Ireland party, but it overshadowed both of these events. "In Irish social and political history," write the editors of a recent and illuminating study, "the famine was very much of a watershed. The Ireland on the other side of those dark days is a difficult world for us to understand; the Ireland that emerged we recognize as one with problems very much akin to our own." [24]

In 1852, when the horrors of the Famine were still fresh in Irish minds, Patrick Murray wrote an important article on Carleton for *The Edinburgh Review*. He praises the novelist on several scores, but the one on which he lays the most stress is this: "It is in his pages and in his alone that future generations must look for the truest and fullest, though still far from complete, picture of those who ere long will have passed away from that troubled land, from the records of history, and from the memory of man forever." [25]

Murray meant the statement to be taken quite literally, for Carleton was the great memorialist of the peasant civilization of Ireland which perished with the Famine. But we may take his observation to hold true, in a sense, for the entire *corpus* of the Irish novel in the early nineteenth century. It has a special value, quite apart from questions of artistic merit, as the unique record of a culture. If we did not have Carleton's novels, we would know much less than we do of the way in which the peasants lived. If we did not have Maria Edgeworth's novels, we would know much less about life in the Big Houses.

[23] *An Irishman's Story*, p. 6.
[24] *The Great Famine: Studies in Irish History 1845-52*, ed. by R. Dudley Edwards and T. Desmond Williams, p. vii.
[25] *Edinburgh Review*, CXCVI (October, 1852), 389.

The topicality of many of the Irish novels, the way in which they are rooted in history as well as in space, forces us to the consideration of controversies which now are long dead, and to the re-living of quarrels which the years have settled. But the relationship is reciprocal. The Ireland which lies on the far side of the Famine is a less difficult world to understand because of the novelists who recorded and interpreted its life. The quarrels and controversies, the passions and aspirations come finally into place as the diverse voices with which a troubled culture spoke to itself and, less coherently, to the world.

3. The Nature of the Irish Novel

NINETEENTH-CENTURY IRELAND was, as we have seen, a land splintered by divided loyalties and ancient hatreds. Sir Walter Scott, visiting the country in 1825, noted with some contempt: "Their factions have been so long envenomed, and they have such narrow ground to do their battle in, that they are like men fighting with daggers in a hogshead."[1] Much later Yeats, writing as an Irishman and in bitterness, would make the same point:

> Out of Ireland have we come.
> Great hatred, little room,
> Maimed us at the start.
> I carry from my mother's womb
> A fanatic heart.[2]

One is tempted to seize upon these quotations as epigraphs to a study of Irish fiction, for most Irish novels accept as given the condition to which they point. The English novelist was concerned with social choice and personal morality, which are the great issues of European fiction. But to the Irish novelist these were subordinated to questions of race, creed, and nationality—questions which tend of their nature to limit the range and power of fiction. Yet for the Irishman these were the crucial points by which he was given social identity.

If the social pattern was much more various than is generally supposed, the popular notion of a dual society, the masters and the ruled, has a large measure of truth. On one side stood "native" Ireland. It had

[1] John Gibson Lockhart, *Life of Sir Walter Scott*, VIII, 25.
[2] From "Remorse for Intemperate Speech," *Collected Poems of William Butler Yeats*, p. 293.

become a nation of peasants, fiercely Catholic, indifferent or hostile to statute law, Gaelic-speaking or at least heavily influenced by the traditions of Gaelic society, nourished by dark and sanguinary resentments and aspirations. On the other side stood the nation of the Anglo-Irish, land-owning, Protestant, and, of course, English-speaking. Though this nation aspired, intermittently, to political independence, in point of fact, its culture and its modes of thought were indisputably English.

The Irish novelists, being men of their generation, realized that the two nations were yoked in a common fate, that despite all hatreds and blood-letting they would have to endure each other. And yet, when all the fair words had been spoken, each writer would find himself pledged to his own people. Maria Edgeworth might reach gropingly, in her last novels, to Gaelic Ireland, but she remained a lady of the Big Houses, anxious for peace, but for peace upon the terms imposed by the Big Houses. And Gerald Griffin, for all the liberality of his sentiments, was haunted by his vision of that older Ireland which existed before the Big Houses, and which remained incarnate in the shattered Norman keeps of the Geraldines. Each novelist was forced to pose to himself the question of what Ireland was and of what it meant to be an Irishman. From tensions of this kind the Irish novels derive their strength.

The Irish novelist, like any writer, was quarreling with himself and with his culture. A special and distinguishing circumstance obtained, however. The quarrel was addressed, in the first instance, not to his own people but to strangers, and it was usually couched in the language of explanation. That is to say, most of the Irish novels were addressed to an English audience, and most of them offered to explain and interpret the sister kingdom. The supposed "editor" of the history of *Castle Rackrent* places his story "before the English reader as a specimen of manners and characters, which are perhaps unknown in England. Indeed, the domestic habits of no nation in Europe were less known to the English than those of their sister country, till within these last few years." [3] Nor is this novel an exception; of the fiction which we shall be considering, only the early stories of William

[3] Maria Edgeworth, *Castle Rackrent*, p. 69.

Carleton were written directly for an Irish audience. And Carleton's stories, when collected and published as a book, were preceded by a note in which the author acknowledged the English reading public as his probable audience.[4]

This circumstance had a decisive effect upon the aims and purposes of the Irish novel. Numberless prefaces, forewords, and introductions make the same tedious avowal of intentions. Ireland, so such statements may be summarized, is for the first time to be represented "as it really is," and in a spirit free of religious and political rancor. Lady Morgan, an inveterate offender in this regard, tells us in the preface to *O'Donnel* that her tale is devoted to "the purposes of conciliation, and to incorporate the leaven of favorable opinion with that heavy mass of bitter prejudice, which writers, both grave and trifling, have delighted to raise against my country." [5] She assures us in the preface to *Florence Macarthy* that her aim throughout her career has been "to sketch the brilliant aspect of a people struggling with adversity, and by the delineation of national virtues, to excite sympathy, and awaken justice." [6] Griffin and Carleton, better and less didactic writers, make similar avowals. And since Richard Lovell Edgeworth, who supplied the introductions to his daughter's novels, was a professional moralist, his remarks may be entrusted to the reader's imagination.

The "editor" of *Castle Rackrent* spoke sober truth: the English reader knew less of Ireland than he did of most European countries. What little he did know was unpleasant. Some hideous insurrection would remind him of its existence, or a reckless Ascendancy duelist would cause a day's gossip. The Act of Union, however, made Ireland a matter of direct concern, and the English public was soon burdened with the rumors of agrarian outrage and armed conspiracies which had hitherto been swallowed by the silences of Dublin Castle. Then, in the eighteen twenties, the mass agitation for the removal of the Penal Laws gave evidence of what was to become a recurrent problem: Ireland's ability to provoke a parliamentary crisis.

[4] Preface to O'Donoghue's edition of First Series of *Traits and Stories of the Irish Peasantry*, I, xxiv–xxvi.

[5] Lady Morgan, *O'Donnel: A National Tale*, I, x.

[6] Lady Morgan, *Florence Macarthy: An Irish Tale*, I, vi.

There was a general desire for information about Ireland, and an interest in the nature of Irish society. Novels were then considered proper vehicles of such information, and writers rushed into print with accounts of "Ireland today." Orange novelists like the aptly named George Brittaine came forward with somber chronicles of brutish, priest-ridden peasants held in check by a devout Garrison of British Christians. Catholic writers like John Banim replied in kind. And liberal Protestants attempted a judicious adjustment of the two extreme positions—a task which was to find more favor in English than in Hibernian eyes. The atmosphere was charged with political passions, and every Irish writer, no matter how far removed he may have been from such concerns, knew that his picture of Ireland would be scanned for its political overtones.

Nor was Catholic Emancipation the only issue which could enmesh the novelist in controversy. The peasant question, the questions of land and of absenteeism are all represented in the novels of the period. All of these, however, came to be overshadowed, in the final decade of the half century, by the single issue of the repeal of the Act of Union, which would mean, of course, the restoration of Irish nationality. The Edgeworths were supporters of the Union, although Richard Lovell, for reasons peculiar to his temperament, had cast his vote against it in the Irish Parliament. And Ireland's claim to nationhood is the chief theme in Lady Morgan's fiction. The issue became one of wide public concern, however, only with the revival of O'Connell's agitation and with the founding of *The Nation* in 1842.

Thus the Irish novel, in one of its aspects, can be termed a kind of advocacy before the bar of English public opinion. In plot and in characterization it often served the interests of special pleading. Maria Edgeworth's scrupulous landlords, venal agents, and irresponsible peasants, like John Banim's oppressed and unwilling rebels and conspirators, are too carefully posed for the vindication of a thesis to constitute a representation of Ireland "as it really was." This propagandistic bent of the Irish novel is its weakest point. That it performed successfully the services of propaganda is doubtful. Very likely the contrasting and conflicting images of Ireland cancelled each other out. The major writers, however much they may have differed, saw Irish experience as being essentially tragic, and this is the one view which English readers were not prepared to accept. The reading public much preferred the Ireland of Charles Lever—an enchanting and dowdy land of *dolce far niente,* in which dashing dragoons and impoverished fox hunters held genial sway over a mob of feckless rustics.

Irish novels were invariably reviewed by British journals on the assumption that they had been written to please English taste or to shape English opinion. John Wilson Croker's slashing attacks upon Lady Morgan in the pages of *The Quarterly Review* were inspired by his fear of the damage which her novels might do to the high-Tory position which claimed his own slippery allegiance. Similarly it was to England that the Irish writer looked for critical judgment. In only a few instances, such as Carleton's remarks upon the novels of Banim and Lever, Thomas Davis's review of Carleton's own work, or an occasional article in *The Dublin University Magazine,* is criticism from contemporary Irish sources relevant or important.

The dependence of Irish writers on an English audience did not seem at all exceptional. London, after all, was indisputably the intellectual and literary capital of the British Isles. The problem, rather, is to define the sense in which their work may properly be called Irish. This problem, which is enmeshed in old and barren controversies and clouded over by doctrinaire political and cultural assumptions, inevitably confronts the student of the literature of nineteenth-century Ireland.

Irishmen, to be sure, had made generous contributions to the literature of the two preceding centuries—Swift, Congreve, Farquhar, Sheridan, Goldsmith, and Burke were all Irish. Except for Swift, however, who in this as in all things is a law unto himself, the fact of Irish birth is irrelevant to their accomplishments. Children of the English garrison, they took quick and natural root in English soil. The attempts which have been made to trace out an "Anglo-Irish"—let alone a "Celtic"—strain in their writings are quite unconvincing.[7] Goldsmith's friends, it is true, made a standing joke of his Irish back-

---

[7] See, for example, William O'Brien, *Burke as an Irishman.*

ground, and his transformation of a Roscommon village into "sweet
Auburn" presents us with a literary oddity. And Burke, who was descended from one of the old Norman families and whose mother was
a Roman Catholic, possessed a familiarity with Irish affairs which
was to stand him in good stead. But Sheridan's Irish birth we are likely
to remember only because of his name and because he was in the
habit of tossing a stage-Irishman into his plays. As for Congreve—we
accept the fact with mild incredulity. The same might be said of the
century's only Irish novelist, Henry Brooke, the author of *The Fool of
Quality* (1765-70).

There did exist in the eighteenth century a literature which was indisputably Irish—the poetry of the Gaelic hedge writers, who had
inherited the traditions of Gaelic letters as fully as had Goldsmith
those of English poetry. This literature was "hidden"—to employ
Daniel Corkery's evocative phrase—but it was not unknown. Goldsmith himself glimpsed Turlough O'Carolan, "the last of the bards,"
and recorded his impressions in a brief essay.[8] It was a dying tradition,
however, and might have perished without record had it not been for
the retentive memory of the peasantry and the devoted labors of a few
amateurs from within the Garrison itself. But the development of an
interest among members of the Ascendancy in the literature of the
older Ireland is discussed at greater length in Chapter Eight, and need
not be anticipated here. It will suffice, for the moment, to realize that
high walls of language and caste separated the two cultures of
eighteenth-century Ireland. Nor were these the only barriers. Brian
Merriman's brilliant poem, *The Midnight Court,* is remarkable as
much for the sophistication as for the antiquity of its traditional form.[9]

A single incident may bring the issue close to our own subject. In
1805 Arthur O'Neill, old and blind, sat dictating the story of his life
to a clerk named Tom Hughes, who served the M'Cracken family of
Belfast. O'Neill was one of the last of the race of Irish harpers, and

---

[8] Oliver Goldsmith, "Carolan," in *Miscellaneous Writings,* I, 208-10.
[9] It has been put into admirable English verse: *The Midnight Court: A Rhyth-
mical Bacchanalia from the Irish of Bryan Merryman,* translated by Frank
O'Connor.

his attachments were to that aristocratic world of the Gael which had almost vanished.

"When dinner was announced," he says, speaking of an assemblage some sixty years before, "very near a hundred of the O's and Macs took their seats. My poor self being blind, I did what blind men generally do, I groped a vacancy near the foot of the table. Such a noise arose of cutting, carving, roaring, laughing, shaking hands, and such language as generally occurs between friends, who only see each other once a year. While dinner was going on, I was hobnobbed by nearly every gentleman present. When Lord Kenmare hobnobbed me, he was pleased to say, 'O'Neill, you should be at the head of the table, as your ancestors were the original Milesians of this kingdom.' " [10]

Behind the darkened eyes of Art O'Neill, an old man talking out his life to a clerk of the family upon whose charity he depended, the Gaelic world lived and glowed in the bright colors of heraldry. This is not surprising, for in his youth he had had another patron—Murtough Oge O'Sullivan, the half-legendary swordsman of Fontenoy and the Kerry coast. And he had crossed the sea in 1745 to play at Holyrood before Charles Edward Stuart, the "saviour and deliverer" of the Munster poets. Indeed, it has been supposed that he was present when the Irish lords met to decide whether they would risk one last throw of the dice on the Jacobite cause.[11]

O'Neill, who like all the Gaelic artists was proud to the point of snobbishness, naturally sought out the hospitality of those few titled O's and Macs who had survived the penal legislation, but he could be sure of a welcome in many a Protestant Big House. In this fashion, amicably but with little real understanding on either side, the two cultures touched one another. One such Big House is of particular interest to us. "Always," O'Neill says, "on my return from the

[10] "The Memoir of Arthur O'Neill" was first published in full by Charlotte Milligan Fox, in *Annals of the Irish Harpers* (London, 1911), pp. 137–87. Samuel Ferguson had drawn upon material from the manuscript in preparing the notes to the 1840 edition of Bunting's *Ancient Musick of Ireland*. The passage quoted appears in Fox, *Annals*, p. 147.

[11] *Ibid.*, p. 146n.

Granard Balls, I stopped at Counsellor Edgeworth's of Edgeworthstown, where I was well received." [12] In this house, which we will visit
in the next chapter, the first and perhaps the finest of Irish narratives
was written.

The "Granard Balls," which in fact were harp competitions, were
held for three years running, beginning in 1781. When Lady Morgan
was writing *The Wild Irish Girl,* she gathered a certain amount of
information concerning the famous harpers, which she incorporated
in the footnotes of that curious novel. Richard Lovell Edgeworth read
the novel when it appeared in 1806, and it stirred a dim and inaccurate
memory. "I believe that some of the harpers you mention were at the
Harpers' Prize Ball at Granard in 1782 or 1783. One female harper, of
the name of Bridget, obtained the second prize; Fallon carried off the
first. I think I have heard the double-headed man." [13]

In Lady Morgan's misty imagination the harpers and bards trailed
clouds of Ossianic grandeur—an attitude which Edgeworth would
have called damned folly. Edgeworth was a generous man, in his brisk,
hard-tempered fashion, and Art O'Neill was surely received with
kindness. But O'Neill was one in an endless stream of mendicants
who came to the gates of the Big House at Edgeworthstown—harpers,
pipers, pilgrims, prophecy-men, fiddlers. This stream troubled Edgeworth's orderly mind and stirred his conscience, but it never touched
his imagination. But then neither did O'Neill truly see "the Counsellor," as he calls Edgeworth, since every gentleman must have a title,
and "the Major" or "his Reverence" or "his Lordship" did not apply.

Between these two men of the eighteenth century—the friend of
Murtough Oge O'Sullivan and the friend of Erasmus Darwin—there
could be no communication. Maria Edgeworth shared, in part, her
father's impatience with the world which Art O'Neill represented. In
the pages of *The Absentee* she deals satirically with life at Kilpatrick
House, which was everything that Art O'Neill expected a Big House
o be—festive, improvident, and swarming with retainers and "folly-
rs." But if she knew little of his Ireland and cared less, she under-

---

[12] *Ibid.,* p. 178.
[13] *Lady Morgan's Memoirs: Autobiography, Diaries, and Correspondence,* I, 293.

stood the moral life of her own caste with an artist's piercing, intuitive understanding. Out of her knowledge she created *Castle Rackrent*.

With this novel a tradition begins, for it is the first fictional narrative of Irish life to be written in the English language. The writers who followed Maria Edgeworth display an equal concern with the Irish scene. Are their novels to be called Irish or English or, by way of ambiguous compromise, Anglo-Irish?

Douglas Hyde dismisses them in magisterial fashion from his *Literary History of Ireland,* telling us that he has "abstained altogether from any analysis or even mention of the work of Anglicised Irishmen of the last two centuries. Their books, as those of Farquhar, of Swift, of Goldsmith, of Burke, find, and have always found, their true and natural place in every history of *English* literature that has been written, whether by Englishmen themselves or by foreigners."[14] And it is true that the nineteenth-century Irish writers have found a place in English literature, but whether, like Farquhar and Goldsmith, they have found their true and natural place is another matter. In most such histories they are to be found huddled together, a worried Hibernian band, with Marryat and Surtees pressing them hard from one side and "The Imitators of Scott" from the other.

Hyde is perfectly justified in excluding them from his own work, for he is writing the history of "the literature produced by the Irish-speaking Irish." But his statement remains somewhat disingenuous, for the point upon which he insisted throughout his distinguished career was that only the literature of the "Irish-speaking Irish" was truly Irish. To the Gaelic enthusiasts of Hyde's generation Ireland's English-language literature was in every way deplorable. It was committed to the representation of Irish life in alien and unassimilable forms, and it had resigned itself to a humiliatingly "colonial" status. In its attempts to "explain" and to "show" Ireland, it was inevitably defensive in tone and attitude.

The argument rested upon false assumptions, for a culture must be judged by what it is and does, not by what it *should* be doing. If Irish culture is to be defined by the Gaelic language, we must conclude

14 Hyde, *A Literary History of Ireland,* p. ix.

that when the last of the hedge poets died, Ireland ceased to have a culture. Long before the Church and O'Connell cast the heavy weight of their authority on the side of English, and long before famine and emigration had thinned the ranks of Irish-speakers, it had become clear that such literary and intellectual life as Ireland possessed would find expression in English.

There is no strong reason why we should not join Professor Corkery in calling this literature Anglo-Irish. And there remains considerable point to the questions which he addresses to it:

The answer to the question: Is there an Anglo-Irish literature? must depend on what regard we have for what Synge spoke of as collaboration—without, perhaps, taking very great trouble to explore his own thought. The people among whom the writer lives, what is their part in the work he produces? Is the writer the people's voice? Has there ever been, can there be, a distinctive literature that is not a national literature? A national literature is written primarily for its own people: every new book in it—no matter what its theme—foreign or native—is referable to their life, and its literary traits to the traits already established in its literature. The nation's own critical opinion of it is the warrant of life or death for it. Can Anglo-Irish, then, be a distinctive literature if it is not a national literature? And if it has not primarily been written for Ireland, if it be impossible to refer it to Irish life for its elucidation, if its continued existence or non-existence be independent of Irish opinion—can it be a national literature? [15]

Professor Corkery, as the reader may have inferred, is an extreme cultural nationalist, and is happiest when a work of art is Gaelic, patriotic, Catholic, and puritanical (though the latter two terms are, in the Irish context, interchangeable). Fortunately, the brilliant accomplishments of modern Irish writers have not depended for a warrant of life or death upon the official opinion of the Republic of Ireland. The warrant for the continued existence of Yeats and Joyce and Synge is in the keeping of the republic of letters, which is at once more just and more generous.

Corkery has, however, defined somewhat inadvertently the anomalous status of the Irish literature of the nineteenth and twentieth centuries. It is a literature which has never been able to depend for its existence on Irish opinion; only rarely has it been written primarily

[15] Daniel Corkery, *Synge and Anglo-Irish Literature*, p. 2.

for its own people; more rarely still has it drawn upon "traits" established in the literature. And yet it is a literature rooted in Irish life and
experience, a literature which often forces us to turn for elucidation to
the thought and culture of Ireland.

Whether a body of literature which must be defined in these terms
may properly be called national, whether it should be spoken of as
Irish or as Anglo-Irish or as Colonial are questions which might be
set forth at greater length, but not, I think, with much profit. Speaking
of "that literature which had no existence until towards the end of
the eighteenth century," Corkery says: "In our youth and even later
it used always to be spoken of as Irish literature: and this custom old-
fashioned folk have not yet given up: to them, Thomas Moore's
Melodies are still Irish Melodies." [16] I have chosen to follow the practice of these old-fashioned folk. For one thing, they seem to have an
old-fashioned preference for accuracy: *Irish Melodies* is the title which
Moore, however mistakenly, gave to his work. It is also true that the
word "Anglo-Irish" has slippery political and social connotations. If
Maria Edgeworth belonged by class and allegiance to the Anglo-Irish,
Gerald Griffin most certainly did not.

The novels of nineteenth-century Ireland were always spoken of as
Irish, and we may accept the term with a full and clear understanding of what it meant. To be sure, we must also bear in mind implications which were not then clear. We have a deeper sense now of the
interdependence of language and culture. We can appreciate that much
which was rich and various, much which was uniquely Irish perished
when Gaelic fell into disuse. O'Connell, in a remark which the Gaelic
League would later make notorious, said that "although the Irish
language is connected with many recollections that twine round the
hearts of Irishmen, yet the superior utility of the English tongue, as
the medium of all modern communications, is so great that I can
witness without a sigh the gradual disuse of Irish." [17] We may agree
with the judgment and yet wonder if he realized how final a sentence
he was passing on much that he cherished.

We must also bear in mind the validity of certain of Corkery's

[16] *Ibid.*
[17] W. J. O'Neill Daunt, *Personal Recollections of Daniel O'Connell,* I, 15.

strictures. A literature which seeks to vindicate and justify the culture from which it draws its being labors under a heavy burden. (Although one which announces truculently that its heroism, suffering, and ineffable purity place it beyond the need of vindication bears a much heavier one.) When these have been taken into proper account, however, and when the limitations and particular merits of each novelist have been recognized, it becomes clear that the major Irish novelists were engaged upon a subtle and profound study of a complicated and self-contradictory society.

I have singled out those novelists who attempted such a task, whether successfully or not. It is for this reason that I have not considered the work of Lover and Lever, whose names, inevitably and indecently yoked, are the first to occur to many readers. In neither writer is there any real tension or any sense of felt experience. It is not true, though many nationalist critics have made the claim, that Lever was engaged in the task of deliberately travestying his countrymen. His novels, nonetheless, are travesties, because they are not written out of any deep concern with his subject—but this is true of all poor novels. At times, as in *The Martins of Cro' Martin* (1847), he seems to be fumbling toward a subject which might engage his feelings, but never with complete success.

On quite different grounds I have excluded certain novelists of unmistakable talent. Charles Maturin launched his career with two bizarre imitations of Lady Morgan—*The Wild Irish Boy* (1808) and *The Milesian Chief* (1812), but it must be said that the true interests of the author of *Melmoth, the Wanderer* lay elsewhere. Joseph Sheridan Lefanu, whose reputation rests most firmly on works of another order, wrote two extraordinary Irish romances, *The Cock and Anchor* (1845) and *The House by the Churchyard* (1862). It is significant, perhaps, that both of these highly gifted members of the Ascendancy should have turned to tales whose somber and uncanny atmosphere seeks to transcend the immediacies of social fact. Maturin's lonely and forbidding country houses, set in frightening isolation upon the bogs, and the strangeness of Lefanu's Dublin suggest the disquiet and desolation which subsequent members of their social class took to be the predominating fact of the Irish scene. Miss Elizabeth Bowen, herself an Anglo-Irishwoman, has suggested that much of what is odd and puzzling in *Uncle Silas,* Lefanu's best novel, is explainable if we assume that he has transferred to the English countryside a tale of the Irish Big Houses.[18]

For our purposes, however, it is preferable that we concentrate upon those writers whose involvement with the Irish scene was deep and steady, and in whose work we can trace the changing pressures of Irish life. Of these, five claim our attention by reason of talent and accomplishment. Three of these, Maria Edgeworth, Gerald Griffin, and William Carleton, will not prompt questions as to the wisdom of my choice. They are writers of great, if often unrecognized, power. Lady Morgan and John Banim are much more uneven writers, and their native endowments are not so large. Though they were capable of fine work—Lady Morgan in *The O'Briens and the O'Flahertys* and Banim in *The Nowlans*—my reasons for discussing them at length are more nearly those of the literary and cultural historian than of the critic.

Lady Morgan's novels afford us an understanding of the way in which cultural and political myth was created in nineteenth-century Ireland, and of the uses to which writers put the romantic conception of an immemorial Irish "nation." The discussion of her novels leads us, inevitably, into a consideration of the literary and political *milieu* within which she worked, for she was involved in the great public issues of the day, and this involvement is reflected in her work.

John Banim's fiction is of interest to us on two counts. The Irish novel is supposed by some literary historians to have been inspired by the example of Scott. The impression is not altogether erroneous, for the bibliographical record of Irish fiction is heavily weighted by historical novels in Scott's vein. No study of the fiction of the period could claim thoroughness, therefore, if it did not deal with a writer whose imagination was fired, as Scott's was, by the clash and clatter of old battles. John Banim is probably the ablest, as he is also the first, of the Irish historical novelists. *The Boyne Water,* his best novel of

[18] Introduction to Lefanu's *Uncle Silas: A Tale of Bartram-Haugh,* pp. 8–9.

this kind, is discussed in Chapter Twelve, together with *The Con-formists* and *The Last Baron of Crana.*

Chapter Eleven, however, discusses another and perhaps a larger claim which Banim has on our interest. Banim was one of the first of those writers who attempted the representation of the life of the Irish peasantry. It was a subject with many political and cultural reverberations, and these are set forth in "Irish Peasants and English Readers." The tales of peasant Ireland which were written by Banim, Crofton Croker, and Eyre Evans Crowe constitute a kind of public debate on the Irish character, set against a lurid background of agrarian crime and near-insurrection.

The careers of the five novelists with whom we will be concerned assume their full interest, however, only when they are placed in the proper relationships to one another. For these writers, differing in talent and intention, differ as markedly in social class and background. It is by virtue of coincidence that they come from the four provinces —Leinster, Munster, Connaught, and Ulster—but the coincidence per-mits us to examine the sharp contrasts which obtained between the West of Ireland and the more Anglicized counties, and the special way of life which obtained in Presbyterian Ulster. The division along religious lines is almost *too* neat. Maria Edgeworth and Lady Morgan were Protestants—though Lady Morgan's faith was a precarious pos-session. Griffin and Banim, following the precedent set by Moore, were members of that first generation of Irish Catholics for whom the re-laxation of the Penal Laws opened careers in the world of English letters. And in spiritual matters William Carleton was a bewildering nondescript—not least bewildering to himself.

By birth they run the gamut of the social classes: the Edgeworths were of that Anglo-Irish county stock which, if not titled, had loftier claims than many of the nobility, and they were landowners of a truly impressive kind; Gerald Griffin was descended from the dispossessed Catholic gentry, though his immediate forebears were strong farm-ers; Banim's father was a petty tradesman, perhaps the least regarded of all Irish social types; William Carleton was able to boast, accurately and often, that he was sprung from the heart of the Gaelic-speaking peasantry. And Lady Morgan's most delightfully Hibernian trait is that in matters of genealogy she was an inveterate liar, concocting once in each decade some new and mendacious pedigree.

Because religion, social position, racial heritage, and family loyalties necessarily engaged their imaginations, these novelists yield to us a surprisingly complete understanding of nineteenth-century Ireland's complex and stratified culture. It is an understanding which sharpens our awareness of the instinctive value which all men place upon culture, the apprehensions with which they view a culture which is shattered, incomplete, or imperiled. The very richness and variety of the forms of Irish life, that tumbling heterogeneity of social types and customs which so charmed readers, bespoke not healthy diversity but Kettle's "unimaginable chaos."

These apprehensions mark the thought and the literature of nineteenth-century Ireland, which found itself confronted by its own unique problems. The Anglo-Irish of Goldsmith's generation pondered but briefly, and probably balefully, the question of nationality. To the Anglo-Irish of Grattan's generation, it was an accomplished fact, and one which held no riddles. But in O'Connell's Ireland the Ascendancy discovered that it was in sober fact a garrison, and a beleaguered one at that. Its Big Houses and law courts and Dublin mansions, which had seemed as firmly built and as imperishable as the prose of Cicero and Plutarch, seemed now to be standing naked and desolate on the dark, treacherous bogland.

The native writers, who were beginning now to think and to write in English, found themselves beset in other ways. They had been cut off, it is true, from the world of Art O'Neill and Egan O'Rahilly and Owen O'Sullivan, but the Gaelic hedge poets, while deserving of most of Professor Corkery's encomiums, had been hopelessly provincial. They had been adrift upon a river, somewhere outside of history and circumstance, and the river had been at last sucked down by the bogs. Brian Merriman had been the only one of them to come to terms with the world around him, and of Merriman Frank O'Connor has aptly written: "He had that sort of clear, objective intelligence which rarely attaches itself to lost causes, and he may well have turned with a wry smile from the dream of a modernized Gaelic Ireland to the teaching of trigonometry." [19]

Merriman died in Limerick in 1805, reduced no doubt to woeful virtue by his son-in-law, the respectable tailor. For Gerald Griffin, who had been born in Limerick two years earlier, the notion of Gaelic Ireland would hold great meaning, and he was to attach much of his passion to it. By that time, however, it lay in the past, and he had to seek it out in the tumbled ruins above the Shannon and among the clansmen of wild Clare and Kerry. It was as dead as the Ireland of the Rackrents, those cruel, fearless, and fatal rakes of the Georgian Ascendancy.

Yet both of these worlds, though dead in fact, were fully and vividly alive in the imaginations of Maria Edgeworth and Griffin, for the Irish novelist, whether settler or Celt, was fierce in his loyalty to the particular "Ireland" which was his. But he knew that others had opposing visions and aspirations—opposing "Irelands." At times, as in Maria Edgeworth's *Ormond,* he wrote out of a conviction that these oppositions might some day be reconciled. But at other times, as in Griffin's *Tracy's Ambition,* he drew a picture of a land whose people, driven by old hatreds, would turn upon each other.

"Great hatred, little room,/Maimed us at the start," Yeats was to write. The novels which we are about to examine will supply us, in unhappy abundance, with proofs of how much hatred there was, and how deeply felt. But they will suggest also that the power to love, to enjoy, and to create, though maimed, was still strong. "The old men," Yeats has also written, "tried to make one see life plainly but all written down in a kind of fiery shorthand that it might not be forgotten." The time has come to read the shorthand and to search out the sources of the fire.

[19] From the introduction to his translation of *The Midnight Court,* p. 10.

Maria Edgeworth

4. Maria Edgeworth: The Crisis of the "'Protestant Nation'

IN JANUARY of the year 1800 an Irish landlord, Richard Lovell Edgeworth, left his home in County Longford to attend the session of Parliament in Dublin. The management of his estate and the care of his numerous family he entrusted to his daughter Maria.

This was the final session of the centuries-old Parliament, which was convening to vote upon the question of its own extinction. The Protestant Ascendancy, with its strong sense of colonial autonomy, felt itself to be independent of England, bound only by a joint allegiance to the crown. It had therefore been necessary for Cornwallis, the Lord Lieutenant, and Castlereagh, the Chief Secretary, to buy votes for the Act of Union by bribery and promises of place. Of necessity the secret had been badly kept, and in the final session member after member arose to recount the offers which had been made to him. These men, the so-called patriot party, rallied around Grattan, the spokesman, the finest example and in a sense the creator of what would be known to history as the Protestant Nation. They were in a minority. The Irish Parliament proved itself to be venal almost without modern parallel, and the Act of Union was passed.

Some members, of course, were Unionist on principle, and of these Richard Lovell Edgeworth was one. Though his family had been settled in Ireland since Elizabethan days, he had been educated at Oxford and had long been resident in England. Under the guidance of, among others, Thomas Day and Erasmus Darwin, he had developed a remarkable taste for the application of rational inquiry and legislation to the various disorders of existence. In particular he was a radical theorist of education; in general he was an eccentric rationalist of a type not infrequent in the eighteenth-century aristocracy. One of his daughter's biographers has summed him up:

To Richard Lovell Edgeworth, life presented a number of problems but few mysteries. Although officially a Protestant (an important circumstance in Ireland) he cannot be called a religious man. Lacking spiritual depth, his mind turned to other problems than those of faith. . . . He made clocks, he invented a sailing carriage, patented a signalling apparatus which he called a telegraph, tried to construct a wooden horse that would jump over stone walls . . . , built a new spire for the village church and had it hauled to the top of the tower by rope and pulley while one of his sons played on a bugle, is regarded by some people as the father of modern road-making, and filled his house at Edgeworthstown with gadgets and contrivances so that for decades after his death unwary guests were trapped in their rooms by complex locks that only members of the family knew how to deal with.[1]

This is too neat. Edgeworth had larger ambitions and, to further these, he decided to return home to Ireland in 1782. "I returned to Ireland," he tells us in an autobiographical fragment, "with a firm determination to dedicate the remainder of my life to the improvement of my estate, and to the education of my children; and further, with the sincere hope of contributing to the melioration of the inhabitants of the country, from which I drew my subsistence."[2]

He chose an auspicious moment. When he landed at Dublin with his daughter Maria, Grattan had just moved an address to the throne, asserting the independence of their nation, a pronouncement which the Crown officials were in no position to deny. Edgeworth was sitting in the gallery of Commons when the nation voted Grattan a testimonial grant and, though he shared the hopes of the patriot party, he edged them with anxieties and dour reflections. The "Nation" was threatened far less from England than from within—it was badly split on the question of Catholic Emancipation and shackled by a system of rotten boroughs which usually kept the parliamentary majority in the control of Dublin Castle's greedy and irresponsible hench-

[1] P. H. Newby, *Maria Edgeworth*, pp. 11–12.
[2] Richard Lovell Edgeworth and Maria Edgeworth, *The Memoirs of Richard Lovell Edgeworth*, II, 1.

men. Moreover, this irresponsibility, Edgeworth felt, and probably rightly, was a condition less of political life than of the peculiar society which the eighteenth century had created in Ireland. Being gifted with a considerable shrewdness in practical affairs, which he passed on to his daughter, he thought this through as he sat watching the exuberant House.

As Maria was to write, "While the volunteer patriots, in the general exaltation of their spirits, anticipated a variety of future undefined advantages to Ireland, his hopes fixed on that which in his view was the most important object, and without which all others, as he foresaw, would be of no avail." [3]

This most important object was a reform of Parliament, and a few days later he made public a characteristically blunt letter to the Volunteer corps of his county of Longford: "At this moment of universal joy and exultation, let me recall to your remembrance, that without an effectual Reformation of the House of Commons, no solid advantage can be obtained from our present success. A venal Parliament may, by degrees, yield everything but the name of Freedom; and the slow but certain influence of corruption may, in a few years, reduce you to the same subjection, which you have so well shaken off by the well-timed exertions of national courage and unexampled prudence." [4] At a Longford meeting he put forward and carried a petition for reform, and other counties followed the example.

The movement for reform was broken, however, and the Volunteers disbanded. Parliament, which sustained such oddities as Duigenan and Sir Boyle Roche, became Fitzgibbon's subservient creature. Flood and Charlemont, patriots in the national sense, were intransigent against Papist claims. A group of young idealists, disgusted by the state of matters, withdrew their loyalty from Parliament to form the United Irishmen, dedicated to the idea of a rebellion in support of an invasion by the armies of the French Revolution; they were joined by large numbers of Dissenters and Catholics, who had cause to be distrustful equally of the Nation and of England. Against this combination Grattan struggled brilliantly but without success.

[3] *Ibid.,* II, 48.　　　　　　　[4] *Ibid.,* II, 49.

Edgeworth, however, a man who could draw an iron conclusion from iron premises, turned his back on Dublin, and his attention to Edgeworthstown and "the melioration of the inhabitants." Unlike many Irishmen, he had no affinity for lost causes, and he came to the conviction that the only solution to the problems of the wretched island lay with a Union which would bring her within the governance of the immeasurably more responsible parliament in London. He formed this view after tedious and public soul-searching.

Now, in 1800, the Act of Union which would bring this about was before the Dublin Commons, but Edgeworth was traveling down to Dublin to vote against it. It was what he would have called a "very Irish" mission. He was a friend of Union, but he would have no part in its enforcement by the sword or by gold. The officials at Dublin Castle, laboring late at corruption and bribery, would have agreed that this was a "very Irish" attitude. They offered him, Maria says,

temptations in every possible form, in which they could *flatter* personal ambition or family interest; he had offers of all that could serve or oblige his dearest friends, and the choice of situation, in which he might, it was said, gratify his peculiar tastes, serve his country, and accomplish his favorite object of improving the education of the people. Opportunity for convenient distinctions in his case appeared also; since he was avowedly of the opinion, that the measure in question would be ultimately advantageous to that country, though he thought the means of carrying it, and the forcing it, at this time, contrary to the sense of the people, was wrong. But, however plausible, he would not admit of such nice casuistry in a case of conscience; he would not palter with the fiend Ambition.[5]

This was partly the stubbornness of a doctrinaire, but it drew strength from his loyalty to the Protestant Nation, and his belief that his people had the right to govern or misgovern their own affairs. For Richard Lovell Edgeworth was more complicated than his dogmatic rationalism might suggest. He was also an Anglo-Irishman, a member of that proud people whom Yeats would celebrate:

> The pride of people that were
> Bound neither to Cause nor State,

[5] *Ibid.,* II, 254–55.

> Neither to slaves that were spat on,
> Nor to the tyrants that spat,
> The people of Burke and Grattan
> That gave though free to refuse—[6]

Edgeworth's closest friends were Thomas Day and Lord Longford, his neighbor in Ireland. Longford was a crusty, hotheaded Anglo-Irishman who had marched and countermarched against the rebels with much bravery and beating of drums. "Little valuing the form of logical argument," Maria observes, with a faint touch of her deft, poised irony, "but arriving by some quick, short and sure mental process at just conclusions, he generally formed right judgments of persons and things; yet he was ever unwilling, perhaps unable, to detail in words the reasons on which his opinions were founded." [7]

This is at a far remove from the Thomas Day whose garrulous speculations gave such piquancy to educational theorizing of the Rousseauan variety. Of his most remarkable exploit Edgeworth has left us a brief account. Day's plan was "to breed up two girls as equally as possible, under his own eye; hoping that they might be companions to each other while they were children, and that, before they grew to be women, he might decide which of them might be most agreeable to himself as a wife. I was not with my friend, when he and Mr. Bicknel selected from a number of orphans, one of remarkably promising appearance. It was necessary that the girl should be apprenticed to some *married* man. I was the person whom Mr. Day named, and to me Sabrina Sidney was apprenticed." [8] Of all the accounts of this celebrated experiment, his is the most casual and matter-of-fact.

It was this philosophical radicalism, tempered by political conservatism and loyalty to class, which made Edgeworth so singular an Irish landlord, for the spirit of Rousseau and Erasmus Darwin dwelt uneasily within the grandson of "Protestant Frank," who had raised a troop to fight for William at the Boyne. He passed on these contradictions to the devoted Maria, in whom they fostered a heightened awareness of the paradoxes and ambiguities of Irish culture.

[6] "The Tower," in *Collected Poems*, pp. 228–29.
[7] Edgeworth, *Memoirs*, II, 10.   [8] *Ibid.*, I, 214.

For father and daughter this culture was synonymous with the Ascendancy, and the Ascendancy was separated from the rest of the population by class, race, and religion. It had every reason to believe that beneath a surface obsequiousness, the peasantry was sullen, savage, and vindictive. A series of risings, bloodily conducted and as bloodily suppressed, haunted the memories of ruler and ruled. In England, with which the Edgeworths were more familiar than most, an increasingly diversified social structure had long been shaping itself, while Ireland had remained feudal. England did not bother itself about race, either as fact or as superstition; in Ireland race and the passions associated with it were as old as the Conquest, and the wounds had been widened by religious persecution and the wholesale expropriation of land. The Protestant of Ireland was a conqueror and yet a colonial, a patriot, but one whose interests set him against the majority of his countrymen. In a word, and a famous one, he was a member of the Garrison.

The members of the Garrison thought of themselves as Irish. Grattan or Burke, Wellington or Castlereagh would have made the claim without hesitation. What they meant by this has been a puzzle both to other Irishmen and to the English. Macaulay points out with gleeful inaccuracy that Swift was no more Irish than an Englishman resident in Madras was Hindu. Yet to Macaulay's dismay Swift *thought* of himself as Irish, though he regarded the "aboriginal inhabitants" as "hewers of wood and drawers of water." He was a member of the proud but insecure "middle nation" which held itself to constitute "the people of Ireland."

It is true, however, that they were a distinct cultural type, proclaiming themselves with belligerent self-contradiction anything but English and at the same time the apotheosis of English rectitude. This can be explained, in part, by the degree to which their social position lacked any equivalent in English life. No Yorkshire squire, even in the year of Peterloo, considered himself entrenched in a fortress against an alien and savage people. No farmer in Sussex felt that he held his land by right of conquest, the opinions of his tenants notwithstanding.

Sir Jonah Barrington, the shady "Judge of the High Court of Admiralty in Ireland," has left us a classic picture of the Ascendancy society of which he was himself so rare a blossom. The peasants, he says, divided the gentry into three classes, "half-mounted gentlemen," "gentlemen every inch of them," and "gentlemen to the back-bone." He begins with the first of these, whom he describes as the only species of independent yeomanry.

They were the descendents of the small grantees of Queen Elizabeth, Cromwell, and King William; possessed about two hundred acres of land each, in fee farm, from the Crown, and were admitted occasionally into the society of gentlemen—particularly hunters—living at other times amongst each other, with an intermixture of their own servants, with whom they were on terms of intimacy. They commonly wore buckskin breeches, and boots well-greased (blacking was never used in the country), and carried large thong whips, heavily loaded with lead at the butt-end, so that they were always prepared either to horse-whip a man or knock his brains out, as circumstances might dictate. These half-mounted gentlemen exercised the hereditary authority of keeping the ground clear at horse-races, hurlings, and other public meetings, as the soldiers keep the line at a review. Their business was to ride round the ground, with becoming spirit, trampling over some, knocking down others, and slashing everybody who encroached on the proper limits. . . .

The second class, or gentlemen every inch of them, were of excellent old families, whose finances were not in as good order as they might have been, but who were popular amongst all ranks. They were far above the first degree, somewhat inferior to the third; but had great influence, were much beloved, and carried more sway at popular elections and general county meetings than the other two classes put together.

The third class, or gentlemen to the back-bone, were of the oldest families and settlers, universally respected, and idolized by the peasantry, although they also were generally a little out at elbows. Their word was law; their nod would have immediately collected an army of cottagers, or colliers, or whatever the population was composed of. Men, women, and children were always ready and willing to execute anything the squire required, without the slightest consideration as to either its danger or propriety.[9]

The picture which he presents is a generally accurate one; it is also, which is not the same thing, the picture of the Anglo-Irish gentry

[9] Sir Jonah Barrington, *Personal Sketches of His Own Times*, I, 103–4.

which obtained in England, where Sheridan and Farquhar had made the "Sir Lucius O'Triggers" conventional stage figures—boastful, peppery, gullible, quick upon a point of honor, and mouthing an erratic gasconade. In Charles Macklin's *The True-Born Irishman* (Dublin, 1783) a Londoner compliments the Irish as being "a damn'd honest, rory-tory, rantum-scantum, daring, singing, laughing, boozing, jolly, friendly, fighting, hospitable people." An Irishman, as peppery as Macmorris, thanks him "on behalf of the people of Ireland," for this "helter-skelter, rantum-scantum, portrait." Macklin had something of Maria Edgeworth's acid understanding of the way in which caricature creates its own object, but by and large the Anglo-Irish would have subscribed to the picture with delight, for these were the qualities and defects which they most honored.

They were notorious, in particular, for their dueling and their drinking. The question of why Irishmen drank so much is almost metaphysical, but the countless charges are scarcely exaggerations. The owlish Samuel Hall, who, for his sins, spent some time in the country, reports upon it with due reproof:

Drunkenness was the shame and bane of Ireland; an Irishman had become proverbial for intoxication. . . . Ingenious devices were invented for compelling intoxication; glasses and bottles so formed that they could not stand, and must be emptied before they could be laid upon the table—the object being to pass the wine rapidly round—were in frequent use. We dined once with a large party where the tea-kettle—from which the tumblers were supplied—had been filled with heated whiskey; the partakers of the "cheer" being too far "gone" to perceive that they were strengthening their punch instead of making it weaker. If a guest were able to mount his horse without assistance, in the good old times, he was presented with a "deoch an durrass," which he was forced, literally against his will, to drink at the door.[10]

Barrington, who himself had nicked his man, and whose brother had been murdered in the brutal travesty of an affair of honor, has personal recollections of several hundred encounters, involving every Irishman of note, almost without exception. The otherwise amiable and graceful Grattan had a truly wicked temper, and this told, if any-

[10] Mr. and Mrs. Samuel Hall, *Ireland: Its Scenery, Character, Etc.*, I, 13.

thing, in his favor. Most of the gentry belonged to dueling clubs, and their pistol cases contained printed regulations, "that ignorance might never be pleaded."

What is appalling in Barrington's description, however, is the revelation of the near-anarchy to which centuries of misrule, oppression, and rebellion had brought the country. Much of Irish history is compressed within the loaded whips of the buckeens and the cudgels of the peasants, for on both sides the absence of substantial law had bred a contempt for its forms. For many of their masters the peasants felt a vast affection which went far beyond "danger or propriety." "Fighting" Fitzgerald maintained his tenants as a kind of murder gang. And it was Barrington's aunt whose cry of vexation at a neighbor, uttered in the presence of a house servant, brought her the man's ear on a platter and supplied Yeats with one of the incidents in "The Tower." But the gentry, when all is said, knew less of their peasants than they did of Hindus, and their sketchy benevolence could be swept away by a moment's whisper of a slave rising.

Of the lot of the peasants enough is known for us to imagine some fraction of it. The families, usually quite large, lived huddled in mud cabins, through whose walls moisture constantly seeped. Their fires lacked proper ventilation, and at night the near-naked people squatted beside them on the earth, the smoke yellowing their skins and, eventually, blinding many. A shocked traveler reported that peasant villages resembled towns less than "heaps of dung reeking with the steam of their own fermentation." [11] Of the traditions of Gaelic poetry and manners which, however debased, these cabins maintained, and which were beginning to interest the dilettantes of Dublin, the landlords knew little and cared less. This neglect was most often the consequence of indolence and ignorance. But by an unhappy coincidence those humanitarian landlords who were not unnerved by the immense task of reclamation were usually, like Richard Lovell Edgeworth, the last people to pry into peasant superstitions, which would have been the

[11] Quoted by Constantia Maxwell in *Country and Town in Ireland under the Georges,* p. 124.

surest way of understanding their tenants. The Gaelic world, therefore, remained submerged, and as unknown as the language by which
its values were transmitted.

Edgeworth's ambitions may be thought of as concentric rings: he
aimed first at the education of his children, then at the improvement
of his lands and the schooling of his peasants, and finally at the perfection of his nation and the world at large. Ireland, at least, could
have profited from his ministrations, and his unique position as a
theorist and an absolute landlord offered him such scope as reformers
rarely enjoy. "So great the difficulties appeared to me," his daughter
remarks, "that I could not conceive how he got through them, nor
could I imagine how the people had ever gone on during his absence." [12] To her second point it may be observed that this was a
people considerably practiced in getting on without absentee landlords. As for the first problem, Edgeworth freed his mind for weightier
matters by making Maria the agent of his estate, the rent-roll of which
was well in the thousands. It was an unusual responsibility to place
upon a girl in her teens, but she was in every way his daughter and the
art of ruling came to her easily.

Between the two of them, father and daughter did what could be
done to get the estates in order and to better the lives of the peasants.
Edgeworth's long residence in England must have been responsible
for some part of the conditions which greeted them, though Maria
would never have admitted that, but the root of the trouble was buried
in the centuries. Since the peasants held their lands upon will, thanks
to the perverse ingenuity of the Penal Laws, his family had taken
care, in each generation, to add conditions which bound landholders
as oppressively as though they were slaves. Edgeworth abolished the
future of such clauses, and refused either to demand or to accept those
which existed. He also remitted the huge accumulation of feudal fines
and penances. He built a school for the village, and supervised its
operations with more energy than a board of governors.

[12] Edgeworth, *Memoirs*, II, 3.

But little can be done, in Maria's philosophical phrase, "by any private individual to alleviate the misery necessary in the passage from one stage of civilization to another." [13] That Edgeworth's neighbors regarded his philanthropic zeal as an instance of his eccentricity was not likely to hamper a man of his stamp, but the peasants were another matter, and he was tempted to think of himself as a benevolent despot guiding the destinies of aborigines, laying down penalties for drunkenness which must often have been as irksome as the duties which he had removed. Yet Maria has summed him up in a way which his actions support: "Generous himself, yet not easily to be duped; willing to give and able to serve, yet neither afraid to refuse or punish; humane, but not meek; just, but not to that extreme where justice becomes injustice." [14]

In the autumn of 1798 all of these virtues were put to the test. The Wexford rising had affected Longford not at all, but through the long summer the landlords grew increasingly apprehensive, and they had organized bands of yeomanry of the usual terrorist stripe. Edgeworth refused to follow suit until it became clear even to his sanguine temper that measures of some sort needed to be taken. He thereupon organized what he magniloquently called the Edgeworthstown Infantry, but this move further infuriated his neighbors, since he admitted his peasants, nearly all of whom were Catholic, to its ranks. For this strict impartiality he came within an ace of losing his life to each party.

The French landed in Killala, in Connaught, on the twenty-second of August and, after administering a sharp defeat to the startled British, moved rapidly inland, in the direction of Edgeworthstown, under the command of the enterprising Humbert. Large numbers of peasants, in the hazy belief that this was the cause of "Robespierre and the Blessed Virgin," joined them as they marched. By September 4, they were reputed to be a few miles away, and one of Edgeworth's servants came upon a band of pikemen with green boughs in their hats. They explained artlessly that they had armed to protect themselves against Orangemen, but Edgeworth knew better. The Edge-

[13] *Ibid.*, II, 19.   [14] *Ibid.*, II, 4.

worthstown Infantry had become an object rather than a source of protection, since Dublin Castle, with an equal display of bland innocence, had "forgotten" to send it any arms.

He packed up his troop with his family and took them to Longford, only to discover that he had delivered a body of defenseless Catholics into a nest of Orangemen. For the next few hours he was busy persuading the carbineers, who had been on the point of retreat, into preparing a defense against the French, while at the same time he was protecting his peasants from the townspeople. He next discovered that his son, who had taken a spyglass to the courthouse roof to watch for enemy movements, had been arrested as a spy. His efforts to extricate his son resulted in his own arrest. At Ballinamuck, however, Cornwallis checked and defeated the French, which made it possible for the Edgeworths to return home. The village to which they returned was "a melancholy spectacle; windows shattered and doors broken." [15] Edgeworth House had been attacked, but one of the pikemen with green boughs in his hat was a tenant, and at his insistence it was not looted.

A few days later they rode over to the sorry field of Ballinamuck. The French had been granted amnesty, but the Irish had been bayonetted almost to a man, and their bodies lay in heaps upon the ground.

After the Rebellion the days of the Protestant Nation were numbered, and the question of Union was broached at the next session of Parliament. The crisis reawakened Edgeworth's interest in politics and he resumed his seat, where he treated Commons to a long, scrupulous speech in which it never became clear whether he favored Union or not. One bellicose member, having forgotten Edgeworth's face during his long absence, declared that he was an impostor, brought over from England "to impose upon the House." [16] Edgeworth took advantage of his transient presence to bring in a bill for the improvement of education. "In the shock of contending parties," he wrote complacently to Erasmus Darwin, "seizing a moment of temporary calm, I found an opportunity of laying the foundation of a system,

[15] *Ibid.*, II, 231.   [16] *Ibid.*, II, 244.

by which the wretched poor of this country may be rendered less savage."

When the session had ended and the Kingdom of Ireland had vanished forever, he summed up matters in a brisk letter to Darwin, and then, with the same resiliency which he had exhibited in 1782, went on to describe his new project: "Mechanoiconomia, or a Description of Machinery for Domestic Purposes." "Maria," he says casually, "continues writing for children, under the persuasion that she cannot be employed more serviceably." [17] In this he was not quite accurate, for she had been taking advantage of his preoccupation with national affairs to write *Castle Rackrent,* the only important work which she did without his guidance, and the one on which her fame rests most securely. Despite his many virtues he had a very slender endowment of modesty, and he would henceforward have to accommodate himself, in awkward ways, to a reputation as Maria's father.

Edgeworth's educational schemes, which so easily embraced a village, a county, and a nation, had not ignored his family. A much-married man and a prolific father, he had experimented in sundry ingenious ways with his children, but Maria, who had been educated in English seminaries, was his only success. She was only fifteen when they returned to Ireland, having been born in 1767, but within a few years she was keeping the accounts of the estate, collaborating on his treatises, and helping to train her numerous brothers and sisters.

It was through this latter task that she discovered, by accident, her flair for fiction. Every evening the Edgeworths crowded into the living room (Richard Lovell hated solitude) to work, read aloud, and pay heed to their father's matchless talent for logical and endless discourses. At odd moments Maria would scribble down the plots of stories for children, and these, if he considered them worthy, would be read to the gathering. He was then working on the system of pedagogy which he later published, with Maria's help, as *Practical Education*. A ruthlessly didactic theory of fiction played its part in his formula, since, like his friend Day, he saw great value in exciting

[17] *Ibid.,* II, 253.

the moral faculties of children through "the application of philosophic principles to trivial occurrences." Maria's stories seemed instances of this properly guided application, and he arranged for their publication. They were important events in the history of such literature— *The Parents' Assistant* in 1796; then *Moral Tales,* for older children; and then *Early Lessons.* Generations of British and American children were to become familiar with Lazy Lawrence and Simple Susan.

Edgeworth's attitude toward his daughter's talent and fame was proprietary to a degree which caused during his life some tittering scandal, and he displayed it with unabashed candor. The explanation is simple: he regarded Maria as his creation in the same way as he did his four-pointed phaeton and his wooden horse which jumped stone walls. As her tales and novels appeared, he bustled before them with forewords and prefaces, halted them with footnotes, and swept them up with explanatory conclusions. After his death Maria faced the fact that his own writings were slender and fragmentary: his literary genius, she says, was of the critical order, and "all his literary ambition, then and ever, was for me." [18]

To the end of her life she continued his habit of writing in the crowded, noisy common room, working on the small and ingenious desk which he had designed for her. It carried the following touching, outrageous, and accurate plaque:

On this humble desk were written all the numerous works of my daughter, Maria Edgeworth, in the common sitting-room of my family. In these works, which were written chiefly to please me, she has never attacked the personal character of any human being or interfered with the opinions of any sect or party, religious or political; while endeavoring to inform and instruct others, she improved and amused her mind and gratified her heart, which I do believe is better than her head.[19]

That she wrote chiefly to please him is unfortunately the case. It has been assumed that his relentless dogmatism is responsible for the uneven quality of her work, but a critic has sensibly remarked that "Edgeworth's crime was not so much that he was a rather pompous and opinionated utilitarian but that he so conducted himself as to

[18] Edgeworth, *Memoirs,* II, 336.
[19] *The Life and Letters of Maria Edgeworth,* II, 688–89.

cause his daughter to love him uncritically and therefore adopt his precepts on life and literature unquestioningly." [20] Yet there is a stronger case to be made. "He inspired in my mind," Maria says, "a degree of hope and confidence essential in the first instance to the full preservation of the mental powers, and necessary to ensure perseverance in any occupation. Such, happily for me, was his power over my mind that no one thing I began to write was left unfinished." [21] Her father was recently dead when she wrote this, and thirty sterile and unproductive years stretched ahead of her.

Adam Buck visited Edgeworthstown around 1790, and made a pastel of the family. Maria and Richard Lovell Edgeworth sit facing each other across a plain table.[22] She is a slight, straight-backed girl, the very image of docile intelligence. Her father has a plan or chart of some sort unfurled on the table; one hand is holding it down and the other, inevitably, is gesticulating. Behind him, holding an infant, is his third and penultimate wife. Seven other children—eight, if you look closely—swarm around them. It is difficult to realize that they are not in Sussex, but in the untamed and bewildering island to which he had committed them, the Ireland of gunmen and drunkards and beggars on the road.

When Irishmen fell to squabbling over their fiction and to testing it for "Irishness," they found cause to regret that Maria's youth had been spent in England. She had not drawn from the soil, by that obscure osmosis of which nationalists possess the secret, a sense of the people, their lore, their beliefs, the gods and demons, and the little people of the bogland. As a matter of fact, she knew a great deal about such matters, because like any good writer she listened to what all kinds of people said, and she put what she heard to good use. Her subject, however, was the Anglo-Irish, the "middle nation," and not the peasantry. The peasantry was important to her, again as a writer, because, ultimately, it was through them that she came to understand the fate of her own class.

[20] Newby, *Maria Edgeworth*, p. 18.   [21] Edgeworth, *Memoirs*, II, 346.
[22] Buck's drawing is used by Isabel C. Clarke as the frontispiece to *Maria Edgeworth: Her Family and Friends.*

She was to explore this fate, with a deepening awareness of its moral sources, in all four of her Irish novels. Because she was herself implicated in it, the later novels reveal in varying ways an attempt to conceal from herself the tragic implications of her theme. But against these, as a standing reproach, is *Castle Rackrent,* which is as final and as damning a judgment as English fiction has ever passed on the abuse of power and the failure of responsibility.

5. Castle Rackrent

CASTLE RACKRENT is that rare event, an almost perfect work of fiction.[1] It is a passionate, elegiac novel, muted and sardonic in tone. In one sense it is less like the novels of its own day than of our own, for all the "set scenes" are deliberately thrown away, and the acts and statements are ambiguous and unsettling. And this is appropriate to its purpose, which is to bring to life, by plot and symbol, a society which was destroyed by self-deception.

It purports to be an account, dictated by an illiterate servant named Thady M'Quirk, of the fortunes of four generations of the Rackrent family, which has ceased to exist in name, though not, perhaps, in blood. Thady is a partisan of the family, or rather, of "the honor of the family." Only when the story is finished does the reader realize that Thady has his own wry view of this matter. But, even so, he does not fully understand the story which he is telling. The meaning and passion with which he instinctively invests the words "honor" and "loyalty" lead him to bring forth evidence which prompts the reader to a quite different judgment of the Rackrents.

"Monday Morning," he begins. "Having out of friendship for the family, upon whose estate, praised be Heaven! I and mine had lived rent-free time out of mind, voluntarily undertaken to publish the

---

[1] *Castle Rackrent: An Hibernian Tale, Taken from Facts, and from the Manners of the Irish Squires of Former Times.* The text followed here is that of the 1802 edition, which includes the notes of Richard Lovell Edgeworth; I have modernized the punctuation somewhat and, in several instances, have made paragraph divisions. Here and in subsequent chapters, page references to novels being discussed are given in parentheses following the quoted material. References to any other sources are given in footnotes.

memoirs of the Rackrent Family, I think it my duty to say a few words, in the first place, concerning myself." (*Castle Rackrent,* p. 7) Every line of his narrative requires either a gloss or a challenge: to the Irish peasant, only Monday morning could see a task auspiciously begun. "Rent-free" sounds pleasant enough, but was the technical term for a special kind of slavery.

To look at Thady in his long, tattered greatcoat you would never think of him as "the father of Attorney Quirk; he is a high gentleman, and never minds what poor Thady says . . . but I wash my hands of his doings, and as I have lived, so will I die, true and loyal to the family." (*Ibid.,* p. 7) The Rackrents have worked their own destruction, but Attorney Quirk, as we will discover, has been its instrument.

The family bears the name of Rackrent, but by blood they are O'Shaughlins. Patrick O'Shaughlin had inherited when Tallyhoo Rackrent died without issue. The novel chronicles his career and that of his successors, Sir Murtagh, Sir Kitt, and Sir Condy. He came into the estates upon the condition, which "he took sadly to heart, they say, but thought better of it afterwards, seeing how large a stake depended on it, that he should by act of Parliament take and bear the surname and arms of Rackrent." (*Ibid.,* p. 8) Thady would have us believe that this reluctance issues from Sir Patrick's knowledge that the O'Shaughlins are "sons of the kings of Ireland." Some of the puzzles of the novel are resolved, however, if we regard this as one of his discretions. It is more likely that Patrick had had to change not merely his name but his creed, which would have seemed to the old Catholic servant the deepest dishonor.

Now it was that the world was to see what was *in* Sir Patrick. On coming into the estate, he gave the finest entertainment ever was heard of in the country—not a man could stand up after dinner but Sir Patrick himself, who could sit out the best man in Ireland, let alone the three kingdoms itself. He had his house from one year's end to another as full of company as ever it could hold, and fuller; for rather than be left out of the parties at Castle Rackrent, many gentlemen, and those men of the first consequence and landed estates in the country, such as the O'Neills of Ballynagrotty, and the Castle Moneygawls of Mount Juliet's Town, and the O'Shannons of New Town Tullyhog, made it their choice often and often when there was no moon to be had for love nor money, in long winter nights, to sleep in the chicken house, which Sir Patrick had fitted up for the purpose of accommodating his friends and the public in general who honored him with their presence at Castle Rackrent; and this went on—I can't tell you how long— the whole country rang with his praises— Long life to him!— I'm sure I love to look upon his picture, now opposite to me; though I never saw him, he must have been a portly gentleman—his neck something short, and remarkable for the large pimple on his nose, which, by his particular desire, is still extant in his picture—said to be a striking likeness, though taken when young. He is said also to be the inventor of raspberry whiskey, which is very likely, as nobody has ever appeared to dispute it with him, and there still exists a broken punch-bowl at Castle Stopgate, in the garret, with an inscription to that effect—a great curiosity. A few days before his death he was very merry; it being his honor's birthday he called my great-grandfather in, God bless him! to drink the company's health, and filled a bumper himself, but could not carry it to his head, on account of the great shake in his hand. (*Ibid.,* pp. 8–9)

Patrick dies "in a sort of a fit" at another and more formidable drinking bout. On the whole, his funeral is a success. "Country people lined the route so thick you might have taken them for an army drawn out . . . and happy the man who could get a sight of the hearse! But who'd have thought it, just as all was going on right, through his own town they were passing when the body was seized for debt." (*Ibid.,* p. 9)

Sir Murtagh, his heir, takes proper umbrage at this insult to the dead, and having gained the support of the county families, properly refuses to pay a shilling of the debt. "But the minute the law was taken off of him, that was an end of honor, to be sure." His career suggests that this was no random improvisation, for he proves to be a rapacious skinflint, though the endless lawsuits which finally ruin him do have a fine, aesthetic pointlessness. Thady feels ashamed of Murtagh during his reign, "and knew not what to say for the honor of the family," though he places much of the blame on Lady Rackrent, one of the unlovely Moneygawl tribe. But he is forced to admit that they make a pair.

Then there was a bleach-yard near us, and the tenant dare refuse my lady nothing, for fear of a lawsuit Sir Murtagh kept hanging over him about the water, of course. . . . As for their young pigs, we had them, of course, and the best bacon and ham they could make up, with all the young chickens in Spring; but they were a set of poor wretches, and we had nothing but misfortunes with them, always breaking and running away. . . . Then his heriots and duty work brought him in something—his turf was cut—his potatoes set and dug—his hay brought home, and, in short, all the work about our house done for nothing; for in all our leases there were strict clauses with heavy penalties, which Sir Murtagh knew well how to enforce; so many day's duty work for man and horse, from every tenant he had to have, and had, every year; and when a man vexed him, why the finest day he could pitch on, when the creature was getting in his own harvest, or thatching his own cabin, Sir Murtagh made it a principle to call upon him or his horse. So he taught 'em all, as he said, to know the law of landlord and tenant.   (*Ibid.,* p. 11)

Murtagh digs up a fairy-mount, which seals his fate, for "though a learned man in the law, he was a little too incredulous in other matters." (*Ibid.,* p. 13) He catches cold traveling to court, and bursts a blood vessel while quarreling about the case with his wife. He might have gone on to great things, Thady remarks, had he not died—"for the best, to be sure."

The estate passes to Kitt, a dashing young officer, who pays a flying visit to the estate, summons an improver for the lands, and fixes a day to settle with his tenants. This spurt of energy is not to the liking of Thady, who suddenly discovers that he had been very fond of Murtagh. A bit of casual generosity on Kitt's part, however, and he is won over:

I was looking at his horses' heels, in hopes of a word from him—and is that old Thady! says he, as he got into the gig—I loved him from that day to this, his voice was so like the family—and he threw me a guinea out of his waistcoat pocket, as he drew up the reins with the other hand, his horse rearing too. I thought I had never set my eyes on a finer figure of a man— quite another sort from Sir Murtagh, though withal *to me,* a family likeness. A fine life we should have led had he stayed among us, God bless him!

                                   (*Ibid.,* pp. 14-15)

But the guinea flung to Thady was to be, so Kitt hoped, his farewell to Ireland. As improvident as Murtagh had been grasping, he cares as little for the land or the people. As soon as he is settled in Bath, where he plans to spend his life gaming, he sends a demand for five hundred pounds. It is the beginning of a process by which he milks the estate dry. Old tenants are evicted and new ones brought in, on steeper rents, and these, in turn, are harried. The peasants, including Thady, blame all this on the middleman, and are convinced that "if his honor Sir Kitt, long may he live to reign over us! knew all this, it would go hard with him, but he'd see us righted." (*Ibid.,* p. 15)

In point of fact, Kitt has come to the conclusion that his agent has been soft and indulgent. The agent had befriended Thady's son Jason, taught him to read and write, and allowed him to help with the accounts. Jason is "a very cute lad—I thought to make him a priest, but he did better for himself." (*Ibid.,* p. 15) As a result of "some private correspondence with his honor," Jason manages to get the middleman turned out, and himself installed in the post. But, strangely enough, this does not reverse Kitt's fortunes, and in a desperate move to recoup them, he marries "the grandest heiress in England."

Bonfires are set along Rackrent Gap to light home Kitt and his bride, but these have burned out, and the castle gate is being locked, when the carriage draws up.

I got first sight of the bride, for when the carriage door opened, just as she had her foot on the step, I held the flame full in her face to light her, at which she shut her eyes, but I had a full view of the rest of her, and greatly shocked I was, for by that light she was little better than a blackamoor, and seemed crippled, but that was only sitting so long in the chariot. . . . His honour spoke never a word, nor so much as handed her the steps; he looked to me no more like himself than nothing at all; I know I took him for the skeleton of his honour. (*Ibid.,* p. 18)

There follows a sequence which must seem entirely bizarre, though the histories of a dozen Irish houses can testify that Maria Edgeworth has drawn upon anecdotes. Kitt's wife is Jewish, belonging to a tribe or nation of heretics of whom Thady has heard rumors. Her family has providently entailed her fortune in such a fashion that Kitt cannot touch it without her consent, and he has brought her to Ireland to force her submission. To the literal-minded servants this fortune consists of a diamond cross which she refuses to take off. When she is not beaten down by ill-treatment or by her fear of the bleak, treeless bogs, Kitt has her locked up in a barrack-room while he entertains in the hospitable Irish fashion.

After some years of this imprisonment she takes to her bed, and is not expected to last the winter. "There were now no less than three ladies in our county talked of as his second wife. . . . I could not but think them bewitched, but they all reasoned with themselves, that Sir Kitt would make a good husband to any Christian but a Jewish, I suppose, and especially as he was now a reformed rake." (*Ibid.,* p. 23) They have no way of knowing, of course, that Kitt's lands are heavily mortgaged to the obliging Jason.

But Lady Rackrent inconsiderately recovers, and Kitt is called onto the field by three outraged relatives of the county girls. His skill carries him through two of the encounters, but he is fatally wounded in the third, and is unceremoniously trundled home on a handbarrow. His widow is now mistress of Rackrent, and her favor is courted. "But when I saw she had made up her mind to spend the rest of her days on her own income and jewels in England, I considered her as quite a foreigner, and not at all any longer as part of the family." (*Ibid.,* p. 26)

Once more, and for the last time, a distant kinsman inherits the fatal estate. Condy O'Shaughlin comes of a lowly branch of that family, and Thady can remember him as an urchin, "running through the streets, and playing at pitch and toss, balls, marbles, and what not, with the boys of the town, amongst whom my son Jason was a great favorite with him." (*Ibid.,* p. 28)

Condy is a finely realized character. His nature is genuinely warm and generous, and his temper is never wasted meanly. But for all this, he has the Rackrent weakness—his duties baffle and overcome him. He is exactly of an age with Jason, moreover, and that young man has at last decided that it is time to take over the property. It is clear, despite the evasions and the significant omissions of Thady's narrative, that this time Jason is moved not merely by gain, but by an active personal dislike.

Condy had grown up among the peasants and, for all his awkwardness, there is an instinctive grace to his dealings with them. "There was not a cabin at which he had not stopped some morning or other along with the huntsman, to drink a glass of burnt claret out of an egg-shell, to do him good and warm his heart, and drive the cold out of his stomach. The old people always told him he was a great likeness of Sir Patrick, which made him first have an ambition to take after him, as far as his fortunes should allow." (*Ibid.*, p. 29) And of these old people Thady has been the most vocal.

The Rackrents who immediately succeeded Patrick had been little impressed by him, but legends had grown among the peasants concerning "the great Sir Patrick," the paragon of Irish grandeur, and Condy does his unlucky best to live up to the myth. He begins by erecting a handsome marble stone to his ancestor and goes on to transform himself into what Patrick is supposed to have been like. He is in love with Thady's niece Judy, a mountain girl, but to further his standing he marries Isabella Moneygawl, a pleasant, indolent spendthrift.

"It's a toss-up with me which I shall marry this minute, her or Mr. Moneygawl of Mount Juliet's Town's daughter—so it is!"

"Oh, boo, boo," says I, making light of it, to see what he would go on to next, "your honour's joking, to be sure. There's no compare between our poor Judy and Miss Isabella, who has a great fortune, they say."

"I'm not a man to mind a fortune, nor never was," says Sir Condy proudly, "whatever her friends may say; and to make short of it, I'm come to a determination on the spot." With that, he swore such a terrible oath as made me cross myself. "And by this book," said he, snatching up my ballad book, mistaking it for my prayer book, said he, "and by all the books that were ever shut and opened—it's come to a toss-up with me, and I'll stand or fall by the toss, and so, Thady, hand me that pen out of the ink-horn."

And he makes a cross on the smooth side of the half-penny. "Judy M'Quirk," says he, "her mark." My heart was all as one in my mouth, when I saw the half-penny up in the air, but I said nothing at all, and when it came down I was glad I had kept myself to myself, for to be sure, now it was all over with poor Judy. "Judy's out of luck," said I, striving to laugh.

"I'm out of luck," said he, and I never saw a man look so cast down. He took up the half-penny off the flag and walked off quite sobered by the shock. Now as easy a man you would think him as any in the wide world, there was no such thing as making him unsay one of those sorts of vows which he had learnt to reverence when young, as I well remember teaching him to toss up for bog berries on my knee. (*Ibid.*, p. 32)

Condy's luck has indeed run out, as Murtagh's had when he turned over the fairy mound. Bella and he start life in great style, "with the finest coach and chariot and horses and livery." It is the high noon of the Ascendancy, and now there are balls finer than Sir Patrick's in the great hall, and a theater in the barrack which had once imprisoned poor Jessica. Condy buys a seat in Parliament, laying out hundreds of pounds on "agents' and lawyers' fees and secret service money," and the Rackrents settle into a Dublin mansion.

His virtues conspire with the usual Rackrent vices, however. He is the only honest member of the clan, and by voting with Grattan's "Patriot Party" he loses his chance of office. And although, as Jason cynically puts it, "he does not care the rind of a lemon" for Bella, he amiably indulges her extravagances. By the next spring Jason has control of his notes, and is able to evict the last O'Shaughlin from Castle Rackrent. His wife leaves him then, though with little ill will on either side, and is soon reported dead.

Condy and Thady move to the old hunting cabin on the edge of the estate, and there Condy enacts the last part of his curious self-identification with "the great Sir Patrick." He is dying himself now, as much from despair as from whiskey, and he remembers that the climax of Patrick's career had been the slow progress of his hearse past the double lines of country folk.

He takes to his bed, feigning death, and Thady spends part of the remaining stocking-full of gold on liquor and pipes for the wake. The cabin is quickly crowded with smoke and peasants, but unfortunately the mourners throw their greatcoats over the supposed corpse, who must come to life to avoid suffocation. "There was a great surprise, but not so great as we laid out it would be." (*Ibid.*, p. 59)

The next morning Judy M'Quirk comes to visit him. She is a widow with children now, and has fallen off in her looks, "being smoke-dried in the cabin and neglecting herself like." But Condy remembers the mornings when he stopped at her cabin for an eggshell of whiskey before the hunt, and Thady decides that she may become Lady Rackrent after all. It is Jason, however, whom Judy has her eye on. She had come to the cabin to make certain that Condy had really signed over the lands to him. "Why follow the fortunes of them that have none left?" (*Ibid.,* p. 65)

A few hours later Condy is dead in earnest, his hand wrapped around his last possession, Sir Patrick's drinking horn. His funeral is a poor thing—not worth Thady's trouble to describe it.

"For my part," Thady says, bringing his story to a close, "I'm tired wishing for anything in this world, after all I've seen in it. But I'll say nothing. It would be folly to be getting myself ill-will in my old age. Jason did not marry Judy, as I prophesied, and I am not sorry for it—who is? As for all I have here set down from memory and hearsay of the family, there's nothing but truth in it from beginning to end; that you may depend on, for where's the use of telling lies about the things which everybody knows as well as I do?" (*Ibid.,* p. 68)

This is a fairly full summary of the plot of *Castle Rackrent,* but it does not suggest the curiously enigmatic quality which is a source of the novel's power. This is earned, in the first instance, by Maria Edgeworth's skillful use of Thady as her narrator. The great advantage of this device, of course, is that it permits a dramatic tension to exist between the narrator's story and his own understanding of it. Critics of the novel have been quick to note the disparity between the family as it exists in fact and as it appears to the imagination of the peasant Thady, but not so ready to admit that a peasant's imagination may be put to complicated uses.

It is Thady who creates the illusion of family, out of the feudal retainer's pride in the house which he serves. But he has the retainer's practicality. He assigns Rackrents their role in the family legend in proportion as they are generous toward him or make life easy for him. In this he reflects the attitude not only of the other peasants in the novel, who turn out to a gentleman's funeral in expectation of liquor and spectacle, but also the peasants throughout Ireland, for whom the feudal ties had in fact dissolved.

But he comes at last to believe his own myth, and even, disastrously, to communicate a sense of its glamor to Condy. Condy's mind is fixed upon an improbable past of great houses and harpists and wine in golden goblets. Because of this, he comes to believe that the Rackrents are indeed an ancient family with an obligation to live honorably. The miracle is that the young man is able to give to the fantasy a kind of fitful existence. There are moments when, because of it, he is able to draw himself up and act like the son of kings. Because the Money-gawls have challenged his claims to gentility, he weds Bella without a dowry. He squanders the last of his coins on a shawl for Judy M'Quirk and gifts for her empty-eyed children.

There is a wealth of wryly observed social fact in the novel. The tactics of Murtagh Rackrent and Jason M'Quirk are case studies in the changing methods by which Irish land was managed, and Jason's character shows a shrewd understanding on Maria's part of the new class which was rising to power. She has drawn on the fondly preserved legends of many an Anglo-Irish family. (Not least upon her own, a fact which would have caused her father, had he been more wary, to tone down the history of the Edgeworths as he relates it in his *Memoirs*.) [2]

But the meaning of these facts is buried deep in Thady's "plain, unvarnished tale." There is a spell upon the Rackrent family. Thady talks of this fate in terms of luck, misfortunes, banshees, spinning coins, fairy mounts, and bog berries, but it is plain. It is a remarkably sterile family. Three times bitter widows quit the castle with no other wish than to be rid of it. The family owes its origins to a triple denial, Patrick's rejection of his name, his blood, and his creed. The denial has been made for the sake of land and the money which land brings, but these, despite every frantic measure, run through their fingers.

Thady's language is thick with the terms by which land is held and exploited—abatements, pounding, canting, replevying, tithes, duty-work, notes, bills of sale, rent-rolls. Patrick defects to get land; Murtagh is crazed by his endless lawsuits; Kitt is turned into a grasping land-lord and a vicious husband. And Condy denies his love. None of them is really sure that the land is his—not even Condy. And all save Condy become mindless looters of their own possessions.

Gold is the dominating symbol of the novel, and the symbol is al-

[2] Edgeworth, *Memoirs*, II, 5–20.

ways hedged by irony. Murtagh levels a fairy mound to increase his tillage, never suspecting that such a mound might conceal gold, buried centuries before. Jessica's wealth is made vivid by her diamond and gold cross—an ornament which her own faith makes entirely inexplicable. Condy's luck runs out when he spins a coin on which he has scratched a cross.

When Richard Lovell Edgeworth returned home from his momentous errand, he dashed off a few brisk lines which he appended to the tale with which his daughter had whiled away the weeks of his absence. The Rackrents, he wrote, were vanishing from Ireland. Perhaps they would be replaced by English manufacturers, which would be all for the best.[3] The nation of Ireland, in any event, had ended with the Act of Union, and he had his own buoyant hopes for the future.

But Maria saw beyond this. Her history of the Rackrent family is the history of the eighteenth century Ascendancy, generation by generation, down to poor Condy, whose pathetic belief in honor and responsibility, born of a servant's chatter, might have sufficed, if only it had come much earlier, to some Rackrent of the past. Instead, he has inherited the sins of Ireland's masters, be they named O'Shaughlin or Rackrent—or Quirk, with the "Mc" dropped off for gentility's sake. Some transaction of the dark past, however, had put a curse upon the blood. The land of this cursed family turned always to gold; the gold turned to wind. And the fine gestures of Condy Rackrent have the weightless inconsequence of nightmare. The peasants may come to his wake, but Judy M'Quirk speaks his epitaph: "Why follow the fortunes of them that have none left?"

[3] *Castle Rackrent*, p. 69.

6. The Landlord as the Hero: *Ennui* and

The Absentee[1]

WHILE MARIA EDGEWORTH was writing *Castle Rackrent,* the bleak implications of her story pressed themselves upon her with inescapable force. For the decade which followed its publication, however, while its fame spread throughout Europe, she was immersed in other business. The moral but sprightly tales for children by which her father set such store continued to appear—more moral, it now seems, than sprightly. In one novel, *Belinda* (1801), she let her imagination carry her from the Ireland of Rackrents and rebellions to the other island, whose forms and graces accorded so well with her own instincts.

The immense, sprawling estate, stretching across bogs and sending its fingers up along treeless mountain sides, needed Maria's steady attention, while Richard Lovell paced the sitting room, improving upon his formidable plans for the betterment of mankind. And there were the myriad social duties and pleasures of the Ascendancy—in 1806, for example, her neighbor and closest friend, Kitty Pakenham, married an Irish officer named Wellesley, who had come home after defeating the Mahrattas, and was marking time until he received another command.

The condition of Ireland, however, was never far from the attention

[1] *Tales of Fashionable Life,* 6 vols. (London, 1809–1812), vol. I: *Ennui;* vol. V: *The Absentee.* Page references here for *Ennui* are to volume VI of *Novels and Tales* (New York, 1859) and for *The Absentee* are to Everyman's Library edition (London, 1910 [with *Castle Rackrent*]).

of the Edgeworths. The Act of Union, in the judgment of Richard Lovell, had given the country its first real chance, and he was soon hard at work urging it out of its sloth. He addressed himself to the problems which for a century would break Irish hearts—land and education. From 1806 to 1811 he acted as one of the commissioners appointed by the Viceroy to inquire into the education of the people of Ireland, and outlined the system of nonsectarian schools which the country would not receive for forty years. At least he wrung from the Charter Schools an ill-kept promise that they would not be used to proselytize. He drafted a number of schemes whereby the vast bogs might be reclaimed and apportioned to peasants, and others designed to improve the methods of agriculture. And in all this thankless work he was assisted by Maria.[2]

The keystone of his system was his conviction that most of Ireland's ills were owing to her foolish regard for some cloudy notion of sovereignty. He observed this among the peasantry, and so laid it down that Greek and Roman history must not be taught in his proposed schools: "They inculcate democracy, and a foolish hankering after some ill-defined liberty: this is peculiarly dangerous in Ireland." [3] But it took a form almost as pernicious among the gentry, whose loose talk of "Ireland's grand and immemorial rights" was something worse than foolish now that Union had come. Ireland might properly be accorded some sort of parochial veneration, and certainly her landlords should hold their country in sufficient esteem to remain resident there. But it was now as much a part of Britain as Scotland or Yorkshire, and that should have been an end to "patriotic" froth.

By way of making this view of things current, Maria published in 1803 an *Essay on Irish Bulls,* which is an ingenious and double-edged argument. In part it is an attack upon the low regard in which the Irish had always been held in England. But it is also a lively reproof to sentimental admirers of the Irish past. A cult of just this sort was growing in Dublin's literary and fashionable circles. Bunting and

[2] The chief of Edgeworth's various reports to government commissions are reprinted in the Appendix to his *Memoirs,* II, 453–89.

[3] Edgeworth, *Memoirs,* II, 457.

Charlotte Brooke had published their valuable collections of the old
music and poetry, and the bizarre pseudo-scholarship of Vallancey and
Cooper Walker was in vogue. The Irish romantic movement, in fact,
was in swing, and the scene was being set for the appearance of
Moore's *Irish Melodies*.

It is a matter of indifference to her, she says, "whether the Irish
derive their origin from the Spaniards, or the Milesians, or the Welsh.
. . . We moreover candidly confess, that we are more interested in the
fate of its present race of inhabitants, than in the historian of St.
Patrick, St. Facharis, St. Cormuc; the renowned Brien Boru; Tireldach,
king of Connaught; M'Murrough, king of Leinster. . . ." [4] And she
takes her stand, as might be expected, with those Irish who had entered fully into English culture, Congreve, Berkeley, Sterne, Sheridan,
and Burke.

It was the daughter of Richard Lovell Edgeworth who wrote thus,
though scarcely the author of *Castle Rackrent*. That the two might be
at variance she did not yet suspect. Lovell Edgeworth, that cross-
grained and upright rationalist, regarded the Irish past much as Gibbon
did the Middle Ages. There was nothing to be gained by contemplating
it save wry amusement at the forms which barbarism can assume.
Ideally, a man should be able to choose a nation as his friend Thomas
Day chose his wife—out of an orphanage, void of memories and hope-
ful of instruction and improvement. Since this was not possible, it was
best to dismiss these memories as so much moonshine, while setting
vigorously to work on the problems which they had created.

Maria concurred, and not merely as a dutiful daughter. The problems at hand—dirt, ignorance, neglect, and poverty—were so large and
so pressing as to make looking back a kind of irresponsibility. Contemplation of the past was Ireland's besetting sin, for the past was a
Medusa head which enthralled the beholder and rendered him powerless to act. But the author of *Castle Rackrent* knew the ways in which
the Irish past had shaped the present, knew how they were wedded.
And she knew, also, the tragic gulf which separated the masters of
the Irish land from its inhabitants.

[4] *Irish Bulls*, pp. 262–63.

These contrary modes of understanding produced the contrasting ways in which her next Irish novels handled a single theme. *Ennui* (1809) and *The Absentee* (1812) are both concerned with the responsibilities of the Irish landlord. The plots are substantially the same: an absentee long resident in England is summoned home, discovers the waste, oppression, and suffering which exist on his estates, and accepts his own guilt in the matter and his duties. But there the resemblance ends.

Although the subject was in its nature a prosy one, its implications were not. Maria Edgeworth conceived of the moral issues of Irish life entirely in terms of its landlords, which may well constitute her limitation, but is not at all unreasonable, for landlords determine the destinies of feudal nations. The difference between the two novels lies in their tone and attack. *Ennui* is animated by Lovell Edgeworth's complacent belief that the Irish gentry could soon put matters to rights once they had developed public spirit. But a shadow of suspicion falls across the pages of *The Absentee:* perhaps too much had happened, perhaps Ireland was not after all a second Yorkshire. It is no more than a shadow, but it suffices to make *The Absentee* a novel, while *Ennui* remains a well-intentioned but rather priggish tract.

Lord Glenthorn, the hero of *Ennui,* had been born in Ireland and nursed in a fosterer's cabin, but since the age of two has lived in England. He decides, out of boredom with the life which he has been living, to visit his birthplace. This is a slender reason for sending a man to a bog and keeping him there for four-fifths of a novel. Maria's intention is that his experiences there should remold his character, but she is successful only in transferring his boredom to the reader.

Much of the novel is not fiction at all, but an exposition of Lovell Edgeworth's theories of politics, economics, social arrangements, education, and morality, and an accompanying explanation of their particular appropriateness to Ireland. The vehicle of this instruction is Glenthorn's agent, a Scotsman named M'Leod, who does nothing to impair the reputation which his countrymen once enjoyed for logical and indefatigable discourse. His ideological opponent is a vicious and opinionated squire named Hardcastle, who believes that every peasant is a rebel fit only for hanging. On several scores, however, a peasant might be excused for preferring hanging at the hands of Hardcastle to improvement at the hands of M'Leod. There is a peculiar insensitivity to human values in his modest but self-satisfied account of the methods by which he hopes to rear up in Ireland "a race of our own training." (*Ennui*, p. 86)

If we exclude Glenthorn, M'Leod, and Hardcastle as conveniences rather than characters, there remain the county gentry and the peasants. The gentry are a pleasure to encounter, not only because Maria knew them so thoroughly, but also because her point of view is the dashing and witty Lady Geraldine, whom she endows with her own carefully hidden gift for malicious analysis. "My plan is much the best," Lady Geraldine says. "To help my friends expose themselves, and then they are infinitely obliged to me." (*Ibid.*, p. 77) Maria feels duty bound to censure such an attitude, but she does not have her heart in the task.

The peasants, however, are a total failure, mouthing mechanical jokes interspersed with "to be sure to be sure" and "not at all at all at all." They have their dark and violent sides—the plot involves Glenthorn in an uprising—but these passions are not given any real life.

The novel comes to a wry conclusion. After Glenthorn has thoroughly mastered the art of administering Irish affairs under M'Leod's guidance, it is discovered that the rightful possessor of his land and title is his foster brother, the illiterate Christy O'Donohue. Ireland's subsequent history has made this ending sardonic in a way which Maria did not intend, for Glenthorn goes back to England sadder and wiser, and Christy burns down the great house as soon as he comes into possession of it.

The reading of *Ennui* is itself a saddening experience. Richard Lovell Edgeworth and his daughter were the first in a line of nineteenth-century landlords whose humane and generous instincts set them apart from their class. As a group they were to fail wretchedly, even on their own estates, for the Irish land problem was hopeless of solution at the level of private action, however self-sacrificing. On the level of national politics they were to be caught between their own class, callous and grasping, and a peasantry which had chosen its own leaders. *Ennui* suggests that they conspired in their own defeat. Only that bloodless paragon, M'Leod, could find nourishment in a social program which runs so athwart the temper of an entire people as that of which he is the mouthpiece.

An awareness that this is so informs *The Absentee,* a novel which reworks the same theme in a richer and more rewarding way. It is, to begin with, much more firmly rooted in social actualities. Lord Colombre, its young hero, is settled in England, as Glenthorn was, but he is very conscious of being "Irish," although he is no surer than anyone else of what this means. He does know, however, that his parents, the Clonbronys, are making themselves butts of ridicule by their attempts to become English. Lady Clonbrony's efforts are particularly strenuous: "You cawn't conceive the *peens* she *teeks* to talk of the *teebles* and *cheers,* and to thank Q, and with so much *teeste,* to speak pure English." (*The Absentee,* p. 84)

The novel is set in the years just following the Union, a period which saw the Dublin of Swift and Grattan reduced to the status of a provincial town. The Clonbronys, following the new fashion, have moved to London, and Colombre has been educated at Oxford rather than Trinity. In London Clonbrony, who had been a great lord at home, is one of the "Irish in society," disdained for his brogue and his gregariousness. The Irishman was expected to be a gallant but cynical adventurer, a role which the heavy but forthright Clonbrony is ill-equipped to play.

Not so his friend Sir Terence O'Fay. O'Fay, who is one of the charms of the novel, had been one of the Dublin Castle understrappers who engineered the Union, and he expresses his principles with a gusto which comes straight out of Sheridan:

I hear great talk now of the Venus of Medicis, and the Venus of this and that, with the Florence Venus, and the sable Venus, and the other Venus that's washing her hair, and a hundred other Venuses, some good, some bad. But be that as it will, my lord, trust a fool—ye may, when he tells you truth—the golden Venus is the only one on earth that can stand or that will stand, through all ages and temperatures; for gold rules the court, gold rules the camp, and men below and heaven above. . . . Deny, if you please, my lord, that it was for a golden pippin that the three goddesses *fit* and that the *Hippomenes* was about golden apples—and did not Hercules rob a garden for golden apples?—and did not the pious Eneas himself take a golden branch with him, to make himself welcome to his father in hell.

(Ibid., p. 105)

Rogues, no doubt, are easier to do than saints, but O'Fay is worth a hundred M'Leods.

Colombre, after studying his father and his father's friends, has begun to ask a question which was to trouble the Anglo-Irish throughout the century. What meaning was there in thinking oneself Irish, now that there no longer was an Irish nation? Lovell Edgeworth had answered confidently that there was little point. But now Maria, at least, was beginning to wonder if the question could be dismissed so easily. To answer the question, Colombre revisits Ireland.

His journey from Dublin to his estates, which he conducts at a leisurely pace, brings him into contact with the types which then composed Irish society. It is a broader canvas than *Ennui* presented, and the observation is much sharper.

The transformation of the vacated House of Parliament into the Bank of Ireland is, it appears, a symbolic change, for the center of Dublin social life is passing from the great houses to the rising class of Catholic merchants, whose wives, bearing such euphonious names as Anastasia Rafferty, hold court in Wicklow villas.

In the country, however, life would seem to have changed little since the days of Patrick Rackrent. The Killpatricks keep an open house which would have delighted Thady M'Quirk.

One hundred and four people sit down to dinner every day, Petito informs me, beside kitchen boys and what they call *char-women*—who never sit down, but who do not eat or waste the less for that; and retainers and friends, friends to the fifth and sixth generations, who "must get their bit and their sup"; for, "sure, it's only Biddy," they say, and "sure, 'tis nothing at all, out of all his honour, my lord, has. How could he feel it! Long life to him!"   *(Ibid.,* p. 185)

But Killpatrick House is a sham, sumptuous and unfinished, "all begun as if the projectors thought they had the command of the

mines of Peru, and ended as if the possessor had not sixpence." (*Ibid.*,
pp. 184–85) Picturesque cottages have been built within sight of the
castle, but beyond these stretch the foul cabins in which the wretched
nurse their grievances.

Colombre's own Nugentstown is in a worse state than this, however. At least the Killpatricks had stayed with the land, dispensing
their slovenly hospitality. But Clonbrony had left his affairs in the
hands of Garraghy, a corrupt middleman who has risen, like Jason
Quirk, from the peasantry.

The town consisted of one row of miserable huts, sunk beneath the side
of the road, the mud walls crooked in every direction; some of them opening
in wide cracks or fissures, from top to bottom, as if there had just been an
earth-quake—all the roofs sunk in various places—thatch off or overgrown
with grass—no chimneys, the smoke making its way through a hole in the
roof, or rising in clouds from the top of the open door—dunghills before
the doors, and green standing puddles—squalid children, with scarcely rags
to cover them, gazing at the carriage.   (*Ibid.*, p. 226)

It is this spectacle of mismanagement and corruption which awakens
in Colombre a sense of responsibility for the lives of his tenants, and a
conviction that he can only fulfill this responsibility by living on the
land. The Clonbronys had surrendered Ireland to merchant vulgarians,
climbing squireens, and predatory middlemen. By returning they will
restore the old feudal relationships.

As a resolution of the novel nothing could be more edifying or less
satisfactory, for Maria knew that while the new Ireland of the nineteenth century was that of the Raffertys and Garraghys, it had only
succeeded the equally squalid world of O'Fays and Rackrents. The
tone of her final lines, buoyant and uneasily optimistic, betrays that
knowledge:

And we leave him with the reasonable expectation that he will support
through life the promise of his early character; that his patriotic views will
extend with his power to carry wishes into action; that his attachment to
his warm-hearted fellow-countrymen will increase upon further acquaintance; and that he will long diffuse happiness through the wide circle which
is peculiarly subject to the influence and example of a great resident Irish
proprietor.   (*Ibid.*, p. 341)

We might therefore be prepared to dismiss *The Absentee* as a superior version of *Ennui*—more vivacious and more brightly colored, but equally implausible as a representation of Irish culture—were it not for a remarkable scene which occurs halfway through the novel and which affects our understanding of its theme.

While Colombre is staying with the Killpatricks, he learns of an eccentric nobleman who lives nearby—a Count O'Halloran, who is reputed to be a great oddity. He is a famous huntsman, which does something to offset the figure he cuts, for he dresses in an antique fashion, with a long queue, laced waistcoat, and gold-laced hat. From curiosity Colombre accompanies two English officers, Benson and Williamson, who are seeking permission to shoot on the Count's grounds.

They find him in a ruined fortress, part of which has been carefully restored. In the great hall stand the skeletons of an elk and a "moose deer," "which had been made out, with great care, from the different bones of many of this curious species of deer, found in the lakes of the neighborhood." (*Ibid.,* p. 194) His library, which is filled with tattered genealogical works and histories of Gaelic Ireland, is also a kind of zoo, with an otter, mice in a cage, a goat, and gold and silver fish in glass globes. Colombre's friends have to fight off an eagle, and are greeted by the menacing growls of an Irish greyhound, one of the last of its species.

O'Halloran himself turns out, despite his reputation, to be a polished and handsome old soldier, who is spending his years of retirement preparing certain maps for the use of the government and hunting down the burial places of the old, vanished families. Benson and Williamson are impressed by O'Halloran, but faintly hostile. Colombre, however, is fascinated by him, and uses him henceforward as a touchstone of moral worth, for he recognizes in him a grace and authority which are lacking in his father and in those Irishmen whom his father knows.

This would be a perplexing scene unless its hints were picked up. The first of these is given when one of the officers pointedly calls him "Mister O'Halloran." We remember then that "Count" is not a British title, but a continental. And O'Halloran's military career has been served in a continental army, which accounts for the hostility of the English soldiers. O'Halloran, of course, is a remnant of that Gaelic aristocracy which fled Ireland after Limerick to form the Irish brigades of France and the Irish regiments of Austria and Spain. During the years with which *The Absentee* deals, the Wild Geese had been driven home by one of the ironies of history: a Europe dominated by Revolutionary France was less congenial to them than even an Ireland owned by Whigs.

They returned as Catholic gentlemen (and very highborn and politically reactionary gentlemen at that) to an Ireland just beginning to emerge from Penal Days, in which their creed and their foreign sympathies made them doubly suspect. Most of them, like O'Halloran, offered their experience and their undoubted skill to the British government, only to be rebuffed as coldly as O'Halloran is by Benson and Williamson.

But if this explains the nature of O'Halloran's "oddness," and his cool reception in his native land, the questions yet remain of why Maria has set this elaborately theatrical scene, and why she has Colombre react so strongly and so decisively to the Count. The answer is that the scene is as much allegorical as it is theatrical.

O'Halloran engagingly reminds his guests that his pets—the mouse, the bird, the fish—are the customary tributes of air, earth, and water, which ancient peoples paid to their conquerors. He might well have pointed out that all the animals in his zoo are allegorical, for the eagle which is stirred to instinctive anger by the English, and the greyhound, "the kind of dog who seizes his enemy by the back and shakes him to death," are the traditional Irish symbols of mastery. The greyhound, like O'Halloran himself, is the last of his breed. The elk and the deer have long been extinct; their skeletons must be dredged from the lake and articulated. And the Count himself, with his antique chivalry and gold-laced hat, is the survivor of a long-dead Ireland.

O'Halloran is Maria Edgeworth's oblique answer to those questions of identity which otherwise the novel poses only to evade. The old man who spends his days hunting the traditional game of the island

and his nights poring over its great names and monuments represents an ideal past. He is wedded to his lands and his crumbling castle, and his tranquillity and moral probity are clearly related to this attachment. His is an Ireland which exists far back in time, far beyond the half-horsed gentry and the half-sirs and the Dublin merchants. It is an Ireland which can and does give Colombre strength and direction.

Maria ignores the obvious irony of this: twenty years earlier O'Halloran would have been an Irish soldier who could not carry side arms in Ireland, a man of piety who could not practice his creed openly, a landlord who could not own land. She ignores, also, a second and less obvious irony. As a literary creation O'Halloran has a faint odor of library oil about him. His is the trumpery Gaelicism of Moore's *Irish Melodies,* with their crumbling walls of Tara and ruined abbeys of the West and their thin, wistful patriotism. It is, in a word, the antiquarian patriotism which she had mocked so cleverly in her essay on Irish bulls.

The old Ireland, with its great strengths and great weaknesses, does exist in the novel, in the careless, slack, generous household of the Killpatricks. And no one who loved the old Ireland as it existed in actuality could have written with Maria's cutting, intolerant scorn of the unquestioning way in which the Killpatricks feed the old women who come to their table. It was, no doubt, uneconomical and improvident, the sort of thing which drove Lovell Edgeworth to despair of his people. And, when we remember those untended hovels of misery tucked out of sight in the Killpatrick bogs, it was morally blind. But it was the enduring Ireland. She would understand this when she wrote her last Irish novel, *Ormond,* with its great figure of Corny O'Shane.

The Absentee is a less ambitious novel than *Ormond,* and its own intentions are significant. They set her out, it might seem, on the road which led to *Ormond. The Absentee* speaks to the need which she felt to relate herself to the Irish past, a need which *Ennui* had explicitly denied. That novel had proclaimed her father's belief that the country should cut itself loose of history and the past. M'Leod, that Adam Smith of the bog-side, is not lyrical by nature, but he approaches it when he describes his success at extirpating the past; when, for example, he points pridefully to the empty ditches where once had huddled the hedge scholars who now attend his model school, a new little race cast in his own spiritless mold.

It is that scene which supplies the key to *Ennui*. The scene in *The Absentee* which counters it is that in which Colombre is led by O'Halloran past locked horns and brass spears and gold ornaments to a table of urns. O'Halloran picks one, at random, as a gift for his young guest; it proves to be an urn lately found in the abbey ground which had been the burial place of the Nugent family. It is this family which had been expropriated, long before, from the lands of Nugentstown, the Colombre holdings. And Colombre, in time, marries Grace Nugent, whose name is entered on the Count's genealogical table as the child of that family. Colombre carries the urn back with him, and carries back also his bride of the old family.

It would stretch matters but slightly, if at all, to suggest that *The Absentee* presents us with the earliest instance of the theme which was to haunt (and in part to create) modern Anglo-Irish literature. For if Irish thought has been obsessed with the past, and with the use of the past to give shape and meaning to experience, the obsession has been, for the Anglo-Irish, an especially poignant one. Their status had always been that of a garrison, and self-interest and natural feeling alike led them to insist upon that status. Their victories had been victories over Gaelic Ireland. These victories alone, save for the brief hour of the Protestant Nation, constituted their only tradition. They might look far into the past, to the Ireland of Finn and Ossian and the sagas; yet between stood history itself.

For the most part, to be sure, this theme found literary expression much later in the century, but Maria Edgeworth's sense of her subject was sure. Her subject was the Irish landlord, and she was concerned with him without apology or guilt or false sentiment. In this she is very much a woman of the Irish eighteenth century—the century of Swift and Grattan. She shared its assumptions naturally and as a matter of course. But she is of the nineteenth century in her awareness that the moral failure of the Ascendancy arose, in part, from its lack of that in which it took the most pride—an aristocratic tradition.

7. In Search of a Hero: *Ormond*

ORMOND,[1] MARIA EDGEWORTH'S final novel of Irish life, was written in 1817, at the urging of her dying father. The old man, who had been told by Crampton, the celebrated Surgeon-General, that he had but a few months to live, was anxious to fight off the "superstition and bigotry which press upon the enfeebled mind, and enhance the terror of death." [2] And so each day, with the tears cutting her eyes "like knives," Maria sat at her table, and each evening she read aloud what she had written.

By June the book was finished, and there remained for Richard Lovell Edgeworth two last and characteristic acts. He dictated a memorandum of the ignoble transactions which accompanied the Act of Union, and he issued instructions for his burial: "I have always endeavored to discountenance the desire which people of this country have for expensive funerals. I would have neither velvet, nor plate, nor gilding employed in making my coffin, which I would have carried to the grave, without a hearse, by my own laborers." [3]

Ormond, oddly enough, comes to its close with two funerals. One is as expensive, feudal, and wild as that of Patrick Rackrent; the other accords to the letter with Edgeworth's directions. But the first is the funeral of Corny O'Shane, whom the reader has come to love, and the second is that of his brother Ulick. And Ulick is buried by his own laborers not to commemorate his Spartan austerity, but because he has lost the affection of the countrypeople.

[1] Page references are to vol. XVIII of *Novels and Tales.*
[2] Edgeworth, *Memoirs,* II, 445.   [3] *Ibid.,* II, 449.

Ormond is clearly Maria Edgeworth's finest work after *Castle Rackrent*. Perhaps it does not deserve the qualifying phrase, for *Castle Rackrent* is a long, brilliantly sustained sketch, while *Ormond* is a novel on the fullest scale, ambitious in conception and bold in execution. In it the themes which for seventeen years she had been turning in her mind come to full and unexpected expression.

It is set in the past, in the Augustan Ireland of the seventeen sixties and seventies; both scene and time are created with a depth and complexity which she had never before attempted. And they are well-chosen, for here at last she is considering not the decline of the Ascendancy, but the years of its flowering.

Harry Ormond is the orphaned son of an army officer. His name joins that which is bluff and British to one of the oldest and proudest of Anglo-Irish titles. Young Ormond has been raised in a fosterer's cabin, and his quick, generous temper has received no chastening discipline. When he comes to manhood, however, he encounters three possible models. One of these is Sir Herbert Annaly, a resident landlord of English stock. The second is his own uncle, Sir Ulick O'Shane, one of the government's "Undertakers," and an important figure in the management of national affairs. The third is a second uncle, "King" Corny O'Shane, a kind of chieftain, who leads on the Black Islands the half-feudal, half-outlaw existence of the proscribed Catholic gentry. Ormond lives, for long stretches of time, with each of these, and becomes immersed in the three worlds which they inhabit. These worlds are various and are richly created: for the first time since *Castle Rackrent*, Maria has created a sense of the actual and the unexpected. She has lost nothing, however, of her interest in emblem and allegory: Ormond is being confronted by Ireland's three "nations."

The O'Shanes are her most brilliant creations. Both have energy and wit, capacity for strong affections and passions, and an instinctive preference for devious action.

Ulick has made his way out of the world into which he was born in a fashion which his three marriages commemorate: "The first he loved, and married, imprudently, for love, at seventeen; the second he admired, and married, prudently, for ambition, at thirty; the third

he hated, but married, from necessity, for money, at five-and-forty."
(*Ormond*, p. 7) The first of these marriages, however impetuous it may
have been, brought him into the world of the Annalys; in the process,
he discarded his faith and his Gaelic, though not his brogue. The
Annalys, however, are county people in the English manner, forthright, honest, and lacking any taste for meddling in politics. His second marriage, to Lady Theodosia, gained access for him to the circle
of Dublin Castle grandees. As the novel opens, however, Ulick has
suffered a temporary reverse—his cabal has fallen and the canal scheme
which he engineered has absorbed more O'Shane money than it has
bog water. To recoup, he has married the widow of a wealthy London
tradesman named Scraggs.

Any fear that this might be too schematic to make for a successful
novel is dissolved by Ulick's first entrance, affable, ill-tempered, shrewd,
and dissembling. We meet him at his home, Castle Hermitage, where
he charms one of his wife's dour friends out of her incivility, and then
walks away muttering, "Wouldn't you swear to that being the voice
of a Presbyterian?" (*Ibid.*, p. 6)

A few hours later, however, we see another side of his character.
Ormond has killed a man and must be hustled to the Black Island.
Ulick accomplishes this easily enough, but as an O'Shane, rather than
a knight and a friend of the Viceroy. For Ulick has forgotten the
spirit of his people, but not their ways, and when occasion arises can
summon up his follower, Tim Kelly the *stalko*. No one understands
this side of his character save his cousin Corny. To Corny, Ulick is a
twister and a renegade, a man who has betrayed his clan and is
capable of equal disloyalty to his present allies. By the same token,
Ulick thinks Corny a fool, clinging suicidally to a way of life which is
being pushed out of history. But at bottom the two men have a grudging respect for each other. They talk together with the mocking,
sly, tortuous indirection of enemies who understand each other.

And so they do, for Ulick and Corny have been enemies for centuries. Ulick is the man who has made peace with the foe and now
wears his colors; Corny is the wily old chief who can be driven from
the bogs to the hills and from the hills to the islands, only to grow
more hardy.

Corny keeps the state of an impoverished king on his Black Islands, greeting his guests in a six-oared boat, with streamers flying and a piper playing. In his battered house (*"Palace* I would have said, only for the constituted authorities of the post-office, that might take exceptions and not be sending me my mail right") he rules with the easy authority of an hereditary monarch. Half the population swarms in to sit at his table each night, when he holds court. Beside him sits "Father Jos," the chaplain whom he maintains in defiance of the law.

In one of her letters Maria describes the man who sat for Corny:

A man I believe like no other, who lived in the remote part of Ireland, an ingenious despot in his own family, who blasted out of the rock on which his house was built half a kitchen, while he and his family and guests were living in the house; who was so passionate that children, grown-up sons, servants and all ran out of the house when he fell into a passion with his own twisted hair; a man who used, in his impatience and rages, to call at the head of the kitchen stairs to his servants, "Drop whatever you have in your hand, and come here and be d—d!" He was generous and kind-hearted, but despotic, and conceited to the most ludicrous degree; for instance, he thought he could work gobelin tapestry and play on the harp or mandolin better than anyone living.[4]

One after another, as she says, she transformed these hints in working out King Corny, and yet she gave to him the tang and color of that old feudal Ireland. She makes something more of him than that, for the affection which Ormond feels toward him is shared by the reader.

King Corny, who had the command not only of boats, and of guns, and of fishing tackle, and of men, but of carpenter's tools, and of smith's tools, and of a lathe, and of brass and ivory, and of all things that the heart of a boy could desire, had appeared to Harry, when he was a boy, the richest, the greatest, the happiest of men—the cleverest, too—the most ingenious: for with his own hands King Corny had made a rat-trap; and had made the best coat, and the best pair of shoes, and the best pair of boots, and the best hat; and had knit the best pair of stockings, and had made the best dunghill in his dominions; and had made a quarter of a yard of fine lace, and had painted a panorama.   (*Ormond*, p. 46)

There is a wonderful scene (too long, unfortunately, to be quoted) in which Corny and Ulick stalk each other, discuss Ormond's future,

[4] *The Life and Letters of Maria Edgeworth*, II, 600.

measure their plans, and offer savage insults, while apparently discussing the most inconsequential affairs. And as they talk Corny is carving a whistle for a peasant boy who sits at his feet. Maria, by some grace of language, convinces us that Corny values the boy's opinion more than he does Ulick's. (*Ibid.,* pp. 50–57)

Ormond falls in love with Corny's daughter Dora, but he has as rivals the Connal brothers, White and Black. (This is less allegorical than it sounds. Maria has probably put awkward English to *dhuv* and *bawn*—"dark" and "fair.") White has amassed a fortune as a grazier—one of the few roads to wealth open to Catholics. Black is an officer in the Irish Brigades of France. With his talk of "operas, wine, women, cardinals, religion, politics, poetry, and turkeys stuffed with truffles," Black is the reality of the type whom Count O'Halloran had represented in ideal form. It is Black who tricks Dora into marriage, to her sorrow.

One of the triumphs of the novel is the skill with which Maria creates the world of the old Catholic gentry. She knew it only slightly, if at all, at first hand, and yet the letters and memoirs of "the old stock" confirm the accuracy of her picture. The scenes in Paris, where Ormond is forced to witness Dora's decline into a petty noblewoman, catch perfectly the atmosphere which surrounded the families of Brigade members.

As Ormond grows older his admiration first for Corny and then for Ulick is subdued. Corny's instinctive skill with his hands, the deepseated authority which permits him to play the buffoon, now seem elements of a tarnished and ludicrous grandeur.

Harry, having now seen and compared Corny's violin with other violins, and having discovered that so much better could be had for money, with so much less trouble, his admiration had a little decreased. There were other points relative to external appearance on which his eyes had been opened. In his boyish days, King Corny, going out to hunt with hounds and horn, followed with shouts by all who could ride, and all who could run, King Corny, hallooing the dogs, and cheering the crowd, appeared to him the greatest, the happiest of mankind. (*Ibid.,* p. 47)

Sir Ulick, by contrast, is the great world, and would polish Ormond into his own image, for he prefers Harry to his own son, Marcus. To

Ormond Ulick seems the perfection of the Irish gentleman, knowledgeable, dexterous, and able. Ulick trains him up as a duelist, introduces him to his old friend the Viceroy, and sends him off to Dublin. But as Ormond moves in the new circles to which Ulick has gained entrance for him, he discovers that Ulick is a sinister joke among the Dublin wits:

> *"Upon his faith."—"Upon his word,"*
> Oh! that, my friend, is too absurd.
> *"Upon his honour."*—Quite a jest.
> *"Upon his conscience."*—No such test.
> *"By all he has on earth."*—'Tis gone.
> *"By all his hopes of heaven."* They're none.
> How then secure him in our pay—
> He can't be trusted for a day!
> How?—When you want the fellow's throat—
> Pay by the job—you have his vote. (*Ibid.*, pp. 187–88)

The Annalys, however, rise steadily in Ormond's esteem—old Lady Annaly and her son Sir Herbert and his sister Florence. The novel ends as the reader had feared it would from the first, with Ormond married to Florence and patterning himself on Annaly. And Annaly, it need scarcely be said, is a doleful composite of Richard Lovell Edgeworth, O'Halloran, M'Leod, and a certain treaclish rectitude which is uniquely his. This, of course, is a major flaw, and a significant one. Maria Edgeworth was as much at home in England as in Ireland, as her novels set in England bear witness. But when she transposes English characters to Ireland, they cease immediately to be believable. Her knowledge that their culture had made possible for them the deep-grained responsibility which she wished so ardently for her countrymen changes them into figures of pasteboard virtue.

Reading *Ormond,* we are apt to dismiss this, however. It is not Ormond, for all his choices and adventures and decisions, who engages our interest, but the O'Shanes, and theirs is a tragedy perfectly worked out. All choices are fatal to the O'Shanes. To act in the great world of wealth and mastery, as Ulick does, is to live without integrity. But Corny—that rare event in fiction, a truly lovable character—is marooned in the past, changing more and more, as the years pass, from

a king to an eccentric. In the collision between Irish and English
values, they had been sentenced to defeat, for assimilation demanded
of them prices too high for honor to pay.

Ulick dies without friends or mourners at Castle Hermitage, whose
name had always implied his isolation. It is said that he died of
sorrow at the collapse of his ambitions, but "some people in the
neighborhood was kept mighty busy talking how the coroner ought
to be sent for." (*Ibid.*, p. 294) Ormond arrives for the funeral to find
the gate locked: there had been talk that Ulick's body would be seized
for debt, but no creditors are foolish enough to imagine that this
could impress his son Marcus.

There was no attempt to seize upon the body; only the three workmen, the
servants, a very few of the cottagers, and Harry Ormond, attended to the
grave the body of the once popular Sir Ulick O'Shane. This was considered
by the country people as the greatest of all the misfortunes that had befallen
him; the lowest degradation to which an O'Shane could be reduced. They
compared him with King Corny, and "see the difference!" said they; "the
one was the true thing and never changed—and after all, where is the great
friends now?—the quality that used to be entertained in the castle above?
Where is all the favour promised him now? What is it come to . . . ?
(*Ibid.*, p. 294)

Corny, too, comes to a fitting end: a fowling piece whose barrel
he had enlarged explodes on the hunting field and kills him. Ormond,
despite his distaste for such customs, attends the wake and accompanies the body to the O'Shane burial ground in a remote abbey.
The coffin is followed by "an immense concourse of people, on horseback and on foot; men, women, and children; when they passed the
doors of cabins, a set of women raised the funeral cry—not a savage
howl, as is the custom in some parts of the country, but chanting a
melancholy kind of lament, not without harmony, simple and pathetic."
(*Ibid.*, p. 150)

Ormond, who is the heir in spirit to both the O'Shanes, has now
the chance either to buy the Black Islands from M. de Connal, or
Castle Hermitage from Marcus. It is the last and most crucial of his
decisions, and of course he chooses the Black Islands. The people "considered Prince Harry as the lawful representative of their dear King

Corny, and actually offered up prayers for his coming again to reign over them." (*Ibid.,* p. 301)

One may doubt if they really did. Corny *had* been a king, for he had been the chieftain of the clan. But the ways in which a chieftain commands respect and love are not to be had for the asking, or the learning. It is a bleak vista which stretches out beyond the deaths of the O'Shanes. Marcus, neither a good Englishman nor a good Irishman, though aping the manners of the former, is living abroad. M. de Connal barters away the Black Islands so that he may pursue his career at Versailles. White Connal is driving off peasants so that their lands may be turned to pasturage. And against this Maria offers us the magic resolution toward which the novel has moved: Ormond's inheritance of the old Gaelic chieftain's moral authority. It is a resolution so impossible of acceptance that it becomes a mocking epitaph.

When Richard Lovell Edgeworth was buried, "there was the most respectful and profound silence. His remains were deposited in the family vault in the churchyard of Edgeworth's Town. No monument of inscription, but one precisely similar to that which he had erected for his father, has been erected for him—a plain marble tablet within the church, on one side of the communion table, bearing his name, and the date of his birth and death." [5] And his virtues and principles, here made incarnate in Ormond, made as slender a mark on the face of Ireland.

The end of the Edgeworthstown drama was played out not in the novels of Maria Edgeworth, but in her life. She was to survive her father by thirty years, and to see the face of Ireland change beyond her recognition. She published little—various sequels to *Early Lessons,* and, in 1834, *Helen,* a novel with an English setting. But there were to be no more Irish tales from the Big House at Edgeworthstown. The irony was that in the increasing turbulence of Irish life, she was the one figure who commanded the disinterested respect of all parties, the one writer to whose voice Europe would have attended.

In the years between 1800 and 1817, her reputation as an interpreter

[5] Edgeworth, *Memoirs,* II, 449.

of the Irish scene had become formidable. "Indeed," she had written, "the domestic habits of no nation in Europe were less known to the English than those of the sister country, till within these last few years." (*Castle Rackrent,* p. 69) Maria had greatly modified this ignorance, not only through her own work, but through its example, for she had begun the tradition of the Irish novel. But the novelists who followed close upon her heels had each his ax to grind that he might bring it keen and murderous to the battlefield which Ireland was becoming, while through her own books, despite their uncompromising message, there shone for all to see her intelligence and love.

Nor did the kind of novel which she had written set a model for Irish writers alone. In 1814 the author of *Waverley* sent her a copy of that novel. No name appeared on the title page, but Maria, who was addicted to puns, decided that it must be "aut Scotus aut diabolus," and addressed to Scott a long letter in which she set down her stunned admiration.[6] But Scott's admiration for her was as large as was his sense of debt. He made generous acknowledgment of both in the General Preface to the Waverley Novels. Speaking of the influences which decided him upon these novels, he says:

The first was the well-merited fame of Miss Edgeworth, whose Irish characters have gone so far to make the English familiar with the character of their gay and kind-hearted neighbors of Ireland that she may be truly said to have done more toward completing the Union, than perhaps all the legislative enactments by which it has been followed up.

Without being so presumptuous as to hope to emulate the rich humour, pathetic tenderness, and admirable tact, which pervade the works of my accomplished friend, I felt that something might be attempted for my own country, of the same kind with that which Miss Edgeworth so fortunately achieved for Ireland. . . .[7]

Maria was both too sensible and too modest to accept this praise at face value, but a strong friendship developed between the two writers, the intentions of whose work seemed so evenly matched. Certainly they had struck out together upon a field new to English fiction—the romance of nationality, or of national character. That a novel should

---

[6] Edgeworth, *Life and Letters,* I, 239-44.
[7] General Preface to The Waverley Novels, 1829.

take as its theme the shape and feel of the culture itself was an assumption which ran counter to the English novel, because it ran counter to English life. Fielding and Richardson and Jane Austen wrote English novels, to be sure, but not novels "about England." Only a culture which felt urgently and consciously a need for definition could have produced the novels of Maria Edgeworth or Scott or Fenimore Cooper.

But this generalization, though it is true and has great consequences, suggests its own qualifications. We must ask, in a later chapter, why the Irish novelists who followed Scott's pattern for historical novels were so manifestly unsuccessful. The chief of these reasons is foreshadowed, indirectly, in the contrast between the public careers of Maria Edgeworth and Scott. Scott's novels are celebrations of an accomplished fact, the peace between the long-warring cultures of Highlands and Lowlands and their reemergence as one of the British peoples. It was Maria's profoundest wish that some such process would knit her own land, but history and present circumstance combined to mock it. And while Scott moved blithely on from one triumph to the next, Maria was retreating within Edgeworth House and silence, until at last despair bade her put down her pen.

She visited Abbotsford in 1823 with her sisters Harriet and Sophy, in response to Scott's urging that she should come "as the Irish should to the Scotch, without ceremony." He had arranged for them a treat which he was sure they would enjoy. The boatman of the Laird of Straffa came to lead the Scotts and their guests and followers in a Gaelic song and dance. Maria somewhat reluctantly took her end of the handkerchief while the others stamped their feet loudly and roared out a chorus "which, as far as I could hear, sounded like 'At am vaum! At am vaum!' frequently repeated with prodigious enthusiasm. In another, I could make out no intelligible sound but 'Bar! bar! bar!' But the boatman's dark eyes were ready to start out of his head with rapture as he sung and stamped, and shook the handkedchief on each side, and the circle imitated." [8]

The breadth of sympathy which Maria's novels display had led Scott to forget that she was also a lady of the Ascendancy, a great

[8] Edgeworth, *Life and Letters,* II, 443–44.

landowner to whom Gaelic was the barbarous tongue of slaves. The only "intelligible sound" she heard was the etymologically exact one. Had she not written to him, in reference to *Waverley:* "Flora we could wish was never called *Miss MacIvor,* because in this country there are tribes of vulgar Miss *Macs,* and this is unfavorable to the sublime and beautiful of *your* Flora—she is a true heroine." [9]

A second difference was pressed upon Scott two years later when he returned the visit, for in 1825 the Irish air was heavy with the mutinous rumbles which would shortly shake the country to its foundations. "Here," Lockhart, who accompanied him, wrote of Edgeworthstown, "above all, we had the opportunity of seeing in what universal respect and comfort a gentleman's family may live in that country, and in far from its most favoured district, provided only they live there habitually, and do their duty as the friends and guardians of those among whom Providence has appointed their proper place. Here we found neither mud hovels nor naked poverty, but snug cottages and smiling faces all about." [10]

But Scott was to discover, before leaving the country, that: "Their factions have been so long envenomed, and they have such narrow ground to do their battle in, that they are like people fighting with daggers in a hogshead." [11]

Maria chose to cultivate the snug cottages and smiling faces of her lands, and to withdraw from the warring Ireland of the Agitation and the Tithe War, in whose tumult she saw overturned her last hopes for a prosperous and united country. The son who had inherited from Richard Lovell Edgeworth proved to have more than a touch of Rackrent blood, and after a luckless attempt to act as his own agent he gladly returned the post to Maria. Henceforth she devoted much of her energy as well as her remarkable talent for practical accomplishments to the improvement of the large estate and the welfare of its small army of tenants.

She kept up her correspondence with the great literary figures of

[9] *Ibid.,* I, 243.
[10] John Gibson Lockhart, *Life of Sir Walter Scott,* VIII, 25. See also Edgeworth, *Life and Letters,* II, 479–81.
[11] Lockhart, VIII, 57.

London and Paris, and found time to read with judicious impartiality the scores of Irish novels "of the school of Maria Edgeworth"—foolish novels by Lady Morgan, hysterical ones by George Brittaine, passionate ones by Gerald Griffin—all of them echoing the tumults of the day. And as the years since *Ormond* stretched into decades, her puzzled readers continued to ask why they had not heard from her on the subject which had once been her own. At last, when her brother Pakenham asked the question, she answered it.

It is impossible to draw Ireland as she now is in the book of fiction—realities are too strong, party passions too violent, to bear to see, or care to look at their faces in a looking glass. The people would only break the glass, and curse the fool who held the mirror up to nature—distorted nature, in a fever. We are in too perilous a case to laugh, humor would be out of season, worse than bad taste. Whenever the danger is past, as the man in the sonnet says, "We may look back at the hardest part and laugh." Then I shall be ready to join in the laugh. Sir Walter Scott once said to me, "Do explain to the public why Pat, who goes forward so well in other countries, is so miserable in his own." A very difficult question: I fear above my power. But I shall think of it continually, and listen, and look, and read.[12]

And while she was thinking and listening, the neighboring great house of Castle Forbes was burned to the ground. The fire attracted much attention throughout the country, but it stuck in her mind for one reason. While the servants rushed through the blazing building carrying out folios of the statutes of the old Parliament, Lord Forbes was "by force of motive, endued with such extraordinary strength in the midst of that night's danger," that he wrenched from its iron spike and pedestal a marble bust of Oliver Cromwell, and threw it onto the grass. "Next morning he could not lift it! and no man who tried could stir it." [13]

She retained the novelist's necessary luck, which is to hear of just the right detail, and the novelist's eye, but these were wasted now in letters. For, though she points no moral, the scene stands out as picturesquely as any in *Castle Rackrent,* and with as clearly defined a meaning. All of Ireland seemed to her to have gone mad. How better could this be said than by recording the preservation of the dead laws of a suborned

[12] Edgeworth, *Life and Letters,* II, 550.   [13] *Ibid.,* II, 483–84.

parliament, and the tribal piety of the Ascendancy landlord who ripped from its moorings the heavy marble head of Cromwell? What better emblem of nineteenth-century Ireland than Castle Rackrent in flame? Before a hundred years had passed, half the Big Houses of the island would be gutted ruins.

From both the ambitions and the methods of the Agitation she was alienated by her loyalties, her tastes, and her prejudices. O'Connell regretted that she did not lend her pen to "liberation," as Lady Morgan was doing, but it was O'Connell above all others whom she detested and feared—the brilliant, foul-mouthed demagogue in whom "the tribes of the O's and Mac's" had found a champion.

There is literally no reign of law at this moment to hold the Irish [she wrote to her step-mother in the very tone and accent of Richard Lovell] and through the whole country there is what I cannot call a spirit of *reform*, but a spirit of *revolution*, under the name of reform; a restless desire to overthrow what *is*, and a hope—more than a hope—an expectation of gaining liberty or wealth, or both, in the struggle; and if they do gain either, they will lose both again and be worse off than ever—they will afterwards quarrel amongst themselves, destroy one another, and again be enslaved with heavier chains.[14]

Then, in 1835, she discovered that Edgeworthstown itself, despite its snug cottages and smiling faces, was not immune to the restless desire to "overthrow what *is*." The general election that year was a fiercely contested one in Ireland; nerves had been drawn taut by four harrowing years of the Tithe War. The landlords of Longford had, as usual, put up their candidate, but this time his victory was not a matter of course. "The priests," who were O'Connell's lieutenants, instructed the peasants to vote against him. It was the picture which was becoming a familiar one in Irish life. And Sneyd Edgeworth, the nominal landlord of his father's estates, wanted to take the familiar revenge— to punish the refractory tenants by forcing them to pay the hanging-gale rent. Maria put a stop to this with a sharp letter:

Because the priests have used force and intimidation, such as their situation and means put in their power, are landlords to do likewise? And are the poor tenants in this world and the next to be ruined and excommunicated

14 *Ibid.*, II, 511.

between them? Are we to recriminate and revenge because the priests and the people have done so? Beaten or beating as brutal force decides? [15]

With that letter, as perceptive of consequences as it is honorable of sentiment, Maria ended the political power of Edgeworth House, for that power had always resided, ultimately, in the power to evict. A year later Miss Farrar, visiting the town, was to write that though Maria had been for so many years the local patroness, now "there were no bows for her or her friends, no making way before her, no touching of hats, no pleasant looks. A sullen expression and a dogged immovability were on every side of us." [16] Men fighting with daggers in a hogshead, Scott had said. To the peasants of Longford, who had not read her letter, Maria stood for one thing only—the Big House and the English interest.

She persisted, however, in the ways which had been taught her by the wise, foolish Lovell Edgeworth. A legacy of diamonds (shades of Jessica Rackrent!) came to her unexpectedly, and she sold it to buy a market house for the town. And visitors continued to make pilgrimages to Edgeworth House to honor the woman who had done "so much practical good to Ireland, and not alone to Ireland but to the civilized world." [17] The irony could scarcely have escaped her, but she met them all with smiling courtesy and discussed the newest improvements in the nondenominational school.

At last, in 1846, when she was past eighty, the Great Famine struck. She set to work at once to take care of her people. When her funds were exhausted, she made "bould to axe my friends" for charity. She had a great many friends, she discovered. The Quaker Association in Dublin and the Birmingham Relief Committee sent money. A group in New York sent barleycorn which Irish porters loaded without taking payment. The children in Boston raised a subscription and sent rice "to Miss Edgeworth for her poor."

The funds were dispersed with her usual vigor. Her brother-in-law, Barry Fox, was put to work teaching the potato farmers how to sow grain. Leather and soles were brought in so that the poorer peasants

[15] *Ibid.*, II, 613.   [16] *Ibid.*, II, 615.
[17] Hall, *Ireland: Its Scenery, Character, Etc.*, III, 275.

might have shoes to their feet when they went to work on the ditches
—this being the form of relief which the government offered. And
above all, she instructed Fox, the people must somehow be permitted
to keep their self-respect. They must not become "craving beggars."

In those last years of her life, the blackest in modern Irish history,
she found her purpose again, and discovered that "her poor" still
needed her. In truth the people were beyond help. The Famine was
to sweep all the players from the board, O'Connell among them. She
had begun her career with the Union, and she was ending it with the
Famine. For more than half of those fifty years her pen had been still.
Now there was time only to scratch out letters asking for charity
and orders to workmen. Yet, had there been time, she would still
have had nothing to say. Her Ireland was as dead as Count O'Halloran's
castle or the Black Islands of Corny O'Shane.

She died on the twenty-third of May, 1849, in her eighty-third year.
She had recorded the burials of many men, and had sent long, cere-
monial processions across the pages of her novels. Of her own funeral,
however, we have only the scantiest of records.

Lady Morgan

8. Sentimental Patriotism: *The Wild Irish Girl*

IN 1806 A GOVERNESS named Sydney Owenson published a novel, immensely popular in both islands, called *The Wild Irish Girl*. It was the first of what she was to call, in a phrase suggestive of one direction which the Irish novel took, her "National Tales." In later years she fondly recalled the triumphant visit to London which followed upon its success—"freshly launched," as she describes herself, "from the barony of Tireragh in the province of Connaught," and wearing the simple frock in which, "not many days before, I had danced a jig, on an earthen floor, with an O'Rourke, prince of Brefney."[1]

Her account is characteristically accurate in the letter and misleading in its implications, for she was not the wild Connaught girl she pretended to be. Her father, Robert Owenson, was a familiar figure in eighteenth-century Dublin and has been described for us in some detail in the memoirs of Barrington, O'Keeffe, and others. He was an actor-manager at the Theatre Royal and the Fishamble Street, a handsome, deep-chested man whose forte was the delineation of "the middle class of Paddies," the braggart, thick-tongued O'Triggers and O'Flahertys of Anglo-Irish comedy. At the height of his career he was managing his own house, but he was cursed with financial ineptitude, and by the 1790s, when his older daughter Sydney was in her late teens, he was wandering from town to town in the west and north, organizing performances for the military garrisons and

[1] Lady Morgan, *The Book of the Boudoir*, I, 73–74.

living off the charity of kinsmen. He made his final stage appearance in 1808, in a play of his daughter's devising, swinging a shillelagh and singing, "An Irishman All The World Over."

In a phrase, he was that bugbear of later generations, the stage Irishman, parading and travestying the foibles of his fellow countrymen. Although Sydney was to hint that his circle of acquaintances was wide, it was composed largely of political hangers-on, hack writers, and minor functionaries at Dublin Castle. It is true that in his successful years he had entree to the salon of the lionizing Countess of Moira, but only on sufferance; his begging letter, asking her to further Sydney's career, was coldly rejected.

Sydney had received a gentlewoman's education at the fashionable Huguenot school which Madame Terson conducted at Clontarf House, and both father and daughter were humiliated when Owenson's financial condition made it necessary for her to take employment as a governess, first with the Featherstones of Westmeath and then with the Crawfords of Tipperary. The downfall was especially calamitous in so provincial and caste-ridden a society as Ascendancy Ireland. Her efforts to extricate herself were strenuous, calculated, and understandable.

She had early given indication of an interest in literary pursuits; we find her name appearing, in 1793, on the list of sponsors of the brilliant and short-lived *Anthologia Hibernica*.[2] By 1801 her father was able to superintend the publication of a number of stilted poems, modeled on the current English fashions. These verses, however, give almost no hint of the subjects which were shortly to claim her attention. For she had been discovering that the well-born ladies and gentlemen into whose company she had been thrust were much less interested in such derivative effusions than in the reels and planxties, the Gaelic songs and airs, which her father had taught her as a parlor accomplishment and which she had augmented during her visits among his kinsmen.

[2] The *Anthologia Hibernica* began publication in 1793 and ceased the following year.

Literary fashions were changing with the generations. In 1776 *The Freeman's Journal* criticized Owenson for "droning out" the songs of Connaught, the guttural chants of savages. Now, however, the more perceptive members of the Ascendancy were beginning to realize that these songs were part of the traditional music of Ireland, composed in its difficult tonal system, and passed down through generations of "bards" and harpers as an hereditary possession. The English interest had for centuries regarded the arts of native Ireland with shuddering disdain. Every educated man knew that early in the Christian era the Gaelic language had been a repository of piety and culture, but he also knew that it had degenerated into a peasant *patois,* willfully clung to by Papist bogtrotters.

But toward the end of the eighteenth century the Ascendancy felt itself to be so firmly entrenched that it could afford to cast a glance at such relics of the ancient order as had managed to survive. This curiosity was quickened by the rage throughout Europe for Macpherson's versions of the Ossianic poems and by the cachet which romanticism had placed on ruins both physical and social. Dilettantes like Ledwich[3] and Vallancey puzzled over the round towers and other "antiquities of Ireland." Societies for the study of Gaelic and for the preservation of the traditional modes of composition were formed. In 1786 Joseph Cooper Walker, a scholar remarkable more for enthusiasm than for sense, published his *Historical Memoirs of the Irish Bards,* with its lovingly gathered recollections of O'Carolan and Cormac Common. Three years later his friend Charlotte Brooke produced her influential *Reliques of Irish Poetry.* From the lips of peasants she took down the well-remembered Cycle poems, peopled with the heroes of Red Branch and Fiann—Deirdre and Cuchulain and Finn. And those dialogues between Ossian and Saint Patrick in which wit and passion conspire to celebrate the coming of one order and to mourn the passing of another. As scholars Cooper and even the perceptive Charlotte Brooke had the insouciance of a Schliemann, and leveled flat the complicated structures which they had

[3] *Antiquities of Ireland,* London, 1790 (second edition, 1804).

unearthed. Scarcely less impressive than the poems themselves, however, was the sheer fact of their existence, their delicate fabric unwinding itself in the talk of *seanachies* by turf fires.

Then, in July of 1792, the Gaelic enthusiasts of the fiercely Presbyterian city of Belfast summoned to a contest the last surviving harpists, using as bait "such prizes as may seem adequate to the subscribers." Ten of them arrived, headed by "Denis Hempson, blind, from Co. Derry, aged 97 years or more, exponent of the old style of playing with long crooked nails." [4] To take down the music, the sponsors hired a dissolute and accomplished young organist named Edward Bunting. The task kindled in him a fire which was to burn throughout the course of a bitter and disappointed life—an ambition to study and record the music of Ireland. For the next two years, accompanied by a hedge master named Pat Lynch, he roamed throughout Ulster, Munster, and Connaught on this mission. In 1796 he published the fruits of his labor, the first volume of *The Ancient Music of Ireland*.

Bunting lived to see his work exploited by Moore and Stevenson and Sydney Owenson herself, and the wild music of the harp, which had stretched through mud cabins, transcribed for tinkling pianofortes. He was still at work in 1840, appending to his sheets of music the increasingly caustic footnotes of the scholar who feels himself misused. All the old men were long dead by then—Art O'Neill, who had traveled to Scotland in 1745 to play "The King Shall Enjoy His Own Again" before the Jacobite prince at Holyrood, and that muchtraveled man Denis Hempson.

By that time the flimsy bridge of Moore's *Irish Melodies* had been flung up, those sugar-sweet confections.[5] But it *was* a bridge between the two Irelands, and a second stood beside it. Through the Belfast harp festival strode, angular and impatient, the obsessed figure of Theobald Wolfe Tone. One soft Dublin night Tom Moore played

[4] From a contemporary list quoted by Charlotte Milligan Fox, *Annals of the Irish Harpers.*

[5] Moore's *Irish Melodies* were first published by Power in Dublin and London in April, 1808. For a brief summary of the confused history of subsequent editions, see H. M. Jones, *The Harp That Once . . .* , Chapter Five. Page references in the present study are to Power's Dublin edition of 1820.

"The Red Fox" to a Trinity College friend, and the friend, Robert Emmet, cried, "Oh, that I were at the head of twenty thousand men marching to that air!" [6] A few years later Emmet himself had become a song in the peat smoke.

Echoes of Bunting's first fame reached the castle of Bracklin ("Brack Lynn," in her stylish orthography), where Sydney Owenson was instructing the daughters of the Featherstone family. She complained in later years of the onerous duties imposed upon governesses, yet she had had time to scribble incessantly, producing, with other work, two novels, *St. Clair* and *The Novice of St. Dominick*. She was also fashioning her most carefully wrought and most successful work of fiction. This was the legend of Sydney Owenson, the Wild Irish Girl from Connaught, reticent and ill at ease in London drawing rooms, and anxious to return to her barbarous and enchanted Barony of Tireragh.

In 1859 there were those still living who would read with some bewilderment the fanciful autobiography of the then Lady Morgan, for they could remember the veritable Robert Owenson, well-proportioned and rubicund, swaggering down the Sligo parade flanked by his dutiful daughters, Sydney and Olivia. A half-dozen houses in Connaught, Protestant and Catholic, gentle and common, could have recalled the girl who bided her time in that province while her father pursued his luckless trade. Their deaths ended the possibility of ever knowing in its entirety the origins and early life of Sydney Owenson.

Mythopoeia was a family trait. Robert Owenson, the hail fellow of Moira House and Dublin Castle, and husband to the very English and very Methodist Jane Hill, had been born as plain Robert MacOwen in the County of Roscommon. His father was "a jolly, racketting Irish boy . . . , a gentleman according to the genealogy of Connaught, but a farmer by actual position." The Penal Laws had robbed the MacOwens of their wide acres, which had passed to the Blakes of Ardfry. His mother was the orphan daughter of Sir Malby Crofton, the head of Sligo's most illustrious English family. As a result of this misalliance with a Papist peasant, "the fair Queen of Beauty who then

[6] Justin McCarthy, *Ireland Since the Union*, p. 67.

graced Longford House" was disowned and forced to live in the humblest circumstances. Sydney "Crofton-Bell" MacOwen became famous throughout Connaught as a poet and musician (*Clasach na Valla,* the Harp of the Valley) and transmitted her gift to Robert.

Robert was educated jointly by the Protestant incumbent of the parish and Father Mahoney, "ex-member of the Jesuit College of Liége." Each Sunday he sang low mass at the Catholic chapel and vespers at the Protestant church. The beauty of his voice attracted the sinister attentions of a Blake of Ardfry, "an intellectual epicurean . . . confirmed in celibacy." Blake took MacOwen into his household, changed his rateen suit, and raised him as a gentleman. Then the young man was brought to London, where he soon won a role at Covent Garden. Somewhere on the road he anglicized his name and discarded his creed in preference for the uses of the Established Church. In 1776, accompanied by his determinedly anti-Irish wife, he returned to Dublin.[7]

The tangled skeins of Irish family relationships form the substance of what is best in Lady Morgan's novels, and they gain interest by comparison with the situation of the actual families who furnished her material. The writer of a much lengthier study of her novels than this could make no better preparation than the resolution of fact and fancy in the above legend. And no more relevant preparation, for the hidden energy of those novels derives from her quintessentially Irish preoccupation with pedigree.

It may suffice here to remark that Sir Malby Crofton had no grand-daughter named Sydney Crofton-Bell, nor any answering to her general description, whether owned or disowned. Robert's mother was the daughter of a cadet, if quite genteel, branch of the family, though there is a very shadowy bar sinister.[8] The suspicion that Robert himself was illigitimate is stronger still. MacOwens *were* a Roscommon clan. (Had poor Owenson known it, they were Hibernicized Normans —originally Sinnott.) *Some* MacOwens were landed, and were forced

[7] Lady Morgan, *Memoirs: Autobiography, Diaries, and Correspondence,* I, 41–58.

[8] Henry Thomas Crofton, *The Crofton Memoirs.*

to forfeit tenure, but scarcely to the Ardfry Blakes, who were themselves Catholic.

Yet somewhere within the legend are bones of fact; therein lies the charm of the puzzle. The idea of Owenson singing in both churches and being educated jointly by rector and Jesuit (and in Sligo of all counties!) is hard to take, however unquestionable his talent for straddling fences. Somewhere in the shadows of Penal Days lie hidden transactions which Irish genealogists once were schooled to blur. When Sydney was tasting fame in Dublin, she was visited by the venerable Richard Kirwan, scientist, Protestant theologian, and founder of the Royal Irish Academy. But her father could tell her of how, as a small boy, he had seen Kirwan come home as a young priest from the Jesuit seminary at St. Omer, and how he had seen him picking his way along the road to celebrate his first mass, anxious lest the mud ruin his French shoes with their glittering buckles.[9] He told her very little, though, of the boy MacOwen, who had stood by the ditch to watch.

Sydney's knowledge of the feudal houses of Connaught, those that had remained gentle alike with those that had sunk into the peasantry, was too intimate to be faked, and it is a mark in her favor that it is the middle level of that society which she describes most accurately. Owenson claimed kinship with the Tribes—the ffrenches, the Joyces, the Trenches, the Bodkins, the Kirwans. ("Or, as he pronounced it, the O'Quiravans, 'for, my dear, I am sorry to say, the Kirwans dropped the vowel in the *troubles,* like many others who dared not exhibit the O or the Mac—which was our own case, God help us.'") There is reason to believe that Sydney spent part of her youth with these families.

The young, when they must live meanly, can find sufficient nourishment in illusions of ruined grandeur—particularly when the ruin has been accomplished by chivalrous adherence to a lost cause. Sydney, fulfilling her half-servile duties in Westmeath, found solace in embroidering on her father's recollections. Like her grandmother she became proficient at the harp, and when house guests wanted to hear

[9] Lady Morgan, *The Book of the Boudoir,* I, 46.

some of the authentic music for which there was such a vogue, she
was at hand with "Ned of the Hill" or "Castle Hyde." Her early
heroines are sensitive and richly talented girls, insufficiently appreciated
by the surrounding Philistines.

In 1803 she took the judicious step of seeking out Alicia Lefanu,
Sheridan's older sister and a friend of Charlotte Brooke. Under Mrs.
Lefanu's patronage, she published in 1805 *Twelve Original Hibernian
Melodies*. It was a genuine coup, for Bunting had printed only music
and Charlotte Brooke only words, but Sydney gave her public both.
Moore, who was preparing the first series of *Irish Melodies* for the press,
must have viewed its appearance with chagrin, but he later acknowl-
edged an equal debt to Bunting and to "the patriotic genius of Miss
Owenson."

In 1805 she visited her publisher in London. Richard Phillips had
decided, while serving a prison sentence for publishing *The Rights of
Man,* that literature could boast more pleasant fields than those tilled
by Tom Paine, and in Sydney Owenson he saw what he now would
call a "property." *The Novice of Saint Dominick* was having a brisk
sale—Pitt, whose encounters with things Irish were uniformly painful, read it on his deathbed. He also suspected that the appetite for
stories about Ireland which Maria Edgeworth had created but had
not hastened to glut was still strong. But he had his doubts that the
novel was the form best suited to Sydney's talents, and so suggested
that she try her hand at a series of letters, after the fashion of Lady
Mary Montague, "on the state of Ireland, the manners and customs
of its inhabitants, etc., etc." [10]

Sydney was immediately enthusiastic and, after bluffing a most
favorable contract from Phillips (himself no stranger to sharp practice),
she returned to Ireland. She paused in Dublin long enough to invest
part of her advance in one of Egan's pedal harps and in a long blue
cloak, both of which were to mark her subsequent appearances in
public. Then she went to Connaught in search of atmosphere.

Most Englishmen, insofar as they thought of Ireland at all, tended
to make a single and solitary distinction between the propertied Prot-

[10] Lady Morgan, *Memoirs,* I, 205.

estant landlords and the multitudinous swarms of Catholic peasants. But Sydney, being a resident Irishwoman, knew that this generalization was false in the particular. She knew that there were many Irelands: there were Catholics of Norman or English blood, "Old English" Protestants who were more in sympathy with the native nobility than with the Cromwellian interlopers, Gaelic families who had thrown in their lot with the Ascendancy and others who maintained amidst poverty the trappings of feudal splendor. And in Connaught, whence her father had sprung, this rich profusion was most vividly deployed.

Of the four provinces, Connaught had come most recently and most imperfectly under English government. "To Hell or Connaught," in the famous phrase, had Cromwell banished the last of the Gaelic chiefs, hoping to hold native Ireland in a kind of penal colony west of the Shannon. It is not surprising, therefore, to find Sydney writing Alicia Lefanu that she has been staying "among my relations for some time," and has amassed much material. The same letter requests an introduction to Joseph Cooper Walker, to whom she was subsequently indebted for much misinformation. No doubt she visited other, less elevated kinsmen as well, but her accounts mention only the time which she spent with Sir Malby Crofton, at Longford House in Sligo.[11]

In considering *The Wild Irish Girl* and the myth which it made current, there is a certain humor in this fact, for while it is true that Connaught was the last stronghold of the "wild Irish," Sligo was a most striking exception to the rule. Upon no other county did Cromwell's soldiers fasten more voraciously, the land being distributed among them almost in its entirety. "They were destined to become a kind of island," as Lennox Robinson says, "bounded on the south by the banished Irish, on the north by Ulster, and on the east by the Irish of Roscommon. On the west was the wild Atlantic, and what could the little colony do save dig itself in, intermarry and consolidate its position." [12] Which, with a vengeance, they did.

But the Croftons were exceptions in this predominantly Crom-

[11] *Ibid.*, I, 258.   [12] Quoted by Joseph Hone, *Life of W. B. Yeats*, p. 4.

wellian settlement.[13] Their descent from an Elizabethan magnate
rescued them, as it had the Edgeworths, from the sense of social in-
security to which were owing many of the excesses of the more recent
plantation families. Then, too, they were not expropriators, for Thomas
Crofton, a grandson of the Escheator-general, had purchased the lands
of Longford House from their Gaelic proprietor, and had married
a daughter of The O'Conor Don. In Sydney's eyes they were proudly
and immemorially Protestant but, in the "old Irish" fashion, protec-
tive of their peasants and cherished in return.

More important than this is a fact to which Sydney does not allude:
the Croftons had been Catholic in the not-too-distant past. In 1732
James Crofton entered his name in the Book of Converts. Then, his
"eyes now open to the errors of the Roman Church," he denounced
his father and older brother as Papist recusants and seized the estate.
Since it is reasonable to assume that Thomas had embraced Catholicism upon his marriage in 1615, the family had for a century been
intermingled and intermarried with Roman stock. This fact, which
she must certainly have known, would have strengthened Sydney's
myth about the Croftons, but her liberality toward Catholics did not
extend to a desire to graft them upon that miraculous plant, her family tree.

But in any event, when it came to choosing a hero for her novel,
the Croftons would not do, for whatever else they may have been,
they were certainly not wild. By an odd and fortunate chance, however, a genuinely wild Irishman had managed to survive in Sligo down
to her own day. Indeed, if she did make childhood visits to Connaught,
she may have met him, for his death in 1793 is tersely recorded in the
copy of the *Anthologia* which bears her own name. She certainly knew
all the legends about him, for she incorporates most of them.

His name was Myles MacDermott, but he was styled, even by his
enemies, the Prince of Coolavin. The title was doubtless employed
by the Wynns and Coopers and Irwins with superior amusement but

---

[13] For accounts of the Crofton family, see *The Crofton Memoirs;* T. A. O'Rorke,
A History of Sligo, County and Town; W. G. Wood-Martin, *History of Sligo,
County and Town.*

not entire contempt. He was The MacDermott, chief of one of the oldest and proudest families in Irish history. Not a nobleman in Connaught could boast so long or so firmly established a pedigree. No one was more aware of this than MacDermott himself, although his lands had shrunk by confiscation to a few hundred acres of bog and mountainside near Lough Gara. He was, in fact, so proud that he would not allow his own children to sit in his presence, and was implacably condescending to any social claim which was not based on Gaelic genealogy. When Arthur Young was touring Ireland, Lord Kingborough, Mr. Ponsonby, Mr. O'Hara, and others of the local gentry took him to Coolavin. "O'Hara," MacDermott said, "you are welcome. Sandford, I am glad to see your mother's son. As to the rest of ye, come in as you can."[14] This was what Sydney had been looking for.

In response to her letter Cooper Walker had written jauntily, "You are now in a part of the island where many of the Finian tales are familiarly known. You will, of course, collect some of them, and, perhaps, interweave them with the work on which you are at present employed." Then, proceeding to matters of style and tone, he urged, like a true disciple of Macpherson, that "in the impassioned parts of your work, you will employ words that *burn,* or *melt,* as the occasion may require."[15] In this matter she was more than able to oblige, for as Jane Austen was to remark one cold winter evening, "if the warmth of her language could affect the body, it might be worth reading."[16]

Which suggests the unhappy fact—*The Wild Irish Girl* is a bad novel. But it is one of those oddities of literature which, regardless of merit, are deeply influential. Macpherson's *Ossian* is itself a case in point. Sydney's novel, however, made another kind of mark. Together with Moore's *Irish Melodies* it established a sentimental image of Ireland of a specific kind. It was this image which aroused among English readers a sympathetic interest in Ireland's plight and gave first form to the rhetoric of Irish nationalists. Because the image was

[14] Young, *A Tour in Ireland,* I, 205.
[15] Lady Morgan, *Memoirs,* I, 260–63.   [16] Jane Austen, *Letters,* II, 64.

sentimental it was false, and both groups suffered an unpleasant disillusionment.

In accordance with Phillips's instructions *The Wild Irish Girl* is composed of a series of letters, although he misjudged in thinking that he could thereby hold Sydney back from fiction. Henry Mortimer, a young profligate and spendthrift, has been sentenced by his father to a term on the family estates in Connaught. Mortimer anticipates this sojourn with distaste, for what he knows of Ireland, and especially of its West, has led him to think it a barbarous land. His first view of the island does not shake this notion, for while he responds to the classical "coolness" of Georgian Dublin, he sees in it only a boastful attempt to outdo London. It is a little England, a façade in which no one believes and which has no real connection with either island. As he travels to Connaught, he moves through country increasingly desolate, a wilderness broken only by ruins of the old order and the implausible mansions of the new.

Thus far one is moved only to remark that the novel anticipates Maria Edgeworth's *Ennui*. But the mood is quite different. The grandeur of savage, melancholy places greatly affected Sydney, and she awaits with impatience the moment when Mortimer will cease to be bored by it. Innismore is more savage than he had feared, a lonely, almost uninhabitable land pushed up against the rocky coast and the fierce Atlantic. But the natives, although they are impoverished and half-naked, reveal an odd and archaic courtesy which draws his interest. The Mortimer lands had been won by a Cromwellian adventurer, and the family has never lived on the land they exploit, relying instead on grasping and socially presumptuous agents.

The people of Innismore, however, have never wavered in their fealty to their traditional lord, the dispossessed "Prince," who now holds only a shattered fortress by the water's edge. Innismore, of course, bears a hatred and scorn not only toward the Mortimers, but toward all English. Despite the Prince's half-secluded life, for the penal laws have made him an outlaw, Mortimer learns of his existence, and one morning slips into the hidden chapel to observe him. Concealing his identity, he arranges a meeting, and becomes Innismore's house guest. Thus he meets Glorvina, the wild Irish girl, whom he encounters at sunset, posed with her harp against the broken battlements and storm-wracked sky.

The plot is not an inventive one, and it would be cruel to unfold its development. Innismore dies, Glorvina and Mortimer marry, and the young man vows to make Ireland, as much as England, his home. But it is not from plot that *The Wild Irish Girl* derives its interest. In essence, of course, the novel is a passionately imagined fantasy. Innismore is MacDermott of Coolavin, but he is also Robert Owenson of Fishamble Street, whose Gaelic songs and improvident habits had been mocked by the Dublin wits. Glorvina is Sydney herself, improbably versed in Irish history and scholarship, graceful, elfin, a harpist without compare, whose young prince will admit her to the *beau monde* (she is addicted to French tags) of the English nobility. And it was, indeed, as "Glorvina," which became her nickname, that Sydney traveled to London. It was as "the Wild Irish Girl" that she would exist as a legend, charming, then touching, finally ludicrous. In this regard "Glorvina's" native past served Sydney as heraldic background, a social disability transformed by magic into a special cachet.

The fantasy, however, extends beyond the personal and assimilates larger issues. Hepworth Dixon, trying to explain the novel's wide success in England, says that "it conveyed in a vivid and romantic story, curious information about the social condition, the manners, customs, literature, and antiquities of Ireland. There was in it a passionate pleading against the wrongs and injustices to which the country and the people were subjected. The work dealt with the false ideas about Ireland which prevailed in England at this period of misconception and misrule. As these pleas were put forward in an interesting form, they were eagerly read." [17]

If this has a familiar ring, it is because such breviaries, containing the daily offices of liberalism, are now commonplace. But Sydney had in fact caught popular fancy on several fronts at once. It was an audience quite prepared to agree that barbarian chieftains were worthier beings than statesmen or merchants, and Innismore is as much a

[17] Lady Morgan, *Memoirs*, I, 277–78.

barbarian as any Iroquois sachem. But he is not noble merely by virtue of his clan pedigree. He is the rightful heir to a British earldom, which had been stripped from him by his honorable adherence to old loyalties, and this rank is recognized by the courts of Europe as infinitely loftier than any Hanoverian creation. By honoring him it was possible to pay homage at one stroke to liberal principles and aristocratic sentiments.

Moreover, there had always been a formidable baffle to any English sympathy with the plight of the Irish, and *The Wild Irish Girl* confronts it directly. During the Counter-Reformation, Ireland had been not merely a hostile province but an enemy power, treacherously allied with the Catholic powers of the Continent. In the eighteenth century there had been one safeguard only—the brutal fact of the Protestant Garrison. The dispossessed Catholic gentry had every reason for disloyalty—laws which disinherited them and laws which oppressed them, strong ties of cultural and political sympathy with France, a thirst for revenge. By 1806, however, this apprehension preyed only on zealots. But the inveterate English distaste for Popery persisted, and this was to be a fact of the highest consequence.

Throughout the nineteenth century English liberalism would issue from principles which were Nonconformist or Evangelical or Radical or indifferentist, but in any event hostile toward Catholic aspirations. Liberal interest in national movements was linked to other conceptions of human freedom, which precluded any wish to "rescue the Irish from the landlords and turn them over to the priests," as the phrase had it. It is this which accounts for their relative chillness toward Irish revolutionary movements, rather than, as Irish nationalists would have it, vulgar hypocrisy. Garibaldi marching against the pope was one thing; O'Connell kneeling to kiss the pope's ring was something else again.

Now *The Wild Irish Girl,* to put it crudely, offered a formula which could square the liberal conscience on that score, and it was therefore received in liberal quarters with sighs of welcome. But because the novel was in effect a political document, had consequences, and raised a most revealing cultural storm, this aspect demands the attention it will receive in the next chapter. It should suffice here to mention it as being constituent to the novel's success.

But in the final reckoning *The Wild Irish Girl* was less narrowly conceived and more generously accepted. Part of its charm lay in its suggestion that a people still existed unchanged in feelings, habits, and manners since the days of Ossian. Innismore, with its prince, chaplain, bards, and harpers, is a court older than feudalism. More important, it is a court in ruins. Before we have done, the reader is likely to have become quite bored with ruins, just as studies of early American novels weary us with prairies—and for the same unavoidable reasons.

Ireland is a country of ruins. They do not so much define the landscape as exist as part of its being. Especially is this true of the landscape as it stands, in the imagination, for all that land means. The prairie suggests a culture which has yet to create its forms, while the ruin implies a culture whose forms have been shattered. But the fallen stones bear hieroglyphs which the artist tries to read. Even Maria Edgeworth, coolly disdainful of nostalgia, turned to them. In *The Wild Irish Girl,* however (though not in Sydney's final novels), the ruins are exploited for sheer effect.

It records a dying world, and death is essential to its charm. All that Mortimer sees is bathed in the colors of sunset, and we are not allowed to forget that year by year the waves of the Atlantic have been smashing against Innismore, eating away its stone. Macpherson's had not been, after all, an heroic poem but a long, luxuriating sigh for the past. Sydney Owenson and Moore, her counterpart, maintain the tradition. They performed an undeniable service for their countrymen. To the image of Ireland which Sir Lucius O'Trigger had incarnated they added a second, quite different one, whose symbols were the harp, the blasted tree, the ruined fortress, the fallen minstrel.

"I sat down on the tomb of the royal O'Connor, and plucked the weed or blew away the thistle that waved there its lonely head. The sun was setting in gloomy splendour, and the lofty angles of the

Abbey-tower alone caught the reflections of his dying beams, from the summits of the mountains where they still lingered." [18]

The tone of this, the image, the pose, the dying fall, the very false-ness of the attitude, disincline one to the notion that it could furnish the sinew of a liberal political program. And yet it did. For several generations the issues of Irish politics would be argued out in the terms of Sydney Owenson's rhetoric.

[18] Lady Morgan, *Patriotic Sketches,* I, 28.

THE SUNSET and autumnal world of *The Wild Irish Girl* creates the mood which dominates the novel, a graveyard melancholy, a meditation upon the fallen tablets of dead kings. This mood, however, is constantly threatened by a fierce and contrary political passion. It is a passion which, by its nature, engages the present and reaches toward the future. Though it never defines itself, many of its strands are sufficiently plain. It asserts Ireland's historic claim to independence, argues the case for Catholic independence, and invokes the optimistic rhetoric of patriotism. Its author would seem to be summoning her countrymen to some high and cloudy heroism.

The Wild Irish Girl won over the ladies of the viceregal court, who commissioned jewelers to fashion Glorvina brooches and had their hair done up, or rather down, *à la* Glorvina. But then the amiable Duke of Richmond was punctilious in his observance of the tradition that viceroys and their trains should know nothing of Irish affairs. The English public, which took Glorvina and Sydney to its heart, and which sent the book through seven editions in two years, shared his benign ignorance. In Ireland, however, it was accepted as a political document. Dublin Castle marked her down as an enemy, and the enemies of Dublin Castle acclaimed her as a valuable ally.

She had become Ireland's first "national novelist" and would remain for many years its most celebrated. That her patriotism was a nebulous pastel over which some Ossianic coloring had been daubed was, if anything, an asset. Ireland had drunk the first, bitter wine of the Union, and was experiencing a sense of deprivation so sharp as to resemble the apprehension of death. The Parliament House stood

empty on College Green, its silences mocked by the suave authority
of its form. With it had died the graces and splendors of the "Protestant Nation." The Catholic clergy and gentry were repenting at
leisure their complicity in the Act of Union. Those United Irish leaders who had not been executed were mute or in exile. The ideals
which had animated Irish life for a generation had often been foolish,
sometimes wicked, but never mean. They had been exchanged for
what seemed meanness itself. The control of Irish affairs had passed
into the hands of the jobbers and boroughmongers of Dublin Castle
—no great change, perhaps, when one remembered what the Irish
Parliament had in practice been; but reflections of this sort, while
salutary, were scarcely comforting.

It was into this void that Sydney sallied with her "patriotic sentiments." Patriotism is the first refuge of an Irishman, and national
usage has always accorded it the widest possible flexibility. Her countrymen needed reassurance that somewhere in the past lay the fragments of a lost glory and the vague promise that it could be somehow revived. Had the promise been anything but vague, they would
have feared it, for political clarity of its nature dictates choice. And
deep within themselves the Irish nursed the sour knowledge that their
experience had been not melodramatic but tragic. They had not been
betrayed by Castlereagh's gold or Pitt's promises or the tongues of informers, but by their own dark, divided hearts. Sydney offered them
the consoling fiction that this was not so.

The shallow and contradictory feelings of early nineteenth-century
nationalism are nowhere revealed more clearly than in this first of
her "national tales." But they exist there in a form so transparently
bland and innocuous that the English public which had taken the novel
to heart was shocked by an immoderately cruel attack on both book
and author.

In 1809, when the first issue of the *Quarterly Review* was being
made ready, Charles Kirkpatrick Sharpe wrote to Sir Walter Scott,
asking for a chance to give Sydney a slating. Scott was sympathetic:
"I would willingly embrace your offer of currycombing Miss Owenson,
who, judging from her Wild Irish Girl, seems to deserve such dis-

cipline very heartily." [1] Gifford, however, had assigned this task to himself, and the article duly appeared, ornamented by his matchless scurrility.[2] But he had been coached (and, one suspects, inspired) by a pale, sharp-featured young Irishman named John Wilson Croker, who had recently come over as M. P. for Downpatrick.

For the next fifteen years Sydney Owenson and Croker were to pursue each other in the public prints with Hibernian ferocity and an intemperateness beside which Gifford's critical style is pale. In the long run the quarrel did Croker more harm than good, for there was something repellent in the obsessive fury to which Sydney provoked him. ("It was thought," Disraeli would write in a famous caricature, "that no one could lash a woman like Rigby.") [3] In time he was joined by the other Irish Tory journalists—Maginn, Prout, Croly.

Eventually (though only the wise and essentially kindly Maginn saw this), the vendetta came merely to amuse and finally to bore English readers. The incessant burden of the attack was the disloyal and seditious nature of Sydney's work. To the English nothing could have been less alarming. Her fiery patriotism was akin to that of some chieftain's daughter in the Hebrides, toasting the Stuarts "across the water." As for her loyalty, had not the very theme of *The Wild Irish Girl* been that any misunderstanding between the two islands was the deliberate contrivance of the absentee magnates and the Dublin Castle gang?

Croker, Irish himself and a product of the Castle's school of statecraft, knew better. Indeed, as Sydney developed from novel to novel into the unofficial spokesman for "Ireland's ancient wrongs," this intolerant, clear-headed careerist was the only critic who troubled to take her pronouncements seriously. In the name of which of Ireland's many conflicting interests did she advance her theory of Irish nationality? One moment she was championing the aboriginal inhabitants. The next it seemed clear that she was espousing the Jacobin and atheistical principles which had sent the United Irish into open

[1] Sir Walter Scott, *Letters*, II, 166.   [2] *Quarterly Review*, I (1809), 50.
[3] In *Coningsby*.

rebellion and treason. Then again she seemed to be a Grattanite. To Croker she was the quintessence of the feckless irresponsibility which had so far made the permanent conquest of Ireland impossible. And he was quite right.[4]

If the political assumptions of her early novels caught the mood of the moment, it was because, being Irish, she shared that mood. The interest of her novels today lies in the painful way with which she came to terms with these assumptions. Caught up in the momentous rush of events during the next twenty years, playing for a time a real role in them, she was forced at last to a thoughtful, rather disillusioned understanding of her "theme." With a kind of rough justice she is remembered today, if at all, for the foolish extravagance of her "national tales." Her work taken as a whole, however, is a valuable record of the little-understood forces which shaped the Irish nationalist movement.

As we have seen, *The Wild Irish Girl* was harmless stuff. Its chief value in Sydney's own eyes was that it admitted her to those Anglo-Irish circles which, a few years later, would be ranged against her. Within months of its publication, the Countess of Charleville and Lady Asgill were seeking her out. Other ladies of rank and title were consulting her as to the best kind of harp to buy and the proper Gaelic motto to be inscribed on a Glorvina brooch. Dr. Johnson's ageless friend, the Countess of Cork, sponsored her triumphant tour of London salons, where the memory of her slender, blue-cloaked figure would linger long.

It was as though her fantasy had come to life and Mortimer had indeed carried her into that great world where, by right of spirit, she belonged. And in her excitement she forgot her austere patriotism.

When her former patroness, Alicia Lefanu, reproached her on this score, she replied airily that the company in which she now moved had "more acquirements and accomplishments, more literary and general *savoir* than (with almost the single exception of your own family), all

---

[4] The most notorious of Croker's attacks upon Lady Morgan's character and political attitudes were contained in his reviews of her travel books, *France* and *Italy: Quarterly Review*, XVII (1817), and XXV (1821).

the youth of Dublin put together." She had great respect for "the Miss Macguffins and Mistresses O'Shaughnessys" when seen from the distance, but preferred to leave matters so.[5]

She was even swept off her feet by that archfiend and perpetrator of the Union, Lord Castlereagh, who struck her as "one of those cheerful, liveable, give-and-take persons, in private, who are so invaluable to villa life." She launched into him, at first, like a "furious little Irishwoman," but Castlereagh won her by replying, with fathomless irony, that "no one cares for Ireland but Miss Owenson and I." [6]

Toward the end of 1809 she was taken under the protection of the Marquis of Abercorn, a powerful and unmistakably Tory grandee. The Abercorns, a bored and rather dissolute couple, were in the habit of adding interesting people to their entourage. For the next three years she accompanied them on their restless travels through the three kingdoms, in each of which the Marquis held a variety of peerages.

This phase of her career was terminated in a singular manner. Charles Morgan, an English physician who had worked with Jenner, was another in the retinue, and Lady Abercorn decided to marry him off to Sydney, presumably as a measure of domestic economy. Morgan was in love with his intended bride, but Sydney, who had turned down better offers, was uninterested in him. There followed a comic interlude in which Morgan pleaded, the Abercorns coaxed and bullied, and Sydney wavered, delayed, and made excuses. At last, on a cold January morning in 1812, as she was sitting by the library fire, Lady Abercorn opened the door and said, "Glorvina, come upstairs directly and be married; there must be no more trifling." [7] Morgan was waiting there, as well as the family chaplain in full canonicals.

As a wedding present Abercorn had Morgan knighted. It was a poor thing: viceroys still possessed the power to confer such honors, and used it so casually that Dublin was to become known to wits as "the city of dreadful knights." Sydney, however, had acquired the title by which she was subsequently known. The marriage was eminently successful. Sir Charles was a liberal in politics and came to share his wife's

[5] Lady Morgan, *Memoirs*, II, 17–18.   [6] *Book of the Boudoir*, I, 91–92.
[7] *Memoirs*, I, 528.

national sentiments. During the final battle for Emancipation, he was among the small group of Irish Protestants who supported O'Connell and Sheil. The couple extricated themselves from the Abercorn household, and Morgan obtained a post as physician to the Marshalsea. Their house on Kildare Street gradually became Dublin's most powerful literary salon, and a center of political activity.

While these changes were taking place, Lady Morgan was working out her second "national tale." Taking up Joseph Cooper Walker's suggestion, she read extensively in the sources of Irish history. In the *Pacata Hibernica,* a "rare and magnificent copy" of which had been lent to her by Lady Cahir, she found her subject: the romantic career of Red Hugh O'Donnell, the Earl of Tyrconnell. "My book," she wrote excitedly to Lady Stanley, "will be a *genuine* Irish romance of Elizabeth's day, founded on historical fact." [8] She began such a novel, but put it aside, having discovered that she was on the point of raising "a veil which ought never to be drawn," thus renewing "the memory of events which the history of humanity requires to be forever buried in oblivion." Which means that the facts of sixteenth-century Irish history had proved too ugly for even her considerable powers of falsification.

Not for many years would an Irish novelist be tempted to present, in however prettified a fashion, the story of the "arch-traitor," Hugh O'Donnell, who had levied bloody war on England from Donegal to the beach of Kinsale. Instead, Lady Morgan's *O'Donnel,* published in 1814, deals with the "flat realities" of contemporary life. Or at least, what she believed to be such, for flat realities were entirely alien to her pen.

The point of moral judgment, though scarcely the hero, of *O'Donnel* is Glentworth, a liberal and fair-minded Englishman whom Lady Morgan has borrowed from Maria Edgeworth's *Ennui* without performing the common courtesy of entirely disguising his name. His wife, Lady Singleton, though of a more frivolous turn of thought, is equally amiable. But his stepdaughters, Caroline and Honoria, are a dull and vapid pair. In this they contrast painfully with their governess,

[8] *Ibid.,* II, 10.

Charlotte O'Halloran, the orphan of an Irish musician, and a most unlikely blend of patriotism, sprightliness, pedantry, and beauty. About
these are gathered a great variety of English and Anglo-Irish types, the
most sinister being a certain Dublin Castle "loyalist" named Dexter
(*né* Croker).

While exploring a mountainous region in remote Donegal, Glentworth encounters an enigmatic stranger, a proud, melancholy man of
soldierly bearing. The stranger is accompanied by a rough, devoted
servant named M'Rory and a fierce hound named Bran, after Finn
McCool's mastiff. A silver collar about Bran's throat bears a cross, an
earl's coronet, the word "Tirconnell," and the date "1603." The man
identifies himself as Roderick O'Donnel, and Glentworth infers, cor-
rectly, that he is related to the princely family which had ruled what
was then Tirconnell but is now Donegal.

What this relationship is O'Donnel refuses with cold politeness to
disclose, but we learn a few more facts about him. Some time later a
storm drives Glentworth to seek shelter in a house, vaguely Spanish,
set in a deep ravine. The house is bare and impoverished, yet boasts
certain magnificent possessions. The pedigree of the O'Donnel family,
"beginning with Niall of the nine hostages," hangs from the wall.
Near it is the portrait of a man in religious habit, whose handsome,
massive face, resembling that of Wolsey, expresses "grief and disap-
pointment, preying on the energies of genius and ambition." (*O'Donnel*, I, 279) Above the chimney hangs a heavy sword, its basket hilt
worked in gold and its blade thick with crusted blood.

Glentworth's host, O'Donnel, enters unexpectedly by a door which
the portrait conceals and, in the course of the evening, narrates part of
his story. The sword is that of the Red Earl, the Elizabethan traitor.
Of Hugh's direct descendants, four survived in the eighteenth century.
The eldest son, Roderick's grandfather, farmed the few acres which
had remained after the confiscations. The two younger sons had sought
careers on the continent, one taking holy orders and rising to power
in the Spanish court and the other becoming a field marshal in the
Austrian service. The fourth child, a daughter, had married into the
peasantry.

In his old age the Abbé O'Donnel, moved by some unfathomable passion, set aside his ambitions, which had been those of a worldly churchman, and returned to Ireland. In his absence, so he discovers, one of his nephews, apostatizing to the Protestant Church, had seized the family lands. Roderick, a son of the disinherited nephew, he finds running the hills. The Abbé, building his Spanish house, educates the boy and sends him into the Austrian service. Roderick travels from Austria to France with Marie Antoinette, and is a colonel of cuirassiers when the Revolution breaks out.

Possessing the traditional Irish "devotion to hereditary monarchy," Roderick had acted, so long as was possible, in the defense of the royal family, then had hastened to offer his sword to his "natural sovereign," King George. The suspicions of the English government, however, have made the gesture a useless one and, impoverished and desperate, he has returned home. The Abbé is dead now, and has left to his nephew only the ruined house, the portrait with its enigmatic smile, and the sword.

Glentworth hears out this story with much sympathetic indignation, and promises to bring O'Donnel's claims before the attention of government. In the months which follow, however, this plan is continually thwarted. Dexter, who has the ear of English politicians, has persuaded them that O'Donnel, "this Irish, French, Austrian soldier," has come back, like his ancestor, to further some treasonable plot—a theory which takes some color from the old Abbé's reputation for papal intrigue.

In the end it is not Glentworth who rescues O'Donnel from his plight, but—predictably—Miss O'Halloran. To accomplish this Lady Morgan marries her off to an English duke, who, being a duke, is wealthy; being infirm, does not assail her virginity; and being considerate, dies within weeks. Together O'Donnel and his bride, the dowager duchess, reclaim his ancestral lands. Lady Morgan, it need not be noted, tended to regard plot as a tedious necessity.

But a perceptive remark by Stephen Gwynn may suggest why *O'Donnel,* for all its silliness, was an important novel. "In the ordinary acceptation," he says, "the Irish gentleman was a Protestant; the Irish retainer a Catholic: these were ultimate facts to the popular imagination. Early in the nineteenth century, Lady Morgan in her novel *O'Donnel* presented an almost unbelievable thing, an Irish gentleman who was of native race and a Catholic." [9] This is scarcely an understatement. Most of the impact of the novel upon its contemporaries lay in the contrast between O'Donnel's obvious gentility and the contempt with which he is treated.

"The impression given by his air and manner," Glentworth remarks of his new-found friend to an incredulous English company, "is that of a person of a certain high-toned character, little calculated for the rough brakes of everyday life, and with all his foreign airs, he is still *very Irish,* quick, sensitive, I had almost said irritable; and I dare say with all the pride of the Milesian O's and Mac's into the bargain." (*O'Donnel,* I, 237) His conversational style is exaggeratedly correct and formal, as though guarding against a rebuff; his manners are impeccable; his "foreign" and "Irish" airs are visible only to Lord Glentworth and his creator. To the reader, he seems a solemnly intended caricature of an English gentleman, whom the inscrutable gods have chosen to disguise as an alien.

O'Donnel thus takes his place as an early instance of those nerveless paragons sent forth by novelists to plead the case of racial or cultural minorities. That the Irish Catholic makes his entrance into the English novel by way of so exotic a character tells us, more vividly than all the author's sermonizing, how alien to British culture he really was. And, as is often the case in such novels, it suggests a fundamental ambivalence in Lady Morgan's attitude toward her subject. Arguing the Catholic position before an English public, she found it good sense (as it was) to maintain that nothing distinguished O'Donnel from Glentworth save the disabilities imposed by shameful laws. But she is constantly and nervously reassuring herself on the same point.

The three characters in *O'Donnel* who summon forth the author's feelings, the three who dominate the novel, we never meet: the

[9] *Ireland,* p. 36.

Elizabethan Hugh O'Donnel, the Abbé, and the rebel leader of the White Boys. They embody the three forces which had shaped Irish culture into its own, very un-English mold: the Gaelic tradition, the Catholic Church, and anarchic violence. This neat pattern has not been imposed on the story, despite its author's predilection for allegory. It is rather the case that she deliberately refused to deal with the realities of her subject, and these return to haunt and trouble her.

O'Donnel and Glentworth discuss religion with a grave and courteous show of mutual respect. Matching off the Penal Laws against the Revocation of the Edict of Nantes, they agree that in the harsh bigotries of the past, both creeds have sinned against the spirit of Christianity. Much of this animus remains, unhappily, to disturb Irish life. M'Rory jabbers superstitious nonsense about Lough Derg and heretics and miracles, and Dexter is possessed by the narrow no-Popery of the Orange lodges. Glentworth and O'Donnel, however, being each in his own improbable way a disciple of Voltaire and Rousseau, have only scorn for such sectarian excess, and their talk is all of conciliation and understanding. It is as though Lord Chesterfield and the author of *Manon Lescaut* had met at some neutral spa.

Instead they meet at night in an oddly sinister Spanish house hidden by the dark Donegal mountains. O'Donnel has appeared suddenly and melodramatically from the passage which the Abbé's disturbing portrait conceals. And the Abbé, though supposedly a benevolent and paternal figure, is linked with that somber inferno of popular English imaginings, Spain of the Counter Reformation. He had helped to shape "the narrow and illiberal views of a crooked and illiberal power," had been one of the black-hooded intriguers of the Escorial. Later still he had been summoned from Trappist meditations to serve the secret purposes of the Vatican. He dies, we are told, with his ambitions thwarted, but we must conjecture what these may have been. Peasants carry his body to a distant monastery and, so his creator hopes, out of history. Not until her final novel, in the baleful figure of the Abbate O'Brien, would she acknowledge the feelings which in *O'Donnel* lie submerged.

The sword of Red Hugh O'Donnel is a symbol as equivocal as the portrait. Of all Roderick's possessions it is the one most precious to him, and his thoughts recur to it constantly.

> He walked toward the chimney-piece, and fixed his eyes on the sword of the hero whose memory he revered, of whose kindred he was so proud, of whose character he was enamoured. With that sword the chief of O'Donnel had avenged his own wrongs, and redressed those of his country. O'Donnel took down the sacred weapon—sacred at least in his own estimation, and examined it with the scrutiny of one who beheld it for the first time, but it was, in fact, with the emotion of one who feared he was looking on it for the last.   (*Ibid.*, I, 104–5)

The golden hilt, into which chivalric designs have been worked, makes it an appropriate weapon for O'Donnel, whose sense of honor is so scrupulous that, despite service in foreign armies, he has never taken the field against his "legitimate sovereign." But the blade tells a different story, for it is rusted with the blood spilled by Hugh's rebellion and treason.

That all of Roderick's claims to a princely and heroic heritage should depend upon his descent from a traitor who foreswore *his* legitimate sovereign and slaughtered her soldiers proves a great embarrassment to Lady Morgan, and explains why she abandoned the earlier version of the novel. For in its present form the novel contains a number of historical fragments which, she alleges, are the Abbé's translation of the account of Hugh's rebellion as set forth in the *Annals of the Four Masters*.

Hugh O'Donnel, it would appear from this, had been a most loyal servant of the Queen. True, he had harried and burned, but only by way of chastening her perfidious Deputies at Dublin Castle. Having "expelled the unjust stewards of an abused sovereign," he retired from the field bearing the praise and "golden opinion" of Elizabeth. Unhappily, he was lured by his kinsman O'Neill into drawing his sword again, this time in an ignoble cause, which was justly wrecked at Kinsale, where "the red cross banner of the O'Donnel was trampled in the dust." (*Ibid.*, II, 34)

The Four Masters would regard this translation as bewildering confirmation of their suspicion that the English tongue is poorly designed as an instrument of truth. For in their version O'Donnel is a hot-blooded champion of the Counter Reformation, impatient with the stodgy caution of O'Neill, and eager to conquer for the True Faith.[10] But then the Four Masters wrote out of a world of loyalties and passions by which Lady Morgan was at once confused and repelled.

It was pleasant, at any rate, to imagine that these ancient furies of blood were safely buried with the Abbé. Roderick O'Donnel, at least, will never use his sword to "avenge his own wrongs." His figure is entirely passive and pathetic, and he draws the blade only to ponder its riddle and to weep. The cause which is his own he commits to Glentworth and to the Duchess of Belmont.

The Duchess, which is to say Lady Morgan, accepted the cause eagerly. From 1814 on we find her taking an increasingly active role in the struggle for Catholic Emancipation. The actual state of this struggle was such as to encourage, at first, most of the illusions in which *O'Donnel* abounds.

Ever since the first, almost imperceptible, relaxation of the penal statutes, the Catholic gentry had entrusted their fate to the liberal Protestants of Ireland. And they had been as pathetically eager as Roderick O'Donnel himself to demonstrate their disinclination to give offense. A century of restrictive legislation had bludgeoned them into a state of obsequious dependence on the Ascendancy. Their Committees, grateful for the permission to meet, were models of decorous restraint. From time to time they would submit a petition, couched in the most abject terms, and would count it a minor victory if it were read at all. France, the Catholic nation to which they had long looked wanly for succor, was in the control of "godless regicides," and the Pope himself had become an English pensioner. In sober fact, not merely the motive but the opportunity for disloyalty had perished for them.

To understand their attitude (a task which later generations were too angry with them to perform), it must be remembered that, their

<hr/>

[10] *Annals of the Kingdom of Ireland, by the Four Masters* . . . , ed. and trans. by John O'Donovan.

timorousness aside, the Irish Catholic gentry were very much hard-headed men of the eighteenth century. Conservative by instinct, they abhorred revolution, wishing only to be accorded full status within a nation which they assumed would be dominated by the Protestant Ascendancy. In short, their position seemed to them identical with that of their coreligionists in England and with the Protestants of France. Since the peasant population of any nation was usually excluded from conservative speculation, they tended, paradoxical as this may seem, to think of their own as the minority creed.

To this considerable extent the thesis implicit in *O'Donnel* is warranted by the political situation. And it proved a persuasive one. As much as any single force did, Lady Morgan's novels made liberal opinion in England receptive to Irish Catholic claims. In her novels and in a spate of articles she impressed upon the imagination of her public the image of the proud, melancholy O'Donnel who was content to wait, presumably until Doomsday, for recognition of the wrongs which had been done him. It did not occur to her that the fierce passions and murky ambitions of the Abbé had not been put to rest in his remote burial ground, that they were being nursed by the peasants and house servants and postboys who supply her novels with their jolly, happy-go-lucky supernumeraries. Nor that the nephew of Count Daniel O'Connell, upon whom she had modeled Roderick O'Donnel, was preparing to hammer those passions into a blade swifter and more decisive than that of Red Hugh.[11]

In the Irish novel, with its insistence upon literal and emphatic symbols, the ruin, as we have seen, exists in abundance. Its meaning is always clear—whether monastery, Norman keep, round tower, or fortress, it refers backward to the Gaelic order. It is only part, however, of a concern with buildings and with the land so common in Irish novels as to suggest a theme with which the culture itself was obsessed. At times the characters withdraw from a novel entirely, save

---

[11] Lady Morgan's letters mention Shee and O'Rourke, other Brigade officers, as the prototypes of her *O'Donnel*, but his career resembles that of Count Daniel O'Connell much more closely.

as bits of painted cardboard, and surrender all the thrust of meaning to the naked stones.

In this set of emblematic values the world of the Ascendancy was always represented by the Great House. (That phrase, though, is English rather than Anglo-Irish: whatever its size or description, it was "the castle" to the gentry and "the big house" to English-speaking peasants.) Lady Morgan's novel of the Great House is *Florence Macarthy,* a book in which she brings to fuller life than hitherto her romantic conception of Irish experience. What makes it a rewarding novel, however, is her growing awareness that this conception might be inadequate and false.

In superficial ways it resembles *O'Donnel.* Like that novel it bears the name of a Gaelic chieftain, by whose memory the characters are haunted. Once again the hero is a soldier who returns home after years of exile. But the plot is deliberately steeped in deceptions, intrigues, false identities, and clouded birthrights. Though it hinges on the issue of rival, if not multiple, claims to the possession of land, and on the theme of the "rightful heir," the conventionality is here justified by Lady Morgan's true subject.

Land and great houses were at the core of the Irish question. Grievances over lands lost, the guilts attached to the possession of land, social status, religious and political loyalties, even the issues of personal identity, were bound together. And in consequence a plot involving land, houses, titles, and heirs had an intrinsic social relevance. In the present instance Lady Morgan uses a Munster estate to say a great deal about Irish history and the immediacies of the Irish cultural situation.

The great house is Dunore Castle in the province of Munster. It is the seat of the Fitzadelm family, who have become the Marquises of Dunore. But behind this apparently simple fact lies a series of proliferating puzzles and mysteries, connected with one another and locked into the dark and devious history of Munster.

The present Marquis has gone mad, his insanity taking the form of a terrified fascination with the past, from which gaunt and bloody apparitions appear. His brother Adelm, then, is the true representative of the family. Adelm, too, is obsessed with history, in a dreamy, romantic way which prevents him from acting. Both brothers are dominated by their mother, the dowager Marchioness, an English-woman, who looks on Ireland as a "thrilling" and exotic province. The lands, which are heavily mortgaged, have been put up for sale by Darby Crawley, the "new man" who has been slowly consolidating his power.

An inexplicable doom has followed the family. "Ah, then," a peasant woman says, "nothing ever thriv with them Fitzadelms: they had the black drop in them, for all they were the portliest men in the country, and to this day it's a saying in the country, 'comely and wicked like a Fitzadelm.'" (*Florence Macarthy,* I, 175) We are never certain what the black drop signifies, for three or four alternative explanations are given us by interested parties. There is also a mystery as to their identity.

They are, it is clear, a branch of the Norman family of the Geral-dines, who seized control of Munster from the Macarthies in the twelfth century. But they are connected only remotely with the most powerful Geraldines, the ones who became Earls of Desmond. Some time during the centuries in which the Desmonds had become "more Irish than the Irish" the Fitzadelms had vanished beyond the Galtee mountains. They reappeared in Jacobean times, having established an English alliance, and, having helped to wrest the land from Macarthies and Desmonds alike, became Barons of Dunore. The reign of James II, however, found them in alliance with their old enemies, and they shared in the defeat at the Boyne.

At the beginning of the eighteenth century, however, they emerged once more from the shadows. Now there were two brothers, Tierna Dhu and Tierna Ruadh, the black baron and the red. Tierna Dhu, for some unspecified service, receives a marquisate and builds a Georgian mansion commensurate with his rank. His laborers are pressed into service in the construction of a road between Dunore and Dublin. It is begun bravely enough, but straggles away, unfinished, in the moun-tains. But though his road does not reach Dublin, Tierna Dhu himself does. His wife dies in childbirth, and his only son is supposed drowned.

In a frenzy of grief he builds on a more and more extravagant scale, mortgaging his land to the Crawleys. And he dies, bankrupt, in a Dublin garret. His brother Gerald, Tierna Ruadh, a wily fox of a man, who had been in collusion with the Crawleys, inherits, and bids fair, for a while, to escape the Fitzadelm curse. But his marriage, too, is unlucky. His wife is unfaithful. Of his two sons, one is a dilettante who has woven a fanciful legend of the Fitzadelm past, a kind of heraldic tapestry of honor and renown. The other, the present Marquis, is insane.

There sails one day into Dublin Bay a ship portentously named "Il Librador." She has been fitted as a sloop of war, and has seen service in the South American revolutions under her captain—a man calling himself Fitzwalter, but in fact the supposedly dead son of Tierna Dhu. Where O'Donnel had been mostly honor and gloom, Fitzwalter is all Byronic energy, a capable and somewhat ruthless fighting man. His first aim is to right his own wrongs and restore his house, but he has larger, national ambitions.

In the thirty-odd years of his absence the country has suffered a fate as stern as his own. Along the road to Munster he passes columns of English soldiers marching down from the Richmond and Portobello barracks to keep order in the province, in which civil war has been raging. The shabby coach which he rides bears the Fitzadelm arms. He passes glens where tithe proctors and estate agents have been murdered. At a mountain pass in the Galtees he comes upon an inn called Lis-na-sleugh, whose dirty sod walls are plastered indiscriminately with engravings of saints and the dying confessions of cutthroats and rebels. Beggars and old women come and leave, on the service, he later learns, of the White Boy bands who control the hills. In the long memory of the peasants, the Fitzadelms have receded into the past. Like the Macarthies and the Desmonds, they have become the stuff of legends—an accursed but glamorous family. The new "lords of the land" are the Crawleys, at whose behest the soldiers and the yeomanry have racked the countryside.

Nothing remains now to complete the transfer of authority save the actual disposal of Castle Dunore itself. It stands vacant at the moment, for its titular head, having passed the final border of sanity into violence, has been placed in confinement. Shortly, however, his mother will arrive, to exchange the land deed with Crawley, who has agreed to send her other son to Parliament.

Fitzwalter enters the house by night, traveling along the broad road which his father had built. But the road now is choked with weeds, the bars of the gate are broken, and the lodges lie in ruin. The woods have all been cut for timber. The Fitzadelm eagle, carved from the black marble of their quarries, is headless, and the claws have been shattered. Pieces of the white, classic portico lie fallen with the rough stones of other ages.

Within, however, the house is rich with the mementoes of history; these alone the Fitzadelms had not pawned nor the Crawleys sold, and the present Marquis has kept them in repair. For the most part they are portraits of the Jacobite beauties who had held court here during the brave days before the Boyne. But there are also portraits of Tierna Dhu and Tierna Ruagh. Fitzwalter's father has been painted in his parliamentary robes. His face, dark and saturnine in complexion, is compact of passion, ambition, and rage. The brother looks the true Geraldine, fair-haired and blue-eyed, but his hand is holding a mask. Everything else has been stripped away, piece by piece. Fitzwalter's plans have been clear and purposeful:

He would endeavour to redeem the folly and negligence of his ancestors, wrest his paternal demesne from the grasp of fraud, or re-purchase it from the grip of sordidness; he would then raise its fallen towers, reclaim its neglected soil, cherish the miserable population, and expiate the violence and rapacity by which his distant forefathers obtained this still beautiful territory. . . . (*Ibid.*, I, 203–4)

But the visit shakes his purpose, if only for a while. His father's self-destroying rage, the meaningful mask in the other portrait, have hinted to him the nature of the black drop in their blood. The Desmonds had at least conquered openly, but the Fitzadelms had advanced themselves steadily by guile and treachery. To suit the convenience of the moment, they had changed and rechanged their faith, sold their friends, betrayed their allies. And they had built, vainly trying to set their mark upon the land. A streak of madness had been growing in them. It led Fitzwalter's father, with the clarity of obsession, to the grandest and most revealing folly of all, the straight highway to Dublin and power. The present Marquis and his brother, lacking this wild physical energy, have tried, in imaginative frenzy, to transform the past by magic, to rewrite the Fitzadelm history.

They have been defeated by the Crawleys, who, lacking a past, lack also historical preoccupations. Their present activities, however, are multitudinous. Darby, the head of the clan, is "agent, magistrate, county treasurer, land jobber, road maker, landlord, and attorney-at-law, captain of the Dunore Volunteers, and commandant of the New-Town Mount Crawley supplementary-auxiliary volunteer legion." (*Ibid.*, II, 2) His brother is commissioner of "one of those boards instituted and perpetuated for the purpose of paying debts to such creditors as the members of the Crawley family." Tim is being trained up to be high sheriff of the county; an army commission has been wangled for the otherwise useless Thady; and Conway has been despatched to tend the family interests as a member of parliament (and, no doubt, as a contributor to the *Quarterly Review*).

Darby, like Lopahin in *The Cherry Orchard,* bears no animus toward the Fitzadelms, though, unlike him, he is incapable of attaching any significance to his victory over them. Old now, and usually a bit drunk, he remembers of his youth only the skill with which he rose: "a bit of a *dewshure* for the great, a Wicklow pebble, or a lump of Irish diamond; or a hundred of Puldoodie oysters, or a cask of Waterford sprats, or some pretty bougie for my friends." (*Ibid.,* II, 46) He had been of service to the government during the rebellion, but his effective "loyalty" does not extend beyond Mount Crawley.

Fitzwalter has come back to Dunore on a mission of private vengeance against the Fitzadelms, to discover that they have been self-destroyed. It was an eighteenth-century mission, to be settled with swords at midnight; his own republicanism is of that century—stern and Plutarchian. But the century has passed. His opponents now are the Crawleys, who have at their command the government itself, the files of red-coated soldiers from the Portobello barracks, and their own inexhaustible, vulgar strength. His purpose fails him, however, not when he confronts the Crawleys, but when, standing in the picture gallery at Dunore, he acknowledges his own descent from Tierna Dhu and the older exploiters from beyond the mountains.

It is the past, however, a much older past than that of the Fitzadelms, which saves him. It also ruins the novel. Perched romantically on a mountain crag is the last fortress of the Macarthies, "the kings of the county round, of the Coriandri and the Desmondii, and blood relations to the Tyrian Hercules, every mother's son of them." (*Ibid.*, I, 259) There, amidst threadbare trappings of Gaelic splendor, lives the last of the family of Macarthy Mor, the beautiful, talented, and patriotic Countess Clancare. Fitzadelm is led to her by Terence Oge O'Leary, a spoiled priest turned hedge schoolmaster, in whose visionary mind the jagged ruin still exists with its "ballium, barbican, embrasures, parapets, and crenelles." Lady Clancare, by some show of instinctive mastery, can control the otherwise anarchic and murderous peasantry. And with her help and theirs Fitzwalter is able to wage a successful fight against the Crawleys.

The novel is brought to a close in language appropriately hollow:

On the successful termination of the great Fitzadelm cause, which had for some months occupied the public attention, the Marquis and Marchioness of Dunore took possession of their ancient castle and vast possessions in Ireland, and fixed there their chief residence. For, convinced by a close and attentive observation, that the land of their birth was hourly sinking in the scale of nations, under the oppression of delegated authority, and by the neglect and absence of its natural protectors, they acted, with their energy and perseverance, upon the dictates of experience, and illustrated, by their example, the truth of a maxim, now more generally felt and admitted, that Ireland can best be served in Ireland.   (*Ibid.*, IV, 281–82)

Florence Macarthy should not be dismissed on such evidence as a summary of its plot affords. Its allegory is easily riddled out and can be set down without reduction: in this algebra of great houses, the warring fortresses of the past, Dunore and Macarthy, are to league themselves against the usurping Crawleys. The allegory is sustained by an ingenuity and precision of detail quite new to Lady Morgan's work, but for all that is hostile to any vividly represented life. Lady Clancare is the blood sister (or, rather, bloodless sister) of Glorvina and Roderick O'Donnel. The Crawleys are two-dimensional caricatures cut with the shears of snobbery. But with the Fitzadelms Lady Morgan has come, for the first time, to a mystery. She stands beside Fitzwalter as he studies the portraits, and confronts her own loyalties.

She had intended Lady Clancare as the center to her tapestry, but Fitzwalter seizes the position. He is a hero of the Ascendancy, which had been from the first the surreptitious object of her concern. In some "magical" way Lady Clancare lends him the immemorial authority of the Gaelic order, but the battle itself and the hard, masculine will is his. Like Roderick O'Donnel, he comes home to Ireland with a sword, but it is one which he intends to use in his own cause, and he has sailed on the "Librador." For the "wild Irish" are never, in Lady Morgan's novels, the arbiters of their own destinies. They are glamorous but passive victims to be championed by Glentworth or by Mortimer.

In *Florence Macarthy,* however, the hero's boldness, like his guilt, is derived from his swift, predatory stock. On his travels he has met Hyacinth Daly of Daly's Court, a figure based upon Grattan, the chieftain of the Protestant Nation. "Mr. Daly had distinguished himself in the memorable year 1782, when Ireland for a moment was a nation, and had kept his noble mansion in Dublin until the Union: then, having followed the liberties of his country from their cradle to their tomb, he had retired forever from the scene of their ruin. . . ." (*Ibid.,* II, 183) And it is the Protestant Nation, the empty House of Parliament, the abandoned mansion in Dublin, which we remember when Fitzwalter visits Dunore. "The broad approach was still visibly marked out, though now moss-grown and green, winding through beautiful, undulating, but neglected grounds. . . ." (*Ibid.,* I, 197)

Lady Morgan's is the first literary work of the nineteenth century to set forth the passions and the ultimate commitments of those members of the Ascendancy who espoused the nationalist movement. Their role was, in many ways, a decisive one; their roster is impressive. It runs, in politics, from Butt to Parnell. And in literature it culminates in Yeats. Yet it is a mark of the general failure of modern Irish thought that no serious attempt has been made to separate out the complex and entangled strands which went into the weaving of nationalism.

Professor Daniel Corkery, for example, in his angry and singularly ungenerous *Synge and Anglo-Irish Literature,* celebrates each arrival from the camp of the Ascendancy into that of nationalism as, literally, a spiritual conversion, a renunciation of pride, mastery, and sense of caste. Yet the fact is that the nineteenth-century writers who came to nationalism from the great houses came with all that pride in the Ascendancy class which, so Professor Corkery imagines, they had abjured. It is stamped on every line of Yeats, for he scorned to evade the truth of the matter.

We of Protestant Ireland, he told a dumfounded Dublin Senate, "are no petty people. We are one of the great stocks of Europe. We are the people of Burke; we are the people of Grattan; we are the people of Swift, the people of Parnell. We have created the most of the modern literature of this country. We have created the best of its political intelligence." [12] And yet it was a class which had betrayed its own brilliance, as he was to say elsewhere: "Protestant Ireland could never have done otherwise; it lacked hereditary passion. Parnell, its last great figure, finding this lack had made the party of my father's friend Isaac Butt powerless, called in the peasants' tenacity and violence, but for months now the peasants had stood aside and waited, hoping that their old masters might take the leadership again." [13]

Now this, making allowance for the vigor and forthrightness of Yeats's language, is an uncannily exact summary of the theme of *Florence Macarthy.* It goes a long way toward explaining the nature of Lady Morgan's patriotism. And it explains, also, why each of these writers came ultimately to turn away in disgust from the movement he had founded. For, in specifically political and cultural terms, this was all sheer *mystique.* When time and the abnegation of power have conspired to choke with weeds the pathway leading from a great house, the process cannot be reversed. The myth had it that Irish peasants, "hereditary royalists," answered from some instinctual depth the call

[12] Joseph Hone, *Life of W. B. Yeats,* p. 396.
[13] William Butler Yeats, *Dramatis Personae* (New York, 1936), p. 39.

of their "old true masters." Which is a dangerous half-truth. Long subjection had at least made them ruthless connoisseurs of power. The *forms* of power made little impression on them, however heroic the tone.

In Yeats's day they were summoned to their hereditary passion by a schoolmaster, a second-rate poet, and "a drunken, vainglorious lout." In Lady Morgan's day, it was a shout, heard dimly through her Kildare Street window: "O'Connell!"

There is neither instruction nor joy (perhaps there is not propriety) in joining Professor Corkery in the Grand Assize which he holds upon the convictions of his countrymen. The point, rather, is that there went into the shaping of the culture and politics of modern Ireland impulses which were contradictory, warring, half-understood. Lady Morgan's value is that she expresses some of these impulses for us with an unexpected clarity.

10. The Houses of the West: *The O'Briens*

and the O'Flahertys

ON MARCH 12, 1826, a small, private party was held at Dublin Castle by the viceroy, Lord Wellesley.[1] Although it is given only a page in Lady Morgan's diary for that year, the evening marked the climax of her career, both in politics and (since she was then at work on her last Irish novel) in literature. And it was very close, though no one knew it then, to one of the turning points in Irish history—the momentous Waterford election.

But everyone did know that, somehow or other, there would soon be a decisive moment. In the three years of its existence the Catholic Association had brought into being the "army of beggars" who would sweep the country to the edge of civil war. Nothing less than knowledge of this could have persuaded the otherwise sober and sensible Wellesley to arrange his hopeless party. For he had asked to it the chiefs of Ireland's two irreconcilable parties—on one side the Castle officials and the masters of the Orange lodges; on the other the directors of the Catholic Association and their handful of Protestant allies.

Somewhere in the streets which stretched beyond into the slums the mobs of Dublin's Liberties were mustered in that quiet, drilled expectancy which Secretary Goulburn was nervously reporting to London. In a hundred shebeen houses throughout the island pothouse bards were fitting doggerel English to old Gaelic war songs. And in

[1] Lady Morgan, *Memoirs,* II, 225–26.

the hills and lonely glens the White Boys were testing the edges of billhooks tied to pikestaffs.[2]

"I was last night at a private party at the Castle," Lady Morgan notes. "I was, as of late I have constantly been, the center of a circle."

There was a special reason for her being there, though she does not mention it. Sir Charles Morgan had been circulating a petition among the Irish Protestants asking for a repeal of the disabilities which rested on Catholics, and had secured the pledges of those landlords who heard the echoes of Grattan's voice above the booming of the Orange drums. The Morgan house in Kildare Street was one of the meeting places of the Catholic and the liberal Protestant groups.

One of the street ballads of the period runs:

> Och, Dublin city, there's no doubtin'
> Bates every city upon the say;
> 'Tis there you'll find O'Connell spoutin'
> And Lady Morgan making tay.[3]

It is given to few romantics to be swept up into the life of their fantasies, but Sydney Owenson had come at last to the court of her enemy to plead her country's cause. Ranged against her was the ultra-Protestant Colonel Blacker, the "roaring lion" and Orange Grand Master, who had recently given voice to his fear that concessions to the Catholics could only lead to a demand that the statue of King William be removed from College Green.[4] Beside him was the hapless Goulburn, who had once assured Peel that the agitation would amount to nothing.[5] Beyond these low comedy figures, however, stood the true rulers of Dublin Castle, Dogherty and Joy, the Solicitor-General.

At Lady Morgan's side was that easiest and most patient of men, "my ultra-liberal husband." (Poor Sir Charles seems to have been of marked, though obscured, abilities; his own work shows a trenchant and humane mind.) But at her other side was "the Catholic chief," Lord Killeen, the young heir to the earldom of Fingall. Killeen, though

---

[2] See James A. Reynolds, *The Catholic Emancipation Crisis in Ireland, 1823–1829*, Chapter 8.

[3] Lady Morgan, *Memoirs*, II, 231.

[4] J. J. O'Kelly, *O'Connell Calling* (Tralee, 1947), p. 129.

[5] Richard Dunlop, *Daniel O'Connell*, p. 145.

a public-spirited man, had been placed at the head of the Association for one reason only. As the son of the premier Catholic peer, he established for it a continuity with the glamorous names of the past.

He had been dragged along, half-reluctantly, by the man who had transformed the face of Ireland, O'Connell. "The big beggarman," as his enemies were soon to call him, was present that night at the Castle, and his was a presence which not even Lady Morgan could ignore;

That "first flower of the earth, first gem of the sea," O'Connell, wants back the days of Brian Boru, himself to be the king, with a crown of emerald shamrocks, a train of yellow velvet, and a mantle of Irish tabinet, a sceptre in one hand and a cross in the other, and the people crying "Long live king O'Connell!" This is the object of his views and ambitions. . . . O'Connell is not a man of genius; he has a sort of conventional talent applicable to his purpose as it exists in Ireland—a *nisi prius* talent which has won much local popularity.[6]

Lady Morgan was not alone in this underestimation, but it is nonetheless revealing. O'Connell had dragged the people of Ireland out of the mist of nostalgia and the shame of slavery into the modern world. Henceforward whoever treated of Ireland must needs reckon with them. Of the "old Irish" leaders, however, Lady Morgan much preferred to deal with Thomas Wyse, the grave and scholarly strategist of the agitation. Or with the reserved, patrician Killeen, who came from the eighteenth-century Recusant world of the Prince of Innismore. Temperamentally she was closest by far to Richard Lalor Sheil, the careerist and glittering orator, from whom stretches in dreary perspective the multitude of blarneying "patriots." But O'Connell, instinct with genius, bravery, and guile, she could never have understood. In a few years' time the heather of Florence Macarthy's Munster would be afire with the Tithe War, and no landlord, be he Crawley or Fitzwalter, would be safe to ride the road over the Galtees. To Sydney Morgan O'Connell would then be only the demagogue who had posted a White Boy behind each hedge.

This shipwreck of the Ireland of her dreams lay in the future, but

[6] *Memoirs*, II, 226.

her imagination was at work on it. In her last and best novel, *The O'Briens and the O'Flahertys*,[7] she set down this vision in all its compelling power. It is one of the most remarkable and least-known works produced by nineteenth-century Ireland. In its own day, it enjoyed a fair success, though not so large as she expected. Tales about Ireland were in great demand in England in 1827, but tales of another sort.[8] White Boy risings, secret societies and, most especially, the Emancipation agitation had made the public eager to learn about "the Irish peasant as he really was." He was, so it seemed, a being at once murderous, pathetic, and fey—and as incomprehensible as a Tartar herdsman. In Lady Morgan's aristocratic and heraldic world there was for the moment little interest.

And yet she had brought her special kind of novel, with all its marked limitations, to something like perfection. For the first time she had created characters with sufficient strength to implicate readers in their fates. Her attention to setting is as great as ever, but is made to serve the necessities of plot. What gives the novel its subtle and outlandish charm, however, is, of all things, her pedantry.

From *The Wild Irish Girl* on, her heroines had been rendered absurd by their addiction to Irish history. In *Florence Macarthy,* the habit had spread, like some infectious disease, to all the other characters. Only the illiterate peasants were spared, but they had their *seanachies,* the repositories of local lore. Yet all this time Lady Morgan had been involved with a truth: the profound influence of history on the Irish character. In her own case it had taken a characteristic course. To understand herself, she had tried to understand her father, the showman cutting his wretched capers on a Dublin stage, who could also remember standing by a Connaught ditch as Richard Kirwan picked his way to Mass in his jeweled shoes. Behind Robert MacOwen were the peasants and the broken gentry and the half-sirs, Malby Crofton of Longford House, the Blakes of Galway and the O'Rourkes of Brefni.

To the Irish history has the compelling force of a map of one's own countryside. Twenty years had passed since Cooper Walker had urged

[7] Page references are to the New York edition of 1856.
[8] See Chapter 12.

Lady Morgan to "look over the Irish historians, Keating, O'Halloran, Leland, etc."[9] Since then, she had been reading constantly, in a random, undisciplined way, and she had come to know scholars far abler than the silly Cooper Walker, and more responsive to the complexities of their subject. She had also heard The O'Conor Don talking of penal days, and Shee telling of his life in the Brigades, and the stories of the United Irishmen who had served with Bonaparte. And, at last, she had found a story which could summon her talent.

Because *The O'Briens and the O'Flahertys* is a full and various novel, executed on the grand scale, there has always been a certain confusion as to its subject. Hepworth Dixon, of the *Athenaeum,* thought it "a repository of the manners, customs, grievances, and society" immediately before and after the Union.[10] The men of Young Ireland found in it a celebration of Lord Edward Fitzgerald and the '98 Rising.[11] W. J. Fitzpatrick, who thought it less a novel than "a work of some historical importance," was troubled by its exhibition of "a somewhat inconsistent love for republicanism and aristocracy." And the Jesuit, Stephen Brown, notes dourly: "May be said to have for its object Catholic Emancipation, yet the author was no admirer of O'Connell, and in this book keen strokes of satire are aimed at the Jesuits, and even at the Pope."[12]

This might mean only that every reader comes to a novel with his own expectations. And in nineteenth-century Ireland, unfortunately, the first question asked of any writer was, "Where does he stand?" Nor had Lady Morgan ever caused doubts as to her willingness to abide this question: if she was nothing else, she was a cut-and-slash polemicist. But the contradictory judgments of partisans as to the subject of *The O'Briens* is caused by the novel's refusal to be pressed into the service of creed or faction. To be sure, all of its author's old enemies are keelhauled anew, and the perfidious betrayal of "Irish independence" is assailed one last time. But these are gestures only, and they are subordinated to a moving and perceptive representation of Irish life.

---

[9] Lady Morgan, *Memoirs,* I, 314.   [10] *Ibid.,* II, 234.
[11] Preface by Robert Sheldon Mackenzie to the 1856 edition of the novel.
[12] *Ireland in Fiction,* p. 185.

The story has two centers—Dublin and a stretch of wild country, called Iar Connaught, in Connemara. And two points of time—the 1770s, which witnessed both the birth of the Protestant Nation and the first stirrings of the Catholic population, and the years of rebellion which led to the Union. Most readers, understandably, have preferred the second volume to the first, for it contains a tautly constructed romance of revolution and conspiracy. The first volume, a seemingly messy snarl of loyalties and betrayals, has been dismissed as irrelevant and confused. It is certainly difficult to read, being built of supposed letters, diaries, bills filed in chancery, extracts from medieval annals, histories written in exile, reports to government. Events, both past and present, are seen through the eyes of men whose thoughts are guarded, and who take for granted the complicated relationships of Irish life. Then, midway, this method is dropped, and our point of view becomes that of the frank and ingenuous young Murrough O'Brien, a romantic patriot caught up in the heroic world of Lord Edward Fitzgerald. But this is exactly her point: the heroism is tragically unrelated to the actualities of Irish life, and the frankness and ingenuousness are fatal.

One figure whom we meet early in the story is "General Count Sir Malachi O'Flaherty," of the Second Irish Brigade. O'Flaherty, a thoroughly gallicized Wild Goose, is an agreeably sardonic man, witty, intelligent, and urbane. Though his politics have the insolent harshness of the *ancien régime,* he is a skeptic in most matters, and quite indifferent to religious issues. For an exile, he is well-informed on Irish matters, but he finds the subject a tiring one.

He receives one day a baffling letter, signed by his "humble servant, friend, cousin, and kinsman, Terentius Baron O'Brien of the Clan Teigs of Arran." (*O'Briens,* I, 20) It informs him, to the accompaniment of much incomprehensible gibberish, that the O'Flaherty lands of Moycullen in Iar Connaught, presently in the possession of an Archdeacon Hunks, of the Protestant Church as by law established, may shortly be sold to interested parties, "who would fain turn the fine old ruins of the abbey, tower, chauntry, and castle, to some popish and superstitious uses. Some saying that the talk was and is, of the nuns of St. Bridget, now lodged over Blake's shop in the Claddagh of St.

Grellan, that they were to be restored to their ancient premises." (*Ibid.,* I, 19) To prevent this, the writer of the letter offers to recover the land for O'Flaherty, acting as "law-agent, champion, and advocate," without fee or reward.

O'Flaherty can make neither head nor tail of the letter, which expresses loyalist and "no-popery" sentiments but also pious and very Catholic invocations of "Mary, John, and Joseph." O'Flaherty's right to the land is traced back, in the wild fashion of Celtic genealogy, to "Earva, king of West Connaught, Anno 944, lineal descendant from Duaeh Tean *gumha,* or the *silver-tongued,* fifth Christian king of Connaught." (*Ibid.,* I, 17) It is a claim which, O'Flaherty rightly concludes, will carry little weight with the Irish House of Lords. But it is accompanied by the first of many legal documents, drafted by Terentius O'Brien, which, to the contrary, are ingenious and formidable disputations. The father of Hunks, it would appear, had conformed to Protestantism, but had "never filed any certificate of his conformity; and therefore his claims as a discoverer are null and void." (*Ibid.,* I, 21)

Entirely baffled, O'Flaherty forwards the correspondence to his cousin, recently appointed to a Connemara parish "by divine indignation, and the favor of your uncle, the titular Archbishop of Tuam." (*Ibid.,* I, 22) The Abbé, an Augustinian, austere and devout but with a certain wryness and worldliness of his own, is newly returned to Ireland, and equally puzzled. The whole island, he has discovered, is an endless confusion, after a century of neglect, corruption, and persecutions. Like all the exiles to France, he dates events from the Boyne, and thus writes:

The frightful shock, the utter dislocation of society, given by the revolution, is still felt in faint and remote vibration, though at the end of a century. The displaced classes are not yet shaken down into their permanent positions. Many of the gentry have melted into peasants, many of the lowest persons have risen into sudden wealth . . . , a third rebellion has broken out since 1759.   (*Ibid.,* I, 28)

Connemara itself makes no sense to him. Its people are in continuous quarrels over land, and the quarrels are hopeless of resolution. Partitions of the soil had been carelessly made over to successive adventurers, soldiers, palatines, and patentees, in "grants, debentures, regrants, patents, commutations and reprisals, gifts of mitre land consecrated by his Holiness the Pope, and now conferred by our sovereign lord the King." (*Ibid.*, I, 72) To this bitterness has been added all the boundless hatreds of religious zeal, an indifferent government imposed upon a society of half-barbarian tribes, and all the shames and glories of the past.

The two O'Flahertys, the soldier and the priest, are used for reasons which are remarkably ingenious, quite apart from their engaging personalities. Each, to be sure, has his own partisan view of Irish affairs. The Count, for all his immersion in French life, still thinks of himself as an Irish gentleman, and one whose family has been used shabbily. His cousin is eager to raise the moral tone of his community, corroded as it has been by the penal legislation. Essentially, however, they are the civilized products of an ordered society. Their humanity, rather than their "patriotism," is shocked. Many an English visitor would be despatched to Ireland by nineteenth-century novelists for this reason, yet they would lack any intimate involvement in the scene. But the O'Flahertys are discovering their own past, and their own country.

Abbé O'Flaherty reconstructs the story slowly as he makes his rounds through wild Connemara, with its sharply indented coasts, its forfeited abbeys and monasteries, its shattered garrisons. The land is dominated by the ducal residence of the Proudforts, floating like "a fairy structure in a desert, backed by inaccessible mountains and dreary wastes," the model of Georgian magnificence. (*Ibid.*, II, 250) Yet scattered over the countryside are the old families, each nursing its special prides and shames. In the remote past, remembered now in fading pedigrees and half-forgotten annals, and in the talk of old women, the chief clans, ever at war with each other and the world, had been the O'Briens and the O'Flahertys. Then had come the Welsh-Norman families, like the Taafes, who became McTaaf. Then the Elizabethan plantation families, like the Hunkses, and then the Cromwellian settlers. And then, finally, the Proudforts.

Gradually a picture emerges which is itself coherent, if the society it mirrors is not. The Gaelicized McTaafs, "being ever a miserable sept," had been driven to such strips of moorland as the other clans disdained. But in Elizabethan times they threw in their lot with the Elizabethans, remaining thereafter staunchly Protestant and Jacobite. The last male, "the Brigadier," had finally made his peace with the Hanoverians, and had died in the Low Country. The family is now represented by two indomitable old women, Monica and Mabel, whose alliances proliferate endlessly—"the Bells, the Blakes, the Bodkins, and the rest of the thirteen tribes . . . the Fitzgeralds of Maynooth, the Talbots of Malahide, the Barnwells of Turvey, and the most of the great Pale families—to say nothing of the celebrated Granuaile, daughter and sole heiress of Duondarragh, son of Cormac, son of Owen Omailly, the chief of his name." (*Ibid.*, I, 62) With these fierce and admirable ladies the past is not a tapestry of triumphs and sorrows, but a web of living relationships. Of their friends they demand honor and loyalty, to whatever creed or party. But soon the name will die with them.

The O'Flahertys had their moment of glory, under the Stuarts, and exploited it recklessly and with cruelty. And they fell with the Stuarts. They began, after Limerick, to drift to France. Now, save for a bastard son, they are entirely cut off from Ireland. They are wilful, charming, arrogant people, their fire never damped by the shames of penal days.

But the O'Briens, the most royal of all these families, have not fared so well. Not having fled the country like the O'Flahertys, nor been protected by religion like the McTaafs, they have borne the brunt of the Williamite settlement. Some have been forced down into the peasantry or have become hedge priests. Others, determined to maintain their rank, took to the hills as freebooters. "They were in one generation, the fierce, bog-hunted tory; in another, the hunted rapparee; and in the next, were broken down to the mere wood-kern." (*Ibid.*, I, 31–32)

But all have lived to see the proud Spanish city of Galway become a provincial town of the new Ascendancy. The Hunkses have sprung up everywhere, as attorneys, conveyancers, bailiffs, agents, and jobbing clergymen. And the Proudforts have set their incredible mansion afloat upon the bogs.

This social pattern, which here seems forced and arbitrary, is de veloped slowly and indirectly, through the accumulation of accurate and evocative detail. Coming from the novel to one of the histories of Connemara or Galway is to be impressed, chiefly, by the fidelity with which Lady Morgan has rendered her scene.[13]

But the pattern is shattered irrevocably by one of the most remarkable figures in Irish fiction, the "Terentius Baron O'Brien," whose letter to O'Flaherty has set the plot into motion. He had once been *Terneen na garlach* (Terry the bastard), the child of an illicit union between the two Gaelic families. As a boy he had wandered from cabin to cabin, begging his bread, until a priest, taking pity on him, made him a mass-boy. Then he had been able to walk "barefoot and barelegged, after the officiating priest, with his bell and book in either hand, bowing to the left and to the right, according to the forms; snuffing with his fingers at the tallow candles that lighted up the rude rock altar, chanting out the responses, and tingling his little bell, with a low and muffled vibration, as if he feared its muffled sound should be borne on the blasts that rushed through the secret mass cave, to the ears of the bishop, 'by law established.' " (*O'Briens,* I, 43)

When the hedge school where he learned his Latin is raided by the prebend, he attaches himself to Geoffrey Hunks, a rising attorney in a country where land claims involve an immense amount of shady manoeuvring. Hunks's specialty is the "discovery" of land illegally in the possession of secret Catholics, so that it may be bought up by the Proudforts. Terence, who has the well-honed mind of a hedge seminarian, proves a most apt apprentice, is made a "gentleman," conforms to the Established Church, marries Deborah Hunks, and at last succeeds to the business. When Deborah dies, he marries into the McTaaf family, much to the dismay of Monica and Mabel.

The Proudforts belong to the handful of grandee families who con-

[13] See James Hardiman, *History of the Town and County of Galway*. There is an excellent modern work: M. D. Sullivan: *Old Galway: The History of a Norman Colony in Ireland*.

trol the country through Parliament, and under their patronage he becomes a powerful and corrupt politician. At the O'Brien House, in Dublin, he lives the violent, high-colored existence of an Ascendancy gentleman—a reckless duelist, a patron of the arts, a heavy drinker.

In Connemara he has earned the contempt not only of the remaining Catholic gentry, but of the old and honorable Protestant families. "It was yourself, Terry O'Brien," Monica McTaaf tells him, "that had the plunder of it and us, when you had the run of Bog Moy House, as the chartered school apprentice of the Hunks. And a poor creature you were, with scarce a screed to your back, though you ride in your chay now; and you were glad to truck the Brigadier's old black camblet coat for ten masses for your mother's soul, to poor Father Blake, for all your going to church on Sundays, like any kiln-dried Protestant." (*Ibid.*, I, 60) The peasants, of course, though they dare only to remark wryly that "O'Brien was a pretty name to open a pew door," have even stronger opinions.

And yet all feel a sullen, unwilling pride on those Sunday mornings when *Terneen na garlach,* now become the great Lord Arranmore, drives to the cathedral porch with the arms and supporters of the O'Briens blazoned on his coach, and his "boy" decked out in crimson livery. The "old race" is ended. Terry's legitimate brother had gone to the continent as a "poor scholar." The true O'Brien, by right of blood, is Shane na Beirne, an illiterate wood-kern, pillaging by night, and running errands by day. The O'Flahertys, for all their grand living in France, are now only names told by the fire. Of the McTaafs two spinsters remain, keeping alive the memory of "the Brigadier" —who, as we discover, was a decent enough person, but little more than a garrulous drunkard. And so the powerful Terence O'Brien has become both the special shame and the sole pride of his countrymen.

But, though none suspect it, these conflicting passions have ravaged O'Brien himself. Beneath the lawyer's audacity and the imperturbable bravery of the Ascendancy duelist still lives little Terneen who hid shuddering behind rocks while the militia tramped the hills searching for Mass caves. Abbé Flaherty, a shrewd judge of men, suspects that O'Brien still thinks of himself as a Catholic.

> Always ready to risk his life upon a point of personal or national honor . . . yet he shrinks from legal infliction, however remotely threatened, and is ready to prostrate his opinion to any constituted authority, from a king to a constable. Courting the notice of the great, even in the party he hates, he enjoys himself only in the intimate familiarity of the lowly and oppressed. Secretly attached to the national party, without one popular feeling, or one constitutional idea, he is ready to restore, but unwilling to reform. With thoughts ever restrospective to the glories of "ancient ould Ireland," with its green banners, and harps, and collars of gold—and with that religious tendency to passive obedience with which we Catholics are accused, he is a rebel and a royalist on the same principle.   (*Ibid.*, I, 51-2)

Restoration of the "ould Ireland" takes the form of preparing cases for the expropriated Catholic families upon which they can base law suits for restoration. Anyone who has ever looked at such a document of the period is likely to be delighted by Flaherty's description: "He brings up evidences, as Hecate calls up spirits, and marshals a dozen of Irish kings in sad array, to scare the wits of Scotch adventurers, and extinguish the claims of Protestant discoverers: giving to his causes a sort of bardic interest, and making his gifts the very poetry of litigation." (*Ibid.*, I, 52) But Flaherty has been too long from home: he has forgotten what deep springs of will and passion are masked by notions apparently grotesque.

Years pass, and the surface of life remains, seemingly, unruffled. O'Brien's lawsuits, save for that brought on behalf of the O'Flahertys, wither away. The O'Flahertys, once restored, take no firm rooting in the land. Dublin, far east of Iar Connaught, creates its own glittering bog. It struggles to a hard, painful birth under Grattan, then falls again. The engineer of the downfall is O'Brien, resourceful, harsh and venal—the chief bully of Dublin Castle.

But the poles of his mind are moving farther and farther apart. Each night he leaves the serene Augustan world of College Green and the Four Courts, and rides in his darkened coach through the polluted, verminous streets of the city to O'Brien House, the somber mansion set up centuries before by the renegade Murrough of the Burnings.

There he begins work on the plans which obsess him. These center on his son Murrough, who bears a king's name, and in whose veins flows the blood of the tribal families. He has, in fact, gone mad, and has drawn about him men equally fanatic.

Their design is to preach a holy war against heresy, seize the country while England is occupied with the war against revolutionary France, kill or drive out the Protestant families, and restore the old ways and families. The plan itself is less wild than its promulgators. O'Brien detests the "patriots" of the Protestant Nation and the rebels of United Ireland as much as the Ascendancy of the Castle. He knows also that the fine rhetoric of the rebel leaders kindles no flames in the fierce wood-kerns and mountain men upon whom their rebellion will depend. Half-peasant himself, he knows their ways, and knows that their deepest sentiments of nationhood are linked with religious frenzy. Beyond his passion for revenge his thoughts cannot take him. In this, as in much else, he resembles Scott's "Redgauntlet," though he is more powerfully conceived.

Young Murrough, educated openly at Trinity and secretly by Jesuits, is to play the heroic role which his father had shunned. But Murrough has been trained in an age which offers other kinds of heroic opportunity.

Knowing nothing of modern Ireland, but her sufferings and her wrongs; knowing little of ancient Ireland, but her fables and her dreams, his mind had been stored with popular and poetical fallacies relative to all that concerned her in his father's prejudices and sentiments, while he had stood opposed to him in his political and religious opinions—he was, on many points, as visionary and fanciful.   (*Ibid.*, I, 280)

Feeling nothing of his father's shame and hatred, he moves honorably and with aplomb through the Ascendancy world. His patriotic feelings attach themselves easily and naturally to Grattan's party of moderate liberalism, but when this is crushed he turns to the conspiracy of rebellion which the chivalrous Lord Edward Fitzgerald heads. Fitzgerald (or rather, as he is called in the novel, Fitzwalter) shares many of Murrough's feelings. Both come of noble families of the old order who had "crossed over" to the new. Both combine, in the puzzling fashion which characterized the United Irishmen, aristocratic and radical sentiments.

Lady Morgan's is one of the earliest portraits of Lord Edward, and remains one of the best, for she was able to draw on the recollections of Cloncurry and Hamilton Rowan. Impulsive, high-spirited, generous, and melodramatic, suicidally trustful of informers, he responds enthusiastically to snatches of Latin orations, noble sentiments, and the cunning artifices which are bred by secret societies.

Murrough is given pause, however, by the striking similarity between Fitzwalter's brand of idealism and ruthlessness, and that of his father. He remarks on this to Fitzwalter, who eagerly accepts the comparison:

Suppose such a society *did* exist in embryo; as yet but feeling its way to the talent and liberality of the Irish heart; and therefore assuming for the present the secrecy and caution which is unhappily sometimes more necessary for the promotion of good than evil. Suppose such a society found it necessary to observe a discretion bordering on mystery, a secrecy which renders the bond of union more cohesive, its spirit more ardent; for in all human associations, the weakness of humanity must be taken into account, and the imagination enlisted on the side of reason. The lever by which this inert mass is to be moved, is one of infinite delicacy. Its springs must be secret, for they are of no vulgar mechanism.   (*Ibid.,* II, 43)

In the dark, drafty library of O'Brien House the O'Brien shield is surmounted by a crown. It suggests the importance of the choices which have been thrust upon Murrough. Grattan's parliamentary struggle, rigorously honest, is hopeless. Of the two conspiracies, his father's and Fitzwalter's, the latter seems infinitely preferable, yet tainted with the same corruption. Unable to choose, Murrough drifts helplessly. In the end it does not matter, for the government, moving with slothful brutality, crushes them all. And Murrough, compromised yet uncommitted, is forced to flee the country, as other Irishmen had fled a century before. And, like those, he rises to a high rank which seems to him meaningless and futile. We last see him as one of Bonaparte's generals, sitting quietly in a theatre box as Haydn's *Creation* is performed.

The gossiping of the town of St. Grellan had exaggerated circumstances, till, to the heated imaginations of its visionary inhabitants, they appeared a fulfillment of the old prophecy, predicted in the old times, of the inseparable connection between the destinies of the O'Briens and the O'Flahertys.

(*Ibid.*, II, 365)

The reader of this remarkable novel is likely to be put off by what seems to be the priggish rectitude of the hero. It is as though he makes demands of purity in ambition and idea which political life cannot sustain. Unpleasant alternatives, after all, do not absolve men of the responsibility of choice. And certainly the novel is so organized as to permit Murrough to decide that all political parties, all loyalties, are canceled out. Yet the character of Murrough gives the novel its center, and makes clear the degree to which choices in Ireland were rendered fatal.

To act at all meant to act "agin" the government, which had at its disposal sufficient force, moral as well as physical, to shatter any opposition. Moderation and fanaticism were equally futile. Fitzwalter, who seems not only to represent Fitzgerald but to prophesy Emmet, Thomas Meagher, John Mitchel, Roger Casement, speaks scornfully of "sentimental whiggery and poetical democracy." But Fitzwalter's politics are themselves only one kind of poetry, as O'Brien's are another. And Lady Morgan's a third. For in Murrough she has drawn her own portrait, caught as she was between her bright, secular Whiggishness and her hankering after a glamorous and immemorial past, her not unworthy desire for an Ireland which could somehow quarter the arms of O'Brien and O'Flaherty, Geraldine and McTaaf, O'Donnel and Mirabeau.

It was in March of 1826 that Lady Morgan noted down her contemptuous opinion of O'Connell. That summer the Beresford family, upon whom she had based the "Proudforts," were routed by his "army of beggars" in the Waterford election. Two years later, after a still more decisive victory in Clare, he was able to growl ominously, "They must either crush us or conciliate us." In April of 1829 George IV, quite literally writhing in impotent fury, gave his consent to the Catholic Relief Bill. The cause to which Lady Morgan had lent both her pen and her parlor for so many years, the cause which would mark the first step in the national revival, had been won.

And not merely won. The victory was to be so decisive as to determine the course of nineteenth-century Ireland. Yet the working out had not been at all as Lady Morgan planned it. O'Connell had caught up the peasantry into an enormous fist which he smashed against the gates of the Ascendancy. Now this *nisi prius* talent was preparing to wage a fight for the repeal of the Union and the mastery of Ireland, with a million peasants and the Maynooth priests at his back.

It became quickly and painfully clear that O'Connell was no more to be bought off by Lady Morgan's Whigs than by Peel's Tories. "This was to be Lord Anglesea's day of triumph," she notes mournfully in 1830. "What an apotheosis! O'Connell has organized all that is false, bad, and ungrateful against him. . . . Ireland now seems organized for revolution." [14]

During the 1830s she made a brave attempt to maintain her position as Dublin's "liberal and patriotic" hostess. She still "received" on Sundays at Kildare Street, wearing a "red Celtic cloak, formed exactly on the plan of Grannuaille's, fastened with a rich gold fibula or Tara brooch." [15] The battered and compromised members of United Ireland were much in attendance, the devious Cloncurry and the chivalrous Hamilton Rowan. But also Samuel Lover, the artist and Dublin wit, in whose imagination capered Handy Andy, the lovable, harmless stage Irishman of the jaunting car and shillelagh. And the fantastic, tight-corseted Maturin, who achieved fame with *Melmoth,* but who had begun his career with *The Wild Irish Boy,* an absurd imitation of Lady Morgan herself.[16]

But outside the windows of Kildare Street O'Connell stormed and abused, went to prison, sent his voice across the hills to the waiting peasants, made alliances and broke them.

[14] *Memoirs,* II, 313–14.

[15] Quoted in Lionel Stevenson, *The Wild Irish Girl: The Life of Sydney Owenson, Lady Morgan,* p. 295.

[16] For his relationship with Lady Morgan, see Nilo Idman, *Charles Robert Maturin.*

On Christmas Eve, 1833, she reflected solemnly, "I must register an odd thought. The Irish destiny is between Bedlam and a Jail; but I won't pursue it." [17] In May of 1837 Melbourne recognized her services to the Whig cause by granting her a pension, and within months the Morgans had packed up and left Ireland forever. In the privacy of her diary she bade her countrymen a waspish farewell.

You have always slighted, and often persecuted me, yet I worked in your cause, humbly, but earnestly. Catholic Emancipation is carried! It was an indispensable act—of what results, you fickle Irish will prove in the end. To predicate would be presumptuous, even in those who know you best. Creatures of temperament and temper, true Celts, as Caesar found your race in Gaul, and as I leave you, after a lapse of two thousand years.[18]

Remembering her triumphs in London thirty years before, she set up a salon. But another Irishwoman was reigning now in literary circles—the young and bewitching Countess of Blessington. And so Lady Morgan spent the last decades of her life in semiobscurity, remembered by a few as the Wild Irish Girl from Tireragh, who had appeared for a brief season with a harp and a legend.

Of Irish matters her diary records only bewilderment and disappointments—and the deaths of friends and enemies, all of whom she managed to survive. In time the Tories made their peace with her, though its terms were stated by the mordant Maginn: "Prate away then, good miladi, gossip, gossip, bore and bore—all for him who to the grave has gone of years a score—for the sake of old MacOwen and his song of Modereen Roo—for your father's sake we are going never more to bother you." [19]

O'Connell received his final check on the plain of Clontarf in 1843, a year in which Wellington was in a crushing rather than a conciliatory mood. He died in Italy, where his heart was preserved in an urn at the Irish College in Rome. Leadership of the national movement passed to Young Ireland, whose ideology owed more than it cared to recognize to the formulation given by Lady Morgan to "patriotic sentiment."

[17] Lady Morgan, *Memoirs*, II, 379.   [18] *Ibid.*, II, 427.
[19] Quoted in Stevenson, *The Wild Irish Girl*, p. 295.

Lady Morgan died on the sixteenth of April, 1859. By the provisions of her will a bas-relief was erected in Saint Patrick's, bearing the image of Turlough O'Carolan, the old blind harper and poet whose memory her father had both revered and travestied.

In the late summer of 1843, as the English papers were reporting, in unwonted detail, the dramatic events leading up to Clontarf, Lady Morgan's eye had fallen upon a brief story which had been crowded to a back page. The O'Conor Don, that gentle, unworldly country-man who had endured with quiet amusement the cries of extremists that he was the rightful king of Ireland, had died. And the story had prompted in Lady Morgan a memory of her youth, when she had seen the crown of Ireland, or what purported to be the crown of Ireland, on display in a jeweler's window.[20]

[20] Lady Morgan, *Memoirs,* II, 493.

John Banim

11. Irish Peasants and English Readers

ALTHOUGH, IN DEFERENCE to his talents, Dublin readily forgave the fact, it did not forget that Thomas Moore had been born in the rooms above the grocery and wine shop which his father kept in Aungier Street. For Moore came from the rising class of Irish Catholic tradesmen, whose status in the early decades of the nineteenth century was a singularly unenviable one. And from a still humbler walk of life came Ireland's first Catholic novelists, John and Michael Banim.

It was a group ridiculed by the Ascendancy and deplored by the old Catholic gentry. Lacking the recusant traditions of the landed families, lacking blood lines and French counts and colonels, its members hungered for respectability. Because they also lacked the hereditary timorousness of the Kenmares and the Fingalls, they were able to play a more manly role in the struggle for Emancipation. During the eighteenth century it had been the Ascendancy boast that a Catholic in Dublin could be recognized at once by his shuffling gait and apologetic manner. O'Connell, and John Keogh before him, changed that. But the mantle of reform sat uneasily on many of the O'Connellites. Indeed, *The Nation* was to maintain that Emancipation had exhausted most of their political and intellectual energies. Theirs was a class painfully emerging from the shadows of Penal Days, still bearing the marks of servitude, and puzzled as to their role in a country where the institutions of government and the sources of social prestige rested securely with those who differed from them in points of creed and racial origin.

John Banim, once grandiloquently hailed as "the Scott of Ireland," was born on the third of April in the fateful year of 1798. His father, Michael, "united business and pleasure, pushing his way into the world as a trader in all the necessities of a sportsman's and angler's outfit. . . . He was a farmer, too, and kept a pair of well-bred horses."[1] Moore tells us, more succinctly, that the elder Banim kept "a little powder and shot shop" in the town of Kilkenny.[2] Banim intended that his sons, John and Michael (who was two years older), should be trained for the learned professions, but his ambitions overreached themselves, and Michael was forced to join him in the shop. John, however, thanks to his brother's sacrifice, was able to study first at Kilkenny College and then at the Royal Dublin Academy.

Kilkenny is one of the best preserved of the Irish counties. For the most part it had been not only within the Pale, but under the powerful protection of the Ormondes, whose castle still dominates the landscape. Across the Nore stood the Protestant College of Saint John, founded in the sixteenth century and reendowed in 1689. In the nineteenth century, it was "the most famous as well as the most ancient preparatory school in Ireland."[3] Swift, Congreve, Berkeley, Farquahar —hardly an Anglo-Irish writer of the Augustan age had not attended it. And John Banim was proud that his name, too, was entered on its rolls. It was a close thing, because in 1819 the redoubtable Doyle, "J. K. L.", succeeded Corcoran as the Catholic Bishop of Kildare and Leighlin, and Doyle took a very bleak view of mixed education.

Whenever John Banim wanted to suggest that a hero, of either faith, was a gentleman born and bred—Pierce Shea in *Crohoore of the Billhook* or Tresham in *The Fetches*—he established him as a graduate of Kilkenny College. Whatever may have been their sectarian pride or their hope for the future, it seemed patent to Catholics of the period that the instruments by which gentility was conferred were in the keeping of the Protestant Ascendancy. Only the very wealthy, such as the O'Connells of Derrynane, had been able to send their sons to Saint Omer or Douai, and the French Revolution had made

[1] Patrick Joseph Murray, *The Life of John Banim, the Irish Novelist . . . with Extracts from His Correspondence*, p. 103.
[2] Thomas Moore, *Memoirs, Journals, and Correspondence*, VI, 136.
[3] Introduction to John Banim's *The Fetches*.

even this impossible. But the O'Connells, connected in countless ways with the world of continental Catholicism, belonged to the eighteenth century. The Banims grew up in a much more provincial country.

There was much agrarian unrest in Kilkenny. By 1823 White Boy activities, shortly to be diverted to the Emancipation agitation, had reached the proportions of guerilla warfare. But the county had earned itself a reputation as "the Versailles of Ireland," thanks largely to the lavish way of life which the Ormondes maintained. A theater had been built at Kilkenny Castle by no less a person than Robert Owenson, and private dramatics were a seasonal event. Young Banim managed an invitation to one of these, and his literary ambitions were kindled, for it happened to be the occasion on which Thomas Moore delivered his tedious *Meleologue on National Music.*

Early in 1820 he left home for Dublin, intent upon a career. With him he brought an uncompleted poem, which he persuaded Charles Phillips to read. Phillips sent it on to Sir Walter Scott, who professed to find "much beauty of language, with a considerable command of numbers and meters," and with this recommendation, the poem was published the following year as *The Celt's Paradise.* Its material and form are familiar, a dialogue between Saint Patrick and Ossian in which the Christian and pagan positions are argued out. Imitations of the Gaelic of this sort had been popular since Charlotte Brooke first published her specimens, and it cannot be said that Banim's version, despite Sir Walter, is at all exceptional.

In the meantime a friendship had ripened between Banim and Richard Lalor Sheil. Sheil, too, came from the Kilkenny trading class, but was several cuts higher in the social scale. His father, having made a tidy fortune in Spain, had returned to Ireland and bought out a Cromwellian landlord. Sheil himself had been educated in England, at the college for Catholic gentry which the Jesuits had begun at Stonyhurst. The specialty of the first Jesuit schools in both Ireland and England seems to have been training in ornate rhetoric and social pretentiousness. Sheil was a prize scholar.

A frail, fiery young man with a very good opinion of himself, he took particular pride in his "eloquence," a gift much cherished by his countrymen. He discovered upon his return home that the Catholic Board was split on the Veto problem, and at once chose the side of the conservative landlords and hierarchy, with that unerring instinct which would carry him, in his old age, to a colonial judgeship. Unfortunately he chose to first display his talents by launching a wicked speech against O'Connell. He discovered, as many others would, that O'Connell could crush talented young men with one careless paw. When Banim met him, he was pondering this lesson, and would shortly emerge as an O'Connell lieutenant.

Sheil now became Banim's mentor, and encouraged him to write a very dull tragedy, *Damon and Pythias,* which was produced in 1821, with Macready and Kemble in the leading roles. The friendship was to prove Banim's only brush with the world of active politics, but it is a significant one. Both had received an education of a more worldly sort than obtained among most Irishmen of their station, and both looked for an English as well as an Irish reputation.

The Celt's Paradise enjoyed a critical success, and *Damon and Pythias* a financial one. On the strength of these Banim married and set off with his bride for London. His hopes were pinned on that most sterile of nineteenth-century ambitions, classical verse tragedy. Instead he found himself living precariously as an assistant at the English Opera House and writing copiously for the annuals and the popular magazines. Fortunately for him, his hack journalism brought him into contact with the scapegrace but comradely gang of Irish literary freebooters whom Thackeray hits off so remorselessly.

In the months before he left Kilkenny he had discussed with his brother Michael a vaguely held notion of turning his knowledge of Ireland to account. Patrick Murray tells us that from the first he had the idea of acting as an interpreter of Ireland to England, but this puts his missionary instinct too high. Most of the Irish writers in London during the 1820s hit, sooner or later, on the fact that they possessed inimitable and very salable material.

These writers—Maginn, Croly, Mahony, Crofton Croker, John Wilson Croker bear the most familiar names—were unexpected and fairly unwelcome benefits accruing to England from the Union. Insofar as they wrote and acted from principle, they were incarnations of the post-Union Ascendancy, Tory in politics and alienated in every sense from either country. William Maginn, who set the tone, is unrepresentative only by virtue of the breadth and virtuosity of his talents.

A few years later another and much better Irish novelist than Banim would write home, after meeting Maginn: "A young man about twenty-six years of age, with grey hair, and one of the most talented eyes, when he lets it speak out, I ever beheld. Banim, who is his bosom crony, considers him the most extraordinary man he ever knew."[4] But Gerald Griffin, who had a talented eye himself, and who moved through London like an Indian scouting hostile territory, became quickly aware of Maginn's limitations. Brilliant and reckless, as generous as he was improvident, Maginn had carried with him to England a hatred of Ireland which might not have been unwarranted, but which found venomous ways of expressing itself. He incorporated his own "Hibernian charm" into his role as a literary adventurer, using it to excuse the multifarious varieties of his irresponsibility. The very fact of swarms of Irish free lances descending upon London in a kind of retaliation for the Invasion touched his highly developed sense of the ridiculous.

But he was aware that Ireland, if served up with the proper sauces, made excellent copy for the English market. His own efforts have been collected in *The O'Dogherty Papers*.[5] But he urged Irishmen of every persuasion to write up the strange doings and sayings of their island, and the pages of the magazines which he edited with such attentive nepotism were always open to their work. Sheil had passed young Banim on to a second mentor, almost as shrewd as the first.

In the years 1825 and 1826 four books appeared on the London market which shaped, in important ways, the nineteenth-century image of Ireland. It is a mark of Maginn's hitherto unnoticed influence that each of the four was either begun at his suggestion or completed with his encouragement. It is a mark of the changing times that each

---

[4] Gerald Griffin, quoted in Daniel Griffin, *Life of Gerald Griffin, Esq.*, p. 181.
[5] Volumes I and II of William Maginn, *Miscellanies: Prose and Verse*.

is directly concerned with the peasantry. They were: *Tales of the O'Hara Family,* which John Banim wrote with the collaboration of his brother Michael; *Today in Ireland,* by Eyre Evans Crowe; *Fairy Legends and Traditions of the South of Ireland,* by Crofton Croker; *Tales of the Munster Festivals,* by Gerald Griffin.

The Irish peasantry was astir in the year 1825, and the noise had reached a puzzled England. Early in the year select committees of both houses of Parliament were given the unenviable duty of inquiring into "the state of Ireland," a task which would preempt much legislative energy for a century to come. The immediate issue was the Catholic Association, which had taken on all the aspects of a dangerous mass movement. There appeared at the hearings, however, an endless procession of magistrates, ministers, priests, police officers, tithe proctors, and judges whose testimony presented, in the aggregate, a bewildering picture of an island where law and order in the English sense could hardly be said to have existed.

O'Connell, Sheil, Bishop Doyle, and a surprising number of conscientious magistrates argued impressively that agrarian crime and secret terrorist societies among the peasants were the inevitable consequences of the harsh and inhuman methods used by landlords to ensure their profits.[6] But the crime and the terror themselves held for English listeners an appalled fascination which explanations as to cause scarcely appeased. The Irish peasant seemed to belong to some other and abominable branch of the human family.

Prophecy-men were walking the roads of Ireland, selling chapbooks which proclaimed that "Twenty-five is the year." Beggars were on the roads in their tens of thousands, families thrown out upon the world by clearings and evictions. In the valley of the Black Pig in Ulster not a farm remained standing. Every peasant knew what that meant: the deliverer of Ireland was at hand. It might be O'Connell, who had made his boast that he could drive a coach-and-six through any English law. It might be a huge, red-haired miller with two thumbs on his right hand: several people had seen him. A man went to a fair to sell a horse and was led into a *rath* where armed men of another age lay sleeping. One of them awoke and, drawing his sword,

[6] *Account of the Select Committee . . . ,* London, 1826.

asked, "Is the time in it? Is the time arrived?" The time was Twenty-five, marked down in the prophecies of Columkill and Pastorini.

The time had at least arrived for Crofton Croker's *Fairy Legends*. Croker was an amateur antiquarian and folklorist, brilliant, resourceful, and imaginative. For ten years he had been roaming the south of Ireland, talking to peasants and taking down what they said. As Charlotte Brooke had learned from the peasants the remembered poems and heroic legends, so had Croker gone to gather magic of another kind and to suggest in another fashion the highly poetic imagination of the most brutalized peasantry in Europe.

His method was to center each chapter on a tale more or less contemporary—a peasant who dreams a dream, a *spalpeen* who meets a fairy on the road. Often these are poor stuff. But he loaded each chapter with a heavy freight of notes, and these are fascinating. Everything went into them—the remarks of a Tipperary farmer, the account of a murder trial, bits of local history, odd superstitions, the personal prejudices of Crofton Croker.

Croker knew what he was about. Both Douglas Hyde and Yeats were to complain that Croker and his followers warped their material to suit the English market. They might have added that he was virtually a travel agent, puffing the legendary charms of the Killarney lakes, and thus helping to create the dreary tourist trade which still flourishes. But Croker also knew that the great age of folklore study had arrived, and that he had stories which had never before been told.

He had tapped the inexhaustible vein of Irish lore. In his pages appear for the first time, save in the chapbooks of peddlers, tales and creatures that seem always to have been with us—the banshee, the leprechaun, the cluricaune, the magic land of Thierna-na-oge. These appeared overnight, summoned from their Hibernian mists, before the delighted eyes of Europe, and won the excited admiration of Scott and Grimm. Within a year Grimm was comparing the measurements of the leprechaun with those of various sprites in Holland, Lower Brittany, and the Servian Vilieu.[7]

Croker shared the Tory and Orange sympathies of his unlovely

[7] *Fairy Legends* (1888 edition), p. x.

kinsman and namesake, Lady Morgan's *bête noire*. Yeats, writing
of Crofton Croker and Samuel Lover, has said: "The impulse of the
Irish literature of their time came from a class that did not—mainly
for political reasons—take the people seriously, and imagined the
country as a humorist's Arcadia; its passion, its gloom, its tragedy,
they knew nothing of. What they did was not wholly false; they merely
magnified an irresponsible type, found oftenest among boatmen, car-
men, and gentlemen's servants, into the type of a whole nation, and
created the Stage Irishman." [8]

The charge is substantially just. Poverty, disaster, and dirt were
picturesque settings for Croker. At best he sighs wistfully that these
charming and imaginative people seem chained by sloth, ignorance,
and superstition. And yet in many ways Croker knew Ireland more
intimately than Yeats did. He was lacking less in political virtue than
in the imaginative power necessary to bridge the enormous gulf which
separated Irish peasants from the other social classes.

Eyre Crowe, the author of *Today in Ireland,* was also a Tory, but
a humane and thoughtful one, and a merciless critic of the Ascendancy.
And yet he could see only a dark, murderous land of Ribbonmen and
secret societies, blood, and senseless violence. He communicated these
dark revelations through his novels and through a series of influential
articles for *Blackwood's*. Other writers came forward to show English
readers the Irish peasant "as he really was." In the circumstances
such works were implicitly polemical, for they were written to influence policy toward Ireland.

Against this background Banim's novels were, almost avowedly,
counter-propaganda. "Banim resolved," Patrick Murray says, "to raise
the national character in the estimation of other lands, by a portrayal
of the people as they really were, but at the same time to vindicate
them from the charges of violence and bloodthirstiness, by showing,
in the course of the fiction, the various causes which he supposed concurred to draw forth and foster these evil qualities." [9]

[8] From the Introduction by William Butler Yeats to his *Fairy and Folk Tales
of the Irish Peasantry.*
[9] Murray, *The Life of John Banim,* p. 102.

This is the kind of laudable ambition which, by the operation of inexorable law, produces poor fiction. Banim's career as a writer lasted only some six years, for he was stricken while still young with a fatal and immediately incapacitating illness. Because they were the years in which many grave political issues were at stake, his work tends more toward "vindication" than toward a representation of Irish life "as it really was." Judged on this ground, he was successful. He was a kind and eminently fair-minded man, and was welcomed in England as an honorable champion of Catholic claims and as an interpreter of the Irish peasant. But his natural endowment as a writer was slender as compared with that of either Gerald Griffin or William Carleton, his brilliant contemporaries.

Banim's novels appeared under the pseudonym of "The O'Hara Family," and he had envisioned a series of tales, for which he would write the more serious stories and his brother Michael the "filling." But Michael was neither a well-educated nor an ambitious writer. The controlling genius was always John's; he wrote most of the important novels and made extensive revisions of Michael's contributions. For this reason it seems sensible to depart from the usual practice of referring to "the Banim brothers." [10]

Banim's work falls into two distinct categories, which it will be

[10] The publication history of the Banim novels is a somewhat complicated one, and may most usefully be set forth in the convenience of a single footnote:

Tales of the O'Hara Family (first series), 3 vols., London, was published in 1825. It includes: *Crohoore of the Billhook, The Fetches,* and *John Doe: or, Peep o' Day.* These stories were republished with additional notes by Michael Banim in 1865, under the general title of *Peep o' Day.* Page references are to the New York edition of 1896.

The Boyne Water, 3 vols., London, 1826. Page references are to the single-volume New York edition of 1880.

The Last Baron of Crana and *The Conformists* were published together under the general title of *The Denounced,* 3 vols., London, 1830. Page references are to this first edition.

Tales of the O'Hara Family, second series, 3 vols., London, 1827. Contains *The Nowlans* and *Canvassing.*

The Croppy, 3 vols., London, appeared in 1828. Page references are to the two-volume Philadelphia edition of 1839. The novels written by Michael Banim after the death of his brother in 1842 need not concern us. Of the novels which we will be considering in this chapter and the one following, Michael collaborated on *Crohoore* and *The Croppy.*

convenient to place in separate chapters. He wrote stories of peasant life and he wrote historical novels. The differences between the two in tone, atmosphere, and attitude are great, but they are linked by a common intention: "the formation of a good and affectionate feeling between England and Ireland." It was an admirable purpose, but he was convinced that whatever did not serve it had to be pruned away, for he believed that affection and strangeness could not exist together. The profound differences between the cultures had to be minimized, the bitterness and the estrangements rationalized. He was determined to remain above the self-lacerating pity with which Ireland called the attention of the world to its miseries, but the determination exacted its price. Only by accident does the pen of the O'Hara Family leap beyond its intention to create surely and powerfully. The most vivid instances of this are *Crohoore of the Billhook* and *The Nowlans*.

Crohoore is the story of eighteenth-century life as it was experienced by the Catholic peasants and strong farmers. From its opening pages we are in a world for which neither the novels of Maria Edgeworth nor those of Lady Morgan have prepared us—the secret, strangely self-sufficient Gaelic world. We are gathered around the turf fire of the Dooling family—Tony, his wife, and his laborers are seated on benches; beyond them the servant girls squat on their haunches. It is a cheerful, even a comfortable, house, yet disturbing because it does not have the indrawn and sequestered privacy to which English novels have accustomed us. Muldowny the piper comes in to gossip and hug the fire. Paudge Dermody, the local wit, wanders in as a matter of course. Old women "begging their way" come and go. The house is open to the country, and no store whatever is set by privacy.

But one of Dooling's workmen, Crohoore, sits apart from the others, breaking the cozy, inglenook atmosphere:

His cheeks were pale, hollow, and retiring; his nose, of the old Milesian mold, long, broad-backed and hooked; his jaws, coming unusually forward, caused his teeth to start from his face; and his lips, that, without much effort, never closed over those disagreeable teeth, were large, fleshless and bloodless, the upper one wearing, in common with his chin, a red beard, just changed from the down of youth to the bristliness of manhood, and, as yet, unshaven. These features, all large to disproportion, conveyed, along with the unpleasantness deformity inspires, the expression of a bold and decided character, and something else besides, which was malignity or mystery, according to the observation or mood of an observer.

(Crohoore, pp. 10–11)

Crohoore, leaning forward to catch the light from the fire, is slowly and lovingly whetting a pike blade to razor sharpness. The noise grates against the melody of Muldowny's pipes.

In the morning Dooling and his wife are found hacked to death, and Crohoore has fled with their daughter Ally. Pierce Shea, her lover, sets out in pursuit, and the reader is plunged into a world of almost incredible violence. Highwaymen, White Boys, and Ribbonmen lie in wait in the hills and glens beyond the farm land. Gallants seize women and force them, weeks later, into tardy marriages. Orange gunmen open fire on peasants huddled in a cave to hear Mass. The garrison of soldiers is in the county to protect property, not life. Mobs of peasants are liable at any moment to hurl themselves against their muskets.

The peasants have their own riah, or king, Jack Doran, a half-sir who has turned gunman. The point on which the plot turns is that Doran's men have murdered the Doolings; Crohoore has taken Ally away for safekeeping. But this is only a device; the substance of the story lies elsewhere. It begins with the simple fact that neither Crohoore nor any of the peasants loyal to the Doolings consider for a moment turning to the law for protection. Nor does Pierce Shea, whose feelings we are to share, expect them to do so.

There are two reasons for this. Doran is playing his own hand, but he is also a White Boy captain, and the peasants are banded together in a war of terror against proctors and bailiffs. Doran is the only man of sufficient education and training to act as their leader. Yet, even if this were not so, none save informers would cooperate with the law. No facts about Ireland unearthed by the various select committees so shocked the English public as these: that large numbers of the peasants periodically banded together to enforce a rough justice through

terror and that the population as a whole passively condoned such activities.

There is a scene in *Peep o' Day* which is startling precisely because
Banim presents it so casually. A young English officer is set upon by a
footpad in a lonely glen. A farmer named Kavanagh rescues him and
kills his assailant. Then he rifles the dead man's pocket, picks up the
body, and tumbles it into the lake. The dead are best sunk under
water and forgotten. The ablest of Ireland's social critics, from Gustave
de Beaumont to George Cornewall Lewis, took great pains, as Banim
does, to place the Irish peasant's hatred of the law in historical perspective.[11] But Banim was under a special burden, that of making
such a world believable as fiction.

It was a problem which he was never able to solve. *Crohoore,* that
"dark and terrible" story, as Stephen Brown calls it,[12] is founded on
fact, and yet one instinctively rejects it as being lurid beyond belief.
He was faced with the task of writing about a bloody and violent
land, in which justice was measured out by hanging judges and
packed juries, and exacted by the loaded whips of squireens and the
brandings and mutilations of secret societies. But there no longer
existed in English fiction conventions by which such a society could
be represented. In default, he accepted the conventions of the shilling
shocker.

The central scene in *Crohoore,* and the one which is most vividly
represented, describes the torture and mutilation of a tithe proctor.
Doran's men meet to plot the crime in a mud cabin, where they are
roused to fury by one of the hedge schoolmasters who acted as the
ideologists of the White Boy movement:

I say once again, that you're not like a son of green Ireland, the crature,
doin' as much as you can, an' sorry in your heart you can't do more, against
the rievin', plunderin', murtherin' raparees o' tithe proctors, the bitther
foes of ould Ireland's land—slingein' at home, because the blow doesn't
strike hard on yourself, an' never heedin' the moans o' the poor neighbors,

---

[11] Gustave de Beaumont, *Ireland: Social, Political and Religious* (2 vols., London, 1839); George Cornewall Lewis, *On Local Disturbances in Ireland* (London,
1836).
[12] *Ireland in Fiction,* p. 20.

that are left to starve, or rot like old horses in the ditches, because the Sassanach clargy, that doesn't care a crooked straw for them or theirs, must have grand houses to live in, brave horses to hunt, coaches to take their pleasure in, an' costly fastes, where there's the mate of all kinds, every day in the year, Fridays an' all, an' wine galore to drink. . . . Hasn't the Sassanach clargy, I say, all Ireland to itself every tenth year? (*Crohoore,* p. 88)

Clancy, the proctor, is routed out of his bed and dragged through the village, as the children shout their consent, and the women peer approvingly from the doorways. A hedge poet accompanies the expedition so that it may fittingly be commemorated, and a fiddler and a piper improve the occasion. Clancy is buried to his neck beside a ditch, then Yemen O'Nase, "the finisher of the law," whets his pruning knife and sets about his task:

Well, we're all ready; an' it's a sweet bit of a blade that's in it, for one knife. Och, bud it's none of your blades that's fir nothin' but cuttin' butther. I gi' you my conscience, this holy an' blessed night, 'twould take the horns of a ten year old bull, not to speak of a poor tithe proctor's ears, though them same does be hard enough in regard of all the prayers they won't hear, an' all the lies they tell. Come, come, none of your ochowns, Peery. Don't be the laste unasy in yourself, agra. You may be right sartin I'll do the thing nate and handy. Tut, man, I'd whip the ears of a bishop, not to talk of a crature like you, a darker night nor this. Divil a taste I'd lave him; and wouldn't bring back any o' the head wid me neither—musha, what ails you, at all? You've a better right to give God praise for gittin' in the hands of a clever boy like me, that—stop a bit, now—that'ud only do his captain's orders, and not be lettin' the steel slip from your ear across your wind-pipe— Lord save the hearers! Stop, I say! There, now; wasn't that done purty?

(*Ibid.,* p. 100)

In the speech of Yemen O'Nase and Mourteen the schoolmaster, we have for the first time the tang and vigor of peasant speech put to dramatic use. In Mourteen's case it is hedge oratory at its most incendiary, and yet the ghost of an old, debased culture lurks in its cadences. Measured against it, Pierce Shea is a lifeless stick of prim good will, and Riah Doran the ranting villain of a Surrey Theatre melodrama. It is essential to Banim's scheme that Shea should be wrongfully accused of being a White Boy, and that Doran should be a White Boy leader but also a cold, Machiavellian criminal. For Doran and Shea are "gentlemen," capable of either heroic and unbelievable virtue or Byronic villainy, but never of the full vigorous life which his peasants possess.

This is the central weakness in his fiction. In each of his novels there is a sharp division between the peasants and the "gentlemen"— as indeed there should be, since his culture imposed the division. But his peasants are created with swift and certain skill, while his gentlemen are mere cardboard figures. The saddening explanation is that he knew next to nothing about the latter class. The English ideal of the gentleman, as it was formulated in the nineteenth century, bore no correspondence to Irish life, yet for Banim it was the only available image.

In *Peep o' Day,* while commenting on the ghastly humor which characterized Irish violence, and on the gunmen who took part in outrages as though playing Tom Fools to a company of Christmas mummers, he says, "There is a mockery of the heart by the heart itself. . . ." (*Peep o' Day,* p. 26) In some measure Banim mocks himself, for too often he sees to the tragic heart of Irish experience, and then denies what he has seen in the interest of some conventional and trumpery plot.

This is particularly true of the way in which he has used the figure of Crohoore himself. Crohoore is "the aboriginal inhabitant of the island," the quintessence of the world which produced Yemen O'Nase and Peery Clancy and Mourteen. He is the dark, unknowable figure who sits in every cabin, whetting the pike on which the blood-red fire plays. He will reappear as Shane na Gow in *The Croppy,* and as Rory na Chopple in *The Boyne Water.* He is "malignity or mystery, according to the observation or mood of an observer." But we are asked to believe, before the story is done, that he is only a variety of the faithful retainer, serving in his own whimsical fashion the best interests of "the young master," Pierce Shea.

Mary Russell Mitford, having in mind the way in which his novels contrasted with those of Maria Edgeworth, accused Banim of having introduced into Irish fiction the lurid melodrama of Eugene Sue.[13]

[13] *Recollections of a Literary Life* . . . , I, 33.

The truth, rather, is that Banim was writing of a land so dark and bloody that Sue's methods would have been overly genteel.

When Thackeray was taking his leisurely and condescending journey through Ireland, he was held down by rain at Kilroy's Hotel in Galway. It was a mean and tedious town: from his window he could see an enclosure of gaunt iron railings, within which stood three gibbets. Upon close inspection, however, these proved to be mere machines for weighing potatoes. Thus marooned, Thackeray stretched out with his cigars and a selection of those penny romances which peddlers hawked throughout Ireland, and which formed part of the curriculum in many hedge schools. One of these, *The Adventures of Mister James Freney,* he describes wittily and at length. The story ends with a hanging upon the very real gallows which stood outside Kilkenny Courthouse. It is on this gallows that Riah Doran is hanged in *Crohoore of the Billhook.* The coincidence is worth our attention, for Freney was one of the two originals of Riah Doran.

The Adventures of Freney is the atrociously written account of an eighteenth-century highwayman, whose outrages are celebrated beneath a thin veil of unctuous moralizing. "The best part of worthy Freney's tale," Thackeray says, "is the noble naïveté and simplicity of the hero as he recounts his adventures, and the utter unconsciousness that he is narrating anything wonderful. It is the way of all great men. . . ." [14] His encounter with *Freney* prompted Thackeray to write *Barry Lyndon,* the literary joke in which he expresses his contempt for glorifications of the criminal à la Harrison Ainsworth. And yet he was not prompted to wonder, all through the rain-filled night in that town which so easily suggested prisons and gibbets, why the imagination of the Irish peasant reacted so strongly to the story of a cutthroat and ruffian.

In the same fashion he treats his readers to copious selections from a popular verse drama called *The Battle of Aughrim,* to the accompaniment of his unflagging and inimitable facetiousness. One point puzzles him: the play, which had become a kind of underground classic among Catholics, was "evidently by a Protestant author, a great

[14] *The Irish Sketch Book of 1842,* p. 163.

enemy of popery." [15] Had he sought an answer, he would have found that the author, the better to celebrate their eventual downfall, had painted Sarsfield and the other Irish officers in bold and mock-heroic colors. And for that pitiful reason the common people had come to cherish a work written in exultation at their downfall. A famous chapbook called *Irish Rogues and Raparees* served the same purpose. [16] But Thackeray did not trouble to seek an answer: he was off the next day for Connemara, where a glimpse into the Petty Sessions confirmed his opinion that the Irish were an innately barbarous and lawless race. "There is a mockery of the heart by the heart itself. . . ."

But the shadow of the Kilkenny gallows fell across John Banim's path each day as he walked to school. He had been taught to fish by old Tom Gwynn, the White Boy captain. His father had told him of how Kilkenny's Irishtown had turned out to see "Riah Doran" hanged. And he had heard the ballads about Freney, who was descended (so it was said, and perhaps said truly) from the Norman house of de la Frene. The country people had showed him the ruins of Inch House, which had been one of the great houses of the Ascendancy, and which Freney raided and looted. "Tom Gwynn," Michael Banim says, "laughing his assured laugh, for he loved a merry reminiscence, assured me that his experiences at clipping the ears of puppy dogs into a close resemblance to the ears of a fox, was acquired by the exercise of his shears on the obnoxious tithe gatherers." (*Peep o' Day*, p. 22, *n*.)

Between Thackeray in Kilroy's Hotel or at the Connemara Petty Sessions and the Banim brothers listening to Tom Gwynn on the banks of the Suir stretched the gulf which separates two profoundly different cultures. But John Banim wrote a great amount of bad fiction in an effort to persuade himself and his readers that the cultures were really not very different at all. When he forgot this noble intention he wrote well.

He is happily forgetful during most of the novel called *The Now-*

[15] *Ibid.*, p. 182.

[16] For a description of this hedge literature, see Patrick John Dowling, *The Hedge Schools of Ireland*, Chapter 8.

lans, a book which is remarkable for its realistic portrayal of Irish life. The scene is set in Tipperary, one of the "disturbed" counties, and the story opens and closes with talk of "O'Connell and of the wars to be expected in Ireland in the year '25, 'according to the prophecy.'" (*Nowlans,* I, 10) But the talk is only a nervous attempt on the part of the Nowlan family to forget for a moment that their son John is lying gravely ill. The illness is mental: John is a priest who had fallen in love and married. Now he has come home to die.

The Nowlans are strong farmers, fairly prosperous and socially conservative. Banim knew their world well—what their parlors looked like, what books a seminarian would read, how farmers and laborers addressed each other. And here, for once, he knew all the subtle divisions of caste and class. Daniel Nowlan, John's father, has married a "black protestan'." She has become a Catholic herself, more or less as a matter of form, and her evening prayers are a blend of piety and social chitchat: "An' I offer up a pattherin' avy for the sowl of my poor dear George Wilkins, of Ross Lodge, Esquire, now and forever, amin." (*Ibid.,* I, 38) His younger brothers have set themselves up in trade in Limerick; one is a saddler and the other a grocer.

But his older brother, Aby, aspires to gentility. He wears a blue coat, a canary waistcoat, and top boots, and longs for the friendship of Squire Adams, of "Mount Nelson, or some such ridiculous name conferred upon a bit of barren ground once called Killavochery, or Ballybrocklehin, or Coolavoorlich." (*Ibid.,* I, 47) In his imitative passion he has transformed himself into one of the heedless, hell-fire Ascendancy rakes. He keeps open house for the county families, staggers under an accumulation of mortgages, and has a veritable harem of peasant mistresses. He takes John Nowlan under his wing and, after a boyhood spent among Aby's squabbling retainers and favorites, the boy is sent to the "Bishop's school" in Limerick, in preparation for Maynooth. John has no real vocation for the priesthood, but his parents view it as a step upward and Aby operates on the old Irish theory that it is a good idea to have at least one priest in the family.

Banim firmly establishes the rich, confusing relationships of the

Nowlan clan, but is less successful, because less familiar, with the Protestant households. Nevertheless, the liberal Longs and the bigoted Adamses have a real existence in the novel. They exist, that is to say, as perils for the Nowlans. Old Mister Long comes from a family with an honorable tradition of friendly relations with his Catholic neighbors, while Adams is an Orange zealot. Protestantism itself, however, is the real threat to the Nowlans, for they are a pushing, aspiring family, and the Established Church is a badge of status; it represents both power and the cachet of gentility.

Banim's first intention was to make *The Nowlans* a novel with a thesis. The early nineteenth century saw the rise in Ireland of a proselytizing movement which called itself, with undue optimism, the New Reformation. In point of fact it was the equivalent of the Evangelical movement in England, but its consequences were much less happy. The Church of Ireland had not hitherto been remarkable for spiritual enthusiasm, and Irish Catholicism, barely emerged from Penal Days, felt itself confronted with a new and more insidious peril when Bible associations, tract societies, Sunday schools, charter schools, and all the apparatus of evangelical zeal suddenly manifested themselves. The result was an acrimonious and singularly ugly warfare.

A group of Evangelical emissaries arrives on the scene in *The Nowlans,* under the patronage of Sirr, the local parson, and Adams. The Reverend Mister Stokes is "an English clergyman, sent from a Bible Society in London to investigate the progress of their benevolent efforts among the peasantry of Ireland." (*Ibid.,* I, 268) He is assisted by a former Catholic priest named Horragan, who has been entrusted with the conversion of the Gaelic-speaking population. Banim wants to convince fair-minded Englishmen, the audience he kept constantly in mind, that, while the motives of Stokes and his associates may be worthy, their ignorance of the Irish scene has made them the inevitable dupes of men like Adams and Horragan—bigots and renegades. To this end he develops a number of lengthy exchanges, in which Long upholds a worthier Protestant position, and the Catholic stand is set forth by an old Dominican.

Most Irish novelists of the period felt themselves impelled to write at least one novel on this topical issue, and never with much success. Banim puts appropriate speeches in the mouths of his characters, but he is entirely unable to respond to the spiritual life of Protestantism. The figure of Horragan is especially unworthy of his usual sense of fairness. Mortimer Sullivan, on whom he is modeled, was a sufficiently wretched being, but Banim represents him with a ferocity of caricature which defeats its own purpose.

But the tone and intensity of the novel change abruptly when requirements of the plot cause Letty Long and Father John Nowlan to fall in love and marry. The other elements of the plot continue to function, but they pale beside Banim's fascinated concern with Nowlan's psychology. It is as though he had discovered, for the first time, that differences of religion and culture can be both profound and determining.

John and Letty elope to London and are married by a Protestant clergyman, and John finds work in the city. To Letty their only offense has been in running away and, although she knows that John has broken his vows, she can only guess at the consequences to him. John is caught in a special and ghastly hell, in which he must continue to think of himself as a priest, and of Letty, despite her virtue, as little better than a mistress. After a short and miserable existence together, Letty dies and John returns home to place himself under the discipline of his bishop.

Banim is respectful of Letty's feelings, which he knows to be connected with her religious training, and yet he is so far removed from the world of Protestantism that he writes tentatively. The fact is reflected in Letty's pathetic attempts to communicate with John and in John's stricken muteness. But with John, Banim is on sure ground and writes with instinctive skill. The special role of the priest in the Irish Catholic imagination is such that few Catholic novelists approached this theme, and none so openly as Banim.

He comes to see, and to make us see, that the issue is not merely one of sect, in the strict sense of the word. John's identity had depended upon a world of feelings and loyalties of which his Catholicism was a part. When he leaves Tipperary for London he changes one existence for another—or, rather, for a state which cannot properly be called existence. In describing this Banim's language is charged beyond its usual range, for he is describing a descent into hell.

If, as his unwinking eyes strained through the blank at the window, perception brought, now and then, a notice of anything to his mind, it was only to encourage the mood that was upon him. The howling of the midnight wind over the black bogs of Tipperary; the gusty beating of the rain against the glass; the feeble glimmering of lanterns at the door of miserable inns, or cabins, as the coach stopped to change horses, and the miserable, half-dressed ghostlike figures appeared and disappeared in the dreary light and engulfing darkness; such circumstances or sights, if at all observed by John Nowlan, could only tend to answer, in an outward prospect, the inward horror of his soul.   (*Ibid.*, II, 37–38)

In Dublin the Nowlans take lodging with an English Protestant family named Grimes. It is a well-conducted family, honest, church-going, neat, and industrious. But to John "it was all mean, pinching economy, miserly comfort, unwarranted neatness, and propriety; cold, heartless, worthless independence. . . . The whole house and its inhabitants had an air of looking better than they really were or ought to be." Old Grimes, who has a minor job with the government, likes to spend his Sunday evenings with his friends, pottering about the yard, mending the sheds or watering the single, sickly laburnum tree. John, watching them from his window, "felt an odd sensation of disgust, such as he thought might be aroused by the sight of so many old shining black beetles, the insects that, of all that crept, were his antipathy and loathing." The two young girls of the family "gave no idea of flesh and blood. They never looked as if they were warm, or soft to the touch. One would as soon think of flirting with them, as with the old wooden effigies to be found in the niches of cathedrals." (*Ibid.*, II, 60–70) The feeling deepens and extends itself:

No charity was in the house, nor in a heart in the house. In the face of all professed beggars the street door was slammed without a word, but with a scowl calculated to wither the heart of the wretched suitor; and with respect to such as strove to hide the profession under barrel-organs, flutes, flageolets, hurdy-gurdies, or the big drum and pandean pipes, their tune was, indeed, listened to but never requited. . . . But nothing irked him so much as the ostentatious triumph over starvation, the provoking assumption of comfort, nay, elegance, as it were, and the audacious independence which resulted from the whole economy. (*Ibid.*, II, 74)

Nowlan is puzzled by the intensity of his dislike, and John Banim seems clearly to share the feeling. He is at least embarrassed by the undue intensity of the language. Committed as he was to a moralistic theory of fiction, he could not acknowledge that for once his imagination had been liberated from its everlasting fairmindedness. He says elsewhere, speaking of the Irish peasant, "those secrets of his inner heart he keeps concealed to the present hour, as well from the oppressor he hates, as from the friends who, if they knew him better, could better serve."

The observation, which is well taken, could be applied with equal justice to Banim himself. Because he had accepted the task of mediating between the two cultures, he could not bring himself to admit how much he cherished the one and detested the other. It is an honorable failure, one must say, remembering how much of Ireland's fiction is animated by a mean and soul-destroying hatred. But tolerance and accommodation wreak their own havoc upon art. Banim had himself taken John Nowlan's journey across the black Tipperary bogs to the house of the stranger.

In John Nowlan's room in the city there is but one concession to ornament, "a long, narrow chimney glass, set in a frame about an inch deep, and presenting to the eye about as faithful a reflection of the human face, as might a river or lake with the wind blowing high upon it." (*Ibid.*, II, 64) Banim's art is like the Grimes's chimney glass. Somewhere, far beyond its flawed and deceptive surface, we can sense, in all his fierce irreducibility, Crohoore of the Billhook, but we are given only as much of him as can be accommodated to an inch of frame. Only rarely, though with pleasure, do we realize that his creator, too, was a man of passion and feeling. *The Nowlans* affords such an occasion.

12. The Historical Novel

IN ONE OF THE MANY ESSAYS which he wrote for *The Nation,* asking for a patriotic and intensely national literature which could create for young Irishmen powerful and compelling images of their past, Thomas Davis moves to an eloquent conclusion:

This country of ours is no sandbank, thrown up by some recent caprice of time. It is an ancient land, honored in the archives of civilization, traceable into antiquity by its piety, its valour, and its sufferings. Every great European race has sent its stream to the river of Irish mind. Long wars, vast organizations, subtle codes, beacon crimes, leading virtues, and self-mighty men were hers. If we live influenced by wind and sun and tree, and not by the passions and deeds of the past, we are a thriftless and hopeless people.[1]

Davis's demand was answered in mocking abundance. If we were to judge it by its bulk alone, we would be tempted to say that nineteenth-century Irish fiction was devoted primarily to the production of historical novels, sumptuously bound in green and lavishly decorated with gilt shamrocks. For the most part they have fallen into a merciful oblivion. It could be argued that their lack of literary worth reflects invidiously upon the shallow and constrictive nationalism to which Davis committed his contemporaries and his successors. It was upon this charge that Davis would be arraigned by a later generation of Irish writers. But in fact Davis's larger error lay in his failure to see that the Irish mind had always been influenced, to the point of obsession, "by the deeds and passions of the past." And when, at his bidding, Irish writers turned directly to national history for material, they brought

[1] "The Library of Ireland," in *Essays of Thomas Davis,* p. 355.

with them the old, sullen grudges and the old, delusive lies. He had asked for a school of historical fiction which transcended hatred, accusation, and guilt. He had forgotten that these were the very forces which had shaped and determined the history of Ireland.

All save one of the historical novelists lie outside the chronological limits set for this study but, by fortunate chance, that one is by far the ablest. John Banim was the earliest writer of the school, and he brought to his work a vigor and an intellectual curiosity lacking in his successors. If he failed in his ambition, the failure is instructive and exemplary. He had a genuine historical imagination, and a generosity and sympathy oddly similar to Davis's. And, unlike Davis, he had a wry knowledge that "in Ireland truth dwells at the bottom of a muddy well." [2]

Banim wrote, in all, four historical novels, and their subjects are chosen with singular skill. The first, *The Boyne Water,* deals with the impact upon Irish life of the struggle between James and William. *The Last Baron of Crana* is set in that period, which still remains obscure and puzzling to scholars, when the Irish forces had capitulated at Limerick and a frightening anarchy had settled over the island. *The Conformists* is a novel of the Penal Days. Finally *The Croppy,* on which Michael Banim collaborated, turns to account the Rising of 1798.

Taken together, the novels should form a coherent pattern. Unhappily, they are of uneven merit, none of the latter three approaching the first in accomplishment. But *The Boyne Water* sets a standard which no other Irish historical novel was to meet. Subject to several strong reservations, it is the best work of its kind since Scott.

The comparison is inescapable, for Scott was Banim's absolute master. As much might be said of any historical novelist; Scott set the mold, and few of his successors either dared or troubled to break it. In most cases, however, his imitators contented themselves with a slavish conformity to the kinds of plot and character which he developed. Banim, as we shall see, can scarcely be excused on this score. But he also had a sense, rare in his generation, of what Scott was about, and of the sources of his power; he knew that beneath the brightly

[2] John Banim, *The Boyne Water,* p. 13.

colored surface of the *Waverley Novels* lay a deep and urgent knowledge of history as tragic experience.

For Banim, as for Scott, past and present were in continuous debate. The feelings, passions, and loyalties which worked upon his countrymen had their sources in past centuries, and hence to understand the past was to gain mastery over the present. "I will tell you, Barnes, what I would like to aid," he wrote. "I would go far to assist in dispersing the mist that hangs over Irish ground. I would like to see those dwelling on the Irish soil looking about them in the clear sunshine—the murkiness dispelled—recognizing each other as belonging to a common country. . . . We, here in Ireland, ought to be anxious to ascertain our position accurately, if for no other reason than that we may give ourselves a common country." [3]

The intention to "ascertain our position accurately" led Banim straight to a single day, July 1, 1690, when, on the shores of the Boyne River, the armies of William of Orange shattered those of James II. G. M. Trevelyan would one day set down the considered judgment of history upon that battle:

The outcome of that day subjected the native Irish to persecution and tyranny for several generations to come, but it saved Protestantism in Europe and enabled the British Empire to launch forth strongly on its career of prosperity, freedom, and expansion overseas. But while Enniskillen, Londonderry, and the Boyne were but a stage in the forward march of British and world history, they became the central point of time in the imagination of the ruling race in Ireland. With equal intensity of recollection, the oppressed Celt continued to think of the gallant defence of Limerick, and the subsequent breach by the conquerors of the treaty signed there with the vanquished race. Sarsfield, the hero of the Limerick campaigns, stood to the conquered as the representative man of the new Ireland, the faithful son of the *mater dolorosa*.[4]

It is suggestive of the nature of Banim's accomplishment that, while the nineteenth century had to run its full course before any historian, English or Irish, could arrive at this just and sympathetic formulation, it could easily be taken as a gloss upon *The Boyne Water*. And yet *The Boyne Water* was written when the battle for Emancipation, in

[3] *Ibid.*, p. 13.   [4] *History of England*, p. 484.

which Banim stood unequivocally with his own people, was at its height, and partisan feeling had reached a pitch of unprecedented bitterness. Despite its almost painful impartiality, Banim's cautious brother counselled him against publication; the advice was sound, for the novel was roughly handled in the English press.

Today, even though most readers must know that "Orangeman's Day"[5] has a very special meaning in Ireland, it is difficult to convey the terrible lacerating fury with which it was charged in Banim's generation. It was to the "glorious and immortal memory" of William and the Boyne that the Dublin aldermen drank their annual toast. It was in the name of that memory that the Belfast shopboys beat their Lambeg drums and shrilled their foolish fifes. And to the Catholic population it was the eternal and unendurable badge of their slavery, for the Boyne had made possible the Penal Laws, and its memory, a scant thirty years before, had sent the Orange yeomanry pillaging and burning across the townlands of the north.

As Banim wrote, O'Connell was rousing his people with memories of another kind, withering Ascendancy pretensions with that astonishing invective of his, compounded of half-lost Gaelic rhetoric and the billingsgate of Dublin law courts. The echoes of his heroic and contemptuous voice would never quite vanish from the hills of Ireland. But it was the voice of a tribal chieftain, putting nerve and backbone into his followers, and sweeping over historical accuracy with lordly disdain. To those followers, though not to O'Connell himself, *The Boyne Water* must have seemed as disagreeable a performance as it did to the Orangemen.

Banim's novel, which is a very long one, travels from the day in 1685 when the news reached Ireland that James had succeeded to the throne to the dark days which witnessed the imposition of the Penal Laws. It is concerned with the contrasting fortunes of two friends on opposite sides: Robert Evelyn, a Protestant who fights under William, and Edmund McDonnell, who serves with Sarsfield. One half of the novel is given over to a slow, but cumulatively powerful, development of the deadly geometry of absolute politics.

[5] Which commemorates, each July 12, a battle fought on July 1.

The ascension of James, which was closely followed by his appointment of Tyrconnel as Lord Deputy of Ireland, strikes the spark. It
came at the close of the most confusing period in Irish history, for
during the Civil War some five armies had been in the field. The
memories of two frightful massacres press upon the people. In 1641 the
Gaelic Catholics of Ulster had risen up to launch a campaign of extermination against the Protestant settlements; in 1649 Cromwell had
put the south to the sword with equal savagery. By the Restoration, it
had become clear that the two peoples of Ireland were pitted against
each other in a way which admitted neither resolution nor mitigation,
for the hatred fed upon the fuels of race and sect, and upon the secret
guilts which each faction nursed.

Now, to the dominant Protestant party, it seems certain that James,
through Tyrconnel, is making ready a final purge, and in their alarm
they plan preventive measures. A portion of the Catholic population
had indeed been awaiting such a purge; the obvious intentions of the
Protestants to strike first drives many others within the Catholic community into the extremist camp. Figures out of some nightmare world
come to dominate the councils of both groups. Noll Whittle, the old
Covenanting mosstrooper, recalls the days when "as a humble doer for
the Lord, forbye a corporal, muckle in favor with that zealous man,
though an Erastian, Charles Coote, I returned to the Papists and
malignants, hilt deep, the sword they had unleashed among the Lord's
people." (*Boyne Water*, p. 131) O'Haggerty, a Dominican fanatic,
tramps the backroads of the Papist counties, preaching a war of blood
and extermination against heretics. *Rory na Chopple,* the bantering,
good-natured cutthroat, waits in the hills to loot and murder the weak
of both factions.

Banim is aware, as most historians of his day were not, that the
struggle in Ireland between the Williamite and Jacobite forces decided
three distinct issues. In its largest terms, those suggested by Trevelyan,
it was the first check placed by the Protestant powers upon the ambitions of the French monarchy. As a dynastic contest it established the
Whig oligarchy in England. But as an issue fought out on Irish soil
it was a chapter in an old story. He sorts out these issues with

care and intelligence, yet mindful of the relationships among them.

The blood spilled at the Boyne Water still ran in crimson channels through the fabric of Irish life; it had become the sacramental wine of rival ideologies. To Irish Protestants William was the champion of the "old cause," brave, pious, and determined. To Catholics he was a cunning hypocrite and tyrant. Both sides were in agreement that James was a coward, who basely betrayed the Irish cavaliers who had flocked to his banners. Banim brushes away both of these convenient fictions. His rival kings are drawn in cold but not hostile lines; they are engaged in a quarrel whose terms are European; fate has drawn them to a country which neither understands nor cherishes.

Behind them move, first as shadows and then as actors, other and more somber figures. The Dominican O'Haggerty and the Covenanting Whittle embody the counter-principles of Ireland's two nations; baleful and fanatic, they suggest the impossibility of compromise. McDonnell and Evelyn, the heroes of the novel, struggle against them, but are at last overwhelmed. As the novel ends Evelyn has shame-facedly taken his place in the Parliament which, at the bidding of Dopping, the sanguinary Bishop of Dublin, has passed the first Penal Laws. And McDonnell is serving in the French army, waiting for the invasion which will begin the wretched struggle afresh. But each young man has come to a sober and ironic sense of the issues which have separated them, and has come to hate the inhuman demands placed upon the spirit by ideologies.

The great merit of *The Boyne Water* derives from those of Banim's qualities which are not of necessity literary. He was a remarkably intelligent man, and it was a specifically political and historical intelligence. He was also, for all his religious piety, skeptical of the social consequences of "crusades." But if these are the virtues which lift *The Boyne Water* above the ruck of its successors, they also impose its severe limitations. We become aware of these gradually, as the pattern of the plot takes shape as a series of annoying parallelisms.

Walker, an Anglican zealot, is paired off against O'Haggerty. A moderate priest, striving for reconciliation, has his opposite number in the Williamite camp. If Evelyn falls afoul of a band of Jacobite terrorists, so must McDonnell, within four or five chapters, be captured by William's brutal mercenaries. Banim does not employ this technique, though it might appear so, to obliterate moral distinctions. If he abjures partisanship, his own loyalties are clear and undisguised, and the judgment which he makes of each of his characters is unequivocal and indeed didactic. And yet one is left with the sense that the pattern, for all its admirable symmetry, lacks a center, lacks some ultimate commitment by Banim to his material.

Perhaps the answer lies with his dependence on Scott. Much of the machinery of *The Boyne Water* has been lifted bodily from *Waverley*. Scott's practice—nowhere more evident than in that novel—was to work with opposites, Scotsman and Englishman, cavalier and roundhead, highland laird and lowland lord, kirk and church. The resemblances to the Irish scene presented themselves to Banim with a dangerous plausibility. He saw Scott's cavaliers as bearing a rough equivalence to the Norman Irish of the Pale, and his roundheads to the Ulster Presbyterians, and his highland chieftains to the "old" Irish. But Scott's recurrent theme, which justifies these polarities, is the death of passion. It is his deep and genuine conservatism which makes legitimate his exploitation of the technique which he invented. Vich ian Vohr, Montrose, "Old Mortality," Rob Roy, all the fierce and splendid fighting men of his novels, are the partisans of causes which have been well and truly lost. Scott played at being a fire-eating Tory, but in truth he was the last of the great Whigs.

Scott had a firm, unshakable confidence in the security of the King, Lords, and Commons of Great Britain, the social worth of the Protestant Succession, and the propriety of the Act of Union which had joined Scotland with England. He turned to the past, as Burke did, to search out those vivid strands which the present had brought into so firm a knot. This deep-felt security permitted his imagination to play with equal sympathy upon Covenanter and Royalist. But it is significant that Redgauntlet, in whom political passion lives beyond its appointed hour, is one of his few tragic figures.

Banim, however, was dealing with a country where the strands of the past still twisted and coiled about men's heads like lethal and uncon-

trollable wires, impelled by some malignant energy. Walker and O'Haggerty were still addressing their bogside conventicles. Even as he wrote,
his *Rory na Chopple,* the blandly smiling murderer with soft brogue
and sudden cruelty, was somewhere in County Clare, leading out a
Ribbon mob against a glebe house—or else he was in the Black North,
at the head of his Orange "loyalists."

Banim's two novels of the Penal Times may be given brief treat-
ment. In *The Last Baron of Crana* he traces the fate of two Gaelic
families in the years following the surrender at Limerick. The hushed
and fearful expectancy which had fallen upon the Gaelic world is
created effectively, and the story has a certain surface excitement, but
the characters are stiffly theatrical. "A stout rebel, as I have ever heard,"
says Sir Redmond O'Burke, accepting Prendergast's surrender in the
thick of a hot action, "and, as I now bear witness, a courageous gentleman; but we waste some time here; I crave your company back to the
hill, whence, after honorably bestowing you, I may again engage in my
duty." (*Last Baron,* I, 9) Prendergast, the Williamite, is afflicted with a
similar rotundity of utterance.

The Conformists takes up a subject to which a real and moving interest adheres, though Banim seems hardly to recognize this. Mark
Darcy returns home from Spain with the education and sword of a
gentleman. His younger brother, Daniel, trained in a hedge school, and
accustomed to accord a sullen deference to the Orange gentry, becomes
increasingly resentful of him, and at last decides upon a dreadful measure. One of the most notorious of the penal statutes was that which
provided that if a son or younger brother conformed to the Established
Church, the law would put him in possession of the lands of his family. The plot is concerned entirely with the motives which tempt
Daniel to this act, its commission, and his ultimate repentance. It is
managed in a style which alternates between the perfunctory and the
lurid.

Banim tells us in a note which introduces these two novels that, because they were being published at a delicate moment in the Emancipation fight, he had carefully pruned and "remodelled" and "rewritten"

so that no passage could possibly give offense to either faith. The thin and watery texture of both stories may, no doubt, be attributed to this absurd decision. But there are other and more substantial reasons.

There is one effective scene in *The Last Baron of Crana*. Young Patrick Burke, who has managed to evade the laws, and who has been brought up as Prendergast's ward, has been searching for the "last baron," Randal O'Hagan. He finds him at last, but can feel only pity and unconquerable disgust. For O'Hagan, who had been an urbane and chivalrous officer on Sarsfield's staff, is now a murdering wood-kern. "Even the expressions of his face, so far as regards indication of rank, were deficient; its colour and texture seemed vulgar; nay, his speech, and the hoarse cadences of his voice, had necessarily acquired their present character, since his abandonment of his name and station in the world. Once or twice, Patrick detected him eyeing askance his own family crest upon articles of plate which lay upon the table. . . ." (*Ibid.*, II, 164)

The effectiveness is accidental. It depends not on the meaning of the scene to us, but on our knowledge of what it meant to Banim. Irish Catholics of his generation took particular and excessive pride in what they imagined their past to have been. Their race had boasted gentlemen as polished as any in the Ascendancy, and as punctilious. They remembered, with a somewhat self-pitying nostalgia, that the ranks of its chivalry had made their last gallant stand at Limerick. Those who remained had not, like Scott's Jacobites, perished in their pride; they had been subjected to a remorseless, if often random, brutalization.

It is not necessary to sort out here the facts and the fancies which were incorporated into the early nineteenth-century myth of Sarsfield and his Jacobite army. The point, rather, is that in the history of the intervening century, rich with the shames, crimes, and glories of the Ascendancy, the history of the Catholic community was, and in part remains, a blank page. Remote country houses might shelter a scholar like Charles O'Conor of Belenagare, who carefully gathered, preserved, and studied the slender memorials of his country.[6] Or a half-proscribed

---

[6] *Dissertation on the Antient History of Ireland* . . . (Dublin, 1753).

squire and smuggler like Maurice O'Connell of Derrynane might toss his correspondence into desks and lockers for the enlightenment of our own age. But for the middle-class Irish who, like Banim, were beginning to find pens and voices, such survivals were themselves inaccessible. And in default they conjectured as to what "things must have been like" in the eighteenth century. An extraordinary talent like that of Gerald Griffin could, by some act of sympathetic magic, recreate that past with surprising accuracy. But most novelists, following Banim's unhappy example, produced cardboard "gentlemen" who nobly endured a puppet-show martyrdom.

In the main these novelists preferred to move further and further into the past, creating out of shroudlike mists a Red Hugh O'Donnell who talked like Sir Philip Sidney and comported himself like Walter Scott welcoming George IV to Edinburgh. But Banim, the evidence of *The Last Baron* and *The Conformists* to the contrary, had no taste for that sort of foolishness. And in *The Croppy* he confronted the most immediate and controversial subject which he could possibly have found.

In 1828 the Great Rebellion was a scant thirty years in the past, and still a subject of empassioned dispute. It had, indeed, its dark significance for the present moment. To the government and to the Ascendancy the most menacing aspect of O'Connell's movement was that it seemed to be fed by the secret White Boy and Ribbon societies which had supplied the '98 with its rebels. But behind this reasonable, though misleading, suspicion lurked a fear which the Garrison had entertained for so long a time that it might well be termed atavistic.

Stated bluntly, it was the fear of a slave uprising. The term suggests the mingled loathing, fear, and contempt with which many in the Garrison viewed the people whom they ruled and exploited. Lord Stanley's description of the Irish peasantry as "bigoted savages" is a mild statement of the case. Fixed in the memory of every landlord, even so enlightened a one as Richard Lovell Edgeworth, were the dreadful massacres which attended the rebellion of 1641. The '98 looked very much like an attempt to repeat the carnage, and confirmed the general notion that the Irish were untamable barbarians, to be kept down by administration of the whip and the pitch-cap as needed.[7]

The liberal minority, however, had from the first put forward the interpretation which serves as the theme as Banim's novel. The peasants of Wexford had been goaded into an insurrection which, once commenced, had taken the unhappy and predictable course of all peasant wars. For the aims of the rebellion very few, and Banim least of all, had a good word to say.

Previous to the insurrection, almost every Protestant, whether sworn or not, chose to be considered an Orangeman; by skillful management, in able hands, the badge of that party became a necessary symbol of loyalty; few of the established religion, therefore, from motives of choice or of prudence, as the case may be, appeared abroad without it. The Catholic peasant confounded all the late adherents of his abhorred enemies with the first and worst who had persecuted him; Protestant and Orangeman became, in his mind, synonymous words; and in this delusion he caught up his rude and formidable pike, when, without time being afforded him to reflect, he was precipitated, by United Irish emissaries on one side, and by monstrous and wanton civil outrage on the other, into the melee of civil strife. (*Croppy,* I, 14)

This is an interpretation which accords with all the evidence we have, save that it is somewhat too eager to exculpate the peasantry on grounds of ignorance. Thirty years hence, however, any Irish "patriot" would reject it with indignation. By that time the '98 had been cast in another, more heroic mold, thanks largely to the spirited efforts of Thomas Davis, John Mitchel, and the Young Ireland group. The United Irishmen, represented by Banim as sinister incendiaries, had become the principal deities of the nationalist pantheon.

Banim's novel is set in Wexford, to which county the actual fighting was more or less restricted. He has allowed himself a canvas of adequate size, and creates a coherent picture of the society within which the violence erupted. It is also, by and large, a convincing picture, although he stumbles into his usual absurdities when dealing with the Protestant gentry. The opening chapters are perhaps too idyllic: "On either side of the river, the grounds rise and fall in every change

---

[7] This position was given its most hysterical formulation in a once-celebrated work, Sir Richard Musgrave's *Memoirs of the Different Rebellions in Ireland.* . . .

of soft form; domain succeeds domain, and mansion is in view of mansion." (*Croppy*, I, 22) But before he is finished, every "domain" and every "mansion" has suffered a hideous transformation. There is also a certain historical justification: Wexford, a peaceful and fairly prosperous county, was the last place in which rebellion might have been expected. But, in a fashion which Banim recreates in all its lurid details, it had been raked over by agitators.

Saunders Smiley, the Orange agent, has his orders from the government to force the peasantry into a premature and hence foredoomed insurrection. He has his counterpart in Bill Nale, a veteran of Ulster's religious battles, who is preaching a holy war of retribution from cabin to cabin. Lastly, and perhaps most fatally, there appears on the scene "the Member from the Committee," the leader despatched by the United Irishmen.

Banim writes of all three with a quiet, bitter contempt, but one scene rises with dramatic force above the level of mere professional competence. It is that in which "the Member," who manages to combine the greatest zeal with the greatest complacence, explains to the men whom he has sworn that they are pledged to a movement whose ideals transcend weak notions of sect and creed. For seated about him are men into whose hearts have been instilled a deep and ineradicable religious hatred, and who will shortly make a travesty of the instructions of their lofty mentors by launching an indiscriminate slaughter of Protestants.

The two great figures of *The Croppy* are Shane na gow and Father Rourke. Both are kindly men goaded into violence; both, transformed by the fury of events, become murderers; both are hanged. The novel closes in the tame fashion which was expected of romances of this sort. Lovers are reunited, faithful servants are rewarded, just punishments are meted out, and Mr. Mossop, the paternalistic magistrate, has regained control of the county. But the final powerful image is of a very different order:

Father Rourke was hanged upon the bridge at Wexford. The weight of his colossal body had broken the rope, however, before Saunders Smiley saw him pending to his heart's content.   (*Croppy*, II, 194)

Like Crohoore, sharpening his pike by the fire's glow, Rourke has a meaning which extends beyond that which the conscious intentions of the novel assign to him. Most of the characters in *The Croppy* had their counterparts in the actual rebellion, and the original of "Rourke" was John Murphy, the parish priest of Boulavogue. Murphy had opposed the rising, both on religious grounds and because like most sensible men he saw that it was suicidal. But when it became clear that his people were being offered the choice of dying with a fight or without one, he took the field with them. When Bagenal Harvey, the country squire under whose command they had been placed, fled in disgust at their uncouth methods of making war, Murphy became their "general." He had been concealing unexpected military acumen beneath his cloth, and led the rebels to their only victories. The yeomanry captured him, hanged him at Tullow, and then burned his body.

Murphy's legend lingered on among the peasantry, and he is the hero of several songs commemorative of the '98. There is nothing heroic, however, about Banim's Father Rourke. He is a determined and capable leader, but action brings out in him a ferocious bigotry, quite equal to that betrayed by his opponents. It is Rourke who directs the murder of innocent Protestant prisoners. There seems no doubt, from any of the evidence, that Banim's portrait is accurate. But when nationalists were constructing their myth of the '98, these harsh lines were carefully sponged away.

In his best novels Banim refused to soften or sentimentalize the issues, and this is a quality so rare in Irish fiction as to excuse his very evident shortcomings. It was a quality which he shared with his much abler contemporaries, Griffin and Carleton. Had the conditions of Irish culture been other than what they were, had not the pressures placed on literature by politics become increasingly sharp, these writers might have marked the beginnings of a tradition. Instead they stand as lonely and broken figures, who failed even to understand each other.

In Banim's work the recurring figure is the peasant, that creature "of mystery or malignity." For Banim, clearly, he was something of both. Dashing Jacobites and disinherited cavaliers and improbable graduates of Kilkenny College make their processional appearances in his stories, but his heart and his wonder are always fixed on the pike-man by the fire and the rebel on the gallows.

When the Land War was at its height in the 1880s, long after Banim's death, *The Daily News* of London despatched a special correspondent named Bernard Becker to "get the facts." Becker was a sprightly and somewhat bumptious young man, full of the breezy journalese of the day. His journey was a sobering and at times a dangerous experience, and he left Ireland shorn of his confidence that "the facts" could be easily obtained. His last recollection was of a shebeen house where he found himself snowbound one December night. It was not the scene which impressed him, but a man whom he found sitting by the fire.

The sulky brute answers me never a word. Probably he knows or suspects where I have been, and if so would let me lie on the ground under a kicking horse till an end was made of me rather than stretch out a hand. He will not speak now, and I observe that the woman, who has kept a tight hold on the shilling, has not poured out any whisky, although she has had the decency to ask me if I wished for any. It is a strange sight, this sullen savage sitting scowling over the fire; but *on se fait a tout* in Disturbed Ireland.[8]

Banim's wish—history was to make it seem an inordinate ambition —was to explain this "sullen savage" to England. As it happens, he lacked the opportunity, for in 1830 a spinal disease paralyzed him, and from then until his death in 1842 he was prevented from writing.

A cottage was procured for him on the Kilkenny road to Dublin, through the generosity of his admirers, who included "that never-tiring friend of the struggling man of genius, the late Sir Robert Peel." To his visitors he discoursed on Ireland by the hour, and on the role which literature was to play in Irish life. The theme was monotonous: "We have been sadly neglected, and the works which have been written on this country seldom give a correct notion of the people."[9]

Once, at least, he roused himself. A new viceroy, Mulgrave, had been appointed, of whom it was predicted that he would be "the

[8] Bernard Becker, *Disturbed Ireland* (London, 1881), p. 338.
[9] Murray, *The Life of John Banim*, p. 296.

greatest and truest friend of Ireland." Banim, an incurable optimist, rode out to meet him in a carriage decorated with green and orange in token of conciliation. Shortly afterwards the Tithe War swept out of Munster into Kilkenny, driving conciliation before it.

Michael Banim, who thought that this newest White Boy rising would make first-rate material, discussed a projected novel with his brother. But John Banim, perhaps admitting at last some defeat of the spirit, advised against it. He had written too much about "the dark side of the Irish character; let us, for the present, treat of the amiable; enough of it is around us." [10]

[10] *Ibid.*

Gerald Griffin

13. *Tales of the Munster Festivals*

THE CHIEF SOURCE of biographical information concerning Gerald Griffin is a life written by his brother Daniel and published in 1843, three years after Gerald's death. It is a disappointing book. The narrative is awkward and repetitious, for Daniel Griffin, a country physician practicing in Limerick, was not a man of letters. A great many questions which Griffin's letters and poems prompt one to ask are left unanswered: he was a puzzling man, and not least so to his family. But, for all its shortcomings, the book is a fitting one. Griffin's fame came to him in London, and he died in a Cork monastery, but his roots were sunk deep in Limerick. A strong and attractive parochialism helped to shape his work.

There had been Griffins in Limerick for centuries. The name suggests that the stock was Welsh, but this matters little; they had become part of the native community and had shared its fate. Gerald's father, Patrick, was the son of a strong farmer, but Patrick Griffin had inherited little of his father's acumen. He had several starts and failures, as a brewer and as a farmer, and finally, in 1820, was forced to emigrate to America, leaving Gerald and Daniel in the care of an older brother.

Patrick Griffin's energies were directed, so we may gather from Daniel's respectful but acidulous remarks, everywhere but to his financial concerns. His generation had seen the rise of the Volunteers, and the spectacular, ephemeral success of Grattan's "Nation": himself a veteran of the Volunteers, he was wont, like old O'Connor in *The Collegians,* to expatiate on the dead glories of those days. He had witnessed the rise and sorry ebb of the early Emancipation movement, and his conversation was rich also in references to this. Of more immediate consequence to his family, the relaxation of the Penal Laws had opened up the possibility of careers for his sons. During the Napoleonic wars his oldest son served as an officer with the Thirty-Seventh, and another was a midshipman aboard the "Venerable."

His wife was descended on the maternal side from the O'Briens of New Ross, a family of the old gentry, and one with a tradition of cultural attainments. She was a well-read woman, and shared, in her own fashion, the interests generated by the national revival. She had a special fondness for the poetry of Goldsmith and Moore, and communicated this to her children. The Irish held Goldsmith in high regard not so much because he was himself Irish as because his *Deserted Village* had created, though in a somewhat inappropriate idiom, an image of their countryside and a sense of the sadness of their situation. As a child Gerald copied out the poem and wrote beneath it, "The Deserted Village, an invaluable treasure." "Irish" poetry, of course, it was not, although Goldsmith's casual account of Carolan suggests that he could respond to the native traditions.

Moore held an even higher place in the esteem of the Griffin family, and understandably so, for in Ireland he summoned special allegiances. When he described a village he may have dissolved its outlines in sentiment, but it was an Irish village and not an anomalous "Auburn." Like Goldsmith he was a product of Trinity College, the citadel of the Ascendancy, but he had been the friend there of Robert Emmett and he was to become the biographer of Lord Edward Fitzgerald. He was a Catholic, a chain which bound an Irishman to his country's somber past. And though, also like Goldsmith, he made his career and his home in England, his affection for Ireland remained. Indeed, at the height of his celebrity, he wore with a flourish his badges of race and creed. For young Gerald Griffin he was the great exemplar of the kind of career in the arts which now seemed to be opening up in London for Irish Catholics. The days of the Wild Geese and the wandering scholars had passed with the Napoleonic wars.

Patrick Griffin remembering the Volunteers and bursting into tears on learning of the death of Romilly; his wife's genteel interest in

Moore and Goldsmith; a son serving with Wellington and one with Nelson; Gerald's aspirations to success in English letters—these suggest the changing face of Irish culture, of which Gerald was to become the chronicler, at once fascinated and austere.

One side of his training led him to look outward, toward England. But another side turned him backward, toward the Irish past. He received his formal training in city "seminaries" conducted by hedge scholars and, in one instance, in what was literally a hedge school. In the century which had just ended, the island had abounded in "scholars," spoiled priests and wastrel poets who taught the classical languages from tattered texts and English from secondhand penny romances. The peculiar circumstance of a people receiving academic and moral instruction almost as though these were outlawed commodities had left its heavy mark, and in Gerald Griffin's day the hedge schools were in decline.

Several of his masters, however, would be remembered long after such schools had become mere legends. One was Richard McEligot, who appeared one day in a Limerick classroom, barefooted and half-clad, and went on to become one of the earliest and most competent contributors to the *Transactions of the Gaelic Society*.[1] It was his boast that "only three people in Ireland know how to read, the Bishop of Killaloe, the Earl of Clare, and your humble servant." He was an absurdly pedantic man, his speech gorged with mouth-filling gentilities of expression, but a first-rate scholar.

McEligot's academy was several cuts above another which Gerald attended, a hedge school proper conducted by a young man named Donovan from the "classical Kingdom of Kerry." Griffin has given us a picture of this school in *The Rivals* (pp. 54–55)—the children arriving in frieze jackets and corduroy trousers, each with his reading book under one arm and a sod for the turf fire under the other. A row of stones stretched across one side for boys, facing another for girls. At the word "Virgil," the class gathers to "consthrue":

Dido, an 'the Throjans, an' all the great coort people about the place, lookin' for shelter, an' peltin' about right and left, hether and thether in all

[1] Patrick John Dowling, *The Hedge Schools of Ireland*, p. 137.

directions for the bare life, and the floods swellin' an' comin' thunderin'
down in rivers from the mountains, an' all in three lines:

> Et Tyrii comites passim, et Trojana juventus,
> Dardaniusque nepos Veneris, diversa per agros
> Tecta metu petiere; ruunt de montibus amnes.

And see the beauty o' the poet, followin' up the character of Ascanius,
he makes him the last to quit the field. First the Tyrian comrades, an effemi-
nate race, that ran at the sighth of a shower, as if they were made o' salt,
that they'd melt under it, and then the Throjan youth, lads that were used
to it, in the first book; and last of all the spirited boy Ascanius himself.

> Speluncam Dido dux et Trojanum eandem,
> Deveniunt,

Observe, boys, he no longer calls him, as of old, the *pius Aeneas,* only
dux Trojanus, the Throjan leader, in condemnation of his crime. That's
where Virgil took the crust out o' Homer's mouth, in the neatness of his
language, that you'd gather a part o' the feelin' from the very shape o' the
line an' the turn o' the prosody. As, formerly, when Dido was asking Aeneas
concerning where he came from, an' where he was born? He makes answer:

> Est locus, Hesperiam Graii cognomine dicunt:
> Terra antiqua, potens armis, atque ubere gleboe,
> Huc cursus fuit:

And there the line stops short, as much as to say, just as I cut this line
short in spakin' to you, just so our coorse was cut, in goin' to Italy. The
same way, when Juno is vexed in talkin' o' the Throjans, he makes her spake
bad Latin to show how mad she is:

> Mene incepto desistere victam,
> Nec posse Italia Teucrorum avertere regem?
> Quippe vetor fatis! Pallasne Exurere cassem
> Argivum, atque ipsos potuit submergere ponto,

So he laves you to guess what a passion she's in, when he makes her lave
an infinitive mood without anything to govern it. You can't attribute it to
ignorance, for it would be a dhroll thing in airnest, if Juno, the queen of
all the gods, didn't know a common rule in syntax, so that you have nothing for it but to say that she must be in the very moral of a fury. Such, boys,
is the art o' poets, and the genius of languages.

Daniel Griffin is defensive in tone when writing of such men as
Donovan, for he knew that by other standards they were self-inflated
ragamuffins. But Gerald knew that they possessed a special gift, one
which laid bare the connections between meaning and meter, gram-

mar and grace. The "dead" language was not dead, and they traced the pulse of its life along the vein of its verse. Rather it was English which had never lived for them. Gaelic and Latin, for centuries, had been their tongues of discourse. English they spoke and taught from expediency. "English sells the cow," the saying went. When they used it, they stumbled and made fools of themselves, advertising in a provincial newspaper that they were available for instruction in "ponderous polysyllables to promulgate professional powers." That is why the wildly gifted Munster poet and scholar, Owen Roe O'Sullivan, turned wooden and callow when he wrote an occasional verse in English to cadge a shilling from a patron.

From the men who instructed him, McEligot, Donovan, O'Brien, Gerald Griffin may have acquired that stiffness which often mars his work, but also the richness of expression, the power of evocation, the ability to seize the one detail which creates the effect.

Above all, however, he was instructed by the countryside. Before he was grown he had roamed over most of Munster, hunting, fishing, asking questions of strangers, and he knew by heart every valley, every village, every point along the Shannon. He had been born on the Shannon, in a sense, for he was born in that part of Limerick town which is a river island, called, significantly, the King's Island. There was much to remind its inhabitants that they were governed by the king of another island. Nearby rested the treaty stone upon which Sarsfield was said to have signed the articles which turned his countrymen over to Dopping's mercies. There was a ropewalk—in Ireland, Gerald was to remark, rope was always in demand, and for a certain reason. He had that kind of eye and mind, one which seizes upon a name, a rock, a length of rope, and makes them represent much.

In 1810, when Gerald was seven, Patrick Griffin moved his family to Fairy Lawn, twenty miles from the town, at the point where the Shannon broadens to its three-mile estuary. There they lived until 1820, when Patrick emigrated. After that Griffin stayed with his brother William in the villages first of Adare and then of Pallas Kenry. Each of these scenes made its particular impression on him. The sheet of river, with Clare on the far shore, is the focal point of many of his stories, just as Adare is the unnamed hamlet of *Tales of My Neighborhood*. Like most regionalists, he decked out his fiction with such items of local interest, but in a more profound sense the genius of place worked on him as it did on all young Romantics.

Near Adare stretched out the wide estates of the lords of Dunraven, the expropriators of much Munster land. On these lands stood ruins which meant little to the Dunravens but much to Gerald. One such ruin had been a Franciscan monastery. Another was all that remained of Desmond Castle, the stronghold of the great Fitzgerald family, knocked down by Cromwell during his pacification of the island. As a boy Gerald climbed over the stones, hunting for flints. When he was grown, he returned and, with the music of an old Gaelic song running through his head, wrote his only poem which is remembered.

> Castles are sacked in war,
> Chieftains are scattered far,
> Truth is a fixed star,
> Aileen aroon.[2]

But the river meant most to him. Rising in Cavan and passing through its many loughs, it connected with Dublin by the grotesque pathway of the Royal Canal, but its true course was westward, past Limerick and Clare, and spilling at last into the Atlantic by the wild Kerry shore, Spenser's spacious "Shenan, spreading like a sea." Gerald used to climb Knock Patrick and, with his back to the King's Island, peer out at the distant and awesome isle of Scattery, whose round towers and crumbled churches suggested the oldest Ireland of all.

There is a kind of geography of the spirit in Griffin's representation of Ireland, and much of this he entrusted to the river. There is also in his work, as he came to have knowledge of himself and of his country, a sense of the conflicting traditions which went into his making—his father's Whiggish patriotism; his mother's responsiveness to Anglo-Irish culture, with all its tense adjustments; the Gaelic underworld of Donovan and McEligot; the time-haunted stones of abbeys, towers, and fortresses.

[2] "Aileen Aroon," *Poetical Works*, p. 148.

In 1823, when he was not quite twenty, Griffin descended upon London, armed with the manuscript of a verse tragedy. He was a singularly handsome young man—tall, slender, and erect, with a pale, intense face, dark eyes, and full, firm lips. Friends were to remark that he kept these looks until his death, despite ill-health and overwork. No one, however, could have been less conscious of such matters than Griffin. He was hardly free from vanity, but it was not the kind which fastens on appearances.

In London he got in touch at once with John Banim, who, with his usual kindliness, set out to find him work of some sort. Banim gave him an introduction to Maginn, whose Grub Street connections were numberless. Griffin was soon able to keep himself perilously afloat by doing translations, making indices, cutting down dictionaries, acting as a parliamentary reporter, and writing reviews, twopenny verse, and literary squibs.

He kept at this work for three years, and it permanently affected his health. His letters home reveal a heart-felt but rather lachrymose frustration. "When I send off my bundle of papers for the evening, I sit down here sometimes to think on my future prospects and go to bed actually feverish with apprehension. There is nothing but doubt and uncertainty about it. No profession, no hold on society, no stamp, no mark, and time rolling on, and the world growing old about me." [3]

A good part of his unhappiness, however, arose not from his lack of accomplishment but from his lack of sympathy with the world in which he found himself. His roots were at home, in Limerick, and he sank no new ones in London. England remained strange to him, and he reacted to it with a countryman's chill, hard hostility. The ordinary people whom he met reminded him of the warmth and quickness of the Irish peasantry, and the extraordinary people put him off in other ways. Westminster Abbey only recalled to his memory the small chapel in Adare.

Banim, who was a journeyman of the arts, had taken his place happily in Maginn's coterie, but Griffin was restless and suspicious.

[3] Griffin, *Life*, p. 191.

He disliked in particular the glib, bantering way in which they turned
their knowledge of Ireland into "good copy." When Banim, with the
best of intentions, offered him a place in "the O'Hara Family," he
refused angrily. Feeling alone and frightened, he put on a mask which
his family would never have recognized—a hard, insolent indifference.
He was not to be the last literary Irishman to strike that pose.

In 1825 the Catholic Association met in London at, of all places, the
Freemasons' Hall. Griffin was present and, though his brain was still
swarming with shapeless classical tragedies, he took note of what
went on. Figures who were idolized back in Limerick he saw clear and
plain—the empty, florid Sheil and the aptly named Lawless. But he also
felt the force of O'Connell, domineering, skillful, and determined.

When his family wrote for news of the meeting, Gerald supplied it
to them, and then added tartly, "You have a queer notion on the other
side of the water, that your concerns are greatly thought about here.
It is a doubt to me if the 'dear little island' were swallowed by a whale,
or put in a bag and sent off to the moon, if the circumstance would
occasion any further observation than a 'dear me,' at one end of the
town, and a 'my eye,' at the other, unless, indeed, among the Irish
mining speculators, or some other gentlemen equally interested." [4]

But he found himself beginning to wonder if Ireland was not a
proper subject for art, just as Greece and Rome were, though not so
grand, perhaps, or so austere. Ireland, he was to remark, had no brilliant drama to dazzle the mind nor any magnificence of decay to feed
contemplation. And yet he felt that somewhere in all that wasted
suffering and vain remonstrance, in "the nightmare of ten centuries,"
the materials for his pen might lie.

In the alarming space of two or three months, and while reviewing
books and scribbling periodical essays at his usual rate, he completed
the volume which he called *Holland-Tide*. He was ambitious that it
should be "illustrative of manners and scenery precisely as they stand
in the South of Ireland"—a fairly typical ambition of the regional
writer, though it was to be redeemed in his case by the freshness of his
imagination.

[4] *Ibid.*, p. 192.

The completion of the book coincided with a complete physical and psychic exhaustion. His brother William, who happened by a lucky accident to be visiting London at the time, arranged with Simpkin and Marshall for publication, and took Gerald back to Limerick. Thenceforth Griffin revisited London only briefly and on business. It remained for him what it had always been, a city as foreign as Moscow.

In its arrangement *Holland-Tide* is a book representative of its type, that is, a series of tales which evoke the atmosphere and characters of a remote and wild countryside. They deal with "fairies, and priests, and joyants . . . wakes and weddings . . . or smugglers, or coiners, or fighting at fairs, or Moll Doyle, or rebellion, or murthering of one sort or other." For this reason a friendly reviewer, by way of praising the book, called it "Crofton Crokerish." The remark put Griffin in a fit of temper, and both the observation and the temper are justified.[5] For it is clear that Griffin was trying for an accomplishment much more substantial than Croker's, and yet had appropriated some of Croker's machinery.

But the longest and most ambitious story, "The Aylmers of Bally-aylmer," bears the marks of his special energy and grace. The setting is Kerry, but not Croker's Kerry, a tinselly county alive with sprites and mischievous tinkers. Griffin's landscape is one of steep, wave-wracked coasts, desolate bogs, and chill mountains. It is a story of smuggling, "the running trade," which supported half the gentry of Munster, and at which the law connived to a degree which would have aroused the shocked envy of Cornwall. Much of the history of hidden Ireland is bound up in the trade, for, if "the gentlemen" smuggled brandies and silks into the country, they smuggled out the young men who fed the seminaries and armies of Europe.

In the background of the story are two chiefs of the trade, William Aylmer and Cahill Fitzmaurice of Kilavariga House, called for his cruelty Cahill-crug-dharug, or Cahill of the red hand. These men are the secret law of their stretch of country, broken gentlemen of the old order who rule the peasants, their "follyers," with iron hands. They

[5] *Ibid.*, pp. 252–53.

live in contemptuous disregard of the law, which is represented by Mr.
Hassett of Hassettville, and the Tralee Assizes. Aylmer is murdered
by Cahill on one of their expeditions, and his son Robert returns home.

The story is framed by Robert Aylmer's journey from Dublin, a
slow and dangerous trip across bog and mountain. In another of his
stories, "Hand and Word," Griffin reminds us of the folk belief that
Cromwell had cursed Kerry because it lacked a tree to hang a man,
water to drown him, fire to burn him. (*Holland-Tide,* p. 147) This is
the land which greets young Aylmer, "a place one of the dreariest that
can be imagined; heath beyond heath and bog beyond bog, as far as his
sight could reach in prospect, canopied over by a low, dingy, and
variable sky, and rendered still more dispiriting by the passing gusts of
wind which occasionally shrieked over the desolate expanse, with so
wildering a cadence as almost to excuse the superstitions of the natives,
that the fairies of the mountains rode the blast." (*Ibid.,* pp. 17-18)

Ballyaylmer House, he finds, is thrown open to the elements, the
forlorn hiding place of his father's peasants.

The entrance consisted of two lean, gawky-looking piers, built of plain
rough stone, and standing bolt upright, like young steeples, on each side of
a low, shattered, paltry, wooden gate, which had long discontinued the use
of its hinges, and was propped up to its office by the assistance of a few
large stones, rolled against the lower bars, the removal of which, for the ad-
mission of cars and horses, usually occupied as much time each day as a
carpenter might have lost in screwing on a fresh pair of hinges. On the sum-
mit of one of these piers, a noseless Banthee or Banathee, done in limestone,
the work of some rural Westmacott, might be observed in the act of comb-
ing her long and flowing hair, an action generally attributed to that warning
spirit. . . . The house itself, a square-roofed, lumpish looking edifice, sadly
out of repair, and destitute of even a solitary twig or fir to conceal its threadbare masonry; its line of red binding-tiles broken and blown away; its
chimneys damaged and menacing; and its slated roof hospitably inviting,
in divers appertures, the visitations of wind and rain—all, together, presented as bleak and comfortless a spectacle as ever greeted even a provincial
eye.   (*Ibid.,* pp. 36-37)

The law, or rather the absence of law, is at the center of every story
which Griffin was to write. Most of his characters stand outside it in

one sense or another, though they may recognize the need to placate or circumvent it. Law makes its first appearance in "The Aylmers" in the person of Mr. Hassett, the landowner and magistrate:

As his carriage turned the angle of a rock, some miles distant from his seat, the sound of all manner of villainous instruments, rattling away to an inspired national planxty, announced the approach of the villagers, and in a few minutes he was encountered by their advance guard, a mounted deputation, headed by a lame carpenter. . . . The music being hushed for a moment into delicious silence, and the open carriage drawn up, the school-master inflicted a harangue on the occupant, which was borne with gracious patience, and suitably acknowledged; after which, with tremendous yells, the crowd bounded on the carriage, emancipated the four-footed cattle, cashiered the postillion, and fastening two ropes on either side, hurried the vehicle across the rough and stony road, which caused an expression of real alarm to take the place of the smiling condescension which had before deepened itself over the gracious countenance of the proprietor. As they hurried him along, amid terrific shouts, and bursts of wild laughter, toward the demesne gate, the walls and the wayside were lined with gaping and noisy crowds, principally composed of the younger urchins, whose scantiness of attire obliged them to make shift in this manner. One of these had clambered up a gate pier and sitting cross-legged on the back of a stone monkey, secured his seat by passing his arm around the neck of the delapidated pug; while with the other he twirled his little hareskin cap above his head, and added his share of noisy triumph to the general voice.

(Ibid., pp. 63–64)

It is a scene quintessential to Anglo-Irish fiction, from Lever to Somerville and Ross, the dear, dirty, touching peasants and the amused, understanding landlord. But Griffin's point is entirely different. There is something sinister in the well-meaning, ineffectual Hassett being bounced along by a people whose true life is secret, violent, and conspiratorial. Griffin says it all in a felicitous and characteristic stroke: the contrasting figures of the broken but balefully potent banshee and the ludicrous, ignoble monkey.

The story reaches its climax at the Tralee Assizes. Griffin sketches the assize town and the court vigorously and with fidelity to facts:

The generally silent and sunshiny streets were now made to echo the frequent tramp of the bespattered and reeking saddle horse, and the lumbering

rattle of the car which brought its load of corn (stacked until now, the
season of scarcity), to the store of the small dealer, a sort of Lilliputian
merchant, who made a new profit by shipping, or rather boating the grain
to the next trading city. The fronts of the inns and *shebeens* were scowered
up, and the rooms made ready for the temporary convenience of petty jurors,
summoned from the furthermost limits of the county; strong farmers anx-
iously looking for the success of their road presentments; Palatines seeking
compensations for burnt hay-ricks and outhouses, fired by the ubiquitous
hand of the White-boy; rural practitioners demanding the legal grant for
the support of a dispensary; middlemen in the commission of the peace,
eager to curry favor with the mighty sojourners by the number and importance of their committals; grey coated rustics, who had come up to town
to stand by a friend and relation whose blackthorn perhaps had been a
little too fatal among the natives at the last fair; country gentlemen willing
to show off as lords of the scene and ambitioning a niche on the grand jury
list. . . .   (*Ibid.*, pp. 121–22)

As we follow the description along through the streets, past the inns
and shebeens, into the courthouse, we realize that this is the most alert
eye which had yet looked upon the Irish scene. Maria Edgeworth
would never have used a court of justice to explain why "ropemakers
thrive at a certain season, why the hangman can endow his daughter
so handsomely, and why the science of anatomy is so attainable, and
so practically understood in Ireland."

But "The Aylmers" reveals more than an accurate eye. Griffin was
always to be intensely concerned with the explosive, anarchic power
which lay at the center of Irish life, unchecked by social forms. The
disparity between the order for which Mr. Hassett presumably stands
and the violence which lies everywhere, just beyond the range of his
eye, is constantly insisted upon. The effect is admirable in some of the
scenes, but in others it dissolves into a lurid melodrama which was
Griffin's besetting sin. It is as though his material is not amenable to
control, or at least to any control within his grasp.

This is borne out more strikingly in the book which he published the
following year, *Tales of the Munster Festivals*. It consists of three short
novels, but one, "Suil Dhuv," overshadows the others. Thomas Davis,
who rarely stooped to qualify his admiration, thought it "one of the

most perfect prose fictions in the world." [6] It is, in truth, a remarkable story, and yet it must be accounted a failure.

It is a sensational and quite blood-chilling re-creation of life in Munster during the Penal Days, when the mountain passes were made dangerous by bands of masterless men and when crime was as natural as breath. Its action is set within a single day, Saint John's Eve, and comes to its climax when the traditional bonfires are lighted. To a stretch of road near Court Mattress Griffin brings a grotesque yet representative company of travelers—a coarse, finely dressed Limerick grazier; a glib-tongued Cork buckeen, a hedge scholar. These take shelter, when night falls, at the inn of Mark Spellacy, the *suil dhuv,* who leads a gang of Raparees. It is the night when Spellacy had planned to loot the village, which he does, though he is killed in the doing.

The halves of the story are badly joined. The figures who appear one by one, on the road or at the inn, are brilliantly sketched, and the story of Spellacy's raid has a certain cumulative force, but the two accounts do not further each other. The murderous natives and the bland, self-righteous expropriators seem involved in a common fate which lies beyond their understanding. As in *Castle Rackrent* the symbols are all of money and the money is all false. *Suil dhuv* has become a forger; the government itself has introduced debased currency into the country; a trickster named O'Neil pretends that he has found a vault filled with "crosses and caps and rings and fine shinin' stones." Spellacy's greed leads him at last to the sacrilegious desecration of the objects of his faith: he loots a church and lays hand on the chalices and ciboria.

But though there are suggestions that through symbol and language we are to find unity in the story, it remains confused and shapeless. The life of the story is local, and lies in the braggart, wonderfully rendered speech of the grazier, in the bare-boned vicious charm of Awny Farrel, the hedge scholar. *Tales of the Munster Festivals* sets

---

[6] Quoted in Ethel Mannin, *Two Studies in Integrity: Gerald Griffin and the Rev. Francis Mahony ("Father Prout"),* p. 66.

out to rival not Crofton Croker, but John Banim. In "Suil Dhuv" Griffin turned, as Banim had done, to the garish literature of the hedges, drenching his story in blood and baleful penitential fires. It secured for him a reputation as the most promising of the young Irish writers. But that reputation was more justly earned by *The Collegians,* which is one of the handful of first-rate Irish novels of the period.

14. *The Collegians*

ONE EVENING IN 1830 Lady Morgan sat up until midnight, gossiping with "Counsellor Curran," the son of the great advocate and brother to Robert Emmet's Sarah.[1] The most talked-about book in Ireland at that moment was "the good, but coarse Irish novel, *The Collegians,*" which dealt with a recent and notorious criminal case. Curran, having been associated with the trial, had the inside story, and Lady Morgan, who dearly loved such accounts, listened avidly. She thought his narrative to possess high qualities of style lacking in the novel, which, if we may judge by the version which he wrote for the *New Monthly,* is most unlikely.

As with many murders which have been turned to literary account, it is difficult to understand why this one so impressed its generation, and our interest centers rather on the way in which the novelist has transformed it. The hero (for want of a better word) of the real crime was a young man named Scanlan, whose family was securely placed among the small gentry, or "half-sirs," of Limerick. A dashing and colorful young man, though a dissipated one, he was greatly liked throughout the county, and idolized by the peasants. Having seduced a village girl named Ellen Hanlon, he convinced himself, for the usual reason, that she would have to be killed, a task which he assigned to a "follower" named Sullivan, whom he would seem almost to have hypnotized. Sullivan made one attempt, but was so moved by pity that his nerve failed him. Scanlan then ordered him to take the girl out in a boat, shoot her, and tumble the body into the Shannon, promising to wait on the shore until he "saw him come back without her."

[1] Lady Morgan, *Memoirs,* II, 287–90.

The girl's body was washed ashore near Kilrush, and her murder was traced, without much difficulty, to Scanlan. Scanlan had powerfully placed friends who intervened in his behalf, and this, along with much sensational information, sufficed to attract national interest to his fate. He was hanged in Limerick.

In the pages of Griffin's novel, *The Collegians*,[2] the sottish murderer of the newspaper accounts becomes the brilliantly created Hardress Cregan, and his crime is made to serve as a mirror of the culture in which it occurred. But Griffin has set his story in the seventeen-seventies, when Ireland was astir with news of the Volunteers, of Grattan, of the first Catholic concessions. A rent had been made in the dark curtain of the Penal Days, behind which could be discerned the shifting forms of the Ireland which was to emerge. Those were the days of Patrick Griffin's youth, and he had told his son of their excitement.

The novel involves, eventually, the entire structure of provincial Irish society: the gentry, from the Chutes of Castle Chute to the Creaghs and Connollys and Cregans of Roaring Hall; middlemen like the Dalys, torn in their feelings between the Gaelic past and the Anglo-Irish present; the English of the Garrison: Leake, a physician, Gibson, the commandant of militia, Warner, the magistrate. Below these the peasants, the landless men, the shopkeepers of Limerick town, the horse traders of the Kerry mountains, the boatmen.

Castle Chute is the Great House of the county. In the hall of its keep, the Munster chieftains had assembled, Gaelic and Norman, to take counsel during the Elizabethan wars. The dour stone fortress has proved uninhabitable, however, and a new residence, to suit the needs of a new age, has been reared beside it. It is thus that its details impress themselves on young Kyrle Daly:

A rusty gate-lock—piers, lofty and surmounted by a pair of broken marble vases, while their shafts . . . were adorned in all their fissures by tufts of long grass—an avenue, with rows of elms, forming a vista to the river— a sudden turn, revealing a broad and sunny lawn—haycocks, mowers at work—a winding gravel path lost in a grove—the narrow-paned windows glittering above the boughs—the old ivied castle, contrasted in so singular a manner with the more modern additions to the building—the daws cawing

---

[2] Citations are to the one-volume edition of 1847.

above the chimneys—the stately herons, settling on the castle turrets, or wing-
ing their majestic way through the peaceful kingdom of the winds—the
screaming of a peacock in the recesses of the wood—a green hill appearing
sunny-bright against a clouded horizon—the heavy Norman archway—the
shattered sculpture. . . .   (*Collegians,* p. 53)

It is a household of women—old Mrs. Chute and her sister and her
daughter Anne—and for this reason we are reminded of that similar
household in Lady Morgan's last novel. But the Chutes are haunted
by no memory so proud and pleasant as that of Brigadier M'Taaf,
who died in the service of King George. For them it is the grim
specter of "the ould man of all," the Chute who made his profitless
peace with the new order of things, and is seen by the peasants by
night, returning to repent his bargain.

This new order is the world of the fast-rising middlemen and the
buckeens with their loaded whips and the drunken heirs of broken
or corrupt families. It is Hepton Connolly, the bloody-minded duelist,
who has managed to keep afloat by at once racking his tenants and
eluding his creditors. It is Barnaby Cregan of Roaring Hall, a middleman who has moved up in the world by marrying into the Chute family—a coarse, violent man given to fits of idle generosity. It is the
world of Barrington's memoirs, Castle Rackrent, and the rakes of
Mallow. Griffin gives it all its scapegrace attractiveness: Hyland Creagh,
who has run through his property and is now the guest at other men's
tables, has his share of that abundant and fatal commodity, Irish charm.

Roughly equal in status to these are the men of the Garrison, Leake,
Warner, and Gibson—quizzical, detached, concerned with the country only so far as their duty extends. They are sober, conscientious men,
and just according to their lights. But those lights never burned
brightly in Ireland.

Far below these are the other folk of Limerick. Mihil O'Connor,
the ropemaker, plies his sinister trade by the historic walls of Garryowen. His brother Edward is parish priest on Castle Ireland, a firm
but faded old man, who remembers the warm sun of Salamanca.
Donat O'Leary is a wild fox of a man who has become, quite inap-
propriately, a tradesman. Lowry Looby is a landless man who has
attached himself to the Dalys as a "follyer"; through his memory jingle

the old songs of another dispossessed family, the royal Stuarts. There
are a score of other, often nameless, characters, like the "turner," or
apostate, who "makes little boxes, and things that way, of the arbutus
and the black oak of the Lakes, that he sells to the English." (*Ibid.*,
p. 178) Beyond Limerick and the Lake country are Poll Naughten
and her husband, who live uneasily on the verge of outlawry. And
far to the west of them all lives Miles na Coppaleen, the Kerry horse
trader, who holds seven hundred acres of barren soil and gray limestone.

The Collegians is a "social" novel, embracing all classes and conditions. But what strikes one immediately about the culture which
Griffin has created is its lack of cohesiveness. The great Norman house
of the Chutes, with its pride and its kindliness, has been emasculated,
peopled by women and haunted by the scheming but defeated "ould
man of all." It has been replaced by the gentlemanly, ineffective
Garrison and the cunning and blackguardly half-sirs. The peasants,
their actions shaped by their affections for a proscribed creed and a
vanished order, are the followers of men who have themselves been
robbed of all sense of social responsibility. The consequence is something more than mere disregard of law. "There is scarcely a cottage
in the south of Ireland," Griffin tells us, prosily but accurately, "where
the very circumstance of legal denunciation would not afford, even
to a murderer, a certain passport to concealment and protection."
(*Ibid.*, pp. 287–88) He puts the same point more vividly on the tongue
of the termagant Poll Naughten, whose turns of phrase are unknow-
ingly echoed by Synge's Pegeen in *The Playboy of the Western World*:

Do you want me to thrust your scarlet jacket between the tree and the
rind? Let me in, you tall ramrod, or I'll pull the soap an' powder out of
your wig. If I had you on the mountains, I'd cut the pig's tail from your
pole, an' make a show of you. Do, do—draw your bay'net on me, you cowardly
object. It's like the white blood o' the whole of ye! I know fifty lads of your
size that would think as little of tripping you up on a fair-green, and making
a high-road of your powdered carcass, as I do of snapping my finger in your
face! That for your nasty bay'net, you woman's match.   (*Ibid.*, p. 288)

Men in scarlet were to have their troubles with Poll Naughten until
1922. And again, when Mihil O'Connor's daughter vanishes, Kyrle

Daly suggests that he lay information with a magistrate, but Mihil prefers to search out her seducer and "pick justice out of his four bones." It is with Daly that we feel impatient, as with a trifler, for Mihil has invoked justice in its only evident existence.

Critics have always been puzzled by the title of *The Collegians,* finding it "strangely mis-named, since it nowhere treats of college life." [3] Other, that is, than in the seemingly accidental fact that both Kyrle Daly and Hardress Cregan have recently been graduated from Trinity. But these two young men stand at the center of the novel, and the source of their education has its relevance.

Charles Daly, Kyrle's father, is an intelligent and high-principled farmer; like Patrick Griffin he is a liberal and an enthusiastic supporter of Grattan and the Volunteers. Griffin paints a picture of the domestic felicity of this family which seems unduly sentimental, until we are struck by the irony of certain of the details.

The walls are crowded with prints—Hogarth's "Roast Beef," Prince Eugene, Schomberg at the Boyne, Betterton playing Cato. There would be nothing improper in this, certainly, were it an English or an Ascendancy household. But the Dalys are Catholic and native Irish, and this makes their taste in decoration wildly inappropriate, for they have chosen to honor Hogarth's most robustly British scene, an English actor playing a Roman statesman, the ally of Marlborough, and, of all people, the Protestant mercenary who delivered Ireland to William of Orange. Perhaps the full weight of this incongruity needs, for its appreciation, some familiarity with Irish loyalties, but it borders on the grotesque.

It is as puzzling, in its way, as Charles Daly's favorite and never-answered conundrum, "Why is that fender like Westminster Abbey?" We are prompted to wonder why Daly has chosen to send his son to Trinity, the ferociously Protestant stronghold of the Ascendancy. It was possible for a Catholic to do so, by that time, once the student had soothed his own scruples, had overborne the disapprobation of his clergy, and had submitted to the conditions on which he would be accepted. In most instances such a course recommended itself only

[3] Hugh Alexander Law, *Anglo-Irish Literature,* p. 191.

to families of marked social ambition. But there is no question of the Dalys' integrity, nor of the steadfastness of their religious convictions. The puzzle suggests that the novel's title may, after all, have some point.

Griffin introduces his themes in ways as oblique as this. In fact, only late in the novel does he let us know which of certain county families are Catholic and which are of "the genteel religion," although part of the action has turned upon the issue. For his point is that in religious as in cultural issues the old lines of authority and order are being blurred.

Kyrle Daly seems, on first inspection, a hero cut from familiar cloth, judicious, temperate, public-spirited. One deficiency, if it can be called that, nags at him. He is respected, even loved, but he lacks that special quality which in Ireland commanded all others: no retainers follow him, impelled by a loyalty firmer than love. It was thus, in Maria Edgeworth's *Ormond,* that the folk of the Black Island followed Corny O'Shane while his brother went to his unmarked grave. Maria Edgeworth would have us believe that this charismatic power was passed on to Ormond, but we cannot believe her. And young Ormond and Kyrle Daly are blood brothers. It meant much in Ireland, that instinctive fealty which survived conquests and settlements and plantations. Griffin's generation was to see it vanish in the first of the wars against the landlords.

Hardress Cregan possesses this special quality in full measure. Where Kyrle, while blunt and affectionate, is reserved in thought and speech, Hardress is all lazy charm and uncontrived mastery. Casually and almost by accident he has stolen Anne Chute, whom Kyrle loves; a pack of peasants follow at his back. Even Kyrle, who has vague suspicions concerning him, is drawn to his gallant, reckless figure as he rides across the Limerick plain. But Hardress's virtues are not all external, for he is no stage villain. He is instinctively generous, chivalrous toward the weak, and has a deep detestation of hypocrisy and cruelty. The flaw which fatally compromises all of these is well-hidden, even from Cregan himself.

The plot of the novel hinges upon the seduction, desertion, and at last the murder of Eily O'Connor, Mihil's daughter. Eily was the object of much sentimental interest during the novel's nineteenth-century vogue, but she is weakly drawn, and as though to compensate for this, Griffin has thrust upon her a topheavy weight of symbolic detail. Her father pursues a trade associated with death, and his rope-walk is adjacent to a gallows green; nearby stand a pesthouse, a coffin-maker's shop, and a churchyard.

Eily is courted by all the young men of her station—Lowry Looby and Donat O'Leary and Miles na Coppaleen. But it is her misfortune to fall in love with Hardress Cregan. From this issue the dreadful events which culminate in her murder at the hands of Cregan's creature, Danny the Lord. Read in the customary sentimental fashion, the novel is a study of passion and an exercise in pathos. By such standards the figure of Cregan is created with remarkable success. The springs of his actions are probed with the relentless skill of a catechist, until at last his charm and generosity are revealed as forms of self-love.

Beneath his charm lies a sullen refusal to accept responsibility for his actions. This failure is worked upon by the baffling figure who is known variously as Danny the Lord and Danny Mann, though neither is his name. Griffin took his hint from the actual crime, for there was something chilling in the relationship between Scanlan and his brutish accomplice, Sullivan. Danny is genuinely and slavishly eager to do Cregan's bidding, but he is also the prey of a malignant desire to destroy his master through his weaknesses. On the Purple Mountain, at the Gap of Dunloe, he tells Cregan that he has a means of putting Eily away, though he uses an odd metaphor to make his point. "I'll tell you what it is, Mister Hardress. Do by her as you'd do by dat glove you have on your hand. Make it come off as it come on, and if it fits too tight, take de knife to it. . . . Don't ax me any questions at all, and if you're agreeable, take off dat glove an' give it to me for a token. Dat'll be enough; leave de rest to me." (*Collegians*, p. 164)

The glove is too tight, and Danny takes the knife to it. And Cregan, because the ambiguity of their contract corresponds to one in his own nature, is never certain of the measure of his own responsibility. As a melodrama of murder and conscience *The Collegians* is remarkably effective and much of its power derives from the clarity with which Griffin has seen his central figure.

What gives the novel its richness of substance, however, is the way in which Griffin has related Cregan and his crime to the society which produced them both, and the way in which he has used secondary characters to reinforce his theme. Hardress Cregan is invested with a kind of kingliness, but beneath his graces and powers lie the terror and the ruthlessness of a child. He has come to manhood in a society in which religion has decayed into social ritual—"the genteel religion" —and law into an extension of social privilege. What matters is *code,* that emptiest of moral patterns, which had become synonymous with honor. It had carried him successfully through balls and drinking bouts, duels and hunts. But, for the moral choice which lies at the novel's core, it has left him stripped of every weapon save the knife in the hand of Danny the Lord.

For Griffin the hunt, that most cherished of Ascendancy accomplishments, is the symbol of its anarchy. The book begins with a hunt, and it ends with one. The sounds of the novel are those of horns in the morning and hoofbeats at night. From the hunt he draws his most vivid images. A peasant is hunted down for sport by hounds and their drunken masters. An old huntsman lies dying outside a cabin while his master's friends are drinking within. A duel is fought by drunken men, stumbling about in a lodge. It is during a hunt that Eily O'Connor's body is discovered. Cregan himself is run like a stag by the calmly contemptuous Gibson, to whom the gallant squires who have rallied about the murderer are a rabble of "drunken gentlemen." Their defiant bluster crumbles before the icy, resolute officer, even the physical daring of the Ascendancy failing in the last instance.

Against the Cregans of Roaring Hall stand the Dalys, Charles and Kyrle, models of exemplary feeling and deed, who live in the sober, forthright world of the Edgeworth heroes. Charles Daly, like the Scottish factor of *Ennui,* has managed by some unexhibited miracle to deal benevolently with his tenants and honorably with his neighbors; his patriotism is chastened by his sense of the practical. And Kyrle has carried this principled moderation still further,

At one point Hardress Cregan, talking to Kyrle Daly, launches forth upon a Byronic assault upon social convention. Daly, in reproving him, says that "elegance of manner is not finesse, nor at all the opposite of simplicity; it is merely simplicity made perfect. I grant you that few, very few, are successful in acquiring it; I dislike its ape, affectation, as heartily as you do. But we find something that is conventional in all classes, and I like affectation better than vulgarity, after all." (*Ibid.*, p. 92) Molière's Philinthe could hardly have improved upon this. How Kyrle reacts to more ˙solemn matters may be imagined.

But it would be far from the fact to suppose that Daly is intended as a counterweight to Cregan, or as the novelist's didactic voice. He seems to be, certainly, but this is a measure of the novel's skill. The Dalys, father and son, are revealed as tragically inadequate. Cregan damns himself. But to be damned, it is necessary first to be alive. The Dalys have molded themselves to their high, hard principles in so repressive a fashion that they cannot be said to live. There is at the end of the novel a climactic moment of reversal and possibility which makes this apparent. In a manner fittingly Irish the Dalys are summoned back to life by the fact of death.

Kyrle has learned from Hyland Creagh of Cregan's involvement with Anne Chute, and for a moment, losing his self-possession, he thinks murderously of his former friend, "the cool, dark hypocrite." His manner, however, remains calm and considered, and soon he is lecturing Creagh on the viciousness of dueling and of talebearing.

When he returns home, however, he discovers that his mother has died in childbirth. Their friends and tenants are already in the house, and distant kinsmen are beginning to arrive. Whiskey and punchbowls have been set out. The keening women have taken up places for their traditional laments. Mass is being celebrated in one of the rooms. The house servants and the coachmen are gathered in the kitchen. Some are asleep beside jugs of Cork porter. Others are arguing the merits of funerals in the past, with "six men marching out before the hearse, with goold sticks in their hands, an' as much silk about them as a lady." (*Ibid.*, p. 248) The house echoes with the keening wail and the voices of mourners and the murmurs of the priest.

Kyrle and his father react in ways opposite and extreme. The genteel, Anglo-Irish veneer shreds away from Charles Daly. He breaks into wild and inhuman shrieks and must be brought to his senses by force. Kyrle is overtaken by a worse ordeal. He is seized by a numbness and apathy which render him unable either to weep or to pray. He remains thus for two days, bewildered and ungrieving, stirred to interest only by the river beyond the windows, where "the wintry tide was flowing against a sharp and darkening gale," and by the bleak and barren hills of Cratloe, and the harsh wind which moves the dry and leafless woodbines.

On the evening of the second day, however, as he is standing by the window of the death-room, he sees an old, frieze-coated peasant coming up the avenue to the house. He imagines the man at home picking up his stick and telling his family that he will "step over to Mrs. Daly's wake." The incident is slight, "but it struck the springs of wonder in his heart." He thrusts out his arms, his head falls back, and he gives way to hysterical grief. His father comes into the room and they meet beside the bed. They pause, "as if by a consent of the intelligence," and then, holding tight to one another, weep convulsively. It is a moment, as Griffin says, which changes their understanding of their lives.

The Irish wake was a way of accepting death by imposing on it the forms of tradition and passion. The English and the Anglo-Irish regarded it with profound and unvarying detestation. Young Ormond can scarcely bring himself to attend the funeral of his beloved Corny. But it enlisted the deepest instincts of the Irish. It is told in the O'Connell family of Mair-ni-dhuv, Daniel's grandmother, that once when she saw a relative slip into a death-room and kneel down quietly to pray, after the Anglo-Irish fashion, she leaped up and cried out contemptuously, "Where are the dark women of the Glens, who would keen and clap their hands, and would not say a prayer until he was laid in the grave?"[4] That scene, which is more revealing than many

[4] Mrs. Morgan John O'Connell, *The Last Colonel of the Irish Brigade*, I, 23.

Irish novels, may help us to understand the one which we are considering.

The Dalys, with their rectitude and virtues, with a son at Trinity and the victor of the Boyne on the parlor wall, are cut off from the instinctual life of their people, yet remain, at the core, unassimilated to the culture whose manners and whose stoicism they emulate. It is a harsh, perhaps a provincial, moral which Griffin has drawn, yet alienation is one powerful theme of the novel.

His design has a flaw near its center, though. He needed a figure to incarnate what he considered the abiding worth of Irish life. He knew better than to employ some such allegorical offering as Maria Edgeworth's O'Halloran or one of Lady Morgan's elegant outcasts. He knew, indeed, that the Irish past lived most vividly and most fully in its peasants. And peasant types he can create well and without condescension. A reader numbed by Lover and Lever is apt to dismiss his Lowry Looby as another stage servant, but he is more than that. When Looby remembers the past, he begins singing "The Blackbird," with its echoes of another age and a gentility unknown to the half-sirs. Looby himself has an instinctive courtesy and tact. It is through his anecdotes, rambling and seemingly inconsequential, that we learn the history of the intertwined Limerick families. And, each in his way, Father O'Connor and old Mihil are effective figures. But in the third of the novel's three young men, Miles na Coppaleen, Griffin tried for something finer than he could achieve.

Miles is the figure whose kingliness is neither false nor achieved at the expense of life. Griffin places him far beyond Limerick in the rocky hills of Kerry, that proud and isolated land. The peasants honor him for his character, his skill with horses, and his fighting prowess, but the gentry, too, accord him a grudging admiration. He is an attractive character, certainly, striding through the fairs with his straight-handled whip. But he is kept too far from the events of the story, perhaps because Griffin was afraid to risk him against the chances of life which had compromised Daly and Cregan. Miles na Coppaleen was to become a darling boyo of the Dublin stage when the novel was dramatized by Dion Boucicault, but he exists in Griffin's novel as a touching failure.[5]

A special irony attends this novel. A success from the month of its publication, it continued to be for many Irishmen *the* novel about their country. Banim and Lady Morgan were quickly forgotten. Carleton was always too powerful, too blasphemous, too devious in his intentions. Lever and Lover were regarded, with some justice, as depraved English tastes. Griffin's own novels, save this one, were neglected. But *The Collegians* was printed and reprinted and cherished. It suffered the fate common to "beloved" books. Its characters entered everyday speech. Scenes were made into prints to be hung on parlor walls not unlike the Dalys'. It became part of what must be called a debased popular culture, along with jaunting cars, souvenir views of Killarney, shillelaghs, Robert Emmet, and "The Wearing of the Green."

But it won even this popularity on merits which are unique in the nineteenth-century Irish novel. Griffin had not written a novel *about* Ireland; he had written an Irish novel. The Ireland of *The Collegians* is not presented to the reader as an object of sympathy or commiseration or indulgent humor. It simply exists. It exists in rich and exact detail; it is "picturesque" and "romantic," enchanted and accursed. But it is given to us in a work of art, not in a disguised tract. And, even when the complexities and ironies of the novel went unnoticed, its moral feeling struck a responsive chord. Griffin was an acute moralist, and one who lived within the same world of moral experience as did the majority of his countrymen. If the phrase "Catholic novelist" is at all meaningful, it may properly be applied to him.

It had been Griffin's intention that the novel should come to the same close as did the case on which he based it: that Hardress Cregan should be hanged. But it was felt that this would jar upon prevailing tastes, and at the last moment he changed Cregan's sentence to transportation for life. And yet he makes use even of this makeshift.

It allows him a picture of Hardress Cregan aboard his prison ship,

[5] Boucicault's drama, which bears *The Colleen Bawn* as its unfortunate title, was first produced in 1860.

looking out upon the street of the coffinmakers on the King's Island. One shop is open, and through the window he can see "unfinished shells, formed for all ages from childhood to maturity." (*Collegians,* p. 333) Within, the carpenter is at work on Mihil O'Connor's coffin.

O'Connor's people had all been buried at Saint John's, but Mihil, like young Michael in Joyce's story, was to be buried "Westward." Cregan, on his own voyage westward, struggles uselessly to accept his own fate. As the ship moves out other scenes summon him, but Cregan, intent upon the end which he had always been seeking, is waiting only for the chance to kill himself. The final image is a fitting one, for Griffin's story of Ireland has been a story of the coffinmakers of the King's Island, and of the spiritual deaths for which the coffins were being readied.

15. The Dark Land: *The Rivals* and

Tracy's Ambition

THE COLLEGIANS HAD given to Gerald Griffin the reputation which he had sought so intently, but he turned his back on it. For the next ten years he was to make his home in Limerick, save for brief and sometimes puzzling trips to London or the continent. He continued to write, though his work no longer showed that remarkable development of power from book to book. Then in September of 1838, having burned his manuscripts, he entered the monastic lay order of Christian Brothers. Two years later he fell victim to one of the recurrent typhus epidemics which preceded the great famine. Behind this bare statement lies a moving and dramatic story, which, unfortunately, we can touch upon only as it affected his work.

In an afterword to *The Collegians* he tells us with undue coyness that Lowry Looby lived long enough to vote in the Clare Election, "but on which side of the question he bestowed his voice, is more than my utmost industry has enabled me to ascertain." [1] All Ireland watched that contest. Griffin crossed the Shannon to Clare, where from a window he witnessed the tumult in the streets. In his excitement he endured an effusion by Sheil without protest. The habitually cautious Banim sent an anxious letter to him from England, where it was popularly supposed that an O'Connell victory might mean civil war. Griffin replied with easy confidence. [2]

Indeed, even to Banim it seemed that a new page in Irish history had been turned. To Maria Edgeworth O'Connell's victory heralded

[1] *The Collegians*, p. 335.   [2] Griffin, *Life*, p. 335.

the approach of chaos. To Lady Morgan it meant the debasement of all nobility and patriotism, the surrender of the national ideal to the priests and the rabble. But Banim and Griffin, eagerly exchanging literary plans, saw it as a rebirth. Griffin grandly projected a thoroughgoing account of Irish history. Nothing came of this but a long and not very interesting historical novel called *The Invasion*. It was O'Connell's impractical plan that the Catholic and the Orange movements could unite in furtherance of an agitation against the Union, and Griffin composed several poems for this campaign, including one called "The Orange and the Green." [3]

It might be said that nothing came of the poem, either. For the eighteen-thirties was one of those periods in Irish history in which bickering and recrimination formed the substance of political life. The Church, which had been the powerful instrument of O'Connell's ambitions, was largely indifferent to the question of Repeal, preferring rather to consolidate its new-won power, and to fight battles in which it had an immediate interest. Of these two were paramount. One was the issue of education, which would trouble Ireland until the end of the century, and which at the moment was entangled in the bitter sectarianism generated by the Evangelical movement known as the "New Reformation." The other was the campaign against tithes, which, by fanning the flames of agrarian unrest, was to culminate in the ugly Tithe War.

Griffin was to be drawn inexorably into both of these disputes. His involvement, however, was reluctant, for during most of these years he was caught up in an intense personal problem. *The Collegians* had suggested that his rigorous literary intelligence was joined to deep religious feeling. In time he would find it necessary to choose between them. But there was a further complication—he had fallen in love.

Lydia Fisher came of distinguished Irish Quaker stock. Her mother was the daughter of Richard Shackleton, the friend of Edmund Burke. Mary Shackleton herself (or Mrs. Leadbeater, by which name she was better known) played a distinctive role in Irish letters. She wrote a book called *Cottage Dialogues,* an edifying and tiresome work for

[3] *Poetical Works*, pp. 58–64.

which Maria Edgeworth provided an introduction. It was felt by many well-intentioned people that this book was admirably suited to inculcate in the Irish peasantry a desire for neatness and sobriety. Accordingly it was translated into Gaelic and distributed through Connemara, a picturesque and pious enterprise, and one which must have prompted speculation among students of Connemara folkways. But Mary Leadbeater, despite her implacable didacticism, was a woman of charm and character. Her "Annals of Ballitore," which was published posthumously, is rich in wit and understanding.[4]

Lydia, who married a substantial merchant named James Fisher, was also literary, and this seems to have been her first bond with Gerald Griffin. He met the Fishers, who were Limerick neighbors, in the late spring of 1829; by the end of the summer their friendship was intense and intimate. Griffin had suddenly been cut off from a society which, whatever his dislike for it might have been, was intellectually stimulating. Lydia was flattered by the attentions she received from a rising young novelist who was also handsome and witty; certainly she flirted with him outrageously. (The role of James Fisher, who read all the correspondence which passed between them, is a mere matter of morbid speculation.)

Beyond any doubt, Lydia and Griffin were deeply in love. The letters and the poems which Gerald addressed to her are conclusive. This love, because it existed in such strained and hopeless circumstances, makes several of the letters painful to read, but for the most part they are lively and graceful.[5]

And in some ways these first years after the publication of *The Collegians* were pleasant. Griffin rambled afield to the lakes and mountains of Kerry, the pleasant leas of Clare, the wild stretches of Connemara. A skillful sailor, he would take his boat past the Tarbert Race, past the "Holy Island" of Scattery, and out to the Atlantic. And there were always the history-haunted ruins—the abbeys and the old fortresses of long-gone Desmonds and Fitzmaurices and McCarthies.

[4] In *The Leadbeater Papers.*
[5] The great bulk of Griffin's letters is to be found in Daniel's *Life;* a few others were first published by Miss Mannin, in the study cited above.

Once a year, and with great reluctance, he would go to London to settle details of publication. It was a city which he hated, and not merely because of his earlier experiences there. His London friendships were nearly all with Irishmen in brief residence to qualify for some professional post, or else with foreigners—General Riego's widow, Valentine Llanos, Pecchioli. In Ireland, even before meeting the Fishers, he had been interested in the Quakers; in London he was drawn to Jewish circles. He sensed, no doubt, that they too were alien enclaves within a social order which he disliked and failed to understand.

"In Ireland," he remarked in double-edged compliment, "all is quiet and easy, everybody minding his business . . . watching the weather and taking politics rather as an amusement, than from any strong personal interest; letting the world roll by peaceably, and not giving themselves much trouble about the moral condition of its inhabitants." But in England all was turmoil, metaphysics, political economy, and skepticism. He dined once with a group which included the editor of *The Athenaeum,* and was ironically impressed by "such argumentation, such logic and learning, such zeal . . . and all with the most perfect good humor." [6] He thought them especially polite when they concealed their amused incredulity that he should be a Catholic "at this time of day."

His letters from London remind one strongly of those by which the young Yeats sought to impress John O'Leary with his own dislike of that city.[7] But Anglophobia was to become so tiresome an affectation of Irish writers that it is owing to Griffin to say that with him it was genuine and instinctive. It exacted a heavy toll. He lacked connection not only with anything so grand as a literary "tradition" but even with the speculations and chatter and shoptalk of his con-

---

[6] Griffin, *Life,* pp. 329–30.

[7] Yeats, oddly enough, much preferred Banim to Griffin, whom he writes of with an entirely unwarranted condescension. He calls him the most facile of the Irish novelists of the first rank. One feels, he says, that Griffin "is Irish on purpose rather than out of the necessity of his blood. He could have written like an Englishman had he chosen. But all these writers had a square-built power no later Irishman has approached." *The Letters of William Butler Yeats,* p. 143.

temporaries. Of the older Romantic generation he has set down his opinion:

> Wordsworth, and Coleridge, and Landor, and Southey,
> Are stupid, and prosy, and frothy, and mouthy.
> Like a ——— and a ——— they sit side by side,
> True brotherly emblems of dullness and pride.
> From morning till night they sit staring and blinking,
> And striving to make people think they are thinking.
> Like four Irish parsons oppressed with the dumps. . . .[8]

Of the younger generation Keats alone won his admiration, partly, one suspects, because Valentine Llanos, Keats's brother-in-law, was Griffin's close friend, and because Griffin shared the belief that Keats had literally been killed by English venom.

His brother Daniel encountered him during one of these London visits. It was a bitter November night, thick with fog. Daniel, who despite attempts at worldliness was more the countryman than Gerald, found the coach house where they were to meet a scene of alarming noises and confusion. Linkboys, guards, and coachmen were screaming at each other, passengers were jostling him, and horses and coaches were entangled. "The whole place," he concludes flatly and anti-climactically, was "a perfect Babel."

Then at last he saw Gerald, "a tall, slender looking figure, with a Russia leather writing case at his side, which was suspended by a silk handkerchief from the opposite shoulder. He was buttoned to the throat and seemed to address himself to someone who stood before him, but was also invisible in the fog. Like all others, he was white from head to foot with hoar frost, and it required a very close scrutiny and some boldness, to venture to recognize him as an acquaintance. It was, however, Gerald, and he seemed astonished at my having succeeded in finding him in such a blinding fog." [9]

Griffin seems momentarily to have infected Daniel with one of his tricks of style, for the image suggests effectively his isolation from the English scene, his cautious and close-buttoned containment, his

---

[8] Griffin, *Life*, p. 275.   [9] *Ibid.*, pp. 284–85.

feeling that he was addressing an invisible audience, his faint touch of the exotic.

In 1830 events turned Griffin away from the Wardour Street history with which he had been dallying unprofitably and back to the subject which alone gave life to his pen—the troubled depths and contradictions of his own culture. *The Rivals* and *Tracy's Ambition* [10] are attempts to come to terms with contemporary Ireland. The first of these is an interesting failure, but the second a powerful and startlingly prophetic novel.

When Griffin, tense with excitement, had watched the miracle of O'Connell's victory in Clare, he had understood its significance. Out of the turbulent, leaderless mobs of the peasantry, O'Connell had shaped his army of beggars, giving them discipline and purpose. It seemed to Griffin as it did to many, that out of their long need the Irish people had found a way to compel justice from an indifferent government.

But within two years Munster was in a state of rebellion. The days of Suil Dhuv and Captain Rock had returned, terror and counter-terror. There were gunmen behind the hedges once again and troops on the road. Men were on the run in the hills above Griffin's home. Into County Clare, to keep the King's peace, rode an army of regulars under the personal command of the Lord Lieutenant, who ventured out of the viceregal lodge on none save the gravest occasions. Emancipation had been an excellent rallying cry, but it brought no practical relief to the peasantry. Grievances real and delusive floated in their minds, and the chief of the former was Tithe, which assaulted with equal vigor their poverty and their faith. Archbishop Doyle had proved beyond honest dispute the injustice of this levy imposed upon those to whom it afforded neither benefit nor satisfaction, but the White Boys had long before puzzled out this conclusion. Emancipation had been decided in far-off London, but tithe proctors lived conveniently at home, where they could be potted from hedges.

As his father had done fifty years before, Griffin watched the familiar

[10] Page references are to the 1842 edition.

tragedy work itself out. The murders and burnings by the Ribbon-men, he wrote in an impassioned letter, had made him ashamed of his countrymen. He quite understood the reasoning behind the stiff Coercion Act which was being hurried through Parliament. And yet —it was a dreadful law, directed against "unhappy wretches" who were driven by need and rage.[11]

He saw also that an increasingly rancorous sectarianism was feeding the fires of violence. This became one of the themes of his curiously disjointed novel, The Rivals, which is of interest, among other reasons, because it attempts to trace the relationships between agrarian violence and other aspects of a changing Ireland. It is really two novels. One is concerned with the religious issue, and the other with the pursuit of a proscribed patriot, Francis Riorden, by a Tory magistrate.

The central figure of the first is Kirwan Damer, a well-meaning squire who has become a zealous proselytizer. An avid reader of the publications of the Society for the Diffusion of Christian Knowledge and a patron of the Kildare Street Schools, he is one of the New Lights of Irish Evangelicalism. "The duellist, the drunkard, and the gambler have all been exiled from the pale of Irish society," Griffin says, "or compelled to wear their vices in a veil. A class of men has succeeded to which even those who have an interest in its vilification must accord a preference. Those who wish to know the character of that class must know the Damers." (Rivals, p. 12)

No one could fairly have accused the Church of Ireland of being lacking in that splendid torpor which had distinguished its sister establishment, and the field for evangelical work seemed fair. But imports from England had a way of turning rancid during the sea voyage. The New Reformation saw itself entrusted with two missions, the revitalization of the Church of Ireland and the conversion of the mass of the population.

There was high enterprise in the endeavor. The Evangelical ranks included the brilliant Caesar Otway and, as a convert, the most talented Irish writer of the century, William Carleton. But, when the clouds

[11] Griffin, Life, p. 385.

had cleared, the New Reformation had left a single legacy—the word "souper," one of the ugliest coinages in the elaborate arsenal of Irish invective. A final moulding had been given to the face of Irish Catholicism, chill, vindictive, implacable. The Orange lodges and the Ribbon societies had been lashed to fresh fury. Education, one of the nation's most pressing needs, had become a matter of sectarian dispute. And, as Griffin had the wit to see, the Tithe War had been given a savage twist, confounding agrarian and religious warfare in the old fashion.

For this reason he treats his Kirwan Damer with angry contempt. His most acrid criticism is placed in the mouth of Leonard, a generous-minded Protestant. Liberal Protestants were a specialty of Catholic novels of the period. Protestant novelists, on the other hand, were fond of elderly, unworldly priests, who deplored the intrusion of their Church into politics.[12] Griffin, a rare exception, is concerned with a general coarsening of spiritual feeling. Mrs. Keleher, Damer's housekeeper, wears a long rosary twined about her waist, as an assurance to her coreligionists that she has not been corrupted.

Beyond the big houses the air is heavy with sodden, dreary controversy. Aaron Shepherd, a gaunt, grizzled Methodist, and Davy Lenigan, a voluble Papist, harangue each other with material culled from pamphlets and from an alarmingly inaccurate digest of the Council of Trent. The *shebeens* have become platforms for pothouse orators. The swift beauty of Gaelic song has given way to wretched doggerel about "the revolted Father Hannen":

> When woeful heresy
> And infidelity
> Combined for to raise disconsolation,
> You forsook that holy church
> That would not leave you in the lurch,
> And publicly denied your ordination.   (*Rivals*, p. 47)

---

[12] The religious controversies of this period would occupy much space in an exhaustive study of the Irish novel. Fiction, being a powerful instrument of moral persuasion, was harnessed to the service of each camp. The Rev. George Brittaine, for example, sang the woes of Protestant virgins converted to Rome under duress and subjected to other indignities unknown to canon law (*Irish Priests and English Landlords,* Dublin, 1830). His opponents answered with such philippics as *Mr. Moses Finegan, an Irish Pervert.* These works fill, in their hundreds, the subcellar of Irish fiction.

Against this loutish religiosity Griffin places scenes and memories of an older Ireland, drawing upon his own childhood. One of these is his charming recreation of Donovan's hedge school, of which he makes Lenigan's brother a master.

But this story yields precedence to that of "the rivals," Francis Riorden and Richard Lacy. Lacy, a lean, bloodless man, is the rebel-hunting magistrate of the county. His methods are opposed by Riorden, a young gentleman of the neighborhood who has championed the peasant cause. The men quarrel, Lacy is wounded, and a warrant is issued for Riorden's arrest. By a coincidence which only a nineteenth-century novelist could arrange with such casual confidence, Riorden is able to join the band of "patriots" who have formed an Irish brigade for service in South America.

Word reaches Ireland that he has been killed in the course of this nebulous enterprise, but he returns and goes into hiding in the hills. His presence there is discovered by Tobin, Lacy's informer. He manages to elude a police hunt, but his inveterate chivalry soon has him in new meshes. He becomes involved with the Hares, an unsavory clan of mountain folk whom Lacy and Tobin have been hunting down for no very compelling reason. In the final chapters, however, his reputation is cleared at the Assizes by Leonard and Damer, honest men despite the implied unsoundness of their religious position.

Obviously there is little point in hoping for much from a plot of this sort. But the novel fails on other grounds: it is disingenuous, which is unlike Griffin, and it is confused. Although the atmosphere and tone of the background action clearly suggest the agrarian insurrection of the period, this is nowhere brought forward. The Hares and the Naughtens and the other peasants are all represented without false sentimentality but, since they are represented as being entirely innocent of the crimes imputed to them, Lacy's villainy is as fathomless as that of Iago, and much more annoying to the reader. It is true that Davy Lenigan is apt to give vent to solemn denunciations of White Boy conspiracies but, since there are none, he seems unduly concerned for the public weal.

The one character who is seen with sardonic clarity is Tom Tobin.

Informers were a class which Irish writers could always handle with murderous efficiency, and Tobin is a prime specimen. He had been Lacy's discovery—a "tall, hungry rogue" who thought it was "high feeding to sit in the chimney corner, at the sign of the Shamrock, and cook a raw potato in the turf ashes." The other members of the family had already made profitable arrangements with the government, particularly his brother Bill, who "mounts the best coat" in Grafton Street. "That's my pride," Tobin observes. "I pick pride out of that." For Tobin is proud of his tattered Gaelic pedigree, and despises the English whom he serves:

A Mister Johnson. Some fellow of low English extraction, I suspect. A fellow of no family. And yet 'tis such fellows that live in such Elysiums as this, while the Blakes, the O'Donnells, the Fitzgeralds, the Butlers, the O'Shaugnessys, the O'Tooles, the O'Lones, the O'Donohues, the M'Carthys, the M'Gillicuddies, and all the cream and top of the old Irish nobility are scattered over the country, hedging and ditching and tilling, as hired laborers, the lands which their ancestors won in fight, and held from father to son at the point of the sword.   (*Ibid.*, pp. 119–20)

It is this pride of blood which has turned him against his own people. This is the pride which, grotesquely, leads him to save his blood money so that it may be expended on a gaudy Irish funeral. Knowing his people, he does not expect a long wait for this ceremony.

His moment comes when he rides into the mountains to serve a warrant on the Naughtins, a family with a marked prejudice against legal procedures. The Naughtins have summoned allies to their cabin, who assist in feeding Tobin his warrant, followed by a glass of water to wash it down. Swept away by the gaiety of the moment, they proceed to batter him with stones until, as a peasant girl delicately phrases it, "a poor man that was in the place had the misfortune of killing him."

Riorden, whose sympathy with the peasants does not extend to the condoning of such methods, rides over to the cabin, but is too late. When he arrives, the dying man is stretched out, his features visible only by the "dead and perplexing light" of a guttering candle crushed against a mud wall. Tobin's victims crowd in gleefully to taunt him, the major air being carried by a parcel of shrill women whom he calls, with accuracy, "cabin curs." Their speculations are theological, centering on his future in the afterlife, concerning which they can offer him little hope.

But Tobin's own concern is of a different order. His father's funeral had covered a mile of the road, and he has begun to worry whether his beloved cousins will spend his money on its counterpart. He runs down their names as though telling his beads, but concludes soberly: "If Bill could take it in hand, I'm sure it would be tasty, but where's the use of talking?"

The scene is brilliantly rendered, in its pathos and its gallows humor, but one figure stands in shadow, as he does throughout the novel—Francis Riorden, the hero. It is important that he should be in some way "involved" with the peasants, but the task calls for all of Griffin's ingenuity. At times he is only a shadowy figure, riding the mountain roads. Our only clue to his role is his participation in the South American expedition.

Griffin gives this expedition only the sketchiest detail, but there seems little doubt that he had in mind the Legion formed by General Devereux and placed at the service of Bolívar, who was far from overwhelmed by admiration of its performance. But for many Irishmen it was a high and gallant moment. To the Irish military valor was an attribute of full manhood. For close to a century, a century which esteemed physical bravery, they had been forbidden to carry arms. Their *émigré* Brigades had earned an almost miraculous reputation on foreign fields, but this fame was only blown back by the winds. From the days of the United Irishmen, however, the Irish soldier of fortune had been associated with the idea of liberation by force of arms.

The shrewd Kirwan Damer realizes this. "He lived and died an honor to his people," Mrs. Keleher says of Riorden, and Damer replies, "I know what you mean by that. He died with a green feather in his cap, and a green sash about his waist, and you are old enough to remember troubled days. There is the secret of your admiration, Mrs. Keleher." (*Ibid.*, p. 20) Of course it is. Robert Emmett had gone to his death with a green feather in his hat and a green sash about his waist. And, in point of fact, Devereux went into battle wearing the cap badge of Lord Edward Fitzgerald.[13]

Behind the puzzling figure of Riorden stands the romantic rebel, who was to haunt the imagination of nineteenth-century Ireland. Riorden is the patriot on his keep in the mountains, the counselor and strategist of the Hares and Naughtins and Lenigans. It is in the language which was coming to be reserved for the rebel chief that Mrs. Keleher describes him:

He had a warm heart in his breast. He had the eye of a hawk and the tongue of an angel in his head. If he burned my house, and then asked me to take him in my old arms, I'd do it. He had ever and always a kind of mournful look in his eyes, and a voice that would coax Europe.

(*Rivals*, p. 20)

Through its conflicting symbols and unstated themes *The Rivals* seeks without success to give expression to the dismay felt by Irish moderates at the degeneration of the Tithe agitation into lawless warfare and merciful repression. A few years later Cornewall Lewis would lay bare, in *Local Disturbances in Ireland,* the economic and cultural roots of agrarian terror. Irishmen, more intimately involved than was Lewis, the English Whig, saw the reemergence of centuries-old hostilities. William Carleton, remembering his own days as a White Boy, was moved to write the most terrible of his stories, "Wild Goose Lodge." [14] In *The Rivals* Griffin took the easy path of evasions which popular fiction left open to him: blameless peasants, chivalrous patriots, and virtuous landlords. But in *Tracy's Ambition* he took the hard road of art.

It is a story told by Abel Tracy, "one of a race who may be considered the only tenants of land in my native island." (*Tracy's Ambition,* p. 160) Above him are the great gentlemen who have reared the big houses, those swaggering expanses of white stone and blinding glass which a more recent generation, in witness of Griffin's warn-

---

[13] W. J. Fitzpatrick, *Secret Service under Pitt,* p. 550.
[14] First printed in *Traits and Stories of the Irish Peasantry.*

ing, saw reduced to charred, untenanted shells. Below him are the multitudinous cabins of the landless poor, into whose secret, communal life he has found it best not to inquire. His estate of Cushlane Beg has been yielding him a profit, and as a Protestant he is an officer in the local corps of yeomanry. He has occasional misgivings. He is a factor of the greater landlords, who have graciously permitted him to bear the burden of taxes, tithes, and county charges and to act as their scapegoat in troubled times. But, being a fair and scrupulously honest man, he is sure that bonds of loyalty hold his own tenants to him. And he is right.

His serenity is breached in two places. One October Fair he meets and falls in love with a girl named Mary Regan, whom he marries despite the scornful disapproval of her brother Ulick. Because the Regans are Catholic, he assumes at first that the scorn is merely sectarian, but learns, much to his mortification, that it is social. The Regans are anachronistic survivals of the old aristocracy. The fact is evident in Ulick Regan's manner and bearing, in his disdainful certainty of self. Tracy, whose "race" of squireens has enjoyed a century and a half of unchallenged complacency, is taken aback by this. Despite the protests of his wife, a gentle and loving woman, he begins to feel a small, rankling discontent. For one thing, she never mentions her brother by name, but searches the faces of her children for a resemblance to him. For another, the peasants, who persist in calling her by her maiden name, show her a deference which Tracy has never known.

"Troubled" times come to the county. The peasants on some of the estates have banded together in a combination so strong that it cannot be suppressed in the usual fashion. Dublin Castle, therefore, despatches a specially empowered magistrate with a detachment of mounted police.

Dalton is Ascendancy Irish of a very different sort from Tracy— urbane, gifted, and arrogant. "This great croppy gardener," Tracy's sardonic friend Clancy says of him, "this weeder out of disaffection." He bears an odd resemblance—of deportment, not feature—to Ulick Regan. His understanding of his duties is that of the stern but just proconsul: "It is nothing to me that Orson, the beast, was once Orson, my brother. I treat him as a beast while he continues so, and as my brother when he resumes the form and manner of a man." (*Ibid.*, p. 193)

In short, he is a member of that nineteenth-century governing caste which was to control Ireland by coercion acts, armed police, and firm notions of racial superiority. Tracy discovers that the easygoing half-sirs of his own class are held in as slight regard as any Catholic smuggler. The local magistrate, Purtill, is one of Tracy's friends. He is not a very creditable person: he is a drunkard, a wencher, and a bankrupt. But he has fallen into the soft ways of the country, a blarneyer and coaxer who has become half a peasant himself. Dalton pushes him aside with casual contempt. *The Collegians* had been an indictment of the squireens with their loaded whips, their hunts, and their duels. *Tracy's Ambition* is their epitaph.

The situation with which Dalton has to cope is complicated, but he has had great experience in such matters. A man named Shanahan has organized a White Boy conspiracy to enforce the rights of tenants and to discourage evictions. The movement is not widespread. Tracy's own tenants at Cushlane Beg, of whom Shanahan's brother is one, will take no part in it. It is tenacious and difficult to uproot, however, because of the peasants' punctilious code against informing and their instinctive hostility to government.

Dalton needs a colleague from the ranks of the small gentry and offers the post to Tracy. Tracy thinks of it as a chance to kill his gnawing sense of social inferiority. The decision is an easy one to make, one might suppose. However real the grievances of the White Boys may be, they are terrorists of the worst sort, and Tracy is a man of substance. But Tracy, being Irish, knows that matters are not that simple. He and his tenants have had a tacit, unspoken agreement: they stayed clear of the White Boys and he stayed clear of the government. When he accepts Dalton's offer, as he does, he accepts the consequences.

He is initiated in short order to the sordid but necessary machinery of repression—*agents provocateurs,* informers, and the rest. Dalton's

plan, which had been used in Ireland before, is to bring the rising
to a premature head and then to crush it by a vivid and edifying display of force. His efficiency is not hampered by squeamish considerations of guilt or innocence in particular instances, since he is convinced
that the peasants are uniformly vicious. He claims to feel great pity
for the people over whom he has been placed, but in an unguarded
moment he pours out his detestation of them.

It is a revealing moment. He has a son, Henry, a charming and high-
spirited young man who has captured the affections of the Tracys,
particularly young Ellen's. Henry has conceived a great liking for the
peasants, who return the feeling, and has been going to their cabins to
take down their songs and poems. After the fashion set by Thomas
Moore, he has been recasting the Gaelic songs in the genteel modes
acceptable to English taste. Dalton takes issue with him on this, and
explains, in a brilliant and sympathetic lecture, the peculiar genius of
Irish song and folk customs. But, as he talks, his language changes
subtly, as though he had no control over it, and he cuts himself short.

Tracy perceives at that moment the sinister complexities of Dalton's
character, and says, wonderingly, "And these are the people whom you
profess to hate." Dalton answers him with forced flippancy, but Tracy
begins to have an understanding of the battle to which he is committed,
one which involves deep and antithetical passions.

Tracy has chosen his side, and now that Dalton's methods have
forced nearly all the peasants to side with the terrorists, he finds that
he can travel only with a police escort. There is civil war in earnest
now, with no quarter and no neutrals.

Phaudrig Shanahan, the White Boy leader, welcomes this as heartily
as does Dalton. The Shanahans have a remarkable history, and one
with which Dalton is oddly familiar. They come from Kerry, he tells
Tracy, and are of a race as old as Noah—the aboriginal Irish. As with
Noah's sons, there is a dark primal stain upon them. They are a race
of parricides and wanderers. For a time, they lived in the Hag's Valley,
then were driven to a wilderness beyond. Dalton, who has already
made a casual reference to Dante, describes this "place beyond" as

being near a lake, "its waters prisoned in by mountain barriers, and fettered in chains of ice."

As Dalton proceeds with his story, we come to recognize its quality as a myth, a kind of unwitting exposure *in extremis* of the bemused dreads which nourished the Garrison. His narrative spells out at last the implications of the hysterical "accounts of the Irish" which the Garrison had for centuries been sending back to England. That it is pathological goes without saying, of course. But this is not quite Griffin's point, for the true substance of his novel is myth itself.

The Shanahans are first presented to us as Dalton was—lurid figures in an implausible melodrama. Two sons, Morty and Phaudrig, have moved with their mother, Vauria, into Tracy's county. Morty, deeply conscious of their evil heritage, has settled at Cushlane Beg; he keeps his passions tightly reined, from a conviction that he has inherited a blind urge to wreak insensate violence. But Phaudrig has gone up into the hills, which resemble the Kerry home from which they have been expelled. Old Vauria is a fierce, almost demoniac, crone, whose troubled mind dwells upon the notion that not merely her family but her race has been uprooted.

Phaudrig becomes the White Boy captain, goading on his people to the worst of their excesses. He is brought to bay and killed in a skirmish in which Tracy has taken part. One night, as Tracy is riding home ahead of his escort, he finds Vauria by her son's grave, which is near a ruined friary. In the harrowing scene which follows, we are intended to take her for that figure of myth, "the ghastly hag, too hideous to be seen." Her wasted, wind-scorched face half hidden by a blue cloak, she has come to mourn her lost son, and to curse on his grave those who killed him. "I have strong friends," she warns Tracy, "an' they have you marked."

Tracy professes to regard a curse of this sort as "a custom of the uninformed portion of the people," and yet from that moment he believes himself threatened by something worse than violence. The land itself has cursed him.

The curse is worked out on the innocent. Tracy and his wife fall into an ambush set by the rebels and Mary is bayoneted. When her corpse is laid out for burial, Tracy, strangely fearful, stands away from it until he has studied his wife's calm, expressionless features. It is a trick of candlelight. When he bends down to kiss her, he sees that her lips are dragged down in a grimace of scorn. He knows that it is intended for him, and not for her slayers.

Sometime after this Tracy and Morty Shanahan, wedded to terror and counter-terror, meet on a road above the Shannon. Loss and bewilderment permit them to talk to each other across the high barriers which divide them. They have almost reached an understanding when Tracy, in the thoughtless tones of social superiority, voices the wish that others beside Morty could learn the folly of rebellion and conspiracy. Shanahan pauses, and when he speaks again it is with the peasant's narrow-eyed, distrustful reserve. The barriers are there, for all of an afternoon's walk by the river.

It is Morty who brings the tragedy to its close. Even when his mother dies he keeps some grip on his reason. He loses it when his sister, whom Dalton has seduced and shamed, comes home to his cabin. Then, at last, he acts with the terrifying savagery which Dalton had ascribed to all his race. He stalks and kills young Henry Dalton, whom he loves and who has harmed no one. "The whole of that family," Moran, a farmer says, "had ever a dark sthrain in 'em."

Dalton's blue-coated police come upon the two young men in a dark gully. Henry Dalton lies dead and stark. Beside him sits the man who strangled him, stunned and imbecile.

Griffin had preached his final sermon, one prophetic of the century which was to follow it. It is less a melodrama than the symbolic representation of a country in which the roots of violence lay tangled deep in the bitter soil. And for him the worst of the story was the inability of those who lived it to perceive its tragic force. "For myself," Abel Tracy says, rounding out his tale, "I now lead a peaceful life among a circle of merry friends. My ambition is entirely set at rest, and I think if I could only succeed in obtaining the commission of the peace, which I am at present exerting every effort to procure, I should be a contented man for the remainder of my days." (*Ibid.*, p. 379)

Griffin relieves by an image the picture which he has given us. The novel ends on Palm Sunday, the day which promises rebirth after bloodshed and death. Since there are no palms in this cold northern island, the churches are decorated with evergreens, and at the novel's close long winding lines of peasants come down from the mountains with boughs of yews across their backs. Not for many decades, however, would there be an Easter Week. Ireland was still the island of the coffinmakers, and an artist could only summon forth the image and then fall silent.

Griffin wrote very little in the years which followed—some volumes of sketches and a historical novel.[15] He filled out his time with the solitary journeys which had taken up so much of his youth. By 1832 he was anxious to end his relationship with Lydia Fisher; in that year it was necessary for the Fishers to leave Limerick, and Griffin thereafter avoided her attempts to maintain the same degree of intimacy. Yet his feelings toward her remained as strong as ever.

In that same year the electors of Limerick asked him to approach Thomas Moore, whom they wished to send to Parliament. There had been a time, as he remarked, when the mere thought of seeing "the Harp of Erin" would have put him in a fever. But now he fulfilled the errand as a matter of duty, and he listened coldly and ironically while Moore expatiated upon his theory that "England will not permit so large a segment of her orb as Ireland to remain forever shrouded in darkness."

For a long time he had felt drawn toward a religious life. In 1830 he had published a curious little book called *The Christian Physiologist*. It follows a traditional pattern of Catholic homily—the anatomy and the physical functioning of each of the five senses is described, each being followed by an ingenious and strained exercise in moral analogy and then by an "illustrative tale" or fable. It remained popular for many years. His family suspected, without evidence, that his mysterious trips to the continent were in some way connected with his resolve to enter the priesthood, and they were not surprised when in 1838 he told them of his intention to quit secular life.

[15] *Tales of My Neighborhood* (1835); *The Duke of Monmouth* (1836).

But they were taken aback when he revealed that he had decided to enter the novitiate of the lay order of Christian Brothers. Like Simon Dedalus, the Griffins were fully aware that the brothers were recruited from the most humble classes, and they felt that the Church would be pleased to make more auspicious terms with a man of Gerald's reputation. But Edmund Rice had founded the order in the conviction that it would become the inheritor of the traditions of the hedge schools, and this seemed to him, as it did to Gerald Griffin, an honor sufficiently high.[16]

In June of 1839 Griffin was assigned back to Munster, to the North Monastery in Cork, where he was kept busy "enlightening the craniums of the wondering Paddies in this quarter, who learn from me with profound amazement and profit that o-x spells ox."[17] In April, 1840, he fell victim to one of the typhus epidemics which permitted English Malthusians to anticipate the day when "the native Irish would be as rare in Kerry as a Red Indian on the banks of the Manhattan." On June 12 he died.

He had begun a story which breaks off at the unfinished sentence, "Of the abyss that lies beyond—"[18] Of that abyss Griffin had seen and told much, but it was deeper than he imagined. The crowds which he had seen at Ennis were to swell into the hundreds of thousands who marched on Clontarf in August of 1843. Upon that shore, under the guns of warships and field artillery, O'Connell's career and the hopes of Griffin's party were shattered. A few years later the nightmare of the Great Famine descended, and in vast sections of Griffin's Munster "tracts of land were simply left to waste, and what rural civilization there remained seemed to fall to pieces."[19]

Griffin had been the chronicler of that civilization. He had recorded its appearance, its manner, its turns of speech. But he had seen some-

[16] For an account of Rice's life, see J. D. Fitzpatrick, *Edmund Rice, Founder . . . of the Brothers of the Christian Schools of Ireland.*

[17] Griffin, *Life,* p. 465.

[18] The manuscript is described by Miss Mannin in *Two Studies in Integrity,* pp. 129–30.

[19] Oliver MacDonagh, "Irish Emigration . . . during the Famine," in *The Great Famine, Studies in Irish History, 1845–52,* ed. by R. Dudley Edwards and T. Desmond Williams.

thing which lay beyond appearances. The people of whom he wrote were his, as they had never been Maria Edgeworth's or Sydney Morgan's. And, like the old fortune teller in one of his early stories, he saw a twisting, bloody road for them, with a gallows at its end.[20]

[20] "Card Drawing," in *Holland-Tide*.

William Carleton

.

16. A Pilgrim to Lough Derg and Dublin

MODERN IRISH LITERATURE, W. B. Yeats has written, begins with William Carleton.[1] His was the richest talent in nineteenth-century Ireland and the most prodigally wasted. For the critic he is a continuous torment, joy, and puzzle. Many of his books, as Yeats discovered, have never been reprinted and are hard to come by. And, as Yeats also discovered, he left a bitter legend behind him; a generation after his death he was still cordially detested by many who acknowledged his great gifts. Those who admired him, from Thomas Davis and Patrick Murray to Yeats himself, were compelled to explain that this profound and sympathetic student of the Irish character was not, after all, merely a hired traducer. His best work lies in parts and fragments; scenes of unmatched power and wit are buried in trumpery plots and harsh polemic.

He was born into the world of the cabins, the lost, splendid, terrible world of the Celtic peasantry, and his life has the charm of his own enigmatic stories. Born of Gaelic-speaking parents, he had trained for the priesthood in hedge schools, tramped the roads as a poor scholar, gone barefoot on his pilgrimage to Lough Derg. One of his earliest memories was of Orange yeomanry smashing open the cabin door with rifle butts. He had been a member of a secret terrorist society, and had seen the body of Paddy Devaun, the Ribbon leader, swinging tarred and chained on its gibbet. He had sung and danced at the fairs and weddings, joked with the friars on the chapel green, and made love to the young girls behind the rowans. He had seen the beggars

[1] Introduction to *Stories from Carleton.*

on the road. He had been a Gaelic poet and rogue, living by his wits from inn to inn, with a copy of *Gil Blas* in his pocket.

Then, quite suddenly, he became Mr. William Carleton of Dublin. One day in 1818, when he was twenty-four, he came down into Dublin to make his fortune. To accomplish this he conformed to the Church of Ireland, went to work for the Erasmus Smith Schools, and married the niece of a Protestant schoolmaster with government connections. In 1825 he met Caesar Otway, the gifted and fiercely sectarian editor of *The Christian Examiner,* by whom he was launched into print as an ex-Papist eager to make public abjuration of his errors and to expose the lurid superstitions of Rome.

Before his career was run he had written for every shade of Irish opinion—stern Evangelical tracts for Caesar Otway; denunciations of the landlords for Thomas Davis; patronizing sketches for *The Dublin University Magazine;* unctuous Catholic piety for James Duffy; a few sketches for Richard Pigott, the sinister mock-Fenian who was to forge the famous Parnell correspondence. By the eighteen forties he was the most celebrated of Irish writers; ten years later he was written-out, a hack whose pen was for hire in Dublin's ugly literary wars. He had but one subject, the days of his youth and the world in which he had lived them. This is the subject which haunted him and drove his pen; to this subject he was faithful, and to nothing else.

Patrick Murray, writing for *The Edinburgh Review* in 1852, defined one of Carleton's claims to our attention: "It is in his pages, and in his alone, that future generations must look for the truest and fullest, though still far from complete, picture of those who ere long will have passed away from that troubled land, from the records of history, and from the memory of man forever." [2] The language should not be dismissed as rhetoric. In 1852 the coffin ships, as they were called, were still crowded with Famine emigrants; on a visit to his native valley during that famine Carleton had found it swept clean of inhabitants.[3] His best and most ambitious book, *Traits and Stories of the Irish*

[2] *Edinburgh Review*, CXCVI (October, 1852), 389.

[3] William Carleton, *The Life of William Carleton: Being His Autobiography and Letters; and an Account of His Life and Writings from the Point at Which the Autobiography Breaks Off,* by David J. O'Donoghue, I, 57–58.

Peasantry, is a record of this peasant society on the eve of its dissolution.[4] It is a work of history, for the history of a nation, as Yeats says, "is not in parliaments and battlements, but in what people say to each other on fair days and high days, and in how they farm, and quarrel, and go on pilgrimages."[5]

But Yeats and Murray are less successful when they try to account, as every critic of Carleton must, for the contradictions in the man: the fierce sense of justice and wrong which existed beside a callous political conservatism; the love and detestation of Catholicism, felt with equal passion; the conflicting emotions of affection, scorn, and anger out of which his stories were created; the confused, groping speculations. In a single year, for example, the year 1845, Carleton published three books. The first, *Valentine M'Clutchy,* is a bitter, incendiary attack upon landlords; its sympathies are so markedly "Catholic" that it was translated at once for *L'Univers,* the organ of French Ultramontanism.[6] The second, *Rody the Rover,* is a harsh attack upon the peasant organization which had been formed to fight landlordism; it helped to restore him in the esteem of the Conservative press. The third, *Parra Sastha,* is a gruesome indictment of the slovenly half-animal life with which the peasants too often were content; it is torn in two by Carleton's affection for the objects of his scorn.

Yeats's explanation limps: "It was not an age of deep thinking. The air was full of mere debaters' notions. In course of time, however, he grew into one of the most deeply religious natures of his day—a profound, mystical nature, with melancholy at its roots."[7] But Carleton's religious sense, like his sense of politics, shows little development—only random, ceaseless change and return. He cut his cloth to suit his odd assortment of employers, and had a chameleon ability to believe, for the moment, whatever he wrote. He was immersed in the troubled and at times bloody politics of a country which he loved and loathed.

---

[4] *Traits and Stories of the Irish Peasantry,* first series, 2 vols., Dublin, 1830; second series, 3 vols., Dublin, 1833. Page references are to the 4 vol. London edition of 1896.

[5] Introduction to *Stories from Carleton,* p. xvi.

[6] *Les chroniques de Château Cumber,* Paris, 1845.

[7] Introduction to *Stories from Carleton,* p. xii.

To understand Carleton in his work and in his life is to understand much of modern Ireland, for in him the values of Gaelic Ireland and those of modern Europe clashed with explosive and tragic force. In his admirable study of Carleton, one of the very few attempts by a modern Irish writer to come to terms with a nineteenth-century writer, Benedict Kiely has written: "Carleton had in relation to the Ireland of his time a significance not shared by his contemporaries, by Lever or Gerald Griffin or the Banims or Mrs. Hall. His life and his writings bridged the Famine. His own character mirrored much of the contradiction and division, political and religious, of that period, just as the journey that brought him from his birthplace in Tyrone to the place where his body was laid in Dublin emphasises the continuance of some of those divisions and contradictions into the present." [8]

"The Poor Scholar," one of Carleton's autobiographical stories, opens with a father and son standing on a hillside. It is winter, and they are thinly clad. The Ulster hill, hard and barren, has been let to them at a rack rent, and soon they will be evicted from it. "Whenever a cold gush of stormy rain came over them, both were compelled to stand against it, and their heads turned, so that the ear almost rested back upon the shoulder, in order to throw the rain off their faces. Of each, however, that cheek which was exposed to the rain and storm was beaten into a red hue, whilst the other part of their faces was both pale and hunger-pinched." (*Traits and Stories*, II, 179) They are looking down into the sheltered valley, where the farms of the Scottish settlers lie snug and warm. Carleton's life, like his story, begins with a boy standing by his father, looking out upon what was at once his own land and the land of strangers.

The name is deceptive: it had once, long before Carleton's time, been O'Carolan. The family was driven from Clandermot during the plantation of Ulster and scattered across the province.[9] James Carleton came into the parish of Clogher in Tyrone sometime in the eighteenth

[8] Kiely, *Poor Scholar: A Study of the Works and Days of William Carleton* (*1794–1869*), p. v.
[9] Carleton, *Life,* I, xiii.

century and married a girl named Mary Kelly, by whom he had fourteen children. William, the youngest boy, was born on February 20, 1794. James Carleton's efforts to wrest a living from inhospitable soil, during a time of troubles, led him to move from one townland to another, but the only town in our sense of the word was Clogher itself.

It is too often forgotten that Carleton, though he wished his stories to be representative of all Ireland, was first of all an Ulsterman, and that this, whether in its Catholic or its Protestant variety, is a special breed—scrappy, pugnacious, and self-reliant. Most of the village streets in Ulster had seen party fights and faction fights long before there were Orangemen or Defenders. In Carleton's Clogher the native Irish and the Scots-Irish were evenly divided, and each nourished a profound, blood-spilling hatred for the other. Carleton grew up accepting violence as one of the casual facts of experience.

Perhaps because the external pressures upon it were so great, the Gaelic population held tenaciously to its language, customs, and traditions; Celtic Ireland lived as fully in Carleton's cabin as it did in Connemara. But in remote Connemara, where most of the landlords were absentee and there were few plantation families, it lived openly. In Clogher it lived despised and hidden. Carleton creates his most startling effects by plunging us suddenly into that world.

His description of Pat Frayne's hedge school in Findramore is a case in point. The village lay at the foot of a long, green hill, which Carleton describes in careful but idyllic terms. The reader is taken down the hill, across the brook, and into the village—two rows of thatched cabins with chimneys of wicker creel plastered over with mud. This "reader" has been given a personality; he responds to the idyllic—perhaps he is an admirer of "The Deserted Village." Now he becomes a traveler on horseback, before whom an urchin is snatched up from the road, "lest the gintleman's horse rides over it." He is a threatening alien, yet it is he who feels fright and disgust. At a cabin door, beside a fetid dung pool, a watery-eyed woman stands watching him. Faces, curious or sarcastic, peer at him from crude window-holes. A lump of clay is hurled at him by a tattered boy behind a hedge. A laborer leans on his hoe, studying him sullenly. The air is thick with

the stench of burning fat. And everywhere there are children, frightened or malicious.

Free of the village at last, the man on horseback rides on toward
another valley, but is stopped by a confused buzz of voices coming
from the mud ditch itself, into which a crude door has been set. A
boy looks out at him, shielding his eyes as if to throw back the light
from the sun. Others join him. And then a ferocious voice sings out,
"Back from the door, boys; rehearse—every last one of you rehearse, I
say, you Boeotians, till the gentleman goes past." (*Traits and Stories,*
II, 210) It is that oddly classical and oddly apt word which tells the
traveler that he is looking at a hedge school. But here the traveler and
the actual reader part company, for the reader lingers to learn the
story of that school, which has a meaning central to the life of Carleton's community and of Carleton himself.

He is taken on a wild journey, for "The Hedge School" is an outrageously funny and bitter story. It is the opening which interests us
now. Carleton has organized his material with great skill—down from
the hill of sentiment, where the writer had spent "many an hour in
solitary enjoyment," watching "the flight of the cloud shadows," into
the mean, ugly life of the village, and at last to the school of mud which
gives meaning to all the scene, to hill and village alike. For "Mat
Kavanagh," as Frayne is called, teaches school by day and leads White
Boys by night, and is the center of the conspiracy of silence which locks
the village. Goldsmith tames his Auburn; Carleton unlocks the untamed heart of Findramore—and it would be so with whatever he
touched.

He always claimed that his skill at storytelling came from his father.
James Carleton is described with great affection in the introduction to
the 1842 edition of *Traits and Stories*—a gentle, humble, and superstitious man who knew by heart "all kinds of charms, old ranns, or
poems, old prophecies, religious superstitions, tales of pilgrims, miracles
and pilgrimages, anecdotes of blessed priests and friars, revelations
from ghosts and fairies." (*Ibid.,* I, xxxvi) William Carleton was to
draw upon his father's rich storehouse of legend when he was tramping the roads, telling a tall tale for a night's lodgings. He was to tell

such tales again in Dublin, pouring them into the shocked ears of the Reverend Caesar Otway.

But one of these stories stood out above all others in his memory. In 1795 a dreadful accident occurred on the pilgrims' route to Saint Patrick's Purgatory on Lough Derg. A boat crowded with pilgrims sank between Pettigo and the island; of ninety-three passengers all but one or two were drowned. But as James Carleton, the *seanachy*, told the story in Clogher, the only survivor was a priest whose saintliness had permitted him to walk safely across the water. This story, as we will see, came to hold great meaning for William Carleton.

Carleton's wide knowledge of the Gaelic oral tradition naturally plays a large role in his stories. Occasionally it lapses into Crofton Crokerism, but most of the time he sees everything that is done or imagined in his stories through a peasant's eyes. Mary Kelly, his mother, was a singer famous throughout her parish, and much in demand at wakes and weddings; he learned from her many of the songs and poems which her grandfather had written in praise of patrons or dead beauties. Once she was asked to sing the English words which had been put to "The Red-Haired Man's Wife," but she said that "the English words and the air are like a man and his wife quarreling— the Irish melts into the tune but the English doesn't." (*Ibid.,* xxxviii)

One clue to Carleton's world is the degree to which it was cloistered and conspiratorial. He was born four years before the '98, became a Ribbonman, and was familiar with political terror and intrigue. He joined the Ribbon Society of his own decision, but he would have had little choice—every peasant in his townland was bound at least to its oath of silence. But the life of his people was secret in other, less melodramatic ways. The Gaelic tongue itself amounted to a secret language. Disputes between peasants were rarely settled by law, but by cudgels or kangaroo courts. Their hedge schools, though the law took no action against them, were technically illegal, and the tang and sting of outlawry were still strong upon them.

But the center of their life was the church, and this too had been outlawed, and now existed upon humiliating terms. Carleton's grandparents could recall the days when priests had been hunted down and altars smashed, when Mass was celebrated in caves. In Carleton's boyhood there was no chapel in his neighborhood. Instead there were what people called "The Three Altars." Each altar stood on the open ground near the road, protected by a few feet of roof; the congregation knelt on the bare earth. Some worshippers, however, brought tussocks of hay or straw on which to kneel, and these lay scattered on the ground from one Sunday to the next. "They presented something very strange and enigmatical to such as did not understand their use." [10]

Carleton was to deal with every mood of the Irish religious impulse, from the exalted to the debased. As a Northerner, however, he was especially sensitive to its social and political implications. In Rebellion time, the Carleton children had somehow come into possession of a toy cannon, which prompted the rumor that the family was concealing arms. The result was a raid by the Orange yeomanry, who treated the family roughly, and prodded one of the girls with a bayonet. James Carleton, that gentle man, packed up at once and sought another farm, but his son swore that he would do something about it when he was older. What he did was to join the Ribbon Society, which was leagued indiscriminately against landlords and Protestants.

As fact and as symbol the Irish peasantry has engaged the imaginative sympathy of writers and intellectuals eager to determine the heart and center of Irish life. The beginnings of this interest we have witnessed in Banim and Gerald Griffin. It was to grow more intense in the course of the century, until, for many writers, only peasant culture would seem truly Irish. This, of course, was Carleton's strongest single claim upon the attention of his contemporaries and his successors. There can be little doubt that Carleton rendered the life of a peasant Ireland with a fullness, a passion, and an accuracy which no other writer has approached. Only to a man who himself had lived that life was such intimacy possible, and the sheer fact that Carleton came from the world of the cabins lent an accidental, dramatic charm to his character and to his work.

[10] Carleton, *Life*, I, 37.

The direction taken by Carleton's critics was properly set by Thomas Davis in 1845:

William Carleton is a peasant's son. His frame and heart are those of an Irish peasant. His intellect and passions are gigantic. No other peasantry have had their tale told so well as the Irish by this Monaghan man. . . . There is nothing in our scenery—from the sunny cornfield and the fierce mountain to the dismal bog and the sequestered glen—from the faction and the party fight to the wedding, the wake, and the funeral—from the land jobber and the usurper and the murderer . . . that he has not put before us. No man who does not know the things he tells, knows Ireland —no man who knows it ever doubted the perfection of these "Traits and Stories." [11]

Yeats, who succeeded Davis in the leadership of Ireland's intellectual life, expands upon this in a marvelous and almost meaningless sentence:

He seems, like the animals in Milton, half-emerged only from the earth and its brooding. When I read any portion of "The Black Prophet," or the scenes with Raymond the Madman in "Valentine M'Clutchy," I seem to be looking out at the wild, torn stormclouds that lie in heaps at sundown along the western seas of Ireland; all nature, and not merely man's nature, seems to pour out for me from its inbred fatalism.[12]

But it is this very general notion of Carleton as "the historian of the peasantry" which has worked against an understanding of all that was hard and unique in the man; in like measure, it has contributed to the sense of confusion and contradiction which he excites in most readers. For Carleton was a "spoiled priest" as well as a "peasant"—no more than in Rabelais, whom in several ways he resembled, should this be overlooked. Oddly enough, it has rarely been considered, save briefly by Catholic writers who wish to enter it as a particular in a bill of indictment or as an explanation of his rough handling of the clergy. By way of three figures may the Gaelic Ireland of the eighteenth century be understood—the priest, the scholar, and the hedge poet, and Carleton —in his own eyes, at least, and those of his neighbors—was all three. These are the arts into whose mysteries he had been initiated, whose

[11] This article first appeared in *The Nation*, July 12, 1845; it was reprinted in *The Essays of Thomas Davis*, pp. 359–60.
[12] Yeats, Introduction to *Stories from Carleton*, p. xvii.

vows he had sworn, from whose nets (to use Joyce's image) he sought
to fly. If we are to understand Carleton's work, we must know what
these meant to him.

The five volumes of *Traits and Stories* range over a wide variety of
subject and theme, yet most of them turn, as though by homing instinct, to the hedge school and the chapel, to the scholar and the priest.
In Irish life, the two were intimately connected. In the eighteenth
century (the century in which, despite chronology, Carleton's Gaelic
life was lived), nearly all the values of the old culture were vested in
these two institutions. One of the *Irish Melodies,* "The Irish Peasant
to His Mistress," suggests, in a way which Moore never intended, the
degree to which even sexual feeling had been invested in the Church.
The Church, of course, is the mistress; her opulent but unsuccessful
rival, honored "while thou wert mocked and scorned," is the Protestant Church of Ireland; the rival lives in a rich temple, the mistress
lies hidden in a cave; "her friends were all masters, while thine, alas,
were slaves." [13] Moore would have justified the image on historical
grounds: it had been employed in the "coded" poems of Penal Days.

Deprived of other leadership, the peasant naturally looked to his outlawed church, whose images and metaphors were feminine—Mariolatry
has always been marked in Ireland—and whose rituals and ceremonies
were the only available instances of formal art. And the leadership was
celibate. There was, of course, an unhappy contingent of priests who
had broken their vows and a larger number of "whiskey priests," but
the overwhelming mass of the priesthood was scrupulous in this matter to a degree which at times excited the incredulous and somewhat
amused admiration of European Catholics. The special and merited
claims of the priest to the affection of his people made him a figure of
uncanny awe—not unmixed, to be sure, with the sardonic awareness of
human limitation which the peasants of all nations possess.

In another respect, however, and one for which the Irish people themselves can scarcely be blamed, the elevated stature of the priest was
harmful to Irish culture. The only road to advancement of any kind lay
through the church, either in its priesthood or in the system of hedge

[13] Thomas Moore, "The Irish Peasant to His Mistress," *Irish Melodies,* p. 73.

schools, which only nominally were free of clerical control. "To the divil I pitch slavery," says Jimmy M'Evoy, the boy on the hillside. "An' now, father, wid the help o' God, this is the last day's work I'll put my hand to. There's no way of larnin' Latin here; but off to Munster I'll start, an' my face you'll never see in this parish till I come home a priest an' a gintleman." (*Traits and Stories,* III, 182) The priest was a splendid and masterful figure, and many young boys "felt the call" for reasons which were, to put it mildly, mixed. Of these Carleton was one.

The ties between the priesthood and education were many. To name the most obvious, the priests, who assumed a despotic authority over the life of the people, were scarcely likely to let the schools pass unnoticed. But the priesthood was recruited from the schools in exactly the fashion that the Irish Brigades recruited their ranks from the heroes of the faction fights. The best scholars were encouraged to stay on for the preparatory courses, or were sent on to classical academies, whence they were passed first to continental seminaries and later to Maynooth. Carleton has explained the method in several stories, most notably "The Poor Scholar" and "Denis O'Shaughnessy Goes to Maynooth."

But the process also worked in reverse, for many of the hedge masters were spoiled priests, or at least had been intended for the priesthood. They were a wild and reckless lot, poets, drunkards, and rebels—both they and the hierarchy profited by the narrow escape. As poets they were trained in the old Gaelic forms; as pedants they were versed in the controversial tactics of the seminaries. As a class they have been both glorified and vilified, but for the most part they were decent men caught up in a freakish system, and many were highly gifted—most of the famous "Munster poets" were schoolmasters and spoiled priests, a bit too fond, for their own good reputation, of whiskey and girls.

For Carleton, the *beau ideal* was his own teacher, "the great Pat Frayne." Frayne was a wanderer from Munster, "the classical kingdom," and hence much sought-after by parents in less erudite provinces. He had a hundred pupils the day after he tacked up on chapel door and at crossroads a notice that he was offering instruction in Greek, Latin, Hebrew, and English, every branch of mathematics, every

classical author, and—a fine Irish touch—"Physics, by theory only; Metaphysics, practically." His true skill was in teaching grammar, arithmetic, Christian doctrine, and some Latin. He carried with him his
library of texts: lives of the saints, denunciations of heretics written in
hudibrastic verse, *The Fifty Reasons, The Grounds of the Catholic
Doctrine, The Battle of Aughrim,* a long eulogy of "Ascanius" (the
Young Pretender).

Despite this literary cornucopia, however, Frayne was not equipped
to prepare youths for the seminary, and accordingly Carleton's father,
who wanted to "see him with his robes on him," transferred him to a
series of classical academies, each of which lasted for a year or so, or
until the master got a new itch to travel. One of the several important
points which is evaded in Carleton's autobiography concerns his decision in favor of a priestly life. He attributes it, in the first instance, to
filial piety; his father very much wanted it, and he loved his father.
Then, too, his "vocation" gave him an undeniable sense of superiority;
he tells us wryly how well he liked to strut about in the "young priest's"
somber black, a tall, big-boned scarecrow, carrying on impressive
theological discussions with fellow aspirants and flirting with impres-
sionable girls. The strongest motive of all, however, was the fierce
thirst for knowledge which he had acquired; he was a born scholar,
who picked up all kinds of knowledge without effort, but classical
studies enthralled him. He tells us with pathetic exactness the book in
Ovid or Virgil on which he was at work when each of his tutors
vanished from Clogher. But there is only the barest hint of any religious emotion, and this, whatever allowance we make for his strong
secular impulses, simply does not ring true. The scrupulous avoidance
tells its own story.

Carleton was about fifteen when his father died and "took the good
luck of the family with him." It was decided by the family, of whom
his invalid brother Jim was now the head, that he should continue his
preparation by going on the road to Munster as a poor scholar, and an
altar collection was taken for this purpose. Of this occasion, a momentous one in an Irish boy's life, Carleton has given us two accounts,

one in the autobiography, and one in the autobiographical story of Jimmy M'Evoy. The two boys, one real and one imagined, started out from the same cabin to take their ways south. But Jimmy M'Evoy went on to Munster and then to Maynooth. Some seven years later, as he was about to make another momentous decision, Carleton paid his first and last visit to Maynooth and, looking through the gate, fancied that he could see "little Jimmy M'Evoy."

But Carleton himself traveled only as far as Granard, which is a few miles from Edgeworthstown. That night, in Grehan's inn, he had a dream which sent him back to his family: a mad bull was pursuing him, and he woke sweating with terror.[14]

For two more years he went without instruction, then found a place in a classical school at Errigal Truagh. He had grown into a tall, strapping young man, a singer at every wedding and a mourner at every wake, an athlete, and a faction brawler. When he was nineteen he joined a Ribbon lodge. The oath was given to him by a red-haired fellow named Hugh Roe McCahy, at a dance on Caragh Hill: "What age are we in? The end of the fifth. What's the hour? Very near the right one. Isn't it come yet? The hour is come, but not the man. When will he come? He is within sight."[15] He would remember the words when he wrote "Tubber Derg." During his time in the lodge, an Orangeman named Jerry Hop-and-Go-Constant and a fellow Ribbonman named Hacket were murdered.

A gypsy to whom he had given a tenpenny bit told him, "He will never be a priest. He will love the girls too well. But when he grows up, he will go to Dublin and become a great man."[16] He was almost grown now, but the only account which the *Autobiography* makes of a change in plans is the abrupt statement, "I now bethought me of opening a classical school."[17] We have one hint as to what had happened. His "classical master" at Errigal Truagh is called Keenan in the *Autobiography*, but he has been identified as the priest of that parish, a Father Campbell. Campbell had had a dispute with Bishop Murphy,

[14] Carleton, *Life*, I, 71. [15] *Ibid.*, I, 85. [16] *Ibid.*, I, 213.
[17] *Ibid.*, I, 95.

"as a consequence of which the latter would not advance any of his students to the church." [18] This would indeed have barred the door firmly.

Carleton describes thus his wild sorrow at the thought of leaving home for his abortive trip to Munster: "All my sorrow, my grief, rather—for my father revived with as much vehemence and power as I first felt on the occasion of his death. I got his clothes—I pressed them to my heart, I kissed them. . . ." [19] And in all his stories the boy who is intended for the priesthood is anxious for prestige, comfort, and advancement, while the father is animated by simple piety. And yet we would know much about Carleton if we knew his feelings when the priesthood was blocked to him.

They would not have been feelings of unalloyed grief, at any rate —he found life much too lively. His most pressing desire was to continue his education. In 1816 Campbell moved his school to Dundalk, and Carleton was left "without a single object or prospect in life." [20] He entertained vague hopes (mistaken, it would seem) that in time Campbell would summon him to Dundalk as an assistant master. In the meantime, though, he was a grown man with a living to make and an obligation to contribute to the support of his family. He made a few desultory attempts to open a school, but "could find only three students whom I could reckon on as certain to attend. I consequently gave all hopes of a school to the wind." [21] Instead he abandoned himself to a lazy and roistering life, a burden to his people.

In "The Hedge School," Carleton has given us a classic account of a hedge master's apprenticeship. A gifted young man would study until he felt himself a match for his master. Then he composed a rhymed challenge and posted it on the chapel door. A formal contest would be held on the green, with the priest sitting in judgment. People would flock in to watch the sport, for these were contests of wit and bluster as well as erudition. If he lost, he went back to school. If he won, he set out on a tour, challenging famous masters in the various villages,

[18] From information supplied to D. J. O'Donoghue by Canon D. O'Connor, who in 1895 was parish priest in Errigal. Carleton, *Life*, I, xiv.
[19] *Ibid.*, I, 68.   [20] *Ibid.*, I, 91–92.   [21] *Ibid.*, I, 95.

"a literary knight-errant, filled with a chivalrous love of letters which would have done honor to the most learned peripatetic of them all, enlarging his own powers and making fresh acquisitions." (*Traits and Stories,* I, 202) After three or four years he returned home for another bout with his old master; if he won this one, the school was his.

Carleton's account of this system of graduate training-by-tournament is somewhat anachronistic. It may well have persisted in some places, just as Munster continued to hold its bardic contests in rural inns, but by the beginning of the nineteenth century the hedge schools were in decline. Carleton's own problem was the more conventional one of finding a community in need of a master. But this he refused for several years to do. The respect in which he had been held by the peasants encouraged his natural talent for indolence and irresponsibility. "During this time," he remarks complacently, "between my studies and amusements I had a very pleasant life, with the exception of some unpleasant glances at the future."

The family was scattered now, and only Carleton and his invalid brother remained with their mother. The Carletons had made great sacrifices for "the young priest," and no doubt they regretted the collapse of his plans, but he was a strong, healthy man, and they needed his help. At last they were evicted, the furniture was seized for arrears, and they had to set out, with twelve sacks of oats, for the home of his married sister Sarah. Sarah's husband soon tired of his idle ways, and turned him out. "I had no fixed residence, no abiding shelter, no home. I passed from one relative to another, and was often asked by my wealthy neighbors to go and spend a week or a month with them." [22]

For a while he stayed with his brother Michael at Aughenclash, where he was once again asked that offensive question, "Why don't you go and learn a trade?" From Aughenclash he went to the cabin of his brother-in-law, Roger Hacket, who wondered, after a few months, "why he didn't get a spade and work?" He had run out of relatives, and his years in Tyrone were at an end. "From that spot I started with a bitter and indignant heart, without one moment's preparation, friend-

[22] *Ibid.,* I, 113.

less, moneyless, and alone—but not without hope, for I had read *Gil Blas.*" [23]

Carleton had discovered Le Sage's great picaresque romance only a week before. A peddler was carrying the book in his pack, and gave it to the young man. Carleton had ransacked the neighborhood for narratives—*The Life of Edward, Lord Herbert* and Defoe's *History of the Devil*—but he knew at once that this story of a Spanish rogue surpassed them all.[24] When he was tramping the roads in search of his own fortune, he would invent parallels between his own adventures and those of Gil Blas.

Carleton's journeying would take him, despite twists and turns, steadily southward, toward Dublin. He made an earlier trip westward, however, to Lough Derg and Saint Patrick's Purgatory, of which he has left several accounts, and it is uncertain where this trip should be fitted into the chronology of his life. It was some months, probably a year, before he left home. The course of his life was set by the roads he took: the Longford road to the seminary, where the dream of the mad bull turned him back; the pilgrim's route to Lough Derg, in Donegal; the road to Dublin, where, as the gypsy had foretold, he became a great man. The second of these was to loom in his own mind as the most important, but we must postpone consideration of it: the account given in the *Autobiography* is merely a close paraphrase of the famous story which he wrote for Otway's *Christian Examiner.*

Dublin lay in the unimagined future the day that Carleton turned on his heel and left Roger Hacket's cabin, with *Gil Blas* tucked in his pocket. Carleton's account of his life on the road supplies the *Autobiography* with its most vivid pages—it is a rambling, jumbled narrative, and there is no need to sort it out here. So far as he had a plan, it was to find a village in need of a schoolmaster, but he fell easily into the wanderer's life. He was not on the roads by himself. The price

[23] *Ibid.,* I, 127.

[24] The novels which Carleton, Banim, and others read were, for the most part, the "cabin classics" hawked by peddlers throughout the island. Most of them were the sixpenny "Burton" books, first published in 1700, in Dublin. An interesting account of these is given in *Irish Book Lover,* II, 110 and 128–29. But how poor Lord Herbert found his way into such lurid company—unless Deism be literally infernal—I cannot say.

of wheat had fallen sharply in the depression which followed the peace, and landlords, anxious to recoup their losses by converting from crops to cattle, had been carrying out mass evictions; special legislation was passed in 1816 to facilitate this process. There followed two severe famines, one in 1817 and a second in 1822. The Ribbon Societies were swelled from the ranks of the dispossessed, and some counties—notably Louth and Tipperary—were under martial law. Thousands of men who had expected to live out their lives in one valley were walking with their families from village to village, begging the bread of charity. Twenty years later, when the country was suffering a worse calamity, Carleton remembered these starving families and placed them in the terrible pages of *The Black Prophet*: "The pictures and scenes represented are those which he himself witnessed in 1817, 1822, and other subsequent years . . . and they not only have escaped contradiction, but defy it." [25]

But Carleton was not yet under the dark star of that novel; he was a strong young man with the world before him, and he naturally gravitated toward the older company of poets, musicians, and vagabonds who had always walked the Irish roads. They were to live in a brighter chamber of his memory, and to reappear in the wild and witty stories which he wrote for the *Irish Penny Journal* in the 1840s.[26] At Peter Byrne's public house he met Talbot and Gaynor, the blind pipers, had his drinks with them, and learned how a man with a pack of entertaining stories could be sure of his bite and his glass at *shebeen* or great house. Unfrocked priests, crackbrained scholars, fiddlers, and wags were his company. And for those who sheltered him he had his father's wealth of stories, as well as "the old classical legends, which I transmogrified and changed into an incredible variety of shapes." [27]

But he came one day to the crossroads of Corcreagh, in Louth, where he saw "something like a tar sack dangling from a high beam of wood, or rather from the arm which projected from it." [28] It was the body of Paddy Devaun, who had been hanged, tarred, and gibbeted in front of his cabin. There were twenty-four bodies hanging from gibbets in

[25] *The Black Prophet: A Tale of the Famine*, p. iv.
[26] Collected in *Tales and Sketches*.   [27] Carleton, *Life*, I, 171.
[28] *Ibid.*, I, 130.

Louth that autumn of 1818, with soldiers standing on guard lest they be taken down. As the bodies decomposed, flies covered them, and "during that autumn, fruit in the county of Louth was avoided, as something that could not be eaten." Nearby stood the burned-out shell of a building called Wildgoose Lodge. Carleton tells us that he had heard "not a syllable" about the atrocity at Wildgoose Lodge, "although the account of it in the newspapers must have gone all over the dominions of George the Third." But he cannot be speaking the truth: Tyrone and Louth are close to each other, and Wildgoose Lodge was a Ribbon affair.

It had been the home of a man named Lynch, a Catholic, who refused to join the Ribbon Society. He was attacked and beaten, for which he named and prosecuted a number of his assailants. In consequence the Ribbonmen turned out in strength, burned his house, and murdered its inhabitants, including a number of children. Twenty-four men, including Devaun, their leader, were tried at the Dundalk Assizes and hanged; many of these were guilty. But the murder gang had numbered in the hundreds, and some of these openly boasted their complicity in the public houses of Corcreagh, where Carleton learned the story. He has told that story, with little invention but with frightening intensity, in "Wildgoose Lodge." [29] It is no more than a sketch, but it makes every line by John Banim seem forced and pallid. The burned house, the stories of children spitted on pitchforks, the tarred, rotting bodies gave him a detestation of violence which he never lost.

After a year or so of the wandering life, however, its charms began to pall, and even Gil Blas could not revive them. "How was I to live now?" began to concern him, and "Where was I to go?" He learned that "Mr. Fitzgerald of the Fane Valley" was looking for a master, and so walked there, but discovered that the post had been filled. Another rumor took him one step further south, into Meath, but this too proved false. At this point, he remembered that someone he had met on his travels had told him of a "society in Dublin, where they trained masters to teach schools" and then found posts for them. Pat Frayne's old pupil had thought that this Kildare Street Society must be a queer place in-

[29] *Traits and Stories*, III, 308-27.

deed, if it set out to teach a man what he already knew. Now he was less sure.

He was almost ready for Dublin, Caesar Otway, and *The Christian Examiner*. There was one more trip to be made:

Here was I left friendless again, with my prospects in life as dark as usual. Where to go, I knew not; but, as in the case of my pilgrimage to Lough Derg, the reader is aware that I went to visit that far-famed locality more from curiosity than devotion, so the idea of a visit to Maynooth seized me, a visit to the town in which the great college was to be seen with my own living eyes. I think I was more anxious to see that college than I had been to see Lough Derg itself.[30]

His road took him to nearby Clane, where he applied for a teaching post in a letter written "at the very top of my skill." But the Jesuits of Clongowes Wood found that they had no vacancy. He was treated to a solitary dinner, and discovered beside his plate a small paper package which contained fifteen shillings. He went then to Maynooth, but of his dealings at the seminary he has little to say: "What communication could a nameless wanderer like me expect with such an establishment?"[31]

Clongowes Wood and Maynooth were at the end of Carleton's road as a "poor scholar" in Catholic Ireland. He was about to enter another world, and for motives which his *Autobiography* do little to put in a favorable light, for his state of mind, as he tells us frankly, was desperate, bitter, and resentful. Thinking better of this, he remarks that he was "on the eve of a change, such as few individuals ever underwent."

A moral gloom seemed to supervene, not only upon the life I led, but upon the general workings of society. My object was to ascertain the causes of things as they appeared to me; but this I could not do. I had no opportunity of making myself acquainted with those works which treat the moral government of life. I had read nothing but a few odd novels and some classics, and was in every way badly qualified to analyze the progress of the world as it went on. Thinking and reasoning had come almost to a standstill with me. . . . What was I to do now? I had tried everything. I felt that I was progressing downwards. Was there a peculiar fate attached to me?[32]

[30] Carleton, *Life*, I, 176.   [31] *Ibid.*, I, 181.   [32] *Ibid.*, I, 188.

And so he walked his way into Dublin, arriving in the evening by the southern road which led into James's Street. "The reader need not expect that I could, even if so disposed, give anything like a detailed account of what I had suffered in Dublin, while an obscure stranger. It is a task through which my memory could not carry me. . . ." [33] He met at last a Mister Fox, who was master of an Erasmus Smith School, and fell in love with his niece, Jane Anderson. He married, became in due time a father, and secured a post with the Sunday School Society —a humble brand, grateful to be plucked from the burning. In exchange for his old friends—Moran, the crazy tailor, who was composing an endless autobiography, and the fiddler Buckramback who had been "out" in the Croppy War—he made others: the brothers Samuel and Mortimer O'Sullivan and Mr. Gallagher of the Santry School, each, like Carleton, a convert who had discovered that "the Government money was very liberal in those days." [34]

There is a genuine pathos, touched though it be with the ludicrous and the sinister, in the story of Ireland's "New Reformation." Many of its leaders were men of spiritual zeal, concerned for the people of Ireland, whose capacity for growth and self-improvement they saw checked, on every side, by the hold of the Church of Rome. They approached the population, therefore, as would a missionary to Africa a horde of brutalized savages held under the sway of despotic witch doctors. Nearly moribund societies for the dissemination of Bedell's Gaelic Bible were given fresh vigor, and bounties, in the form of government funds, fellowships, and appointments were provided for the recruitment of promising converts. In famine times religious instruction was made a condition for charity. From this wretched confounding of piety with bribery the reputation of the New Reformers never recovered. Nor was Carleton ever to shed the obloquy of his association with them. For it was assumed, and with good reason, that his conversion had little to do with any species of spiritual transformation; in a hard hour, he bargained for station, respectability, and security.

"He was the perplexed pilgrim," Benedict Kiely has written, "losing

[33] *Ibid.*, I, 196–97.   [34] *Ibid.*, I, 233.

his balance at the beginning of his journey, staggering on in dizzy bewilderment, anxious to please and pacify as he went, anxious to tell the truth but not always finding it possible, offending all men by the erratic uncertainty of his progress. He wanted to stand high above all the confusion in some cool rational place. But the fact that he had once walked in the procession to the house of Mr. Phineas Lucre, taken his guinea or the proverbial soup with the unfortunate minority of his fellow-countrymen convinced by the crushing power of material things, always retarded his ascent." [35]

This shows more perception than Carleton's career is usually accorded, and yet it is less than a full accounting. Certainly his early involvement with Otway and *The Christian Examiner* thrust him suddenly into a world which he was ill equipped to understand. His conversion to Protestantism was, one might say, accidental and issuing from his circumstances. Yet his attitude toward his life in Gaelic Ireland was deeply ambivalent, and from this ambivalence issues the best of his work. Toward his material he directed at all times the artist's eye, which is at once loving and skeptical. In many ways his transformation from Billy Carleton, the poor scholar on the road, to Mr. William Carleton of Dublin was an escape from the crushing power not merely of material things but of his own heritage, from the haunted past, the obsessions, hatreds, and dark isolation of his own people. No mere convert's zeal, nor desire to please, can account for the extraordinary power with which *The Lough Derg Pilgrim,* his introduction to print, is written.

The way in which it came to be written suggests, in dramatic fashion, the oddly accidental way in which, from first to last, his career progressed. His change of faith had not been attended by the swift shower of benefits which he anticipated. His first hope was that it might procure for him a sizarship at Trinity College, and to this end he sought the support of Charles Maturin, the novelist, "a thin man, not ill-looking, with good eyes," who used to interrupt Carleton by raising his hand as if to say, "Hush! I have an image!" [36] But his marriage to Jane Anderson disqualified him for this. Whether as Maynooth candidate or Trinity fellow, the gypsy's prophecy held: "He will never be a priest; he loves the girls too well."

Through the offices of the Association for Discountenancing Vice, from whose "teacher's list" Protestant clergymen secured masters, he found work first in Mullingar and then in Carlow. His first ambition, which had been "to open a school," was thus, though in an unlooked-for fashion, gratified. But he proved to have several of the besetting sins of the old hedge masters—a propensity for adding yearly to his duties as a father, a taste for whiskey, and a general improvidence. In Mullingar, he was thrown in jail for debt, sharing his cell with an un-frocked priest who lived as a "couple-beggar." Carlow School, to which he was next sent, was in the coal-mining district, where his children fell ill in the wretched cabin, fourteen feet by ten, which had been provided for him. "I found," he says, "that to live there was only another word for death." [37]

Those apt and haunting words, "to live there was another word for death," were the last which Carleton was to write, and they were written on his real deathbed. Here the *Autobiography,* our only source of direct information for the first part of his life, breaks off. Carleton is exceedingly chary about dates, and O'Donoghue, its editor, made no attempt to annotate the *Autobiography,* so that we must proceed from internal evidence. We may fix the date of his trip through Louth at 1819, for example, because we know that Paddy Devaun was tried the spring preceding. We are able, by like argument, to fix the date of his encounter with Caesar Otway.

"In those days," as Yeats writes, "there lived in Dublin a lean con-troversialist, Caesar Otway. A favorite joke about him was, 'Where was Otway in the shower yesterday?' 'Up a gun-barrel at Rigby's.'" [38] Everything, and especially everything in Dublin, was a joke to Sam Lover and the young wits of the Comet Club. But even the more worldly and sensible of the Evangelicals must have felt twinges of embarrassment at the thought of this devoted and eccentric man. He was a writer of talent and a clergyman unstinting in zeal and self-

[37] *Ibid.,* I, 289.   [38] Yeats, Introduction to *Stories from Carleton,* p. xiv.

sacrifice. His sketchbooks show him to have been responsive to the changing Irish landscape and the idiosyncrasies of Irish character. On the subject of the Church of Rome, however, he was quite literally mad, a condition for which his vocation afforded a perfect disguise. Beneath theological and social objections to papist theory and practice lay a mind obsessed by the celibacy of priests, the virginity of nuns, and a hundred other objects of furtive sexual speculation. These thrust themselves to the surface of his books with frightening regularity.

In 1826 Otway made a tour of Ireland in search of mountain scenery, holy wells, "beastly Rites," eagles' nests, and scandals concerning libidinous priests. He turned up some remarkable material, including the case of the unfortunate Mary Riorden, who, at the instigation of the priests, drank water into which "holy clay" had been mixed; some thirteen years later, having taken ill, she disgorged "quantities of insects of the Beetle species, some more than half an inch long, in all stages of their existence—some as larvae, some as pupae, and some in their winged state; which, as soon as they were discharged, flew about the room." [39]

A gaunt scarecrow dressed in flapping russet, Otway explored the island in his carriage—Quixote in a gig. In the autumn of 1826 he visited Lough Derg, jouncing along the roadless bog to Pettigo while questioning—artfully, he believed—the grinning gossoon who acted as guide. Saint Patrick's Purgatory was, he already knew, "the monstrous birth of a dreary and degraded superstition," but he hoped, at least, to find the fabled blandishments of Rome—cloisters, arches, and ivy-covered abbeys. He found, instead, a shabby collection of cabins and slated huts, the penitential circles of jagged rock, and a few priests. Yet he tried to imagine Station Island as it must have looked during the pilgrim season, when bloody-shinned peasants swarmed over it like gulls on a rock, and he felt ashamed for "human nature, and looked upon myself as one of the millions of fools that have, century after century, degraded their understanding by coming thither." [40]

[39] Caesar Otway, *Sketches in Ireland, Descriptive of Interesting and Hitherto Unnoticed Districts in the North and South*, p. 261.

[40] *Ibid.*, p. 154.

Otway returned to Dublin, published his *Sketches,* and then met Carleton. Carleton had somehow escaped the unhealthy airs of Carlow, either on his own initiative or, more likely, his employers'. Once again he was penniless and desperate. He found occasion to remark that he had read and admired Otway's book. Otway, for his part, was impressed with his new acquaintance. Otway's descriptions of the Irish peasantry, when he is momentarily rid of his obsession, are enthusiastic and sentimental; he was especially fond of Carleton's type—strapping, big-boned, fair and reckless. If the Irish soul could indeed be saved, it would be by such instruments, and not the insignificant Maynooth controversialists who had hitherto been the only birds to fly into the nets of the New Reformation.

"In the course of conversation," Carleton says, "I discovered that he had never been present during the season of making the Pilgrimages, and was consequently ignorant of the religious ceremonies which take place in it. In consequence, I gave him a pretty full and accurate account of them, and of the Station which I myself had made there. After I concluded, he requested me to put down what I had told him upon paper, adding 'I will dress it up and have it inserted in the next edition.'" [41]

Carleton had all the skill and brilliance of the professional Irish story teller, and Otway was so impressed that he at once found living quarters for him and accepted part of his financial responsibilities. And into the narrow columns of *The Christian Examiner* Carleton began to pour the rich variety of his stored-up impressions and experiences. "A Pilgrimage to Patrick's Purgatory" ran to the length of forty octavo pages in the April and May issues of 1828. It was followed, in June and July, by "A Broken Oath," and, beginning in August, "Father Butler." At the beginning of 1829 he set to work on a series of "Sketches of the Irish Peasantry." That same year a slim volume was published containing "The Lough Derg Pilgrim" and "Father Butler." [42]

Gerald Griffin, in *The Rivals,* places a copy of this book on the

---

[41] Preface to 1851 edition of *Traits and Stories of the Irish Peasantry.*

[42] *The Lough Derg Pilgrim* and *Father Butler* (Dublin, 1829). Henceforth this was to be the title of Carleton's account of his trip to Patrick's Purgatory.

library table of Kirwan Damer. He does not bother to describe it, nor was there need. For Carleton, within the space of a few months, had become a writer both celebrated and notorious. The eighteen twenties abounded, as we have seen, in controversial fiction, to which *The Examiner* contributed its full quota of dreary bigotry. Carleton had the tone down pat—the fierce, insistent invective, the lurid rhetoric, the shocking abuse, in which all factions indulged. In that first year of his public career Carleton made powerful and unappeasable enemies. The Catholics, of course, abominated not merely what was written, but the renegade who had written it out of his own experiences in Catholic Ireland. And many Protestants, sickened by these inveterate sectarian hatreds, shared the distaste.

But those who were concerned for the development of an Irish literature were also aware of a fact strange to the point of the bizarre. In the pages of this infuriate little periodical, from the pen of an embittered apostate had come stories beneath whose coating of polemic lay a deep persuasive love for the peasants of whom he wrote, and a great though ungauged power.

17. *Traits and Stories of the Irish Peasantry*

I WAS, AT THE TIME of performing this station, in the middle of my nineteenth year—of quick perception—warm imagination—a mind peculiarly romantic—a morbid turn for devotion—and a candidate for the priesthood, having been made slightly acquainted with Latin, and more slightly still with Greek. At this period, however, all my faculties merged like friendly streams into the large current of my devotion. Of religion I was completely ignorant, although I had sustained a very conspicuous part in the devotions of the family, and signalised myself frequently by taking the lead in a rosary. I had often out-prayed and out-fasted an old circulating pilgrim, who occasionally visited our family—a feat on which few would have ventured; and I even arrived to such a pitch of perfection at praying, that, with the assistance of young and powerful lungs, I was fully able to distance him at any English prayer in which we joined. But in Latin, I must allow, that owing to my imperfect knowledge of its pronunciation, and to some twitches of conscience I felt on adventuring to imitate him by overleaping this impediment, he was able to throw me back a considerable distance in his turn; so that when we both started for a *De profundis,* I was always sure to come in second.   (*Traits and Stories,* II, 267)

The story which Caesar Otway had expected of him and the other, very different story which Carleton could not help but write are both present in the first paragraph of "The Lough Derg Pilgrim." This would happen with all of the many stories which he went on to write for the many masters whom he served. Nineteenth-century Ireland demanded of literature the fixed, single vision of explicit commitment. And poor Carleton was only too anxious to oblige, driven by need but also by his fumbling attempts to impose an order upon the rich anarchy of his memories and passions. His pen would move with the swift ease of a skate upon ice across the smooth frigid surface of party cant, but sooner or later some jagged, coarse-grained actuality would stop him dead. He would begin to wonder how that "fact"—scene or person or emotion—really looked, on all of its surfaces. Did he remember it rightly? Is this the way people really had talked on the chapel greens of his youth? Is this really why they fought, argued, went on pilgrimages?

The hero of the story which he wrote for Otway—romantic, warmhearted, and sensitive—is destined for a high spiritual adventure at Lough Derg; he will perceive, in the awful darkness and silence of the Purgatory itself, the monstrousness of Rome and the soul-destroying degradations of her pilgrimages, and he will receive his intimation of the slender crystal stream of true Christian faith. But there is an impudent young countryman lurking behind him, who sees ritual prayer as an endurance contest with an "old circulating pilgrim" and a holy pilgrimage as a grand chance at once to increase his reputation for piety and to see a bit of the world. It is this countryman, as ill-fitted for Otway's church as for the priesthood, who sets out on "a delightful morning in the pleasant month of July with a single change of linen in my pocket, and a pair of discarded shoes upon my bare feet." (*Ibid.,* II, 269)

The meaning of "The Lough Derg Pilgrim" is set by two lakes, that which Carleton leaves and that toward which he travels. The first lies within knolls of mountain pine and glens of hazel and holly; the young man, as he walks beside it, is observant of waterfowl, rapid martins, cock grouse, and quail. The other lake lies far distant, beyond a westward chain of dark mountains. One lake belongs to the world of natural beauty "which the wisdom of God has given as a security in some degree against sin, by opening to the heart of man sources of pleasure, for which the soul is not compelled to barter away her innocence." Lough Derg, the other lake, remote, bleak, and ugly, seems not to belong at all "to the circumference and reality of human life." (*Ibid.,* II, 271)

At last I came out upon the main road; and you will be pleased to imagine to yourself the figure of a tall, gaunt, gawkish looking young man, dressed in a good suit of black cloth, with shirt and cravat like snow, striding solemnly along, without shoe or stocking; for about this time I was twelve miles from home, and blisters had already risen on my feet, in consequence of the dew having got into my shoes, which at the best were enough to cut up any man; I had therefore to strip, and carry my shoes—one in my pocket, and another stuffed in my hat—being thus with great reluctance compelled to travel barefoot. (*Ibid.,* II, 272)

To Carleton neither of these portentous lakes is so real as the road itself, where the dew does not "hang shining upon the leaves," nor "fall in pattering showers from the trees." He is one in a straggling procession of men and women of all ages, "stumping it stoutly" with bags of oats slung across their backs and thick staffs in their hands. He does his best to arrange his fellow travelers into a moral catalogue which will reveal the various ways in which "superstition had exacted from libertinism what fear and ignorance had promised her," but he is constantly distracted by sights and sounds. Two old women mutter to each other about the virtues of the shrine as a cure for heartburn; a schoolmaster tramps along in a shabby black coat, reading the Seven Penitential Psalms; someone else is teaching a young mother a Latin charm against colic; Carleton himself promises to "swap prayers" with Sol Donnel—"everybody that comes here the second time, sure, knows Sol Donnel, the blessed pilgrim." The people on that rocky, blistery Donegal road were Carleton's own—"voteens," publicans, pickpockets, rogues, tailors, fools, and perhaps a saint or two. A few stories more and he would cut them free to go their own gait, and then his usefulness to Caesar Otway would be at an end.

The narrator of "The Lough Derg Pilgrim" has two voices. One is a fair imitation of Caesar Otway, which is to say that it is not a human voice. The other voice, unexpected and spontaneous, is that of a man remembering his magical, preposterous youth, when the pleasure of life was asserted not by allegorical lakes, but by the randy folk whom one met along the road, like Nell M'Collum, the tinker's widow, who lent Carleton a cloak and then picked his pocket. The first voice tells us of how Carleton endured his three days of physical and spiritual torment among the penitents of Station Island; of how, during the midnight watches, it was given him to perceive the dark terrors and superstitions into which his soul had been thrust by the priests; and of "that solemn, humble, and heartfelt sense of God's presence which Christian prayer demands."[1]

But there is nothing very grand or very terrible in the experiences of the second voice. It is the voice of a gawky and conceited seminarian who delights in being mistaken for a priest and convinces himself that his spirit is chastened thereby—"Pride, I trample you under my foot." Otway, seeing the prior's house on Station Island, imagines "the ecclesiastic's avaricious heart" alternately "beating quick with delight as he measured the boatloads of people coming over to add to the store of money he was collecting, and which was to him a God," and contracting with terror at the thought of its own abominable corruption.[2] But when Carleton sees that house, the first thing he notices is a wisp of smoke coming from the chimney, "which at once brought me back to humanity and the thought of roasting meats, boiling pots, and dressing dinners." (*Traits and Stories,* II, 290)

This Carleton, too, ends his pilgrimage in weariness and disillusionment, but of a different sort. Piety, he has concluded, is more sensibly practised by a Clogher fireside than on a barren and comfortless island. Nor, he feels, can there ever be wisdom is tramping barefoot around circles of jagged rocks, as he had done during "the best part of a July day, when the soles of my feet were flayed, and the stones hot enough to broil a beef-steak." Above all, he has learned that he is not the only adept in the art of faking piety, for the respectful old lady who was so solicitous of his blistered feet ("Asthore, it's himself that's not proud, or he wouldn't tramp it, barefooted, along wud two old crathurs like huz; him that has no sin to answer for.") has skinned him of his purse and half his wardrobe. And so he trudges home, "a goose stripped of my feathers, a dupe beknaved and beplundered—having been almost starved to death on the island and nearly cudgeled

---

[1] *Traits and Stories* (New York, 1881), p. 808. This is one of the passages which Carleton later removed from "The Lough Derg Pilgrim" as being "offensive." American editions continued to use the early version, in accordance with the carefree habits of nineteenth-century publishing.

[2] Caesar Otway, *Sketches in Ireland,* pp. 176–77.

by one of the priests." Worse yet, when the priest of his parish, "a small, pleasant little man," heard the story, "he laughed till the tears ran down his cheek." The plucked goose of this sketch set Carleton's imagination working; he reappears in that wonderful story, "Denis O'Shaughnessy Going to Maynooth," Carleton's first major story and the last which he was to write for *The Examiner*.

"The Lough Derg Pilgrim" suggests that Carleton's break with the instinctual life of his people liberated his powers and clarified his vision, yet exacted its own penalties. Those grisly punishments and moans of lamentation beneath the leaden Donegal sky tell us of some dark, debasing medieval world in which the Irish peasant continued to dwell, but say nothing of its bright, heraldic colors. There is a legend that the blind poet, Turlough O'Carolan (who bore Carleton's name in its uncorrupted form), visited Lough Derg in his old age. This would have been during the worst of the Penal Days, for O'Carolan died in 1739. A century had passed since Bishop Spottiswoode, in an effort to extirpate the Romish practice, had leveled the chapels, filled in Patrick's Cave, and smashed the abbey. For fifty years the law had been exerting every effort to break up the pilgrim route, but without success. As the story had it, and every hedge poet swore to its accuracy, O'Carolan, in helping a woman from the pilgrim boat, recognized the girl whom he had loved in his youth, and cried, "That is the hand of Bridget Cruise!"[3] The anecdote reminds us that another poet, Ariosto, made a trip to Lough Derg one of his tests of heroic chivalry; and that Dante used it as one of the patterns for his Hell; and that from the days of *The Golden Legend* it had been a shrine famous through Christendom.[4] The full meaning of Lough Derg to the religious imagination cannot be given by either of the two voices which Carleton here adopts—the chill, hating voice of Caesar Otway, or the wry, self-concerned voice of Denis O'Shaughnessy.

Carleton wrote regularly for *The Examiner* through 1831. These stories, which were collected three years later as *Tales of Ireland*, are

[3] Edward Hayes, ed., *The Ballads of Ireland*, II, 27n.
[4] For the history of Lough Derg and the Pilgrimage, see Canon Daniel O'Connor, *Saint Patrick's Purgatory*, and Alice Curtayne, *Lough Derg*.

slight and are marred by the insistent purposes of controversy. Occasionally they have a bright, fitful life, which characteristically is irrelevant to the stated theme. "The Priest's Funeral," for example, deals with the way in which a priest's dying wish to be received into the Protestant Church is frustrated by his fellow clergy, who are anxious not only for his soul but for the property which earlier he had willed to them. But the story is dominated by two outrageously comic figures, a bishop and a Dominican monk who sit outside the death-room bickering over appointments, obscure points of theology, ecclesiastical scandals, and the old dispute between regular and secular clergy. In genre scenes of this sort, painted with a satirical and affectionate brush, his talent was searching out its true direction. He was already at work on the great series of *Traits and Stories of the Irish Peasantry,* and one of the first of these was to be his final contribution to *The Examiner.*

"Denis O'Shaughnessy Going to Maynooth" appeared in the September-December issues of *The Examiner,* but in a much abridged form. In December it was brought to a swift and bumpy halt; Otway's editorial note explained that it was necessary "to complete all serial contributions by the end of the year." [5] Although the magazine continued just long enough to include an obituary notice of Carleton in its final issue, no more of his work was to appear in its pages. David O'Donoghue's suggestion is that "Going to Maynooth" proved unpalatable to Otway and his readers, since it "promises to be an example of the evils of Popery admirably suited for Evangelical purposes," but turns into something quite different.[6] It would seem the case that Carleton became so fascinated by the full-bodied and hilarious tale which he was telling that he forgot the moral which it was intended to point.

It is one of the very best of his comedies. At its center stands the incomparable Denis himself, at once touching, ludicrous, and insufferable. An entire society, however, is built carefully about him, composed of his adoring family, sweethearts, and neighbors. An ardent controversialist, his nose set in "firm defiance of heretics, infidels, and

---

[5] Carleton, *Life,* II, 18.   [6] *Ibid.,* II, 19.

excommunicated persons," he seems to have been destined from child-hood for holy orders. His mother dreams one night that he is seated, dressed "like the Protestant clargy," at the head of a banquet table. She tells him that he's wanted to anoint Paddy Diarmud, but he re-plies loftily, "He must wait then till morning, or if he chooses to die against my will, an' the will o' the church, he must take the quense-quences. We're wealthy now." The tone frightens her awake, and getting out of bed she discovers him in the kitchen "wid an ould knife in one hand, an' an iron skiver in the other, imitatin' a fork." (*Traits and Stories,* IV, 103-4)

Food and forks play an important role in his own dreams of clerical glory:

I think, father, that upon considering the consequence to which I am now entitled, and the degree of respectability which, in my own person—*in propria persona*—I communicate to the vulgarians with whom I am con-nected—I call them vulgarians from no derogatory motive; but you will concede yourself, that they are ignorant of the larned languages, an' conse-quently, though dacent enough, still, in reference to Latin and Greek, but vulgarians. Well! *Quid multis?*—I say, that taking all these things into speculation, looking at them—*veluti in speculum*—it is neither dacent nor becoming that I should ate in the manner I have done, as vulgarly as them-selves—that I should ate, I say, any longer without knife and fork. . . . Pay attention, therefore, to my words, for I expect that they will be duly ob-served:—buy me a knife and fork; and when I get them, it's not to lay them past to rust, you concave. The beef and mutton must follow; and in future I'm resolved to have my *tay* breakfast. There are geese, and turkeys, and pullets enough about the yeard, and I am bent on accomplishing myself in the art of carving them. I'm not the man now to be placed among the other riff-raff of the family over a basket of potatoes, wid a black clerical coat upon me, and a noggin of milk under my arm! I tell you the system must be changed: the schoolmaster is abroad, and I'll tolerate such vulgarity no longer.   (*Ibid.,* IV, 102-3)

Denis is all language and appetite; he revels in words which are as hard and dazzling as diamonds, and he has a lapidary's sense of their arrangement: "Father, I condimnate you at once—I condimnate **you** as being a most ungrammatical ould man, an' not fit to argue

wid any one that knows Murray's English Grammar, an' more espa-
ciously the three concords of Lilly's Latin one—that is, the cognation
between the nominative case and the verb, the consanguinity between
the substantive case and the adjective, and the blood-relationship that
irritates between the relative and the antecedent." (*Ibid.,* IV, 74) Such
knowledge is second nature to one who can "read the Greek Tista-
ment wid my right eye, an' thranslate it wid my left, according to
the Greek an' English sides of my face, wid my tongue constrein' into
Irish, unbeknownst to both o' them." (*Ibid.,* IV, 75) "Oh, how I scorn
your gravity, man," he says, on another occasion. *"Ignorantia,* as I
said, is your date an' superscription; an' when you die, you ought to
go an' engage a stone-cutter to carve you a headstone, an' make him
write on it, *Hic jacet Ignorantius Redivivus."* (*Ibid.,* IV, 78) But for
the ladies he has a softer voice: "Yes, I know the seven languages;
but what is all that compared to the cardinal virtues? This world is
a mere bird of passage, Miss Norah; and it behoves us to be ever on
the wing for futurity and premeditation." (*Ibid.,* IV, 97)

Beneath all this Denis has a shrewd head, and it is well that he has,
for the negotiations which must precede his appointment to Maynooth
are devious and delicate. Father Finnerty, the parish priest, hints to
him that this appointment may depend on whether or not Old
O'Shaughnessy's *garran* is a forthcoming gift. "I will undertake to
say," Denis at once replies, "if you get me into Maynooth, that my
father on my authority will lend you the colt tomorrow, and the day
of its reclaiming will be dependent upon the fulfillment of your promise, or *votum."* Finnerty, "who had not expected to find such deep
logic" in Denis, agrees, adding dourly, "You will be a useful man in
the church, and you deserve to be pushed on, at all events." (*Ibid.,* IV,
113)

Thus begins the involved epic of the *garran* colt. Denis's family is
taken aback by this intrusion of worldly considerations, until Denis
reminds them that "you may think that this was plain conversation;
but I have read too much for that. In fact, it was logic—complate,
convincing logic, every word of it." Finnerty having agreed to recom-

mend him, he is convinced that "the Irish hierarchy is plased to look on me as a luminary of almost superhuman brilliancy and coruscation." (*Ibid.,* IV, 121)

In his imaginings, as he walks "soliloquising in the glen below, meditating on the transparency of all human events," he is already ordained:

In the morning I rise up in imagination, and after reading part of my office, I and my curate—*ego et coadjutor meus*—or if I get a large parish, perhaps I and my two curates—*ego et coadjutores mei*—order horses, and of a fine calm summer morning we mount them as gracefully as three throopers. The sun is up, and of coorse the moon is down, and the glitter of the light, the sparkling of the dew, the canticles of the birds, and the melodious cawing of the crows in Squire Grimshaw's rookery. . . .   (*Ibid.,* IV, 136)

Unfortunately, Finnerty, too, has a curate, a Father Molony, of whom Denis remarks that "should I ever come to authority in the Irish hierarchy, I shall be strongly disposed to discountenance him, if it were only for his general superciliousness of conduct. So there's another clause disposed of." (*Ibid.,* IV, 111) And Molony has a nephew, Denis's rival for "the Bishop's Maynooth letter." In his nervousness, Denis blurts out the arrangement concerning the *garran* colt during his interview with the bishop, and the appointment goes to young Molony.

But Finnerty, undismayed, lays down a new line of strategy. The next morning he, both of the O'Shaughnessys, and the unlucky colt proceed to the bishop's palace. "Wait till you take a toss on this sofa," he whispers to Denis, "and then you will get a taste of ecclesiastical luxury. . . . Dionysius, look about you! Isn't this worth studying for?" "Yes," says the increasingly knowledgeable Denis, "if it was perusal on the part of his lordship that got it." (*Ibid.,* IV, 170–71)

There follows a long scene of subtle and tactful bargaining, with the interested parties distributed in different rooms. Denis is rightly convinced that the issue turns on the ultimate disposition of the colt, but Finnerty knows that bishops have their odd ways. "My Lord," he says, "the horse is in your stable, and Denis declares he will not take him out of it." "I have not the slightest objection to that," the bishop replies blandly, "upon the express condition that his son shall never enter Maynooth." But the end of the matter is that Denis gets his letter of recommendation and the bishop's brother, who has made a mysterious appearance, gets the horse. (*Ibid.,* IV, 167)

Denis tenders "my most gracious and supercilious thanks to the bishop," and, more enigmatically, "my most obsequious thanks to the furthest extent of my gratitude" to the bishop's brother. Then father and son set off for home on the remaining horse, with the colt's bridle slung about Denis's neck. In their excitement they forget about poor Father Finnerty, who trots behind them shouting, "Do I deserve this?" "What is he saying?" asks the father. "He is declaimin' about gratitude," says the son. "Lay an her," says the father. At home a great feast has been prepared, and neighbors and kinsmen are waiting with gifts appropriate for a seminarian—copies of "The Garden of Love and Royal Flower of Fidelity," "An Essay on the Virtue of Chastity," and "On the Increase of Population in Ireland," and a stout oak cudgel, so that he may end awkward debates "wid a visitation upon the kidney."

Here the story should end, but Carleton has come to a belated sense of his duty, and spoils his effect by a long account of Denis's change of heart. "Ambition loses much of its fictitious glitter" for Denis and he comes to recognize the harsh and overbearing way in which he has used his family. But the reader has come to entertain a high affection for the old, overbearing Denis. The old Denis, taunted by his brother on his lack of horsemanship, had replied grandly, "I'll not tolerate vulgarity any longer; you must larn to address me in a more polite style. If the animal—that purblind quadruped—walked into the mire, by what logic can you produce an association between her blindness and my knowledge of Latin and Greek? But why do I degradate my own consequence by declaiming to you a eulogium upon logic?" (*Ibid.,* IV, 110) The new Denis has lost all traces of this brilliantly comic language: "I have mingled with those on whom before this—that is, during my boyhood—I looked with awe, as on men who held vested in themselves some mysterious and spiritual power. I have mingled with them, Susan, and I find them neither

better nor worse than those who still look upon them as I once did."
(*Ibid.,* IV, 188) And the story ends with the marriage of Denis to
his Susan, their wedding being "the longest, the most hospitable, and
frolicsome that ever has been remembered in the parish from that day
to the present." (*Ibid.,* IV, 207)

But "Going to Maynooth" has been so finely wrought that this
wretched epilogue does little to harm it. Of Carleton, as of Denis
himself, it might be said that he lived by language and appetite. Though
there is a widely held legend to the contrary, the Irish have rarely displayed, at least in their literature, a very rich vein of high comedy, but
Carleton is a genuinely witty and humane writer. His appetite for
sights and sounds was, of course, immense, and has frequently been
remarked upon. "You are never wearied," as Thomas Davis says, "by
an inventory of wardrobes . . . yet you see how every one is dressed;
you hear the honey brogue of the maiden, and the downy voice of
the child, the managed accents of traffic and flattery, the shrill tongue
of woman's fretting, and the troubled gush of man's anger." [7] And,
indeed, at a distance the *Traits and Stories* seems a boundless sea of
murmurous voices. Each story, however, is carefully controlled by
Carleton's selective intelligence. He makes use of a dozen fledgling
priests, and all of them speak the inflated, quasi-theological language
of the hedge schools, yet each exists in his own being.

The first series of *Traits and Stories of the Irish Peasantry* appeared
in 1830, and the second four years later. A preface to the first volumes
assures Carleton's readers that "they contain a greater number of facts
than any other book ever published on Irish life," and insists upon
the author's "intimate and extensive knowledge" of the people; on
these points he was to become wearily repetitious, though the claims
are well merited. They are a people, he says, "the very fittest in the
world for either the poet or agitator—capable of great culpability, and
of great and energetic goodness—sudden in their passions as the red
and rapid gush of their mountain streams—variable in their tempers
as the climate that sends them the mutability of sun and shower—at
times rugged and gloomy as the moorland sides of their mountains—

[7] *Essays,* p. 357.

often sweet, soft, and gay as the sun-lit meadows of their pleasant vales." (*Traits and Stories,* I, xxv)

This sounds very much like rhetoric of the loose, rhapsodic sort in which Irish literature unhappily abounds, and which seeks to link the peasantry, for good or ill, to the primal, mindless forces of nature. It speaks quite accurately, however, to Carleton's imaginative apprehension of his theme. "The red and rapid gush of their mountain streams," here mentioned in passing, is one of his controlling images. Years later, in the months which preceded the abortive rebellion of 1848, Carleton took a walking tour with Thomas Francis Meagher, the most romantic and most eager of the conspirators. Meagher was to remember Carleton's comparison of Old and Young Ireland to "two streams from one source, the one strong and loud but muddy, the other weak and silent but pure." [8] The reference was political and topical, and Meagher, who found it flattering, missed the older man's irony. In Carleton's stories the crystal clarity of lake, stream, and spring suggests an unreal, often a delusive purity of spirit and purpose, while dark, troubled water, stained to the color of blood, has the reality of experience itself.

"Lough derg" means, after all, "the red lake." And of the many prophecies which, so the prophecy men averred, would foretell rebellion, the one which struck him most forcibly was that which spoke of the millstream at Louth running red with human blood. Again, there are two springs in "Tubber Derg," one of his most powerful stories—one is a spring of "delicious crystal" but crimson oozes from the other, and a man walking near it seems "to track his way in blood." (*Traits and Stories,* IV, 2) In the early Carleton these contrasting waters often symbolized a simple, Manichaean dichotomy. One stream "stood for" the Irish capacity for love, affection, and sacrifice; the other stream "stood for" an inclination, equal in strength, toward violence, savagery, and superstition. And this was admirably adapted to the service of the various causes in which his pen was enlisted. But at the root of Carleton's vision lies what Yeats has called a "clay-cold melancholy"; he came to believe that his people were

[8] Carleton, *Life,* II, 92.

stained with saintliness and blood. He could never explain, to himself least of all, what meaning he attached to this, though he availed himself of the glib generalities of the day, which spoke of the "Celtic soul" and its commingling of innocence and crime. But his truest instincts, as Yeats perhaps guessed, were pantheistic and pagan, and his comparison of his people to the moorlands and meadows on which they lived is something more than metaphor.

Carleton's first notion was that the *Traits and Stories* should be a series of tales told about the kitchen fire of Ned M'Keown's mountain *shebeen*. The earliest stories—"The Three Tasks," "Shane Fadh's Wedding," and "Larry M'Farland's Wake"—fall within this scheme, and are pleasant enough stories in Crofton Croker's exuberant and trivial vein. But the convention, which even then was stiff and a bit faded, is in every way alien to his talents. The firelight which glints so merrily from the polished pewter was never drawn from peat bog, but from oak felled in an English forest. M'Keown's public house is no *shebeen,* but an English wayside inn, and the storytellers are not peasants but "rustics." Carleton's borrowed tone, mannered and arch, is appropriate to such an atmosphere.

The fourth story, "The Battle of the Factions," begins as another of these tales told in the inglenook. Then, very suddenly—one can almost mark the line—Carleton drops the device. It has come time for the schoolmaster, Pat Frayne, to tell his story, since each of the rustics, in accordance with this tiresome convention, has his representative trade and his quirk of character. "My grandfather," he begins in the flat tone of the earlier stories, "though a tall, erect man, with white, flowing hair, like snow, that falls profusely about his broad shoulders—" But before he has given a fair beginning to the chronicle of his grandfather's days as a faction fighter, he has remembered his own encounters with the O'Hallaghans, "who had no more discretion in their fighting than so many African buffoons." Remembering it, he cries out, "God be with the days when I and half a dozen gossoons used to go out of a warm Sunday in summer—the bed of the river nothing but a line of white, meandering stones, so hot that you could stand upon them, with a small, obscure thread of water creeping in-

visibly among them, hiding itself, as it were, from the scorching sun
—except here and there you might find a small crystal pool where the
streams had accumulated." (*Traits and Stories,* II, 5)

Carleton, hearing in his mind the voice of Pat Frayne at the school
of Findramore, and perhaps the voice of Billy Carleton telling his
stories on the roads of Louth, had found what he needed. It is a full-
cadenced voice, susceptible of infinite modulation, moving without
effort from the sardonic to the tragic, and intelligent as though on instinct. "Gentlemen," the real Pat Frayne said to his students, one
Easter week, "tomorrow let each of you bring me an egg—one will
be sufficient, but in the meantime I have no objection against two.
When you bring them, I will then go to that field . . . , and placing
every egg upon a spot of ground which I will consecrate by the repeti-
tion of that most charitable of all documents, the Athanasian Creed,
I will cause every egg to rise with the lightness of a soap bubble into
the air, and it will in this manner disappear for ever." [9]

And the "Pat Frayne" of Carleton's invention can use language as
though it had been similarly bewitched. As he talks, the dead world
of M'Keown's inn falls away. It is a Sunday in summer, with the
air "of a fine texture." The people of his village are waiting for Mass
to begin, but Father Luke O'Shaughran, whose horse travels at a dog's
trot, "like the pace of an idiot with sore feet in a shower," has not
arrived. A few *voteens* have gone into the chapel to make "the grand
tower," traveling from station to station on their knees. But the other
members of the congregation are gathered on the chapel green in
small groups—standing or stretched out on the grass or "laired" on
the sunny side of the ditches. Here the schoolmaster is discoursing
upon politics and there the *shanahus* has a story of his own to tell.
Some "walking geographer" of a pilgrim is demonstrating the magic
properties of an amber rosary, "in all the vanity of conscious sancti-
mony, standing in the middle of the attentive peasants, like the knave
and fellows of a cartwheel—if I may be permitted the loan of an
apt similitude." The young girls, screened by hedges, are seated on
the green banks, pulling on the stockings and shoes which they have

[9] Carleton, *Life,* I, 22.

brought with them or peering into a bit of mirror propped against the ditch. Their voices float lazily: *"Musha,* are we alive after that, at all, at all! Why, that bates Molly M'Cullagh and her red mantle entirely! I'm sure that it's well come up for the likes of her, a poor imperint crathur, that's sprung from nothing, to give herself such airs." "What could we expect from a proud piece like her," a second replies, "that brings a manwill to mass every Sunday, purtending she can read it, and Jim Finigan saw the wrong side of the book toardst her the Sunday of the Purcession." (*Traits and Stories,* II, 12-13)

From this genre scene, painted with swift, exact strokes, Frayne moves upon his story, describing in the same easy way how a crab-tree cudgel is dressed so as to give it "a widow-and-orphan-making quality, a child-bereaving touch." But the story ends in murder and bloodshed, and with Rose Galh, whose voice had been the brightest of those which floated to us from the hedges, a spent and broken woman. The world of the *Traits and Stories* has come alive with the rise and fall of Frayne's voice.

These stories are given life by language, by Carleton's discovery of the explosive energies of the word. His characters are realized more vividly through speech than through action. Of his plots it is often possible to say little more than that they are serviceable. "Neal Malone" and "Going to Maynooth," which are two of the best stories, are anecdotes, expanded to *novella* length. "The Hedge School" veers suddenly and disconcertingly from the jubilant account of how Findra-more acquires Pat Frayne by kidnapping him from another village to the dark narrative of Frayne's life as a White Boy and his betrayal by an informer. "The Midnight Mass" is awkwardly transposed from Wardour Street Gothic. Yet these and the other stories by which his reputation must stand or fall are as searching and as moving as any which the nineteenth century produced.

The later Carleton was overconcerned with plot. As we shall see, he took to heart the reproaches of critics in this regard, and cast about desperately for acceptable models. *The Squanders of Castle Squander* and *The Black Baronet,* his late novels, are ambitious attempts at a theme which from the first had attracted Anglo-Irish writers—the decline of the Big House. But he worked very clumsily with such material. His true subject was a people emerging painfully from the submerged, broken world of Gaelic Ireland. In his attempt to record that life he was well served by his first models—his father's long, rambling anecdotes and the loose picaresque of Le Sage.

It was a world to which not merely English forms and customs but the English language itself was alien. And yet, perhaps paradoxically, the people of whom he wrote were obsessed by language, and made drunk by the power of words. *"Oxis Doxis Glorioxis,"* says Darby More, the ragged beggar. (*Traits and Stories,* II, 58) When Lanigan, the wandering scholar, is asked where he comes from, he replies, *"Per varios casus et tot discrimina rerum, venimus a Mayo."* (*Ibid.,* III, 215) To the beggar this garbled Latin is an opaque charm drawn from a language which is literally miraculous, the language of his church. To the scholar it is the language of learning itself, a closely guarded secret of craft and mastery. But for the peasants of whom Carleton wrote, English, too, was an acquired tongue. "Maybe 'tis yourself that hasn't the tongue in your head," an old woman says to a schoolmaster, "and can spake the tall, high-flown English; *a-wurrah,* but your tongue hangs well anyhow, the Lord increase it." "I'll castigate yees in dozens," the schoolmaster says to his class, his tongue savoring the syllables; "I can't spake to this dacent woman, with your insuperable turbulentiality." (*Ibid.,* III, 244) But when Jimmy M'Evoy returns to his family from the roads and schools of Munster, both the high-flown English and the round Latin fall away from him, and he remembers the tongue which goes "directly to the heart": *"Ish maheen a tha in, a vair dheelish machree."* (*Ibid.,* III, 306) Ireland's three languages—English, Gaelic, and Latin—are the knotted veins and sinews of Carleton's prose.

This sensuous delight in the thing said is what Carleton would call a "trait" of Irish character. But his feelings toward it are double and opposite, for he connects this energy and grace of speech with much that was morally ugly in Irish life. " 'May the grass grow before your door!' is highly imaginative and poetical. Nothing, indeed, can present the mind with a stronger or more picturesque emblem of desolation and ruin. Its malignity is terrible." (*Ibid.,* I, 214) "An Essay on Irish Swearing" is a bitter and caustic satire on those writers of the *Blackwood's* school who professed to find "Paddy" a compound of wit and murder, too innocent in his violence to deserve full moral censure. But it is also an angry, self-despising attack upon his own people, who had chosen sound rather than sense. The "poetic" quality of peasant speech could make a chivalric hero of "the poor boy who perhaps only burnt a family in their beds." (*Ibid.,* I, 205) The rich honey of its rhetoric could coat the most savage and degenerate of crimes. Half a century before John Synge put his ear to a Wicklow floor to catch the talk of servant girls, Carleton had caught every turn and nuance of Irish speech. Unlike Synge, he judged, moralized, interrupted himself with sermons and imprecations. And he is, by this measure, the better writer, for he knew that language has moral sources and moral consequences. He had seen the charred timbers of Wildgoose Lodge and the body of Paddy Devaun turning in the August air.

"My friends and good people," says Mat Kavanagh, the hedge schoolmaster, as he stands on the gallows,

in hopes that you may all be able to demonstrate the last proposition laid down by a dying man, I undertake to address you before I depart to that world where Euclid, De Carts, and many other larned men are gone before me. . . . You may curse, but it's too late now to abscond the truth—the "sum" of my wickedness and folly is worked out, and you see the "answer." God forgive me, many a young crathur I inticed into the Ribbon business, and now it's to end in hemp! Obey the law; or if you don't, you'll find it a *lex talionis*—the construction of which is that if a man burns and murthurs, he won't miss hanging. Take warning by me, by us all; for although I take God to witness that I was not at the perpetration of the crime that I'm to be suspinded for, yet I often connived, when I might have superseded the carrying of such intentions into effectuality.   (*Ibid.,* II, 265)

But Carleton also knew the paths which carried better men than Mat Kavanagh to murder and the gallows. There is no wilder or more comic scene in the *Traits and Stories* than that on which "Tubber Derg" opens. The bailiff has come to seize the two Murray cows, and Mrs. Murray hurries for help to her neighbor, Owen M'Carthy.

M'Carthy arrives, to find that the children have taken in hand the task of murdering the agent. They have him wedged securely between wall and dresser, with a large tub beside him. The smallest of the children are running into the yard and then back again at full speed, filling the tub with ditchwater. Other young Murrays are battering his shins with tongs and potatoes. A few specialists are heating sharpened sticks with which they hope to blind him. And Jimmy, the oldest boy, is prepared to drown him as soon as the tub is filled.

"Oh, mudher, mudher," one of the urchins cries, "don't come in yet; don't come in, Owen, till Jimmy, an' huz, an' the Denises, gets the bailey drownded. We'll soon have the *bot* full; but Paddy an' Jack Denis have the eyes almost pucked out of him; an' Katty's takin' the hook from behind the *cuppel,* to get it about his neck." (*Ibid.,* IV, 10)

But "Tubber Derg," which begins on this winsome Hibernian note, is the most heartbreaking of Carleton's stories. It is the story of Owen M'Carthy, that strong, patient bull of a man, and of what happens to his spirit when he must take his family onto the roads to beg their bread from door to door. "When an Irish peasant is reduced to pauperism he seldom commences the melancholy task of soliciting alms in his native place. The trial is always a severe one, and he is anxious to hide his shame and misery from the eyes of those who know him." (*Ibid.,* IV, 29) And so we are put forth upon a long journey along the terrible roads of 1818, when famine, fevers, and mass evictions combined to strip entire valleys of life.

Beg—that ud go hard with me, Kathleen. I'd work—I'd live on next to nothing all the year round—but to see the crathurs that wor dacently bred up brought to that—I couldn't bear it, Kathleen—'twould break the heart widin me. . . . I love them as I do the blood in my own veins; but I'd rather see them in the arms of God in heaven, laid down dacently, with their little sorrowful faces washed, and their little bodies stretched out purtily before my eyes—I would—in the graveyard there beyant, where all belonging to me lie, than have it cast up to me, or have it said, that ever a M'Carthy was seen beggin' on the highway. (*Ibid.,* IV, 16)

But that pride is stripped away from M'Carthy, piece by piece, until he takes his place with the unnumbered thousands, a bundle of rags by the gate to the Big House: "We're axin' your charity, for God's sake!" When pride, shame, and scruples have been crushed, there remains the freemasonry of the outcast. Carleton's story turns a light upon the darkest of Irish scenes, the lines of beggars moving slowly along the roads. "We took no revenge into our own hands," M'Carthy says, "but left everything to God above us. We are poor; but there is neither blood, nor murder, nor dishonesty upon our heads." Yet he is asked, at one of the Big Houses, "Why don't you work, you sturdy impostor, rather than stroll about so lazily, training your brats to the gallows?" (*Ibid.*, IV, 41) Carleton had seen a generation of his countrymen in training to the gallows; he had seen men look with respect and admiration at the ghastly corpse of Paddy Devaun. Bonaparte, the beggars whisper, is to come to Ireland, a man against whom bullets will not avail. The massive, armored giants are rising up out of the earth, and the stream of Louth will run red with blood. Out of these secret dreams, born in the midnight ditches and carried from cabin to cabin, would come the black, hating Ireland of the nineteenth century.

But Carleton could also see the road which Jimmy M'Evoy takes in "The Poor Scholar," the road which led from his father's rocky hill to the schools of Munster. Jimmy moves through the maze of Gaelic Ireland, instructed by good masters and beaten by cruel, taking his dry lodgings in cabins and his wet nights by hedges. In the tender pages of this story Carleton summons up the lost land of his youth, when the roads were for pilgrims and poets and drunkards and young boys bound for Munster. It is a confused story, by turns harrowing and jubilant, with as many odd twists as the road itself, but it ends "in a kind of sweet, musical cadence, the Irish cry of joy."

"I'm a poor scholar," Jimmy says to strangers, "the son of honest but reduced parents; I came to this part of the country with the intention of preparing myself for Maynooth, and if it might plase God, with the hope of being able to raise them out of their distress." (*Ibid.*, III, 251)

Jimmy, like Owen M'Carthy, crosses fever lands and famine lands, and passes through towns where "hundreds lay huddled in cold cabins, in out-houses, and even behind ditches." But Jimmy is too young to know that his world is dying, and he carries his talisman—Creech's *Translation of Horace*. It is a gift from Corcoran, the old schoolmaster whom he meets on the road and who remembers his own journey, fifty years before, to "that counthry where the swallows fly in conic sections, where the magpies and the turkeys confab in Latin, and the cows and bullocks will roar you Doric Greek." (*Ibid.*, III, 211) The last, lingering light of the eighteenth century plays upon Corcoran, though Jimmy mistakes it for the sun.

"He is among the greatest, possibly the greatest writer of fiction that Ireland has given to the English language," Benedict Kiely says of Carleton, in the assertive tone to which many who have discovered his *Traits and Stories* are tempted. "He wrote good stories and he wrote very inferior stories; he wrote well and he wrote at times with an excruciating badness. . . ." [10] The assertion is nearly always followed, and properly, by the qualification, for there is much that must be said of Carleton's broken career and faulty art, his excesses, his foolishness, and his abysmal lapses of taste. Yet the Carleton of *Traits and Stories* remains, for each reader, a discovery, a writer so fine that the reader begins to doubt his own judgment. From the broken land of gunmen and gallows, of bent men upon bitter soil and lovers "scattered like nosegays" across the meadows, came a writer so gifted that he could show us everything at once.

[10] *Poor Scholar*, p. 177.

18. The Dublin Years

WHEN TIM KEARNEY, "the pride of Ireland," had been crammed with so much knowledge that he might have puzzled Scaliger himself, he went up from Munster to Trinity College in Dublin, where he stumped all the "great larned Fellows," and argued the Provost to a draw. A large and fashionable audience witnessed the final contest, and a young gentlewoman with three estates fell in love with Tim because of his erudition. She pledged to marry him as soon as he became a counselor, and placed him in the meantime upon an allowance of thirty pounds a year. (*Traits and Stories*, III, 214–15)

When Carleton put the story of Tim Kearney's heroic accomplishment in the mouth of Corcoran, he may have been thinking of another poor scholar who had come into Dublin along the southern road ten years before. The young man who had spent his first Dublin night in a beggars' cellar off Dirty Lane was now Mister William Carleton, the celebrated writer. Critics whose political convictions led them to differ on everything else were agreed that he had written "an Irish classic," and the Dublin periodicals were bidding against one another for his stories.

A number of such publications made their appearance in the eighteen thirties, flourished for a season, and then died in that climate where only the rhetoric of debate could survive—*The Dublin Monthly Magazine, The Dublin Literary Gazette,* as well as those so obscure and short-lived that they have not been traced. *The Comet* did well for a time, but its mocking and insolent gaze was directed too steadily at Dublin Castle, which found effective means of discouraging the staff.

The National Review collapsed when Charles Lever, a clever young medical student, published an ill-considered defense of Shelley's poetry, and brought down the wrath of the New Reformation. When the Castle and the churches failed to act against the magazines, they attacked each other.

Carleton wrote cheerfully for all of them, out of the abundance of stories which he had yet to tell. There were months when a Whig and a Tory journal, engaged in bitter conflict, would confront each other on quayside stalls, each with its announcement of the latest story by "the peasant novelist." Those early stories have the freshness and wonder of a recent past upon them, and they are written with all the energy generated by his discovery of a way to describe the life which he had left. They were unearthed and reprinted years later, by one editor after another, and most of them are able to stand beside *Traits and Stories*.

In those days he lived half in and half out of the city, in a thatched cabin near Clontarf—a dwelling not unlike those in which he had spent his youth, and swarming with as many children. Indeed, the children, his bottomless thirst, and his improvident habits kept him bogged as deeply in debt as any of his Clogher peasants. Despite these similarities, however, he was no longer a part of the world about which he wrote. He was to remain "the peasant novelist," but he had ceased to be a peasant. Because he was aware of this, he kept firm his hold upon what he knew. When some crisis of the moment prompted him to write about a famine or an insurrection, he would turn his imagination back to the scenes which he had witnessed and the tales which he had heard on the roads. At the end of his life, when his skill failed him, he glossed over his memories with false nostalgia, but until then they retained their harsh, bright colors, and he could summon them at will.

In 1833 a magazine was launched which was to play an important role in the shaping of Irish culture. Carleton, naturally, was an early contributor, but in the course of the decade he attached himself more firmly to its interests and was associated in the public mind with the political position of its editors. The monthly, which called itself *The*

Dublin University Magazine, had no official connection with the university from which it took its name, but its editors were all Trinity College men who were determined to establish an intellectual organ which could rise above the mean controversies of the day while remaining Ascendancy in tone and loyalties.

Politics, they soon discovered, was not to be divorced from any Irish undertaking, and the magazine for a time seemed sentenced to the fate of its predecessors. A dispute as to policy arose between its Tory and Whig editors, and the latter broke away to start a rival publication. This journal perished within the customary year, but *The Dublin University Magazine* survived and flourished, thanks to the resourcefulness of its brilliant young editor, Isaac Butt.

Butt, who had all the makings of an *enfant terrible,* knew that the time was ripe for a forthright, if not a belligerent, statement of the Tory case. The liberals within the Ascendancy were beset upon two fronts. O'Connell, having scored his stunning victory in 1828, had tried to shape his own party, but when this did not prove feasible, he entered upon an alliance with the English Whigs. The alliance was of limited advantage to either of the contracting parties, but fatal to Irish Protestant liberalism. The seeming identity of interests between the liberal party and the feared and despised Catholic demagogue allowed the Tories to come forward as the firm and sole champions of the landlord class. Both as an editor and as a rising barrister, Butt pressed this case with fine Orange fury, castigating the "unprincipled and desperate nominees of an ignorant and bigoted populace," and pledging that the magazine would remain the "monthy advocate of the Protestantism, the intelligence, and the respectability of Ireland." [1]

The success of the magazine owed much to these mosstrooping tactics, but still more to Butt's editorial judgment. He was determined to raise the tone and the standards of Dublin's intellectual life; his taste in literary matters was excellent, and his sympathies generously free of bias. The pages of *The Dublin University Magazine* were open to the generation of trained and disciplined Irish scholars which had

[1] Quoted by Butt's biographer, Terence de Vere White, in *The Road of Excess,* p. 10.

arisen—George Petrie, Eugene O'Curry, and John O'Donovan were to become the most celebrated—and it printed a considerable body of first-rate translations from European literature. Of greater moment, perhaps, was the tact with which Butt sought out and developed talent. He persuaded Charles Lever to try his hand at capturing the life of the hard-drinking, fox-hunting squires of Galway, and published serially Lever's first Irish novel, *Harry Lorrequer.* James Clarence Mangan, Joseph Sheridan Lefanu, Samuel Lover, and Samuel Ferguson, poets of differing but undeniable abilities, enriched the pages of the magazine. Butt's sensibility had its limits—he failed to understand the nature of Mangan's frail, exotic genius—and he was continually distracted by his political ambitions, but full justice has never been done to his accomplishment.

Despite his responsibilities, the years of Carleton's close association with *The Dublin University Magazine,* from 1835 to 1841, were the most pleasant of his Dublin career. He was moving among men who were themselves endowed with talent and who were appreciative of his own. "He was essentially of the people he describes," Samuel Hall was to write contemptuously, "peasant-born and peasant-bred, and most at home in mud cabin or shebeen house." It is true that Carleton gave class-conscious Dublin constant reminders of his origins. His tall, heavy frame, his massive head with its shock of red hair and its long upper lip suggested these as fully as did his ungovernable temper, his sullen suspiciousness, his sudden hatreds and loyalties. The facts, however, all contradict Hall's further assertion that he never obtained "the respect of those whose respect was worth having."[2] His friendships were many and various, and those who held him in particular esteem were men who differed from him in personality and habits—George Petrie, the scholar and musician, and Samuel Ferguson, the poet.

Superficially, Carleton and Ferguson had little in common save an Ulster birth. By class, training, habits of mind, and political convictions, Ferguson was unshakably of the Ascendancy, while Carleton was an unaccountable stray from the Ireland of mud cabins and fac-

[2] *Retrospect of a Long Life,* II, 141.

tion brawls. Ferguson was a gifted poet, disciplined by the traditions of English verse, whose imagination had been captured by the Gaelic songs and heroic legends. Carleton, the son of Gaelic-speaking parents and a product of hedge schools, was trying by main force to bring the Gaelic world within the orbit of English letters. The kinship of these contrasting ambitions formed the basis of a long and lasting friendship.

Ferguson has left a record in his poetry of one of their many walking trips through the Wicklow mountains, of the girl who offered them the hospitality of her cabin:

> Considerate and discreet, she stood
> Apart and listened to the wind.[3]

Ferguson, in his turn, stood apart from the Irish people, though considerate of their interests, but his ear caught the sound of the wind in the Wicklow glens, and the sad cadence of Irish verse.

It seemed to the Carleton of those years that he had left the roads at last, save for those occasions when he walked them for pleasure, as a gentleman might, in the company of a poet. He had learned how to do one kind of story supremely well, and his inherent indolence, his constant need to make money in the surest way, his desire for literary respectability, all prompted him to keep on writing that story. The variety of his work, within this limit, is impressive. In one brilliant sketch, "Barney Brady's Goose," [4] he achieved with careless ease the effect of wild Hibernian hilarity which Samuel Lover worked at through long, strained pages. In the remarkable series of stories which he wrote in 1840 and 1841 for George Petrie's *Irish Penny Journal,* he recorded the lives of the footloose Irish rogues and tinkers whom he had met at inns and by firesides.[5] During 1837 and 1838 *The Dublin University Magazine* published his novel, *Fardorougha, the Miser,* a study of the Irish passion for land.

The Athenaeum found this novel equal in skill and intensity of

---

[3] Samuel Ferguson, "The Pretty Girl of Lough Dan," *Poems,* p. 76.
[4] First published in *The Dublin University Magazine* in 1838; often reprinted in collections of Carleton's minor fiction.
[5] Collected in *Tales and Stories of the Irish Peasantry.*

feeling to *Eugenie Grandet*.[6] It is too generous a judgment, though the comparison is merited, but it suggests the reputation which Carleton now enjoyed. "Ireland in a few years," he wrote confidently, "will be able to sustain a native literature as lofty and generous and beneficial to herself as any other country in the world can boast of."[7] It was a prediction which many Irishmen were making in that year, and Carleton's name was sure to be invoked. So, too, were the names of his associates. The pages which carried *Fardorougha* carried also Ferguson's delicate, cool evocations of life in Norman and Elizabethan Ireland, Lever's rollicking novels of witty ne'er-do-wells, and Butt's swashbuckling rhetoric.

"The man of most authentic genius in fiction," a contemporary wrote bitterly, was allied with that dominant party of landlords whose only remedy for a turbulent people was to "hunt them down like redshanks."[8] And it was true that Carleton, like the bards of an earlier century, believed that it was simple courtesy to sing the praises of his masters and to make their cause his own. Denunciations of "bloody-minded agitators" and "ignorant rebels" came easily to him, and when he had made his duty to party, he was free to tell his story.

The Irish, he says in one of his *Penny Journal* sketches, have always preferred the fiddler to the harper.[9] The songs which the fiddler scrapes tell of love, dancing, and mirth, and he expects for them only a close place by the fire. But the harp has another music, and its songs are of heroism, sacrifice, fate, and death. Carleton had found a snug, dry corner, and he was content with it.

"Do you mind when you and I were at school with Pat Frayne?" a cousin wrote him from the Clogher valley. "Them were the days that we had nothing to trouble us, and poor Jack, too, he was a brave, clever fellow, and a good learner; but the light-footed boy, as we use to call you, could leather us all at the spelling lesson, and run away with the pins." John Carleton of Kilnahushogue had his monthly budget of news. "We buried Johnny McGinn of Lisnamaghery last week—he

[6] *Athenaeum*, No. 613 (July 27, 1839), p. 563.
[7] Author's Introduction (1842) to *Traits and Stories*, I, xxxiv.
[8] Charles Gavan Duffy, *Young Ireland*, p. 69.   [9] *Tales and Stories*, I, 302.

died in four days' sickness." [10] The landlords were still evicting, and
cattle were grazing on the fields which men had farmed for centuries.

Carleton remembered Pat Frayne very well, and every other man
whom he had known in Kilnahushogue. They all existed for him in
the irrecoverable past, the living equally with the dead. They were
the theme of his own song—their sins, their suffering, the shape and
color of their lives. The present lay in Dublin, however, and he could
not have been greatly concerned to learn that his sister Mary had
written a Gaelic lamentation upon his "desertion" of his people. But
the wind can rise suddenly in the Irish mountains, sweeping all before
it and shaking the land. Such a wind was now rising. It would take
him from his safe fireside and send him out into the storm of Irish
politics.

In the spring of 1840 O'Connell broke with the Whigs and determined upon a campaign to secure the restoration of the Irish nation.
He had passed from middle to old age in the years since the Clare
election, but he was prepared to set in motion the elaborate machinery
of agitation, confident that the old methods would suffice. The magic
of his thunderous voice would stir up the masses and his resourcefulness would baffle his enemies. Once again the zeal of his associates
would hammer the peasants into a single and formidable weapon
pointed against England.

Instead he found himself fighting a lonely battle against public indifference. He had one asset of incalculable value, the veneration which
his name inspired among the poor, but little else. The daring lieutenants of twelve years before were now contented Whigs, and he was
forced to rely for assistance upon his personal retinue of place-hunters,
relatives, and adulators. The bishops, upon whom so much depended,
were not hostile to the man who had won Catholic Emancipation,
but neither were they eager to embrace his new cause. A small but
useful group within the Ascendancy was in agreement with him that
the union with England must be ended, but it was not willing to
place itself under his command. Like his uncle "Hunting Cap," the

[10] Carleton, *Life,* II, 46–47.

last of the Gaelic chieftains, he had ruled alone, brooking no insubordination. It had won him his victories in the past, but now he was paying the penalty in wearying speeches to half-deserted halls. His vigor was as yet unimpaired, though soon it would be, and he sat in impotent fury, his hat pulled over his eyes, while his henchmen made their absurd speeches.

It is not surprising, therefore, that the Ascendancy responded to the new agitation not with alarm but with amused contempt. *The Dublin University Magazine* was foremost in the campaign of ridicule, for Butt had become the young darling of the Unionists, a man equal to O'Connell in his capacity for invective. Carleton was not far behind him, denouncing the Irish peasant, that "creature of agitation," as "a poor, skulking dupe" who was at once "insolent and arrogant." Respectability, for which he had hungered so long, had taken visible form for him as *The Dublin University Magazine,* which he astonishingly characterized as blessedly free from sectarian and political animus.

At the end of the second year of O'Connell's wasted efforts, however, an event which neither he nor his enemies had anticipated redressed the balance of political forces. This was the appearance, on October 15, 1842, of a weekly journal called *The Nation,* dedicated to the cause of Irish independence and making its appeal to "the popular mind and the sympathies of educated men of all parties." [11] Its editor was Charles Gavan Duffy, an ambitious Catholic journalist, who was "aided" by O'Neill Daunt, a pious O'Connellite, and James Clarence Mangan, the poet. The guiding spirit of the new journal, however, was Thomas Osborne Davis, a young Protestant barrister who had recently been graduated from Trinity College.

A scant three years of life were left to Davis, who died at the age of twenty-nine, but he was destined to leave a deep impression upon his own and succeeding generations. He had already performed the feat of acquiring patriotic principles while in residence at Trinity College, and he looked with unbounded confidence to a national regeneration. This was the high noon of such aspirations throughout

[11] Prospectus of *The Nation,* reproduced in Duffy, *Young Ireland,* p. 80.

Europe, and young men not unlike Davis were planning and dreaming in the garrets and printing shops of Paris, Warsaw, and Rome. Davis, like them, was at times absurd and humorless, but he possessed qualities which the moment required, a lofty idealism, a consuming energy, and an ability to summon the loyalty of the new generation.

Within a few months *The Nation* was the most widely read journal in Ireland. O'Connell welcomed it eagerly—at the moment he would have accepted the support of a Moslem confraternity—though privately he shared the opinion of *The Dublin University Magazine* that it was a purveyor of wretched doggerel. The ambitions of the editors were boundless; they sought to quicken the national spirit and rouse it to intellectual vigor. Schemes which could not have been completed within decades were blithely drafted—national libraries were to be published, series of biographies written, folk songs to be composed by the hundreds, native industry encouraged; indeed, nothing which the teeming fancy of Davis might imagine was omitted from the program.

To O'Connell only one fact mattered: inspired by the patriotic ardor and bad poetry of *The Nation,* young men of the middle class were enrolling under the banner of Repeal. He had thought Gaelic war chants tedious even when sung in the original; translated into the meters of *Lays of Ancient Rome,* they were insufferable. But Davis and Duffy and John Dillon were taking the places which Wyse and Sheil had held in an earlier struggle; once again he had talented and tireless troops at his disposal. Repeal clubs were founded in every provincial town, in whose assembly rooms was heard a rhetoric to which Irish ears were unaccustomed. O'Connell could harangue a mob, argue a parliamentary issue, or overawe a factious meeting with unmatched skill, but he was unresponsive both to the merit and to the cant of Young Ireland. Of the men who were to play leading roles in the coming drama—Mitchel, Doheny, Meagher, and the rest—all had been recruited by Davis and *The Nation.*

The most unexpected recruit, however, was Carleton. As early as the seventh issue of *The Nation,* Duffy published a coy hint that Carleton had called at the office, asking him to deny the "absurd rumor" that he was the sole writer for the journal. Duffy did so, and then assured his readers that none regretted more deeply than did Carleton himself the way in which he had "wronged and misrepresented the people of Ireland."[12] This remarkable confession by a Conservative writer in a magazine which was being assailed as an agent of sedition had its sequels. The issues of September 23 and October 7, 1843, carried Carleton's long, brutal attacks upon Charles Lever and *The Dublin University Magazine*.

The grounds of Carleton's adherence to the new party were and remain obscure. He had previously been marked down as "an enemy of the people" whose very name was odious, and spirits less generous than Davis viewed the move with suspicion. O'Connell, to be sure, hailed him now as "the Scott of Ireland," but this was an encomium which he distributed liberally. He had earned a reputation in Dublin as a man whose political principles deferred to the needs of his pocket. His present move does not lack particular evidence of this.

In April Charles Lever had succeeded Butt as editor of *The Dublin University Magazine* and the change displeased the more talented of its contributors. Carleton, comparing Lever with other Irish writers, was to say that there was no more similarity between Banim and him than between "John Kemble and a buffoon"—a harsh but apt comparison. A few months later he lost the services of Samuel Ferguson and James Mangan; at the same time he picked a quarrel with Carleton and denied him access to the pages of the magazine. Having unburdened himself of the three writers by whom *The Dublin University Magazine* lives in literary history, he proceeded to mold the periodical in his own image—a task described by Mr. Lionel Stevenson as "lifting *The Dublin University Magazine* to international renown."[13]

Thus, at the time when Carleton paid his visit to Duffy's office, he had lost his most profitable source of revenue. It has been suggested that the visit "displays his offence-avoiding anxiety" to have it publicly known that he had no connection with *The Nation*.[14] But it is equally possible that he had hit upon an ingenious means of informing the

[12] Carleton, *Life*, II, 56.

[13] In *The Showman of Vanity Fair: The Life of William Makepeace Thackeray*, p. 108.

[14] Kiely, *Poor Scholar*, p. 111.

Tories that if some other provision were not made they might expect
to find him writing for the enemy. In August he had made application to Sir Robert Peel for the pension which had lapsed with the
death of John Banim and was curtly refused. Once before, desperation
born of need and a sense that he had been treated shabbily had driven
him to a momentous step. In any event, his two articles of 1843 unmistakably announced his alliance with a cause which was drifting
rapidly into chaos, though it seemed for the moment near the full tide
of success.

The combined energies of O'Connell and the men of Young Ireland
had created a movement of formidable proportions. Hundreds of
thousands turned out for the "monster rallies," marched in orderly
formations by "Repeal wardens." The Church showed its venerable
readiness to accommodate itself to the irresistible by announcing its
support of the principles of Repeal. Many within the Ascendancy itself were willing to cast in their lot with the movement, persuaded by
the examples of Duffy and Davis that Irishmen of both creeds had at
last found common and honorable ground.

Throughout the summer of Repeal Year and into autumn, "musters
of the nation," as they were grandiloquently called, were held at sites
rich in associations—Mallow, Tara, Mullaghmast. O'Connell, the
veteran tactician, had studied his earlier triumphs with a view to re-
peating them. On a dozen platforms, he announced the determination
of the Irish people to insist upon their rights, and to meet with defiance
any attempt at coercion. *The Nation* took an equally belligerent stand;
its pages became thick with references to military triumphs of the past
and to patriotic martyrs who had died while resisting the Saxon cavalry.

Sir Robert Peel had meanwhile been preparing a counterstroke by
which these sweeping if ambiguous pronouncements were to be put to
the test. A "muster" at Clontarf, presumably the equivalent of the
Clare election, had been fixed for Sunday, October the fifth. On Fri-
day the government organ hinted that the meeting might be proclaimed
as a breach of the peace; late the following day, the proclamation was
issued. Regiments of foot, horse, and artillery were brought into position on the heights above the Clontarf plain, and the cannon of the

Pigeon House fort were trained upon the approaches from Dublin. On Sunday the Lord Lieutenant inspected these forces, but it was a needless precaution. Upon receipt of the proclamation, O'Connell had cancelled the meeting. Riders were sent out upon every road to turn back the crowds converging upon Dublin—including, no doubt, the dauntless "Mountaineer Cavalry advancing four deep and filing to the rear with remarkable precision." [15]

One week later O'Connell and Charles Gavan Duffy, the editor of *The Nation,* were arrested on charges of having sought to spread disaffection and to inculcate doctrines "tending to overthrow the Constitution of the British Empire as by law established." In January they were tried before a packed jury upon evidence so flimsy that the inevitable verdict of guilty was reversed by the House of Lords. Upon his release from prison O'Connell was welcomed as a monarch by the adoring multitudes, and a carriage draped in royal purple carried him through the streets of the city. The long shadow which he cast across the land concealed almost to the last the fact that the old man had broken down under the strain of his recent exertions. Impaired in mind as well as in body, he pursued mechanically the courses which had already brought him to defeat.

Only the young men who had served him so tirelessly perceived that some fatal infirmity had sapped his courage and his will. Only vigorous and forthright action could save from disaster the movement which he headed, yet he chose instead to spend his days roaming the rocky fields of Derrynane, entrusting the business of the Repeal Association to his jealous and small-minded son. Whatever powers of mind he retained were devoted to fighting the growing strength of Young Ireland. Four long, bitter years were spent in this ugly and fratricidal struggle.

During these years a conviction hardened in the minds of his opponents. In the years of his strength O'Connell had employed every weapon save one to rescue the country from its disastrous plight. There remained only that one—armed revolt. It would have been better, they came to feel, to have rushed with bare fists against the guns of Clontarf than to acknowledge the hopelessness of their position. An

---

[15] Duffy, *Young Ireland,* p. 360n.

absurd and even sinister doctrine—William Carleton was later to call it insane—was being born in those fierce arguments. While they argued, the sick, vengeful O'Connell on one side and the tempestuous Meagher on the other, the peasants of Louth were making an alarming discovery: the potatoes which they pulled from the ground were black and rotten.

"With all his splendid equipment of brains," Charles Gavan Duffy says of Carleton, "he was incapable of comprehending the principles and aspirations" of Young Ireland.[16] Two men of great literary power wrote for *The Nation* during the years of political crisis, Carleton and James Mangan, and in Duffy's judgment their emancipation from *The Dublin University Magazine* was a victory won for both art and nationality. Yet neither fully identified himself with the movement which the journal served. This left Duffy faced with the puzzling fact that the two indisputable successes of Irish literary nationalism were Mangan's poems and Carleton's novels.

Carleton published no new work in the years between 1842 and 1845. Repeal Year came and passed, the guns of the Pigeon House fort were leveled against Clontarf, Meagher defended the merits of the sword in Conciliation Hall, and O'Connell poured the vitriol of his contempt upon Thomas Davis. By late 1844, however, Carleton had brought a novel to completion. Davis, who read the manuscript with the greatest excitement and admiration, decided that it was too important to be published serially in a political journal, and made arrangements with James Duffy for its appearance as a book.[17]

Valentine M'Clutchy, Davis wrote in *The Nation,* was the most complete and daring picture of Irish country life ever executed.[18] Carleton's earlier admirers received it less warmly. *The Athenaeum* remarked distantly that it was "obviously the production of a partisan, and written for a purpose beyond and independent of the story."[19] The journals of Irish Toryism were incoherent in their fury and could

---

[16] Quoted in Carleton, *Life,* II, 57.
[17] *Valentine M'Clutchy, the Irish Agent: or, Chronicles of Castle Cumber.*
[18] Quoted in Carleton, *Life,* II, 66.
[19] *Athenaeum,* No. 898 (Jan. 11, 1845), p. 39.

only cry out that action should be taken against the writer as "a fomenter of discontent and disloyalty."[20] But Joseph Sheridan Lefanu, editor of the reactionary *Warder,* admitted ruefully that this incendiary novel was one of the most powerful of Irish books.[21]

It is not easy to define the power of this awkward, ill-constructed novel which Yeats so admired and which Benedict Kiely has called "the most important book of the Irish nineteenth century."[22] Scenes of wild comedy and heartbreaking pathos are placed beside each other without regard for effect. At times the narrative gives way to sermonizing, vituperation, and sulphurous prophecies. The central figures are given allegorical names and perform allegorical functions—Valentine M'Clutchy, the agent; Darby O'Drive, the bailiff; the Reverend Phineas Lucre, the absentee clergyman; Solomon M'Slime, "the religious attorney." Judged simply as a political tract, the book is murky and ambiguous.

These very defects, however, are clues not only to the book's importance, but to an understanding of Carleton's puzzling and contradictory interpretation of Irish life. Years later, when his friend John M'Kibben taxed him with having written nothing equal to *Traits and Stories,* Carleton tacitly admitted the charge, and then went on to discuss the characters of those stories: "I found them, and only gave them a linked embodiment, some at school or at college, or amid the lanes and hill-sides of my native Tyrone. I found them at mass, in 'stations,' and pilgrimages, in the company of the priests."[23]

"A linked embodiment" is an admirable description of the way in which the world of Carleton's early fiction is peopled. The stories themselves reinforce each other, creating the cumulative effect of a swarming, tumultuous countryside. "At the time I wrote this story," he says, speaking of "Denis O'Shaughnessy," "I could afford to be laconic and contemn all pride of the literary art, as I had found out by long and wearisome defeat and failure that the true way to acceptance is by following art and nature."[24] It is this confidence in his material which sets the early Carleton apart from other Irish writers.

[20] Quoted in Carleton, *Life,* II, 129.   [21] Quoted, *ibid.,* II, 66.
[22] *Poor Scholar,* p. 111.   [23] Carleton, *Life,* II, 305.   [24] *Ibid.,* II, 306.

He was by instinct an artist, and dealt in the politics of the spirit. For this reason, it did not matter what he wrote, nor for whom, nor what "lessons" he tacked on to his narratives.

But for this reason, too, he had avoided the special burden which pressed upon the other writers—the need to come to terms with contemporary Ireland and the issues which confronted it. He picked up his ideas about politics from his employers or out of the Dublin air. Often they ran counter to the true thrust and power of his stories—in "Tubber Derg," for example. When he met Thomas Davis, however, he came into contact with a mind very different in kind and quality from the mind of a Caesar Otway or an Isaac Butt. The affection and reverence which he felt for the young man twenty years his junior inspired him to eulogies which pass all reasonable bounds, but his praises turn always upon one point—"the ever-living truth which kindled all his purposes into that clear light that dwelt upon all he did, and in all he said." [25] Davis kindled in Carleton the same desire to speak the truth. The fire burned for a few years.

Duffy was quite right in his belief that Carleton was "incapable of comprehending" the principles of Young Ireland—his mind was far too hard and practical. Carleton knew most of the men who led the abortive rebellion of 1848; Thomas Francis Meagher and Michael Doheny had become his close friends. His opinion of them was succinct —"as politicians, they were insane." [26] For that matter, he had the peasant's sardonic distrust of all politicians, and nationalists in particular. "O'Connell, Sheil, and William Smith O'Brien, all devious types of one constraining idolatry—*country*." [27]

Davis worshiped at the same shrine, and more single-mindedly than those named by Carleton. His concept of nationality, however, was wide and generous; it avoided successfully those traditional Irish traps of race, creed, and social class. His grasp of practical political issues was weak and his poetry was wretched, yet like many others in the movement which he headed, he cherished whatever was unique or valuable in Irish life. Under Davis's influence, Carleton addressed

[25] *Ibid.*, II, 89.   [26] Prefatory Note to *The Tithe-Proctor*.
[27] Carleton, *Life*, II, 305.

himself to a difficult task—he tried to bring together his scattered impressions of Irish life, to go beyond the "linked embodiments" with which he had been content.

Valentine M'Clutchy is Carleton's *Castle Rackrent*. It is his attempt to define once and for all the tragic center of Irish life. He intended the comparison: his novel has as its subtitle *The Chronicles of Castle Cumber*. It fails in the way that all of his later novels fail; it is great only in fragments. Carleton lacked the discipline which is necessary to sustain a novel through three long volumes, and the skill which gives thematic unity to diverse material. But it succeeds in the way that the best of the *Traits and Stories* do. He could look steadily at an isolated scene and draw forth the whole of its meaning. He was not afraid of contradiction or paradox or complexity.

Like *Castle Rackrent* and *Tracy's Ambition,* it is a novel of land and money. Its villains are those who grow rich upon land—agents, landlords, absentee clergymen, drivers, attorneys, *shoneens*. Its victims are those whom the land keeps poor—the peasants. Solomon M'Slime, "the religious attorney," uses religion as a cloak, but his true passion is land. Phineas Lucre is powerful because of the land which his church controls, and he uses eviction as a bludgeon to beat peasants into Paradise. In the hands of Valentine M'Clutchy politics is an elaborate fraud which he uses to control land. Land was not an abstraction to Carleton—it was dirt, rocky soil, potatoes, the sole means of sustenance for an entire people.

Valentine M'Clutchy betrayed no secret, for every peasant and every landlord knew from childhood the lesson which it taught. Only the politicians did not. O'Connell in his belief that the restoration of "the old Parliament in College Green" would bring back the Golden Age; Davis with his lofty dreams of Wolfe Tone, Robert Emmet, and the Volunteers; Peel with his self-righteous confidence that all would be well when the rebelly Irish accepted the benefits of English rule were not arguing the issue which put gunmen behind hedges and forced Connaught landlords to travel their own estates under armed guard.

From one of Carleton's poorer novels Benedict Kiely has singled out a telling scene. In *The Squanders of Castle Squander* a scene lives like "a lost fragment from an old Gaelic satire." "And what are you to give us?" the legless beggar Bill-in-the-Bowl cries to the men of Young Ireland who have come to prepare the Rising. "Why," Young Ireland replies, "have you no soul—no spirit for universal freedom? Have you no lofty aspirations?—no humanity?—no fire?—no lightning?—no thunder?" "No," Bill replies, "the devil a taste o' anything o' the kind we have stronger than brimstone." [28]

It is the voice of Brian Merriman and Egan O'Rahilly and Carleton himself. The men who obeyed the nod of Bill-in-the-Bowl had not fought for Wolfe Tone and his "Republic of Ireland." They had melted away to leave Robert Emmet standing alone in his resplendent green uniform, his sword drawn, on a Dublin street. In three years' time, they would greet Thomas Meagher and Smith O'Brien, who had come to Munster to lead them into battle; they would wish those valiant gentlemen every possible success in their rebellion, and then return to their cabins. But for land they would fight to the death. Michael Davitt, the peasant, would one day turn that fight into a war. William Carleton, who was also a peasant, laid bare the sources of their passion.

Perhaps the most terrible scene in *Valentine M'Clutchy* is that in which O'Regan lies dying in his cabin. The evicting party is on its way, and O'Regan's wife, weeping and hysterical, begs her husband to die before they arrive. It was a scene eminently pleasing to the taste of nationalists, for it somehow suggested the cruelty of "the Saxon invader." But Carleton had done more than this. He had touched the raw nerve and root of Irish life, the center at which feeling was strengthened and perverted.

Of the novels which Carleton wrote during this period, O'Donoghue, a sedate and churchly nationalist of a later generation, says that "they are his least valuable works from a literary point of view, but they are almost the only ones the Irish people know or care for. . . ." [29] There are many scales, however, on which a literary work may be weighed. Carleton's work lacks coherence and design when he tries to build on the grand scale. He was "incapable of comprehending" any of the formal ideologies by which the stresses and counter-thrusts of a culture

[28] *Poor Scholar*, p. 125.   [29] Carleton, *Life*, II, 58.

may be given meaning. Like his people, he was, in Yeats's phrase, half-risen from the earth.

As he talks with the English-born dean of studies, Stephen Dedalus, who believes that he is capable of understanding all things, reflects bitterly: "The language in which we are speaking is his before it is mine. . . . His language, so familiar and so foreign, will always be for me an acquired speech. I have not made or accepted its words. My voice holds them at bay. My soul frets in the shadow of his language." [30] What is true of words is true also of the literary forms in which they are deployed. The novels of Carleton's middle years strain and buckle beneath the weight of meaning which he puts upon them. They seek to accommodate his sense of the turbulence and anarchy of peasant Ireland to the structure of the conventional "thesis-novel." Because he is intent upon "explaining," laying bare, exposing, they do not take their own shape with the ease and fluency of the earlier stories.

A remarkable instance of this is the novel called *The Black Prophet*. It was written in 1846, during the months when the Irish people were coming to reluctant awareness of the fact that a calamity of unprecedented proportions was upon them. Carleton writes: "Having witnessed last season the partial, and in this the general failure of the potato crop, he anticipated, as every man must, the fearful visitation which is almost decimating our wretched population; and it occurred to him that a narrative founded upon it, or, at all events, exhibiting, through the medium of fiction, an authentic detail of all that our unhappy and neglected country has suffered during *past* privations of a similar kind might be calculated to awaken those who legislate for us. . . ." [31]

In Dublin and in London the men responsible for the conduct of public affairs were meeting to discuss measures. Although the harrowing knowledge of how full was the sentence of starvation would come only in the following year, a half-spoken fear haunted these assemblies. "For a century and a half," Gavan Duffy was to write, "all

---

[30] James Joyce, *A Portrait of the Artist as a Young Man,* p. 221.
[31] Prefatory Note to *The Black Prophet*.

the epidemic fevers with which Ireland had been visited had one origin. They had occurred under widely different circumstances; in the stifling heat of the dog-days, in the killing cold of December, in a season of rain, in a season of drought, but they were invariably preceded by a famine." [32] Famine and plague besieged the country every decade or two, taking their fearful toll and then subsiding. In their wake they left an uprooted population, terrorist societies, and smouldering resentments. That this should be a recurrent feature of Irish life was itself a shocking and sufficient indication of its abominable economic structure. Now, however, the full and accumulated debt was due. Before the eyes of Europe Ireland was to become a vast charnel house, somber and sickening.

For Carleton famine was the Irish situation *in extremis*. His first story, "The Lough Derg Pilgrim," had been the extended image of a terrestial hell—sufferers moving mechanically along circles of jagged stone beneath a black sky. Paddy Devaun's Louth is posted with rotting, black-tarred bodies, corrupted by the August sun. Owen M'Carthy steps across the bloody ground of Tubber Derg into the nightmare of the beggars' roads. Pat Frayne stands doomed upon the gallows and exhorts his friends to repent. Jimmy M'Evoy, "the poor scholar," sits shivering in a famine shed, his mind sliding into delirium. The tragic scenes which burn themselves upon the reader's memory are so much of a kind that we may give a name to them: they seem fragments of a *danse macabre* contrived by a lurid but powerful imagination.

Yet this was not contrivance. Carleton's brooding, terrible talent had seized and given shape to the substance of experience. Famine, plague, and blood always lay beyond the bend of the next year's harvest. In 1818 and again in 1822 he had walked along the roads dotted with plague huts and had seen the wasted bodies tumbled into their shallow graves. Now, in 1846, he set out to describe what he had seen, to remark upon its causes and its dangers, and to prescribe its remedies. *The Black Prophet* was to be his "big" novel, his final, summarizing statement of the moral and social ills which beset Irish society.

The vividness and clarity with which it reveals a countryside lying

[32] *Four Years of Irish History: 1845–1849*, p. 43.

under sentence of death give the forcefulness of observed fact to the novel. Its background is supplied by a people struggling with dazed incomprehension against starvation and pestilence. In the public Soup Shops, "wild crowds, ragged, sickly, and wasted away to skin and bone" struggle "for the dole of charity, like so many hungry vultures about the remnant of some carcase which they were tearing, amid noise, and screams, and strife, into very shreds." (*Black Prophet*, p. 150) All shame, all modesty, all human restraint crack beneath the insupportable burden which is placed upon them. Wild portents seize the imagination of a population moving toward a kind of mass delirium. "Hearses, coffins, long funeral processions, and all the dark emblems of mortality were reflected, as it were, on the sky, from the terrible work of pestilence and famine, which was going forward on the earth beneath them." (*Black Prophet*, p. 149)

But this background, thick with misery and despair, Carleton knew was insufficient to the demands of a novel. There must be lengthy, didactic, and not particularly wise discussions of the economic causes of famine. There must also be a conventional plot, rich with conspiracy, murder, and retributive justice. The plot is inadequate to Carleton's theme, for Skindacre, his land-hungry villain, possesses neither full existence as a character nor stature as an allegorical figure. The atmosphere, the incidental scenes, the pervasive tone of calamitous horror seek to enlarge the novel, but it remains constricted by the mechanical plot.

Carleton's imagination was most firmly engaged by the figure who gives the novel its title, however, and Donnel Dhu, the "prophecy-man," is the strongest link between the plot and the rich possibilities of the theme. Carleton had always had a sense of the dramatic value of this singular Irish type. "Scarcely any political circumstance occurs," he says in "Tubber Derg," "which they do not immediately seize upon and twist to their own purposes. . . ." (*Traits and Stories,* IV, 32) In the period of the 1818 famine with which both "Tubber Derg" and *The Black Prophet* are concerned, the prophecy-men had seized upon the stories of the black militia and the "Valley of the Black Pig." In a time of great suffering, so the stories ran, the Fenian warriors would rise up from this valley. In early stories from Carleton's pen these tales had been hawked by idle mendicants, toward whom he is aloof and censorious.

But Donnel Dhu, "the black prophet," is a grim and sinister figure, malevolent and cunning, who seems to have been summoned forth by the times. In appearance, habit, and dress he resembles not the itinerant prophecy-men, but the guilty and haunted priest of an *Examiner* story, "The Lianhan Shee." [33] Though his motives are culpable, and he is entangled in the sordid conspiracy upon which the novel hinges, he seems to contradict Carleton's assertion that "nothing so much generates imposture as credulity." (*Black Prophet*, p. 16) For Donnel Dhu possesses genuine prophetic powers:

Look about you and say what it is you see that does not foretell famine— famine—famine! Doesn't the dark wet day an' the rain, rain, rain, foretell it? Doesn't the rottin' crops, the unhealthy air, an' the green damp foretell it? Doesn't the sky without a sun, the heavy clouds, an' the angry fire of the West foretell it? Isn't the airth a page of prophecy, where every man may read of famine, pestilence, an' death? The airth is softened for the grave, an' in the black clouds of heaven you may see the death-hearses movin' slowly along, funeral afther funeral, and nothing to follow them but lamentation an' woe, by the widow an' orphan—the fatherless, the motherless, an' the childless—woe an' lamentation—lamentation an' woe.

(*Ibid.*, pp. 15–16)

Donnel Dhu carries his dark secrets to the gallows and beyond it, dying "firmly but sullenly, and as if he defied the world and its laws." (*Ibid.*, p. 320) Larger and more portentous than the uneven story in which he appears, he carries the weight of apprehensions which Carleton cannot formulate. To Carleton, Patrick Murray would write, had fallen the task of recording the life of "those who ere long will have passed away from that troubled land, from the records of history, and from the memory of man forever." [34] In the pages of *The Black Prophet*, Carleton seems to come to a startled half-recognition that this is indeed the task which fate has assigned to him. The food riots, the sounds of murder and violence, the cries of the dying, the infected

[33] *Traits and Stories,* III, 61–91.
[34] *Edinburgh Review,* CXCVI (October, 1852), 389.

stretched out in their wretched sheds, the straggling lines of mourners bearing cheap, false-bottomed coffins, all the final terrors of a people on the edge of extinction. For Carleton, as for Donnel Dhu, the Irish earth was a page of prophecy which he could almost read.

The land had other prophets who read the signs of "the Great Famine." In Dublin Doctor (later Sir) Dominic Corrigan demonstrated with a scientist's icy logic that this was one disaster which sentenced landlord and peasant alike: soon the inexorable arithmetic of typhus infection would turn the entire island into an undiscriminating trap.[35] The landlords gave heed to this timely warning; meanwhile, however, they pursued their blind and insensate policy of mass evictions and forced surrender of land.

In Queen's County James Fintan Lalor, a hunchback with a touch of genius, addressed "the Landowners of Ireland" through a sardonic open letter in *The Nation:* "And so, it seems, you have doomed a people to extinction and decreed to abolish Ireland? The undertaking is a large one. Are you sure your strength will not be tested? The settlement you have made requires nothing to give it efficacy, except the assent or acquiescence of eight millions of people."[36] The landlords, Lalor believed, had forfeited every right to their land, and the people possessed every right to rise up against them.

Lalor's implied threat of a general rising seemed to have the power of fact behind it, for outbursts of violence were being reported from every province. Late in 1845 Carleton had written and brought hastily into print *Rody the Rover*, which is less a novel than a tract which vehemently cautions the people against secret societies. It was particularly caustic and informative in its explanation of the methods employed by Dublin Castle to secure informers and *agents provocateurs*. This drew the anger of the authorities upon him, but he answered firmly that it was the obligation of every honest man to oppose the police system "so long as Government shall continue to keep such an odious and unconstitutional body in its employment."[37]

[35] *Famine and Fever, as Cause and Effect in Ireland.*
[36] Quoted in Denis Gwynn, *Young Ireland and 1848*, p. 132.
[37] Letter to *Saunders' News Letter*, quoted in Carleton, *Life*, II, 81.

By 1848 Carleton's friends in the Young Ireland movement had determined upon an armed revolt. History has concurred in his judgment against this conspiracy, but even the levelheaded and cautious Duffy had begun to despair of an alternative. Carleton was indecisive and tossed upon crosscurrents. The author of *Valentine M'Clutchy* could understand Fintan Lalor's fury, but he was still the man who had foresworn violence as he stood beneath the gibbets of Louth.

The two novels which he wrote during 1847, *The Emigrants of Ahadarra* and *The Tithe-Proctor,* display the divisions of his feeling. *The Emigrants,* which was written after a visit to his own depopulated valley, is suffused by a feeling of deep and troubled sympathy for the peasants who were being wrenched away from their homesteads and packed aboard "coffin-ships." It argues passionately against extreme measures, however, and won the approval of Digby Pilot Starkey, Maria Edgeworth's friend, who, like most Irishmen of property, had considered Carleton's recent work subversive of the public interest. Starkey welcomed the skill with which he had exposed both the "fatal errors" of the landlords and "the ruinous and criminal delusions" of the peasants and the apostles of revolution.[38]

The Tithe-Proctor is so harsh and uncompromising an attack upon insurrectionists that he was never quite forgiven for it. "It might have been one of his best books," O'Donoghue wrote in 1896, "but for the insensate violence which defaces and destroys it. . . . Carleton characterizes the Irish people in terms which, but for remembrance of his former pictures, would cause his name to be execrated by his countrymen."[39] It was less clear to some of his countrymen, apparently, that his portrait of Purcel, the tithe proctor, is etched in acid, and that Turbot, the absentee clergyman, is shown as a monster of greed and silly vanity. The tone at times is raging and sulphurous, but Carleton's anger is directed against rebels and landlords alike. It was written during the months when Fintan Lalor was organizing the peasants for local campaigns of attrition, and Carleton, the old Ribbonman, knew the horrors of such warfare too thoroughly to countenance them.

[38] Quoted in Carleton, *Life,* II, 102.   [39] Quoted in *ibid.,* II, 102.

It was at this point that, in accordance with the pattern which governed his life, his personal affairs collapsed. Since 1842 he had been agitating for a pension with the dexterity and lack of reticence of an O'Connell henchman, but without success. He now found himself hopelessly in debt, and since these had been his most productive years we must take the fact as a measure of the loose habits at which his friends hint broadly.

In June of 1847 a memorial petitioning the government on his behalf was circulated. In one respect at least it is a curious document, since it bears the signatures of men who were soon to be accused of treason, some of the witnesses against them, the lawyers who prosecuted, and the judges who sentenced them to death. In September Carleton learned that it was not then possible to place him on the pension list, but his hopes were encouraged for the following year.

The motives of the propertied classes in coming to Carleton's support are expressed by Digby Starkey with delightful frankness. As he explained matters in a letter to Maria Edgeworth, he had approached Clarendon, the Viceroy, with the argument that Carleton must, if necessary, be bribed. "I represented to him . . . the importance of detaching a writer of Carleton's powers, who can affect the middle classes so widely, from a connection which would necessitate the application of those powers to a dangerous purpose, and of rendering him, first, independent to follow the bent of his own inclinations, and secondly, inclined of his own generosity and the liberality of Government, to employ his pen in the illustration of the social virtues and the cause of order." [40]

Starkey's letter was written in June of the following year, by which time Carleton's career had taken another of its surprising turns. He was writing for *The Irish Tribune,* an advanced revolutionary organ; there was, indeed, a widespread though inaccurate rumor that he was one of its proprietors, and hence a member of the conspiracy. [41]

The phrase, "an Irish conspiracy," is self-contradictory: all Dublin

[40] Quoted in *ibid.,* II, 125.
[41] *Dublin Evening Mail,* July 3, 1848, quoted in *ibid.,* II, 129.

knew that the Rising had been planned for the weeks following the harvest. *The Nation* was publishing minute instructions for the manufacture of pikes and the construction of barricades; Fintan Lalor's *Irish Felon* was concerning itself with more exotic modes of warfare. *The Tribune,* whose actual proprietor was Kevin Izod O'Dogherty, was, if anything, more romantically desperate than its fellows. Carleton had accepted a position on its staff, through ignorance (so he later and unconvincingly claimed) of its policy. The first few issues carried installments of a novel on which he was then at work.[42] It is fair to assume that he severed his connection when he learned informally that he might be granted a government pension.

Carleton's pension was a Whig contrivance; it would be difficult to refute the charge of the Tory *Evening Mail* that "a hostile pen has thus been purchased off from the ranks of disaffection."[43] Upon learning that his services had been secured by a revolutionary journal, Clarendon sent an anxious letter to Lord John Russell, and "the glad tidings" were forwarded to the novelist almost by return post.[44]

While Carleton was indignantly rebutting Tory charges that he was a "Jacobin," his old friends in the movement made their pathetic stand. Duffy had been imprisoned, but Smith O'Brien, Doheny, and Meagher were at large. "Prodigious meetings" were held on Slievenamon; other assemblies in Meath and Limerick seemed to the dazzled eyes of the patriots "like the muster of an insurrectionary army."[45] Dublin Castle had been carefully prodding the leaders into a premature act of overt rebellion, and the plan succeeded perfectly.

On July 20, as Meagher was later and sheepishly to relate, "I put on my tri-colour sash—green, white, and orange—buckled on my sword belt, cartouche-box—and flourishing a very handsome old sword . . . , gave myself up to the illusion of a gallant fight, a triumphal entry, at the head of armed thousands, into Dublin, before long."[46] Two weeks later the Rising was over—it had amounted to a few scattered shots

[42] Later completed: *The Evil Eye,* Dublin, 1860.   [43] Carleton, *Life,* II, 130.
[44] Starkey to Maria Edgeworth, quoted in *ibid.,* II, 124.
[45] Charles Gavan Duffy, *Four Years,* p. 634.
[46] From Meagher's Narrative, written in Richmond Prison in 1849; it is reprinted as Appendix I to Gwynn's *Young Ireland.*

and much confused marching and countermarching. Smith O'Brien, following the tragicomic "battle of Ballingarry," was ignominiously captured in the Thurles railway station. Meagher, who had more flair in such matters, led his lieutenants to the Kilnemaugh mountains, where he planned to rouse the hillside peasants. The peasants willingly sheltered him, at considerable risk to themselves, but he discovered, much to his chagrin, that they had not been manufacturing pike heads, despite the explicit instructions of *The Nation,* and had no intention of embarking on his suicidal project. He managed to stay on the run longer than most of the rebels, but in mid-August he was taken by a patrol.

In 1847 Meagher and Carleton had vacationed together in Wicklow. Carleton, employing one of his favorite images, "had compared two streams from one source, the one strong and loud but muddy, the other weak and silent but pure, to old and young Ireland respectively." [47] Meagher, we know, remembered that conversation. Perhaps Carleton did, too; at any rate the sentimental gasconades of the young men of "the movement" in *Castle Squander* sound suspiciously like the much-admired rhetoric of Thomas Francis Meagher.

For one reason or another Carleton was sunk in a profound and alarming melancholy in the months which followed the Rising. He heard news of the prisoners from mutual friends. One of them had seen Meagher pacing in the courtyard; he had rushed forward to shake hands, but the gaolers pushed him back.[48] "Speranza," Oscar Wilde's mother and one of the silliest women who ever set pen to paper, wrote a long letter designed to rouse Carleton from his gloom, and reassure him of his talent. She closes: "Our poor friend Mr. Duffy seems very ill, I am really uneasy about him, but that Ballingarry killed us all. I have never laughed joyously since—there, goodnight." [49]

The Tithe-Proctor was the last of Carleton's novels to be written with his old fire and zest. *The Squanders of Castle Squander* has its moments, but the machinery creaks. From that book he moved, in his

[47] Carleton, *Life,* II, 92.   [48] Quoted in *ibid.,* II, 119.
[49] Quoted in *ibid.,* II, 139.

fitful if prolific fashion, to the sheer incompetence of his final years. The explanation, in part at least, is clear. Being assured of his pension, D. J. O'Donoghue writes, he could afford to become careless; many of his later works were written "after their author's intellect had been weakened by trouble and over-indulgence in stimulants." [50] But perhaps "Speranza," in her own gushing way, was right: perhaps "that Ballingarry killed us all." When *The Tithe-Proctor* was being assailed on the grounds that it was fatally marred by political rancor, *The Athenaeum* shrewdly observed: " 'A truce to politics,' we suspect, would be equivalent to 'no more novels from Mr. Carleton!'—and this we are by no means prepared to wish." [51] If we take the word "politics" in its largest sense—the ordering of social life—the reviewer may have defined the problem.

In 1847 Carleton had paid the visit to his native Clogher which he had vowed to make only when he was famous and learned. He was greeted by the great landowner of the region, who amiably escorted him "to what once was Ballyscally, but which was now a scene of perfect desolation." It was the worst of the famine years, and yet "out of seventy or eighty comfortable cottages the gentleman in question had left not one standing. Every unfortunate tenant had been evicted, driven out, to find a shelter for himself where he could." [52]

Carleton and "Mr. B—" walked together along the high, stark mountain, whose slopes, once dotted with cabins, commanded a view of that countryside which had been the world of his youth and of his art—Kilnahushogue and Tulnavert and Findramore. Before them, to the west and north under the hill, stretched a long, narrow depression which had been stripped of all life. All natural life, one must add, for this was the Valley of the Black Pig, where the Fenians dwelt in their long sleep. "My companion brought me up to see an obelisk which he was building, on the top of a much higher hill than Ballyscally. It was nearly finished, but we reached the top with some difficulty, and after all saw very little more than we could see from its base. Like many other similar and useless structures, it was called 'B—'s Folly.' " [53]

[50] *Ibid.*, II, 124.
[51] *Athenaeum*, No. 1121 (April 21, 1849), p. 403.
[52] Carleton, *Life*, I, 56.
[53] *Ibid.*, I, 57.

In that image, full, final, and exact, Carleton has described the Ireland of the later nineteenth century. Famine and fever had swept clean entire districts, and evictions and forced emigration had cut their heavy gashes upon others. The "monster rallies" and the "prodigious musters of the nation" were stilled. These were the years to which Thomas Davis had looked for a rich and various renaissance, splendid in its works of physical beauty, but they may be characterized by the obelisk which a wicked man had erected for the perpetuation of his folly.

"I am not a Young Irelander," Carleton wrote truthfully to *The Evening Mail,* "nor, in a political sense at least, an old one. I am no Republican, no Jacobin, no Communist, but a plain, retiring literary man, who wishes to avoid politics. . . ." [54] He had been surrounded, however, by the schemers and idealists of politics, for it was the Irish fate that the best as well as the worst of his countrymen should feel compelled to commit their energies to political activity.

Now all of the best men, save Duffy, were gone. O'Connell, whom Carleton had never liked but who was great in his way, had died in Rome in 1847. Doheny had managed to escape to America. O'Brien, Dillon, and Meagher had been given life sentences to penal colonies. Duffy, the ablest in his group, had five times stood trial for his life upon manufactured evidence. Upon his release, he resumed the editorship of *The Nation* and patiently began the futile task of piecing together the popular movement. From the ruins of Young Ireland he hoped at least to salvage a plan to secure for peasants a minimal claim on their holdings. But Ireland, as Carleton wrote in a letter, was "as silent as a graveyard." [55]

Carleton emerged from his depression and set to work on three novels. When they were half finished, he packed them up and took them to London, where they were sold—*The Squanders of Castle Squander* to J. R. Maxwell, *The Black Baronet* to Saunders and Otley, and *Willy Reilly and His Dear Colleen Bawn* to *The Independent.* They are painfully inferior to any of his earlier work.

[54] Quoted in *ibid.,* II, 133. The letter was not printed by the *Mail,* but was found among Carleton's documents.
[55] Carleton, *Life,* II, 149.

The Black Baronet (1852) is the first of his unhappy attempts to treat of life among the gentry. Years later, by way of apology, he admitted to M'Kibben that he had not had "access to the higher orders, and, except an occasional peep into a squire's house or an outside glance at a courtly gathering I knew little or nothing of their ways." [56] He was referring to his youth only, of course, but for him that was the sole touchstone of value. *The Black Baronet* is exactly the melodrama of aristocratic heroes and villains which might have been spun by a boy after "an outside glance at a courtly gathering."

In 1845, Gavan Duffy had included in his *Ballad-Poetry of Ireland* a version supplied to him by Carleton of the famous old song, "Willy Reilly." Carleton had heard the song from his mother, Duffy's note says, "and had long intended to make it the foundation of a national novel." [57] In 1850 he did exactly that, for *Willy Reilly* (1855) was perfectly suited to the national mood—soft, sentimental, wistful. It was by far the most popular of his novels, running through at least forty editions. When he appeared at the theater after its publication, the audience greeted him with cheers and cries of "Willy Reilly!" Carleton, somewhat conscience-stricken by the reception of a book which he knew was inferior, made a lame reference in the second edition to the haste with which the book was written, then settled back to enjoy its popularity.

In the 1850s and for several decades thereafter the highest praise which a novel could receive was the assurance of critics that it was "admirably free of political bias and sectarian animus." On these grounds and these alone is the novel deserving of praise. The false, weepy tale enlisted Carleton as an early recruit in the regiment of slack writers who assured a lachrymose public that no sight was more lovely than the "Rose of Tralee" as she stood illuminated by the pale and rising moon. Carleton had lost somewhere the sting and bite of the verses which he had sung to Duffy.

"'Taedet me vitae," runs the refrain of a poem which Carleton published in *The Nation*. It summons forth the other Irish writers whom he admired, "pain-stricken Banim," and "Griffin, master of

[56] *Ibid.*, II, 305.   [57] Quoted in *ibid.*, II, 201n.

the heart, / In nature powerful as in art." But they and his unnamed
absent friends are sent back to the shades, and his unnamed hopes are
dismissed—"My children are my country now. Taedet me vitae." [58]

In 1855 he lost the last of his close friends. For five years Duffy
had waged a great-hearted and hopeless battle. Against formidable
odds he had organized a Tenant-Right League, only to see it wrested
from his control by the priests, who now controlled popular politics.
Duffy was an unpleasant reminder to the bishops of the days when
brash young men had dared to challenge the hierarchy. The clergy
preferred to trust two humbugs named Sadlier and Keogh, whose
piety was so ostentatious that they and their henchmen were known
as "The Pope's Brass Band."

Duffy, in disgust, emigrated to Australia, where in time he became
Prime Minister. In 1856 he wrote to Carleton, "I never for a moment
regretted having left the Ireland where Judge Keogh and Archbishop
Cullen predominate; but the slopes of Howth, the hills of Wicklow,
and the friends of manhood are things not to be matched in this
golden land." [59] For Carleton, however, there remained only the Ireland of Cullen and Keogh, the ravaged valleys of Ulster, and the
shabby streets of Dublin.

He continued to write until his death a decade later, but what he
wrote has no proper place in literary history. He fought with his
creditors, appeared and reappeared in bankruptcy court, steered clear
of politics, wrote gentle folksy sketches for pious Catholic periodicals.
He made other friends, to whom he was "The Great Peasant," a remote figure out of the heroic past. He had his depleted fund of stories
for them, and his unfailing blarney.

There were always a few young men eager to buy him drinks. In
exchange he told them what they wanted to hear, splendid lies for
a drab day. O'Connell? A man of conscience, good humor, and cir-
cumspection who "spoke to the king in the presence of the people."
The men of the '48 Rising? "The most brilliant men that ever broke
a lance with the English in Ireland." Davis and Meagher? "The
heralds of a new oriflamme." Lord Clarendon? A sympathetic noble-

[58] *Ibid.*, II, 190–92.   [59] *Ibid.*, II, 226.

man, "who in the most handsome manner acknowledged his services to the cause of the best interests in Ireland." [60]

But there were stories that more remote and more surprising figures had taken a hand, from time to time, in his affairs; what of that? "Yes, even Sir Thomas Larcom, the far-feared terror of gun clubs and Ribbon-men, was one of my unsought patrons; and, who will deny it, John of Jarlath, the great McHale, and that giant of polemics, Sir Tresham Gregg, were fain to be my friends, and for a time I hoped to temper the blasts of party zeal to the shorn lamb of Irish hope, and was a picturesque peace-maker with a utilitarian ideal." [61]

But *Redmond Count O'Hanlon, the Irish Rapparee* was due at the printers the next day, or perhaps *The Hibernian Magazine* needed copy for "The Vengeance of Shaun Roe." And so he would rise up unsteadily and walk home through the broad, empty streets of the Dublin night. Young Thomas Meagher had dreamed of leading through these streets an army terrible with green and orange banners, but they woke now only to the quick march of the British regiments or the patriotic bands which played "O'Donnell Abu" as young men sailed off to help the Pope fight the patriots of Italy. Some forty years before another young man had wandered into these streets, with a copy of *Gil Blas* in his pocket and the promise of a gypsy that he would become a great man. One night, as Carleton talked with his new friends, there echoed in his ear the cry of old Connor to Denis O'Shaughnessy: "My sowl to glory, you larned vagabond; is this the way you're preparing yourself for the Church?"

He died on January 30, 1869. The Protestant rector of his parish and a near-by Jesuit disputed the possession of his soul. [62]

[60] *Ibid.,* II, 304–5.   [61] *Ibid.,* II, 307.
[62] *Ibid.,* II, 326–27.

Conclusion

19. "Fiery Shorthand"

IN HIS LATE, BROKEN YEARS Carleton boasted that no writer would succeed him until fifty years had passed. There was much vanity in this, but more truth, for the nineteenth-century Irish novel established no tradition. Between Carleton's death and the beginning of the new century Ireland produced no prose writer of real stature. When a novelist of commanding talent did appear—the greatest, perhaps, of his age—he owed little to the work of his predecessors. Ireland was Joyce's theme, as it had been theirs, and he shared their involvement in issues of race, culture, and nationality. But in his work the theme finds its expression in irony, in a passion which mocks both itself and its object.

Impelled by the need to define themselves and their culture, the early novelists had shaped vivid images and scenes; they had drawn an intricate network of symbolic references from the landscape and the monuments of their haunted and fatal island. By Joyce's day, however, these images had lost all resonance, and were no longer capable of sustaining true feeling. They had spent too many years in the service of bad art and provincial politics, and could be appropriated only to the uses of satire.

April 14 [Stephen Dedalus notes in his journal]. John Alphonsus Mulrennan has just returned from the West of Ireland. European and Asiatic papers please copy. He told us he met a man there in a mountain cabin. Old man had red eyes and short pipe. Old man spoke Irish. Mulrennan spoke Irish. Then old man and Mulrennan spoke English. Mulrennan spoke to him about universe and stars. Old man sat, listened, smoked, spat. Then said:—Ah, there must be terrible strange creatures at the latter end of the world.[1]

The West of Ireland had given to the earlier novelists their most powerful images—the Black Islands of Corny O'Shane, the ruined Sligo fortress of the Prince of Innismore, the keeps and towers of Gerald Griffin's Munster, the Kerry of Miles na Coppaleen. But the nationalists of a later generation, who cultivated the myth of the peasant and who thought of the West as the reservoir of a peculiarly Irish grace and power, had managed at once to coarsen and to falsify these strong yet delicate images. Stephen Dedalus, with his terrible, inward-coiling anger, neatly and justly reduces the process to the spectacle of John Alphonsus Mulrennan sitting reverently before an oracular bog-trotter.

The fierce, symbolic wolfhound of Maria Edgeworth's and Lady Morgan's romances had become the abominable cur of the Citizen who patrols the streets of a paralyzed Dublin. Those romances themselves seemed, at the century's end, the faded flowers of a gentler age. Between that age and the age of young Joyce lay famine, bloodshed, stifled rebellions, and heartbreak. In this sense, it matters not at all that there were Irish novelists before Joyce, for their work was entirely useless to him. They had established no conventions by which the actualities of Irish life could be represented.

The history of the Irish novel is one of continuous attempts to represent the Irish experience within conventions which were not innately congenial to it. Maria Edgeworth's novels-with-a-thesis, Lady Morgan's exotic romances, Gerald Griffin's moralities, the picaresque narratives of William Carleton are all encumbered in certain essential ways by the conventions which they have assumed. The best of them, which seek to move beyond these forms, make their strongest points and exist most vividly through indirection, symbol, allusion, and subtle shifts in point of view.

Technique, however, is always correlative to the sense of life which it embodies and makes manifest. The English novels, whether great or good, are concerned with the actualities of social existence, and

[1] James Joyce, *A Portrait of the Artist as a Young Man,* pp. 297–98.

with the heroisms and comedies of social choice. The salient feature
of the Irish novel, as we have seen, is its involvement with issues of
another order, its concern with the ways in which history, language,
and race may define, liberate, or thwart the personality. It is the measure of Joyce's extraordinary accomplishment that he was concerned
equally with the texture and core of the socially existent and with the
more lonely quest to which his countrymen had been sentenced—
the hapless inheritors not of a society but of haunted ruins and "unimaginable chaos."

And yet, enormous though the differences between Joyce and his
predecessors may be, a continuity exists by virtue of the themes upon
which they were all engaged—the twin themes of the Irish fate and
the fate of being Irish. Exile, if not cunning, has been the customary
resource of the Irish writer—Maria Edgeworth to the silence of her
estates, Lady Morgan to her house in suburban London, Carleton
to some remote chamber of his memory and imagination. To these
we might have added others—Maturin's commitment to a romantic
Gothic which required no local habitation or Lefanu's absorbed concern with the supernatural. The fact remains, general beyond the point
of coincidence, that no writer of ability before Joyce found possible
a sustained and successful career in Irish letters. Because the pattern
stretches across the century, there is no villain to single out—neither
England nor the Church nor Nationalism nor the Establishment. The
enemy, if one must be named, was the necessity of choosing among
these.

To be sure, there are specific grounds upon which the collapse at
mid-century of the Irish literary movement may be explained—the
devastating effects of the Famine; the political inertia, born of both
despair and cynicism, which followed upon the '48 Rising; the re-
shaping of the implacable barriers of caste and creed. Yet one can only
assume that a literature so dependent upon circumstance had at best
had a precarious tenure.

From the first the literature and politics of Ireland existed in a relationship which was not merely intimate but incestuous. Its novels and
its poetry created and fed political aspirations, while its commitment

to the political as the highest mode of virtue placed upon literature demands which made it increasingly rigid and brittle. The question first posed by Macmorris—What is my nation?—exacted hard and unyielding answers. There are very few moments in the Irish novel when the writer's will is relaxed, though at such rare times we may find his imagination most powerfully at work.

Yeats was to write, "We and our bitterness have left no traces/On Munster grass and Connemara skies." But the bitterness still lived in the Irish air, and was bred in the Irish bone. The grass, the skies, the rivers and towers served the early novelists as double emblems of hatred and love. Each writer was driven into despairing silence only when the possibility of meaningful choice was removed. We have examined in some detail the ways in which this operated. In the years which followed 1850, the despair was universal. To have supposed during those decades that Ireland possessed the ability to choose its own destiny would have been to indulge the conjectures of sentimentalists or fanatics. And it was in those decades that the tradition of the Irish novel withered.

Ireland in those years worked out the dark, final terms of her fate —that Ireland in which, as Duffy aptly wrote, "Judge Keogh and Archbishop Cullen predominate." Subservient to an alien and indifferent power, its spiritual life confined by the ordinances of a harsh and provincial church, the strict and somber history of its tragic past appropriated by demagogues and clowns, the best of its young men driven into the underground courses of hopeless conspiracy, the island accepted passively the nightmare of its history. Seen in this context, Joyce's *non serviam* is less the mutinous refusal of the artist to accept social responsibility than the necessary assertion of individuality against the abnormal claims imposed by a particular culture.

Carleton, the skillful and inveterate trimmer, could maintain a pale existence in the Ireland of Keogh and Cullen, but steelier souls could not. He seems, in his final years, a figure of parable—an old man bereft of speech, ravaged by cancer, scrawling out painfully upon a slate his messages, his begging letters, his safe inept stories, the bright record of his youth.

About him gather figures representative of the stupor which had fallen upon Ireland—the paralysis, as Joyce was to call it. His friend Cashel Hoey, the aptly named journalist who had reduced Duffy's *Nation* to a treacle compounded of honey manufactured by native and patriotic bees, bogwater gathered from Connemara, and tears shed easily for "our poor, dear old Ireland." The absurd "Speranza," a Celtic version of the parlor revolutionist. Alexander Sullivan, the cautious parliamentarian and professional nationalist, who would one day lead his nephew Tim Healy in the attack on Parnell. The sinister, slouching figure of Dick Pigott, the "procurer" of the Parnell letters, who knew the secrets of a few conspiracies and pretended to know more. These were the leaders who had taken the places in Irish life once occupied by O'Connell and Meagher, Davis and Mangan. Carleton wrote his final stories to suit their wishes and demands. Most of them walked behind his coffin to its grave in Mount Jerome Cemetery, where an embarrassed clergyman remarked that since he had performed the appointed service, no further words should be expected from him.

Ireland possessed only two prose writers of even middling ability at the time of Carleton's funeral, and both of them, in point of fact, were resident in an English prison. During the long year of his wasting, there had been another Rising, more formidable than that in '48, though equally futile. Two of the chief conspirators, Charles Kickham and John O'Leary, were literary men. With that cheerful readiness not merely to meet but positively to court calamity which ever characterized the Irish rebel, they had set up headquarters across the street from Dublin Castle and had admitted an informer to their councils. In consequence they were almost the first of the Fenian leaders to fall into government hands.

Kickham wrote several novels[2] which are not really first-rate (*Knocknagow* is the best), but they were highly regarded by his coun-

[2] *Knocknagow: or, The Homes of Tipperary* and *Sally Cavanagh*.

trymen—on the grounds, no doubt, that special consideration should be given to the literary productions of a political prisoner and a Head Center of the Irish Republican Brotherhood. John O'Leary, however, is quite another matter for, if his own work is rambling and ineffectual, he became in his own right an excellent figure of fiction by virtue of the role assigned to him in the imagination of the youthful Yeats.

In an odd fashion the early Yeats takes up the task with which certain of the older novelists were concerned, for he was attempting to construct a glamorous national myth out of unlikely material. Above all else he was determined to raise his country from its shabby debasement by confronting it with instances of heroic being. O'Leary, who had become a self-admiring windbag, must be transformed into a lean, heavy-maned lion who would hurl forth a Plutarchian sentence "in ignorance of its passionate value and would forget it the moment after." [3] It did not matter that Samuel Ferguson's verses limped, for he was "the most central and most Celtic" of the Irish poets—an "aged sea-king sitting among the inland wheat and poppies—the savour of the sea about him and its strength." [4] Nor did it matter that when Carleton tried to reflect seriously upon the nature of Irish society he produced "mere debater's notions," for in his essence he was "like the animals in Milton, half-emerged only from the earth and its brooding."

In Yeats's "Irish propaganda," to use his own angry, retrospective phrase, the circuit of an earlier generation was closed once more, for he and his colleagues of the Irish Revival had made available a fresh vocabulary of heroic enterprise and feeling. From the dark chambers of the century which was ending he summoned names which might stand as emblems. Mangan, Davis, and Ferguson, Emmett and Lord Edward and Wolfe Tone were the names upon which he worked the magic of his verse.

It is of signal importance, however, that the greatest of Ireland's novelists stood coldly aloof from the passions which the greatest of

[3] William Butler Yeats, *Autobiography*, p. 89.
[4] Quoted in Alfred Perceval Graves, *Irish Literary and Musical Studies* (London, 1913), p. 50.

her poets had done so much to awaken. In Irish matters, though in these alone, it is difficult not to accept as being *ben trovato* the story of the youthful Joyce expressing to Yeats his regret that the poet was too old to learn from him. For Ireland, whether as an issue or as the cause of poetry, was something to which Yeats had committed himself. But Joyce was Irish of the Irish. His was the deep and envenomed hate which a man may feel toward that to which he is bound by love and by spirit. Toward that sense of Irish possibility which Yeats, following Davis and Ferguson, sought to express, Joyce was born wise and mocking.

And yet the wisdom and the mockery came to him as part of his inheritance. The journal entry from *A Portrait* with which we began this chapter ends thus:

I fear him. I fear his redrimmed horny eyes. It is with him I must struggle all through this night till day come, till he or I lie dead, gripping him by the sinewy throat till . . . Till what? Till he yield to me? No. I mean him no harm.[5]

For the Irish novelist, the problem has always been that of coming to terms with that archetypal countryman of his, that "terrible queer creature at the latter end of the world." At times he has felt as foolish as John Alphonsus Mulrennan must have looked. He has worked within a culture which in some ways is very rich, though it is a ruined richness, and which in other ways is as stripped as the Connemara shore. Working with the conventions, the literary forms, the terms of discourse of another culture, he has sought to define himself and to represent his world. It was one of the gifts of Joyce's ruthless genius that he could turn all these difficulties to account—that he could turn them, indeed, into the substance of his work.

To understand the Ireland which shaped two such different men as Yeats and Joyce, one must move back, as we have done, beyond the thronging murmurs of the Dublin streets, beyond the waste of the empty decades, beyond the fields and valleys swept bare of all life, beyond the final delirium of the brave. *Ultimus Romanorum*, Carleton wrote of himself. And, as he was writing, the snow was settling in

---

[5] Joyce, *A Portrait of the Artist as a Young Man*, p. 298.

the mountain passes which had been marked on the maps for the Rising of that year. Modern Ireland had taken shape during his lifetime, and he had played his part in the shaping.

It was in the nineteenth century that Irishmen paused, in the midst of turbulence and anger, to take stock of their various and vivid culture, to reckon up what had been squandered or smashed, and to study that which remained with puzzled affection. Of what they saw and felt the novels which we have been examining are the truest record. The foolish enthusiasms of Lady Morgan and the wisdom of Maria Edgeworth, Griffin's pride and Carleton's fury—it was all written down, as Yeats was to say, in a fiery shorthand, that it might never be forgotten.

Bibliography

Bibliography

ORIGINAL EDITIONS of works of fiction have been listed here wherever possible. Places and dates of publication given in parentheses are those of editions cited.

Austen, Jane. *Letters,* ed. by R. W. Chapman. 2 vols. Oxford, 1932.
Banim, John. *The Boyne Water.* 3 vols. London, 1826. (New York, 1880.)
—— *The Celt's Paradise.* Dublin, 1821.
—— *The Croppy.* 3 vols. London, 1828. (2 vols. Philadelphia, 1839.)
—— *Damon and Pythias.* Dublin, 1822.
—— *The Denounced: The Last Baron of Crana* and *The Conformists.* 3 vols. London, 1830.
—— *Recollections of the Dead-Alive.* London, 1824.
—— *The Smuggler: A Tale.* 3 vols. London, 1831.
—— *Tales of the O'Hara Family.* First series. 3 vols. London, 1825. (Under title: *Peep o' Day.* New York, 1865.)
—— *Tales of the O'Hara Family.* Second series. 3 vols. London, 1826.
Barrington, Sir Jonah. *Historic Records and Secret Memoirs of the Legislative Union between Great Britain and Ireland.* London, 1844.
—— *Personal Sketches of His Own Times.* 2 vols. Philadelphia, 1827.
Beaumont, Gustave de. *Ireland: Social, Political, and Religious.* 2 vols. London, 1839.
Brightfield, Myron F. *John Wilson Croker.* London, 1940.
Brittaine, George. *The Recollections of Hyacinth O'Gara.* 5th ed. Dublin, 1839.
Brooke, Charlotte. *Reliques of Irish Poetry.* Dublin, 1789.
Brown, Stephen, S.J. *Ireland in Fiction: A Guide to Irish Novels, Tales, Romances, and Folk-Lore.* Dublin, 1916.
Bunting, Edward. *The Ancient Music of Ireland.* Dublin, 1796.
Burke, Edmund. *Works.* 12 vols. Boston, 1866.
Butler, William. *Confiscation in Irish History.* London, 1917.
Carleton, William. *The Black Baronet.* London, 1852.

Carleton, William. *The Black Prophet: A Tale of the Famine.* Belfast, 1847.

——— *The Emigrants of Ahadarra.* Belfast, 1847.

——— *Fardorougha, The Miser: or, The Convicts of Lisnamora.* Dublin, 1839. (London, n.d.)

——— *The Life of William Carleton: Being His Autobiography and Letters; and an Account of His Life and Writings from the Point at Which the Autobiography Breaks Off,* by David J. O'Donoghue. 2 vols. London, 1896.

——— *Parra Sastha: or, The History of Paddy-Go-Easy and His Wife Nancy.* Dublin, 1845.

——— *Redmond Count O'Hanlon, the Irish Rapparee.* Dublin, 1862.

——— *Rody the Rover: or, The Ribbonman.* Dublin, 1845.

——— *The Squanders of Castle Squander.* 2 vols. London, 1852.

——— *Stories from Carleton.* Introduction by William Butler Yeats. London, 1889.

——— *Tales and Sketches.* Dublin, 1845.

——— *Tales and Stories of the Irish Peasantry.* 2 vols. New York, 1864. (New York, n.d.)

——— *Tales of Ireland.* Dublin, 1834.

——— *The Tithe-Proctor.* Belfast, 1849. (London, n.d.)

——— *Traits and Stories of the Irish Peasantry.* 5 vols. Dublin, 1830–1833. (4 vols., ed. by David J. O'Donoghue. London, 1886.)

——— *Valentine M'Clutchy, the Irish Agent: or, Chronicles of Castle Cumber.* 3 vols. Dublin, 1845.

——— *Willy Reilly and His Dear Colleen Bawn.* London, 1855.

Clarke, Isabel. *Maria Edgeworth, Her Family and Friends.* London, 1949.

Connolly, James. *Labour in Ireland.* Dublin, 1944.

Corkery, Daniel. *The Hidden Ireland: Gaelic Munster in the Eighteenth Century.* 2nd ed. Dublin, 1925.

——— *Synge and Anglo-Irish Literature.* Cork, 1931.

Corrigan, Dominic J. *Famine and Fever, as Cause and Effect in Ireland.* Dublin, 1846.

Crofton, Henry Thomas. *The Crofton Memoirs.* . . . York, 1911.

Croker, John Wilson. *Familiar Epistles, to Frederick B. Jones, Esq.* Dublin, 1804.

——— *A Sketch of Ireland, Past and Present.* Dublin, 1808.

Croker, Thomas Crofton. *Fairy Legends and Tales of the South of Ireland.* London, 1825. (London, 1888.)

Crowe, Eyre Evans. *Today in Ireland.* 3 vols. London, 1825.

Curtayne, Alice. *Lough Derg: St. Patrick's Purgatory.* London, 1945.

Curtis, Edmund. *A History of Ireland*. 6th ed. London, 1950.

—— *A History of Medieval Ireland from 1086 to 1513*. London, 1938.

Daunt, W. J. O'Neill. *Personal Recollections of Daniel O'Connell*. 2 vols. London, 1848.

Davis, Thomas. *The Essays of Thomas Davis*, ed. by David J. O'Donoghue. Dundalk, 1914.

De Quincey, Thomas. *Autobiography from 1785 to 1803*, ed. by David Masson. Edinburgh, 1889.

Dermody, Thomas. *The Harp of Erin*. London, 1807.

Disraeli, Benjamin. *Coningsby*. 3 vols. London, 1844.

Dowling, Patrick John. *The Hedge Schools of Ireland*. London, 1935.

Downey, Edmund. *Charles Lever, His Life in His Letters*. 2 vols. Edinburgh, 1906.

Doyle, James. *Letters on the State of Ireland*. Dublin, 1825.

Duffy, Sir Charles Gavan. *Four Years of Irish History: 1845–1849*. London, 1883.

—— *The League of North and South: An Episode in Irish History*. London, 1886.

—— *Young Ireland: A Fragment of Irish History, 1840–1850*. New York, 1881.

Duggan, D. C. *The Stage Irishman: A History of the Irish Play and Stage Characters from Earliest Times*. London, 1937.

Dunlop, Robert. *Daniel O'Connell*. New York, 1899.

Edgeworth, Maria. *The Absentee* (vol. V of *Tales of Fashionable Life*). (London, 1910.)

—— *Belinda*. 3 vols. London, 1801.

—— *Castle Rackrent: An Hibernian Tale, Taken from Facts, and from the Manners of the Irish Squires of Former Times*. London, 1800. (London, 1802.)

—— *Ennui* (vol. III of *Tales of Fashionable Life*).

—— *Harry and Lucy . . . being the First Part of Early Lessons*, London, 1801.

—— *The Life and Letters of Maria Edgeworth*, ed. by Augustus Hare. 2 vols. New York, 1895.

—— *Moral Tales for Young People*. 2 vols. London, 1801.

—— *Novels and Tales*. 20 vols. New York, 1859.

—— *Ormond*. London, 1817.

—— *The Parent's Assistant: or, Stories for Children*. 2 vols. London, 1796.

—— *Tales of Fashionable Life*. 6 vols. London, 1809–12.

Edgeworth, Richard Lovell, and Maria Edgeworth. *Essay on Irish Bulls*. 3rd ed. London, 1808.

Edgeworth, Richard Lovell, and Maria Edgeworth. *Essays on Practical Education*. 2 vols. London, 1797.

—— *The Memoirs of Richard Lovell Edgeworth, Begun by Himself and Completed by His Daughter, Maria Edgeworth*. 2 vols. London, 1820.

Edwards, R. Dudley, and T. Desmond Williams, eds. *The Great Famine: Studies in Irish History, 1845–52*. Dublin, 1956.

Ellis, S. M. *Wilkie Collins, Le Fanu and Others*. London, 1931.

Ferguson, Sir Samuel. *Poems*. Dublin, 1916.

Fitzpatrick, J. D. *Edmund Rice, Founder . . . of the Brothers of the Christian Schools of Ireland*. Dublin, 1945.

Fitzpatrick, William John. *The Friends, Foes and Adventures of Lady Morgan*. Dublin, 1859.

—— *The Life of Charles Lever*. 2 vols. London, 1879.

—— *Secret Service under Pitt*. 3rd ed. London, 1892.

Fox, Charlotte Milligan. *Annals of the Irish Harpers*. London, 1911.

Froude, James Anthony. *The English in Ireland in the Eighteenth Century*. 3 vols. London, 1890.

Goldsmith, Oliver. *Miscellaneous Writings,* ed. by John Prior. 4 vols. New York, 1850.

Grattan, Henry. *Memoirs of the Life and Times of the Rt. Hon. Henry Grattan by His Son*. 5 vols. London, 1839–46.

Green, Mrs. J. R. *The Making of Ireland and Its Unmaking: 1200–1600*. London, 1908.

Griffin, Daniel. *The Life of Gerald Griffin, Esq*. London, 1843.

Griffin, Gerald. *The Christian Physiologist: Tales Illustrative of the Five Senses*. London, 1830.

—— *The Collegians: A Tale of Garryowen*. 3 vols. London, 1829. (Dublin, 1847.)

—— *The Duke of Monmouth*. 3 vols. London, 1836.

—— *Holland-Tide*. London, 1826. (London, 1842.)

—— *The Invasion*. 4 vols. London, 1832.

—— *Poetical Works*. London, 1842.

—— *The Rivals* and *Tracy's Ambition*. 3 vols. London, 1830. (London, 1842.)

—— *Tales of My Neighborhood*. 3 vols. London, 1835.

—— *Tales of the Munster Festivals*. 3 vols. London, 1827.

Gwynn, Denis. *Daniel O'Connell*. Cork, 1947.

—— *The Struggle for Catholic Emancipation: 1750–1829*. New York, 1928.

—— *Young Ireland and 1848*. Cork, 1949.

Gwynn, Stephen. *Henry Grattan and His Times*. Dublin, 1939.
—— *Ireland*. New York, 1925.
—— *Irish Books and Irish People*. Dublin, n.d.
Hall, Anna. *The Whiteboy*. 2 vols. London, 1845.
Hall, Samuel C. *Retrospect of a Long Life*. 2 vols. London, 1883.
——, and Mrs. Hall. *Ireland: Its Scenery, Character, Etc.* 3 vols. Philadelphia, n.d.
Hardiman, James. *History of the Town and County of Galway*. Dublin, 1820.
Hayes, Edward, ed. *The Ballads of Ireland*. 2 vols. Dublin, 1857.
Hone, Joseph. *Life of W. B. Yeats*. New York, 1943.
Hyde, Douglas. *Beside the Fire*. London, 1891.
—— *A Literary History of Ireland*. New York, 1899.
Idman, Nilo. *Charles Robert Maturin, His Life and Works*. Helsingfors, 1923.
Jacob, Rosamond. *The Rise of the United Irishmen: 1791–94*. London, 1937.
Jones, Howard Mumford. *The Harp That Once: A Chronicle of the Life of Thomas Moore*. New York, 1937.
Joyce, James. *A Portrait of the Artist as a Young Man*. New York, 1916. (New York, 1928.)
—— *Ulysses*. Paris, 1922. (New York, 1940.)
Kickham, Charles. *Knocknagow: or, The Homes of Tipperary*. Dublin, 1879.
—— *Sally Cavanagh*. Dublin, 1869.
Kiely, Benedict. *Poor Scholar: A Study of the Works and Days of William Carleton (1794–1869)*. London, 1947.
Krans, Horatio Sheafe. *Irish Life in Irish Fiction*. New York, 1903.
Law, Hugh Alexander. *Anglo-Irish Literature*. London, 1926.
Lawless, Emily. *Maria Edgeworth*. New York, 1904.
Leadbeater, Mary Shackleton. *Cottage Dialogues among the Irish Poor*. Dublin, 1811.
—— *The Leadbeater Papers*, ed. by R. D. Webb. 2 vols. London, 1862.
Lecky, W. E. H. *History of Ireland in the Eighteenth Century*. 5 vols. London, 1892.
—— *Leaders of Public Opinion in Ireland*. 2 vols. London, 1912.
Leclaire, L. *A General Analytical Bibliography of the Regional Novelists of the British Isles, 1800–1850*. London, 1954.
Ledwich, Edward. *The Antiquities of Ireland*. Dublin, 1789.
Lefanu, Joseph Sheridan. *The Cock and Anchor: A Tale of Old Dublin*. Dublin, 1845.
—— *The Fortunes of Colonel Torloch O'Brien*. London, 1847.

Lefanu, Joseph Sheridan. *The House by the Church-Yard.* 3 vols. London, 1862.

—— *Uncle Silas: A Tale of Bartram-Haugh.* 3 vols. London, 1864. (With introduction by Elizabeth Bowen. London, 1947.)

Lever, Charles. *Complete Novels.* 37 vols. London, 1897–99.

Lewis, George Cornewall. *On Local Disturbances in Ireland.* London, 1836.

Locker-Lampson, G. *A Consideration of the State of Ireland in the Nineteenth Century.* London, 1907.

Lockhart, John Gibson. *The Life of Sir Walter Scott, Bart.* 2nd ed. 12 vols. Edinburgh, 1839.

McCarthy, Justin. *An Irishman's Story.* New York, 1904.

McCarthy, Justin Huntly. *Ireland Since the Union.* New York, 1887.

Macarthy, Mary. *Fighting Fitzgerald and Other Papers.* New York, 1931.

McCullough, Torrens. *Memoirs of the Right Honourable Richard Lalor Sheil.* 2 vols. London, 1856.

MacDermot, Frank. *Theobald Wolfe Tone: A Biographical Study.* London, 1939.

MacDonagh, Michael. *Daniel O'Connell.* London, 1903.

McDowell, R. B. *Public Opinion and Government Policy in Ireland, 1801–1846.* London, 1947.

Macklin, Charles. *The True-born Irishman: or, Irish Fine Lady.* Dublin, 1783.

Maginn, William. *Miscellanies,* ed. by Shelton Mackenzie. 5 vols. New York, 1857.

Malton, James. *Picturesque and Descriptive View of the City of Dublin.* Dublin, 1799.

Mannin, Ethel. *Two Studies in Integrity: Gerald Griffin and the Rev. Francis Mahony ("Father Prout").* London, 1954.

Mathew, David. *The Celtic Peoples and Renaissance Europe: A Study of the Celtic and Spanish Influences on Elizabethan History.* London, 1933.

Maturin, Charles Robert. *Melmoth, the Wanderer.* London, 1820.

—— *The Milesian Chief: A Romance.* 4 vols. London, 1812.

—— *The Wild Irish Boy.* 3 vols. London, 1808.

Maxwell, Constantia. *Country and Town in Ireland under the Georges.* London, 1940.

—— *Dublin under the Georges.* London, 1936.

Merriman, Brian. *The Midnight Court,* trans. by Frank O'Connor. Dublin, 1945.

Mitchel, John. *Jail Journal: or, Five Years in British Prisons.* New York, 1854.

Mitford, Mary Russell. *Recollections of a Literary Life*. . . . 3 vols. London, 1852.

Molyneux, William. *The Case of Ireland's Being Bound by Act of Parliament in England*. . . . Dublin, 1698.

Moore, Thomas. *Irish Melodies*. Dublin, 1820.

—— *Meleologue on National Music*. Dublin, 1811.

—— *Memoirs, Journals, and Correspondence*, ed. by Lord John Russell. 8 vols. London, 1854.

Morgan, Lady. *Absenteeism*. London, 1825.

—— *The Book of the Boudoir*. 2 vols. London, 1829.

—— *A Few Reflections, Occasioned by the Perusal of a Work, entitled, Familiar Epistles*. . . . Dublin, 1804.

—— *Florence Macarthy: An Irish Tale*. 4 vols. London, 1819.

—— *France*. 2 vols. London, 1817.

—— *France in 1829–30*. 2 vols. London, 1830.

—— *Lady Morgan's Memoirs: Autobiography, Diaries, and Correspondence*, ed. by W. Hepworth Dixon. 2 vols. 2nd ed. London, 1863.

—— *The Lay of an Irish Harp: or, Metrical Fragments*. London, 1807.

—— *The Novice of Saint Dominick*. 4 vols. London, 1805.

—— *The O'Briens and the O'Flahertys: A National Tale*. 4 vols. London, 1827. (2 vols. New York, 1856.)

—— *O'Donnel: A National Tale*. 3 vols. London, 1814.

—— *Passages from My Autobiography*. London, 1859.

—— *Patriotic Sketches*. 2 vols. London, 1807.

—— *Poems; Dedicated by Permission to the Rt. Hon. the Countess of Moira*. Dublin, 1801.

—— *St. Clair: or, The Heiress of Desmond*. 4 vols. London and Dublin, 1803.

—— *Twelve Original Hibernian Melodies; with English Words, Imitated and Translated from the Works of the Gaelic Bards*. London, n.d.

—— *The Wild Irish Girl*. London, 1806.

Murray, Patrick Joseph. *The Life of John Banim, the Irish Novelist . . . with Extracts from His Correspondence*. New York, 1869.

Musgrave, Sir Richard. *Memoirs of the Different Rebellions in Ireland*. . . . 2nd ed. Dublin, 1801.

Newby, P. H. *Maria Edgeworth*. Denver, 1950.

O'Brien, William. *Burke as an Irishman*. Dublin, 1924.

O'Callaghan, John Cornelius. *A History of the Irish Brigades in the Service of France*. New York, 1874.

O'Connell, Mrs. Morgan John. *The Last Colonel of the Irish Brigade: Count O'Connell and Irish Life at Home and Abroad*. 2 vols. London, 1892.

O'Connor, Daniel. *St. Patrick's Purgatory, Lough Derg.* Dublin, 1895.

O'Connor, T. P., and Katherine Tynan, eds. *The Cabinet of Irish Literature.* 10 vols. London, 1879–1903.

O'Conor, Charles. *Dissertation on the Antient History of Ireland.* . . . Dublin, 1753.

O'Conor, Matthew. *The Military History of the Irish Nation.* . . . Dublin, 1845.

O'Donoghue, David J. *The Life and Writings of James Clarence Mangan.* Dublin, 1897.

O'Donovan, John, ed. and trans. *Annals of the Kingdom of Ireland, by the Four Masters.* 7 vols. 2nd ed. Dublin, 1856.

O'Faoláin, Seán. *The Great O'Neill: A Biography of Hugh O'Neill, Earl of Tyrone, 1550–1616.* London, 1952.

——— *King of the Beggars.* New York, 1938.

O'Hegarty, P. S. *A History of Ireland under the Union, 1801–1922.* London, 1952.

O'Keeffe, John. *Recollections.* London, 1826.

Oliver, Grace. *A Study of Maria Edgeworth.* Boston, 1882.

O'Rorke, T. A. *A History of Sligo, County and Town.* 2 vols. Dublin, n.d.

Otway, Caesar. *Sketches in Ireland, Descriptive of Interesting and Hitherto Unnoticed Districts in the North and South.* Dublin, 1827.

Parker, Charles S., ed. *Sir Robert Peel from His Private Papers.* 3 vols. London, 1880.

Paul-Dubois, L. *Contemporary Ireland.* Introduction by T. M. Kettle. Dublin, 1908.

Raymond, James Grant. *The Life of Thomas Dermody.* 2 vols. London, 1806.

Reynolds, James A. *The Catholic Emancipation Crisis in Ireland, 1823–1829.* New Haven, 1954.

Scott, Sir Walter. *Letters,* ed. by H. J. C. Grierson. 12 vols. London, 1932–37.

Simms, J. G. *Williamite Confiscation in Ireland, 1690–1703.* London, n.d.

Smith, Charles. *Antient and Modern State of the County of Kerry.* Dublin, 1753.

Spenser, Edmund. *Poetical Works of Edmund Spenser,* ed. by J. C. Smith and E. de Selincourt. Oxford, 1940.

——— *A View of the Present State of Ireland,* ed. by W. L. Renwick. London, 1934.

Stevenson, Lionel. *The Showman of Vanity Fair: The Life of William Makepeace Thackeray.* New York, 1947.

—— *The Wild Irish Girl: The Life of Sydney Owenson, Lady Morgan* (*1776–1859*). London, 1936.

Sullivan, M. D. *Old Galway: The History of a Norman Colony in Ireland.* Cambridge, 1942.

Swift, Jonathan. *The Drapier's Letters,* ed. by Herbert Davis. Oxford, 1935.

—— *Irish Tracts: 1728–1733,* ed. by Herbert Davis. Oxford, 1955.

Thackeray, William Makepeace. *The Irish Sketch Book of 1842.* Boston, 1889.

Tierny, Michael, ed. *Daniel O'Connell: Centenary Essays.* Dublin, 1949.

Tone, Theobald Wolfe. *The Letters of Wolfe Tone,* ed. by Bulmer Hobson. Dublin, n.d.

—— *The Life of Wolfe Tone; Written by Himself and Continued by His Son.* 2 vols. Washington, 1826.

Trevelyan, G. M. *History of England.* London, 1926.

Walker, Joseph Cooper. *Historical Memoirs of the Irish Bards.* 2 vols. Dublin, 1786. 2nd ed., 1818.

White, Terence de Vere. *The Road of Excess.* Dublin, 1946.

Wood-Martin, W. G. *History of Sligo, County and Town.* 3 vols. Dublin, 1882.

Wyse, Thomas. *Historical Sketch of the Late Catholic Association of Ireland.* 2 vols. London, 1829.

Yeats, William Butler. *Autobiography.* New York, 1938.

—— *Collected Poems.* New York, 1947.

—— *Fairy and Folk Tales of the Irish Peasantry.* London, 1888.

—— *The Letters of William Butler Yeats,* ed. by Allan Wade. New York, 1955.

—— *Letters to the New Island,* ed. by Horace Reynolds. Cambridge, 1934.

——, ed. *Representative Irish Tales.* 2 vols. New York, 1891.

Young, Arthur. *A Tour in Ireland.* 2 vols. Dublin, 1780.

Zimmern, Helen. *Maria Edgeworth.* Boston, 1891.

Acknowledgments

A NUMBER of friends and colleagues were of help to me while I was planning and writing the present book. Some of these may properly be mentioned within the conventions of this note.

My interest in the literary culture of the nineteenth century was quickened by work under Professor Lionel Trilling of Columbia and Professor Jacques Barzun, present Dean of Faculties of that university. Professor Trilling read the manuscript in its several stages, as did Professors Susanne Nobbe and Jerome Buckley. I was helped by the further suggestions of Professors Charles Everett, William York Tindall, and Robert Webb. My debt to Charles Everett, grounded upon both friendship and profession, includes and extends beyond his interest in this book. To my friend Kevin Sullivan I am grateful for a number of pleasant discussions, and more pleasant arguments, upon the issues which the book considers.

Miss Elisabeth Shoemaker edited the finished manuscript with exemplary care and skill, despite only our divergent views on capitalization of class nouns.

Part of the book was written in Virginia, at the home of Leonard and Stasha Berman. The acknowledgment of this act of hospitality does very little to suggest the depth of my indebtedness to each of them.

The greatest of these debts is also the oldest. It is to Ellen Treacy Bonner of Fermanagh, whose name lives now in that of her great-granddaughter. Many of the stories which the book discusses I first heard of from her; much of the history was for her the remembered past.

New York   Thomas Flanagan
May 31, 1959

Quotations from "Dedication to a Book of Stories Selected from the Irish Novelists," "Remorse for Intemperate Speech," and "The Tower," by William Butler Yeats, in his *Collected Poems,* New York, 1947, are used with the permission of The Macmillan Company.

Index

Abercorn, Marquis of, becomes patron of Lady Morgan, 129

Absentee, The, see Edgeworth, Maria

Act of Union, passed in 1800, 23; Daniel O'Connell and, 27

Adventures of Mister James Freney, The, 181

"Agitations," Daniel O'Connell's, 30

"Aileen Aroon," *see* Griffin, Gerald

"Altars, The Three," 262

Anarchy, near, in eighteenth-century Ireland, 61

Ancient Music of Ireland, The, see Bunting, Edward

Anthologica Hibernica, 110 and *n*

Antiquities of Ireland, The, see Ledwich, Edward

Ascendancy, characteristics of men of, 19; attitude of Maria Edgeworth to, 58

Athenaeum, The, on William Carleton, quoted, 326; on Carleton's *Valentine M'Clutchy,* quoted, 312

Austen, Jane, on Lady Morgan, quoted, 119

Banim, John, 47, 48, quoted, 201, 202; ancestry, 167-68; birth, 168; education, 168; goes to Dublin, 169; Richard Lalor Sheil becomes mentor, 169-70; marriage, 170; goes to London, 170; death, 201; called "the Scott of Ireland," 167; novels, central weakness in, 178, 179-80; as a historical novelist, 189-90; *Works: The Boyne Water,* discussed, 189-95, quoted, 189-92, *passim; The Celt's Paradise,* 169-70, praised by Sir Walter Scott, 169; *The Conformists,* discussed, 195; *Crohoore of the Billhook,* discussed, 176-80, quoted, 176-79, *passim; The Croppy,* discussed, 197-200, quoted, 199-200; *Damon and Pythias,* produced, 170; *The*

Last Baron of Crana, discussed, 195, 196, quoted, 195, 196; *The Nowlans,* discussed, 182-87, quoted, 183-87, *passim; Peep o' Day,* discussed, 178, 180, 182

Banim, John, and Michael Banim, collaboration of, 175 and *n; Works: Tales of the O'Hara Family,* 172; *Peep o' Day,* quoted, 182

Banim, Michael, ancestry, 167-68; birth, 168; *see also* Banim, John

"Barney Brady's Goose," *see* Carleton, William

Barrington, Sir Jonah, *Personal Sketches of His Own Times,* quoted, 59

Barry Lyndon, see Thackeray, William Makepeace

Battle of Aughrim, The, 181-82

"Battle of the Factions, The," *see* Carleton, William

Battles, in Irish fiction, 15

Beaconsfield, 1st earl of, *see* Disraeli, Benjamin

Becker, Bernard, *Disturbed Ireland,* quoted, 201

Belinda, see Edgeworth, Maria

Black Baronet, The, see Carleton, William

Black Prophet, The, see Carleton, William

Book of the Boudoir, The, see Morgan, Lady

Bowen, Elizabeth, comment on Lefanu's *Uncle Silas,* 47

Boyne, battle of, 9-10

Boyne Water, The, see Banim, John

Brittaine, George, 38

Brooke, Charlotte, 82, *Reliques of Irish Poetry,* 111-12

Brown, Stephen, *Ireland in Fiction,* quoted, 151

Bunting, Edward, 81, *The Ancient Music of Ireland,* 112

Burke, Edmund, "A Letter to a Peer of
Ireland," quoted, 11
Butt, Isaac, 302-3, quoted, 302

Campbell, Father, 267-68
Carleton, James, 260-61
Carleton, Mary Kelly, 261
Carleton, William, 9, ancestry, 258-59;
birth, 259; background and early life,
255-56; death of father, 266; further
education, 267; joins Ribbon lodge, 267;
prophecy of gypsy to, 267; interruption
of education, 268; begins wandering,
269-71; goes to Dublin, 256, 274; conforms to Church of Ireland, 256; works
for Erasmus Smith Schools, 256; marriage, 256; diversity of writing, 256;
meets Caesar Otway, 278; writes for The
Christian Examiner, 278-79; association
with The Dublin University Magazine,
303-4; begins to write for The Nation,
308-10; financial troubles, 323; petition
to government for pension for, 323-24;
visit to Clogher, 326-27; last days,
329-30; death, 330; unaffected by memory of Protestant Nation, 23-24; as historian of Irish peasantry, 33; representative of modern Ireland, 258; knowledge
of Gaelic oral tradition, 260-61; Thomas
Osborne Davis on, quoted, 263, 312;
Sir Charles Gavan Duffy on, 312; Benedict Kiely on, quoted, 258, 274-75, 299;
William Butler Yeats on, 255, 257, 263;
Works: Autobiography, see Life; "Barney
Brady's Goose" (in Tales and Stories
of the Irish Peasantry), 304; "The Battle
of the Factions" (in Traits and Stories
of the Irish Peasantry), discussed, 292-94,
quoted, 292-94, passim; The Black
Baronet, 294-95, 327, 328; The Black
Prophet, discussed, 318-21, quoted, 271,
319, 320, Prefatory Note, quoted, 317;
"Denis O'Shaughnessy Going to Maynooth" (in Traits and Stories of the
Irish Peasantry), discussed, 285-90,
quoted, 285-90, passim, Carleton's comment on, 313; The Emigrants of
Ahadarra, discussed, 322, Digby Pilot
Starkey on, quoted, 322; "An Essay on
Irish Swearing" (in Traits and Stories
of the Irish Peasantry), 295-96, quoted,
295-96; Fardorougha, the Miser, 304-5,
compared to Eugenie Grandet by The
Athenaeum, 304-5; "The Hedge School"
(in Traits and Stories of the Irish Peasantry), 259-60, 268-69, quoted, 260,
269, 296; Life, quoted, viii, 262, 267,
268, 269, 270, 271, 273, 274, 275, 305-6,
313, 314, 325, 326, 327, 328, 329, 330;
"The Lough Derg Pilgrim" (in Traits
and Stories of the Irish Peasantry),
278-79, 278n, discussed, 280-84, quoted,
280-84, passim; Parra Sastha, 257; "The
Poor Scholar" (in Traits and Stories of
the Irish Peasantry), 258, 298, quoted,
258, 265, 298, 299; "The Priest's Funeral" (in Tales of Ireland), 285; Rody
the Rover, 257, 321; The Squanders of
Castle Squander, 294-95, 315-16, 325,
327; "Taedet me vitae," quoted, 328-29;
Tales and Sketches, 271n; Tales of Ireland, 284-85; The Tithe-Proctor, discussed, 322, Prefatory Note, quoted, 314;
Traits and Stories of the Irish Peasantry,
256-57, 264-69, 290-99, quoted, 260,
261, 290-91, 295, 305; "Tubber Derg"
(in Traits and Stories of the Irish Peasantry), discussed, 296-98, quoted, 297,
298, 319; Valentine M'Clutchy, 257, discussed, 312-16, critical comments on,
312-13; "Wildgoose Lodge" (in Traits
and Stories of the Irish Peasantry), 272;
Willy Reilly and His Dear Colleen Bawn,
327, 328
Case of Ireland's Being Bound by Act of
Parliament in England, The, see Moly-
neux, William
Castle Rackrent, see Edgeworth, Maria
Castlereagh, Robert Stewart, 2d Viscount,
and Act of Union, 23
Catholic Association meeting (1825), 212
Catholics, in Ireland, legislation against,
10-13, effects of, 14-15; and Protestants,
evasion of laws by, 12
Celt's Paradise, The, see Banim, John
Christian Physiologist, The, see Griffin,
Gerald
Clare, John Fitzgibbon, 1st earl of, and Act
of Union, 23
Coleridge, Samuel Taylor, 236
Collegians, The, see Griffin, Gerald
Conformists, The, see Banim, John
Coningsby, see Disraeli, Benjamin, 1st earl
of Beaconsfield
Contemporary Ireland (L. Paul-Dubois),
see Kettle, Thomas
Controversy in the novel, 38

Corkery, Daniel, *Synge and Anglo-Irish Literature*, 145; quoted, 44, 45

Corrigan, Sir Dominic, 321

Counter-Reformation, Celtic Ireland espouses, 5

Crofton family, 117-18

Crohoore of the Billhook, see Banim, John

Croker, Crofton, *Fairy Legends and Traditions of the South of Ireland*, 172, 173-74

Croker, John Wilson, attacks on Lady Morgan, 39, 127-28, 128n

Croppy, The, see Banim, John

Crowe, Eyre Evans, *Today in Ireland*, 172, 174

Damon and Pythias, see Banim, John

Daniel O'Connell: Centenary Essays, see Tierney, Michael

Davis, Thomas Osborne, 307-8; quoted, 216-17; "The Library of Ireland," quoted, 188; on William Carleton, quoted, 263, 290; on Carleton's *Valentine M'Clutchy*, 312

Day, Thomas, 57

"Dedication to a Book of Stories Selected from the Irish Novelists," see Yeats, William Butler

"Denis O'Shaughnessy Going to Maynooth," see Carleton, William

Devaun, Paddy, 271-72

Disraeli, Benjamin, 1st earl of Beaconsfield, *Coningsby*, quoted, 127

Disturbed Ireland, see Becker, Bernard

Dixon, Hepworth, quoted, 121, 151

Drama, English, the Irish in, 60

Dramatis Personae, see Yeats, William Butler

Drapier's Letters, The, see Swift, Jonathan

Dublin under the Georges, 1714–1830, see Maxwell, Constantia

Dublin University Magazine, The, 301-3, 307, 309

Duffy, Sir Charles Gavan, 329; quoted, 312, 329; arrested for sedition, 311; returns to editorship of *The Nation*, 327; *Ballad-Poetry of Ireland*, 328; *Four Years of Irish History; 1845–1849*, quoted, 317-18, 324; *Young Ireland*, quoted, 305, 311

Edgeworth, Maria, 36, birth, 65; education, 65; first attempts at writing, 65-66; first published works, 66; supports Union, 38; attitude to Daniel O'Connell, 28; visits Sir Walter Scott, 101-2; Scott returns visit, 102; comment on Scott's *Waverley*, 102; devotes her later years to care of the peasants, 102-6; peasants deny gratitude to, 104-5; and the Great Famine, 105-6; death, 106; *Works: The Absentee*, 42, 83, discussed, 85-91, quoted, 85-88, *passim; Belinda*, 80; *Castle Rackrent*, discussion, 69-79, quoted, 36, 69-77, *passim*, 100, as first Irish novel, 6-7, as requiem for Protestant Nation, 23; *Ennui*, discussed, 83-85; quoted, 84; *Essay on Irish Bulls*, 81-82, quoted, 82; *Helen*, 99; *Life and Letters*, quoted, 66, 95, 101, 103, 104, 105; *Ormond*, 92-99, discussed, 92-99, quoted, 93-99, *passim*

Edgeworth, Richard Lovell, background of, 53-54; opposes Act of Union, 23; supports Union, 38; advocates reform of Parliament, 55; attends last session of Parliament, 53 ff.; philosophical radicalism of, 57; ambitions of, 62; philanthropy of, 62-63; attitude to work of Maria Edgeworth, 66; appointed commissioner of education, 81; reforms proposed by, 81; theories of, in Maria Edgeworth's *Ennui*, 83-84; death, 98; quoted, 42; *Works: Memoirs*, quoted, 54, 55, 56, 57, 62, 63, 64, 65, 66, 67, 81, 92, 99; *Practical Education*, 65-66

Edgeworthstown Infantry, organization, 63

Edward III, laws concerning Irish, 4

Edwards, R. Dudley, and T. Desmond Williams, *The Great Famine: Studies in Irish History, 1845–52*, quoted, 33

Emmet, Robert, 113

"English in Ireland," the, 10

Ennis Election, 27-28

Ennui, see Edgeworth, Maria

Essay on Irish Bulls, see Edgeworth, Maria

Fairy and Folk Tales of the Irish Peasantry, see Yeats, William Butler

Fairy Legends and Traditions of the South of Ireland, see Croker, Crofton

Family relationships, in the novels of Lady Morgan, 114, 115

Fardorougha, The Miser, see Carleton, William

Ferguson, Sir Samuel, 303-4; "The Pretty Girl of Lough Dan," quoted, 304

Fiction, Irish, Anglicization of, 39-40, 43-47; see also Novel, Irish

Fisher, Lydia, 233-34, 249

Fitzgibbon, John, earl of Clare, *see* Clare, John Fitzgibbon, 1st earl of

Fitzpatrick, W. J., quoted, 151

Florence Macarthy, see Morgan, Lady

Frayne, Pat, 259-60, 265-66, 293, 305, quoted, 293

Gaelic literature, revival of interest in, 111-13

Gaelic tradition, survival of, 15

Garrison, the, social position of, 58

Gifford, William, attack on Lady Morgan, 127

Gil Blas, see Le Sage, Alain René

Goldsmith, Oliver, admiration of Gerald Griffin for, 206

"Granard Balls," 42

Grattan, Henry, secures concessions from England, 20; dilemma of, 20-21; loses backing of Volunteers, 21; aims of, 21; asserts Irish independence, 54; opposition to, 55

"Great Famine, The," 317-21; as landmark in Irish history, 33-34

Great Famine: Studies in Irish History, 1845-52, The, see Edwards, R. Dudley

Great House, the, as symbol in the Irish novel, 138

Great O'Neill, The, see O'Faoláin, Seán

Griffin, Daniel, *The Life of Gerald Griffin,* quoted, 236

Griffin, Gerald, 36, 50; quoted, 211, 212, 235, 250; on William Maginn, quoted, 171; ancestry, 205-6; childhood homes of, 209-10; influence of Munster on, 209; effect of father's memories on, 23; admiration for Goldsmith and Moore, 206, for Keats, 236; education, 207; goes to London, 211; friendship with John Banim and William Maginn, 211; hack work, 211; lack of sympathy with English life, 211-12; illness, 213; return to Limerick, 213; and Lydia Fisher, 233-34, 249; dislike for older Romantic poets, 236; visit to Thomas Moore, 249; joins Christian Brothers, 232, 249-50; death, 250; *Works:* "Aileen Aroon," quoted, 210; "The Aylmers of Ballyaylmer" (in *Holland-Tide*), discussed, 213-16, quoted, 214-16, *passim; The Christian Physiologist,* 249; *The Collegians,* discussed, 219-31, quoted, 220-31, *passim,* 232, basis in fact, 219-20,

Irish acceptance of, 230; *Holland-Tide,* discussed, 212-16, compared by reviewer to work of Crofton Croker, 213; *The Invasion,* 233; "The Orange and the Green," 233; *The Rivals,* 237, discussed, 238-43, quoted, 207-8, 238-43, *passim;* "Suil Dhuv" (in *Tales of the Munster Festivals*), discussed, 216-18; *Tales of the Munster Festivals,* 172; discussed, 216-18; *Tracy's Ambition,* 237, discussed, 243-49, quoted, 243-48, *passim*

Griffin, Patrick, reaction to Act of Union, 23

Gwynn, Stephen, *Ireland,* quoted, 132-33

Gwynn, Tom, 182

Hall, Samuel C., *Ireland: Its Scenery, Character, Etc.,* quoted, 60, 105; *Retrospect of a Long Life,* quoted, 303

Harp contest (1792), 112

Hedge literature, 181-82, 182*n*

"Hedge School, The," *see* Carleton, William

Hedge schools, 207-9, 259-60, 264-66

Hedge writers, patriotism in, 40

Helen, see Edgeworth, Maria

Hempson, Denis, 112

Henry V, see Shakespeare, William

Historical Memoirs of the Irish Bards, see Walker, Joseph Cooper

History, in Irish fiction, 16; influence of, on the Irish character, 150-51

History of England, see Trevelyan, G. M.

History of Ireland in the Eighteenth Century, see Lecky, W. E. H.

Hoey, Cashel, 337

Hughes, Tom, 40

Hyde, Douglas, *A Literary History of Ireland,* quoted, 43

Insurrection Acts, Daniel O'Connell and, 27

Invasion, The, see Griffin, Gerald

Ireland, Elizabethan view of, 3-5; English measures against, result of, 8-9; government of, in the eighteenth century, 18; Rebellion (1798), 22-23, consequences of, 23; invasion of, by French troops, 63-64

Ireland, see Gwynn, Stephen

Ireland: Its Scenery, Character, Etc., see Hall, Samuel C.

Ireland in Fiction, see Brown, Stephen

Irish Brigades, 10, 12

"Irish Emigration . . . during the Famine," *see* MacDonough, Oliver
Irish Melodies, see Moore, Thomas
"Irish Nation," rise of, 14-15
Irish novel, *see* Novel, Irish
"The Irish Peasant to His Mistress" (in *Irish Melodies*), *see* Moore, Thomas
Irish Rogues and Raparees, 182
Irish Sketch Book of 1842, The, see Thackeray, William Makepeace
Irish writers, eighteenth-century, uninfluenced by nationality, 39-40
Irishman's Story, An, see McCarthy, Justin

Jacobitism, survival of in Ireland, 12
Jail Journal, see Mitchel, John
Joyce, James, 333-40, *passim; A Portrait of the Artist as a Young Man,* quoted, 317, 333-34, 339; *Ulysses,* quoted, x, 16

Keats, John, admiration of Gerald Griffin for, 236
Kelly, Mary, *see* Carleton, Mary Kelly
Kettle, Thomas, introduction to L. Paul-Dubois' *Contemporary Ireland,* quoted, 6
Kickham, Charles, 337-38
Kiely, Benedict, *Poor Scholar,* quoted, 258, 274-75, 299, 309
Kilkenny College, 168
Kilkenny County, 168-69
Kinsale, battle of, 5-6
Kirwan, Richard, 115

Lalor, James Fintan, quoted, 321
Landor, Walter Savage, 236
Last Baron of Crana, The, see Banim, John
Leadbeater, Mrs. (Mary Shackleton), 233-34
Leaders of Public Opinion in Ireland, see Lecky, W. E. H.
Lecky, W. E. H., *History of Ireland in the Eighteenth Century,* as monument to the Protestant Nation, 25; *Leaders of Public Opinion in Ireland,* quoted, 12
Ledwich, Edward, *The Antiquities of Ireland,* 111
Lefanu, Alicia, becomes patroness of Lady Morgan, 116; reproaches Lady Morgan for forgetting patriotism, 128
Lefanu, Joseph Sheridan, 46-47; *Uncle Silas,* 47, comment on, by Elizabeth Bowen, 47; on Carleton's *Valentine M'Clutchy,* 313

Le Sage, Alain René, *Gil Blas,* 270
"Letter to a Peer of Ireland, A," *see* Burke, Edmund
Lever, Charles, 46, 301; preferred by English readers, 39; *The Martins of Cro' Martin,* 46; becomes editor of *The Dublin University Magazine,* 309; is attacked by William Carleton, 309
"Library of Ireland, The," *see* Davis, Thomas
Life and Letters, see Edgeworth, Maria
Life of Gerald Griffin, The, see Griffin, Daniel
Life of John Banim, The, see Murray, Patrick
Life of Sir Walter Scott, see Lockhart, John Gibson
Life of William Carleton, see Carleton, William
Literary History of Ireland, A, see Hyde, Douglas
Literature, Irish, unifying theme of, 6-7; and politics, 335-36
Lockhart, John Gibson, *Life of Sir Walter Scott,* quoted, 102
Longford, Lord, 57
Lough Derg, significance of, 284; *see also* Saint Patrick's Purgatory
"Lough Derg Pilgrim, The," *see* Carleton, William
Lover, Samuel, 46, 174
Lynch, Pat, 112

McCarthy, Justin, *An Irishman's Story,* quoted, 32-33
MacDermott, Myles ("The Prince of Coolavin"), 118-19; quoted, 119
MacDonough, Oliver, "Irish Emigration . . . during the Famine," quoted, 250
McEligot, Richard, 207
Macklin, Charles, *The True-Born Irishman,* quoted, 60
MacPherson, James, *Ossian,* 111
Maginn, William, 171; instrumental in appearance of books about Ireland, 171-72
Maria Edgeworth, see Newby, P. H.
Martins of Cro' Martin, see Lever, Charles
Maturin, Charles, 46, 275
Maxwell, Constantia, *Dublin under the Georges, 1714–1830,* quoted, 25-26
Meagher, Thomas Francis, 324-25; Narrative, quoted, 324
Memoirs, see Edgeworth, Richard Lovell

Memoirs, see Morgan, Lady

Merriman, Brian, 49-50; *The Midnight Court,* 40

Midnight Court, The, see Merriman, Brian; *see also* O'Connor, Frank

Mitchel, John, *Jail Journal,* quoted, 29

Mitford, Mary Russell, on John Banim, 180

Molyneux, William, *The Case of Ireland's Being Bound by Act of Parliament in England,* publicly destroyed, 17-18

Moore, Thomas, admiration of Gerald Griffin for, 206; *Irish Melodies,* 112 and *n*; "The Irish Peasant to His Mistress" (in *Irish Melodies*), 264

Morgan, Sir Charles, 129-30, petition for repeal of laws penalizing Catholics, 148

Morgan, Lady, 47, ancestry, 109-10; education, 110; early interest in literature, 110; romanticization of self and ancestors, 113-18, *passim;* chooses Connaught as setting for *The Wild Irish Girl,* 116-19; becomes Ireland's first "national novelist," 125; novels of, political aspects, 125-46, *passim;* opposition to, 125, 126-28; attacks on, by William Gifford, 127, by John Wilson Croker, 39, 127-28, 128*n;* marriage, 129; attitude to Daniel O'Connell, 28; referred to in street ballad, 148; political activity, 148-49; receives pension, 163; returns to Ireland, 163; spends her last years in semiobscurity, 163; death, 164; *Works: The Book of the Boudoir,* quoted, 109, 129; *Florence Macarthy,* discussed, 138-46, quoted, 17, 139-44, *passim,* Preface, quoted, 37; *Memoirs,* quoted, 128-29, 130, 149, 162, 163; *The Novice of St. Dominick,* 113, 116; *The O'Briens and the O'Flahertys,* discussed, 150-61, quoted, 152-61, *passim,* conflicting opinions on, 151; *O'Donnel,* discussed, 130-37, quoted, 131-35, *passim,* Preface, quoted, 37; *Patriotic Sketches,* quoted, 123-24; *St. Clair,* 113; *Twelve Original Hibernian Melodies,* 116; *The Wild Irish Girl,* 109, discussed, 119-24, influence of, 119-20, 121-23, 125-28, secures entree into Anglo-Irish society for author, 128-30, Jane Austen on, 119, Sir Walter Scott on, 126-27

Movements, popular, joined by peasantry, 14

Murphy, Father John, 200

Murray, Patrick, quoted, 33, 256-57; *The Life of John Banim,* quoted, 174

Nation, The (periodical), 307-12

Newby, P. H., *Maria Edgeworth,* quoted, 54, 66-67

"New Reformation," 274

Novel, English, subjects of, 35

Novel, Irish, bibliographies of, viii*n;* topicality of, 34; subjects of, 35; addressed to English readers, 36-37; effect on aims and purposes, 37; English attitude to, 38-39; criticism of, 39; and uncongenial conventions, 334-35; common themes of, 335; stocktaking in, 340

Novelists, Irish, quarrel with Irish culture, 36; differences among, 48-49

Novice of St. Dominick, The, see Morgan, Lady

Nowlans, The, see Banim, John

O'Briens and the O'Flahertys, The, see Morgan, Lady

O'Carolan, Turlough, 284

O'Connell, Count Daniel, as model for Lady Morgan's *O'Donnel,* 137

O'Connell, Daniel, 149, 161-62, 191; quoted, 29, 31, 45; and the Catholic peasantry, 26-27; and Emancipation, 27; and the Act of Union, 27; stands for Parliament, 27; impact on Irish history, 28-33; English view of, 28-29; victory of, differing attitudes to, 232-33; fights for restoration of Irish nation, 306 ff.; supported by *The Nation,* 307 ff.; arrested for sedition, 311; final defeat, 163; death, 163, 327

O'Connell, Maurice, 197; quoted, 13

O'Connell, Mrs. Maurice ("Mair-ni-dhuv"), quoted, 228

O'Connell, Richard, quoted, 24

O'Connor, Frank, introduction to Merriman's *The Midnight Court,* quoted, 50

O'Conor, Don, The, death, 164

O'Donnel, see Morgan, Lady

O'Donnell, Hugh, Earl of Tyrconnell, 130, 197

O'Donoghue, David, quoted, 285, 316, 322, 326; *see also* Carleton, William, *Life*

O'Faoláin, Seán, *The Great O'Neill,* quoted, 8

"O'Hara Family, The," pseudonym of John Banim, 175

Old Pretender, the, *see* Stuart, James Francis Edward (Prince)

O'Leary, Ellen O'Connell, quoted, 32

O'Leary, John, 337, 338

O'Mahony, Diarmuid, quoted, 30

O'Neill, Arthur, 40-42, quoted, 41, 42

O'Neill, Hugh, Earl of Tyrone, forms coalition against England, 5

O'Neill, Shane, 3-4

"Orange and the Green, The," *see* Griffin, Gerald

"Orangeman's Day," 191 and *n*

Ormond, see Edgeworth, Maria

Ossian, see MacPherson, James

O'Sullivan, Owen Roe, 209

Otway, Caesar, 276-78; *Sketches in Ireland,* quoted, 277; and William Carleton, 278-79

Owenson, Robert, 109-10, 113-14, 115

Owenson, Sydney, *see* Morgan, Lady

Pacata Hibernica, 130

Parliament, last session of, 53 ff.; reform of, advocated by Richard Lovell Edgeworth, 55

Parliamentary Wars, confusion of, 9

Parra Sastha, see Carleton, William

Parsons, Sir Laurence, quoted, 19

Patriotic Sketches, see Morgan, Lady

Peasant, as recurring figure in Banim's novels, 200-1

Peasantry, Irish, appeal to writers, 262

Peasants, misery of, 61-62; unrest among (1825), 172-73

Peel, Sir Robert, quoted, 27

Peep o' Day, see Banim, John

Penal Days, in novels of John Banim, 195-97

Penal Laws, 10-13

Periodicals, Irish, 300-3

Personal Sketches of His Own Times, see Barrington, Sir Jonah

Phillips, Richard, becomes Lady Morgan's publisher, 116

Pigott, Richard, 337

"Pilgrimage to Patrick's Purgatory, A," *see* Carleton, William, "The Lough Derg Pilgrim"

Politics, and literature, in Ireland, 335-36

"Poor Scholar, The," *see* Carleton, William

Poor Scholar, see Kiely, Benedict

Portrait of the Artist as a Young Man, A, see Joyce, James

Practical Education, see Edgeworth, Richard Lovell

Prendergast, J. P., quoted, 10-11

"Pretty Girl of Lough Dan, The," *see* Ferguson, Sir Samuel

"Prince of Coolavin, The," *see* MacDermott, Myles

Protestant Nation, rise of, 14-15; significance of, 17-33; limitations of, 22; dissolved by Act of Union, 23; attitude of Catholics to, 24-25; attitude of Protestants to, 25; Dublin as legacy of, 26; extinction of, 64-65

Protestants, and Catholics, evasion of laws by, 12

Reliques of Irish Poetry, see Brooke, Charlotte

"Remorse for Intemperate Speech," *see* Yeats, William Butler

"Repeal Year," musters, 310-11

Retrospect of a Long Life, see Hall, Samuel C.

Rice, Edmund, 250

Rising (1848), 323-25

Rivals, The, see Griffin, Gerald

Robinson, Lennox, quoted, 117

Rody the Rover, see Carleton, William

Ruin, the, as symbol in the Irish novel, 137-38

Russell, Father Matthew, vii

St. Clair, see Morgan, Lady

Saint Patrick's Purgatory, accident on pilgrim's route to, 261

Sarsfield, Patrick, 10

Scott, Sir Walter, quoted, 35; attitude towards the Irish, 19; on Maria Edgeworth, quoted, 100; on Ireland, quoted, 102; on Lady Morgan, quoted, 126-27; on Banim's *The Celt's Paradise,* 169; as master to John Banim, 189-90; *Waverley,* comment on, by Maria Edgeworth, 102, influence on John Banim, 194

Shackleton, Mary, *see* Leadbeater, Mrs.

Shakespeare, William, *Henry V,* III, ii, quoted, x, 3; V, Prologue, quoted, 5

Sharpe, Charles Kirkpatrick, 126

Sheil, Richard Lalor, 169-70; friendship with John Banim, 169-70

Smith, Goldwin, quoted, 8

Southey, Robert, 236

Spenser, Edmund, *View of the Present State of Ireland,* quoted, 8, 9
"Speranza," *see* Wilde, Jane Francisca Elgee
Squanders of Castle Squander, The, see Carleton, William
"Stage Irishman," the, 60
Starkey, Digby Pilot, on Carleton's *The Emigrants of Ahadarra,* quoted, 322; on petition for Carleton, quoted, 323
Stuart, James Francis Edward (Prince), 10
Sullivan, Alexander, 337
Swift, Jonathan, *The Drapier's Letters,* defense of Irish claim to independence, 18; quoted, 10
Synge and Anglo-Irish Literature, see Corkery, Daniel

Tales of Ireland, see Carleton, William
Tales of the O'Hara Family, see Banim, John
Thackeray, William Makepeace, travels in Ireland, 181-82; *Barry Lyndon,* 181; *The Irish Sketch Book of 1842,* quoted, 181
Tierney, Michael, Preface to *Daniel O'Connell: Centenary Essays,* quoted, 29
Tithe War (1830–1837), effect on movement for Repeal, 31
Today in Ireland, see Crowe, Eyre Evans
Tone, Theobald Wolfe, character of, 21-22; forms United Irishmen, 22
"Tower, The," *see* Yeats, William Butler
Tracy's Ambition, see Griffin, Gerald
Trevelyan, G. M., *History of England,* quoted, 6, 190
True-Born Irishman, The, see Macklin, Charles
Twelve Original Hibernian Melodies, see Morgan, Lady

Ulysses, see Joyce, James

Uncle Silas, see Lefanu, Joseph Sheridan
United Irishmen, formation of, 22

Valentine M'Clutchy, see Carleton, William
Vallancey, Charles, 82, 111
View of the Present State of Ireland, see Spenser, Edmund

Walker, Joseph Cooper, *Historical Memoirs of the Irish Bards,* 111-12; advice to Lady Morgan, quoted, 119
Waverley, see Scott, Sir Walter
White Boys, 14
Wilde, Jane Francisca Elgee ("Speranza"), 325, 337, quoted, 325
"Wildgoose Lodge," *see* Carleton, William
Wild Irish Girl, The, see Morgan, Lady
William of Orange, victory at the Boyne, 9-10
Williams, T. Desmond, *see* Edwards, R. Dudley
"Willy Reilly" (song), 328
Willy Reilly and His Dear Colleen Bawn, see Carleton, William
Wordsworth, William, 236

Yeats, William Butler, quoted, 145, 276; on Gerald Griffin, quoted, 235n; on William Carleton, 255, quoted, 257, 263; admiration for Carleton's *Valentine M'Clutchy,* 313; on Irish literature, 338, quoted, 338; "Dedication to a Book of Stories Selected from the Irish Novelists," quoted, vii, 336; *Dramatis Personae,* quoted, 145; Introduction to *Fairy and Folk Tales of the Irish Peasantry,* quoted, 174; *Letters,* quoted, vii, viii, 50; "Remorse for Intemperate Speech," quoted, 35, 50; "The Tower," quoted, 56-57
Young, Arthur, 119